The Mass Psychology of Fascism

ALSO BY WILHELM REICH

WILHELM REICH

The Mass Psychology of
FASCISM

Edited by Mary Higgins
and Chester M. Raphael, M.D.

The Noonday Press
Farrar, Straus and Giroux
New York

The Noonday Press
A division of Farrar, Straus and Giroux
19 Union Square West, New York 10003

Distributed in Canada by Douglas & McIntyre Ltd.
Printed in the United States of America

Library of Congress catalog card number: 78-113776

Twelfth printing, 1998

CONTENTS

Love, work and knowledge are the well-springs of our life. They should also govern it.

WILHELM REICH

PREFACE

to the Third Edition,
Revised and Enlarged

Extensive and painstaking therapeutic work on the human character has led me to the conclusion that, as a rule, we are dealing with three different layers of the biopsychic structure in the evaluation of human reactions. As I demonstrated in my book *Character-Analysis,* these layers of the character structure are deposits of social development, which function autonomously. On the surface layer of his personality the average man is reserved, polite, compassionate, responsible, conscientious. There would be no social tragedy of the human animal if this surface layer of the personality were in direct contact with the deep natural core. This, unfortunately, is not the case. The surface layer of social cooperation is not in contact with the deep biologic core of one's selfhood; it is borne by a *second,* an intermediate character layer, which consists exclusively of cruel, sadistic, lascivious, rapacious, and envious impulses. It represents the Freudian "unconscious" or "what is repressed"; to put it in the language of sex-economy, it represents the sum total of all so-called "secondary drives."

Orgone biophysics made it possible to comprehend the Freudian unconscious, that which is antisocial in man, as a secondary result of the repression of primary biologic urges. If one penetrates through this destructive second layer, deeper into the biologic substratum of the human animal, one always discovers the third, deepest, layer, which we call the *biologic core.* In this core, under favorable social conditions, man is an essentially honest, industrious, cooperative, loving, and, if motivated, rationally hating animal. Yet it is not at all possible to bring about a loosening of the character structure of present-day man by penetrating to this deepest and so promising layer without first eliminating the nongenuine, spuriously social surface. Drop the mask of cultivation, and it is not natural sociality that prevails at first, but only the perverse, sadistic character layer.

It is this unfortunate structuralization that is responsible for the fact that every natural, social, or libidinous impulse that wants to spring into action from the biologic core has to pass through the layer of secondary perverse drives and is thereby distorted. This distortion transforms the original social nature of the natural impulses and makes it perverse, thus inhibiting every genuine expression of life.

Let us now transpose our human structure into the social and political sphere.

It is not difficult to see that the various political and ideological groupings of human society correspond to the various layers of the structure of the human character. We, however, decline to accept the error of idealistic philosophy, namely that this human structure is immutable to all eternity. *After social conditions and changes have transmuted man's original biologic demands and made them a part of his character structure, the latter reproduces the social structure of society in the form of ideologies.*

Since the breakdown of the primitive work-democratic form of social organization, the biologic core of man has been without social representation. The "natural" and "sublime" in man, that which links him to his cosmos, has found genuine expression only in great works of art, especially in music and in painting. Until now, however, it has not exercised a fundamental influence on the shaping of human society, if by society we mean the community of mankind and not the culture of a small, rich upper class.

In the ethical and social ideals of liberalism we recognize the advocacy of the characteristics of the surface layer of the character, which is intent upon self-control and tolerance. This liberalism lays stress upon its ethics for the purpose of holding in suppression the "monster in man," our layer of "secondary drives," the Freudian "unconscious." The natural sociability of the deepest third layer, the core layer, is foreign to the liberal. He deplores the perversion of the human character and seeks to overcome it by means of ethical norms, but the social catastrophes of the twentieth century show that he did not get very far with this approach.

Everything that is genuinely revolutionary, every genuine art and science, stems from man's natural biologic core. Thus far, neither the genuine revolutionary nor the artist nor scientist has won favor with masses of people and acted as their leader, or if he has, he has not been able to hold them in the sphere of vital interest for any length of time.

The case of fascism, in contrast to liberalism and genuine revolution, is quite different. Its essence embodies neither the surface nor the depth, but by and large the second, intermediate character layer of secondary drives.

When this book was first written, fascism was generally regarded as a "political party," which, as other "social groups," advocated an organized "political idea." According to this appraisal "the fascist party was instituting fascism by means of force or through 'political maneuver.' "

Contrary to this, my medical experiences with men and women of various classes, races, nations, religious beliefs, etc., taught me that "fascism" is only the organized political expression of the structure of the average man's character, a structure that is confined neither to certain races or nations nor to certain parties, but is general and international. Viewed with respect to man's character, *"fascism" is the basic emotional attitude of the suppressed man of our authoritarian machine civilization and its mechanistic-mystical conception of life.*

It is the mechanistic-mystical character of modern man that produces fascist parties, and not vice versa.

The result of erroneous political thinking is that even today fascism is conceived as a specific national characteristic of the Germans or the Japanese. All further erroneous interpretations follow from this initial erroneous conception.

To the detriment of genuine efforts to achieve freedom, fascism was and is still conceived as the dictatorship of a small reactionary clique. The tenacity with which this error persists is to be ascribed to our fear of recognizing the true state of affairs: fascism is an *international* phenomenon, which pervades all bodies of human society of *all* nations. This conclusion is in agreement with the international events of the past fifteen years.

My character-analytic experiences have convinced me that there is not a single individual who does not bear the elements of fascist feeling and thinking in his structure. As a political movement fascism differs from other reactionary parties inasmuch as it is *borne and championed by masses of people.*

I am fully conscious of the enormous responsibility involved in making such an assertion. And in the interest of this lacerated world I should like the toiling masses to be just as clear about their responsibility for fascism.

A sharp distinction must be made between ordinary militarism and fascism. Wilhelmian Germany was militaristic, but it was not fascistic.

Since fascism, whenever and wherever it makes its appearance, is a movement borne by masses of people, it betrays all the characteristics and contradictions present in the character structure of the mass individual. It is not, as is commonly believed, a purely reactionary movement—it represents an amalgam between *rebellious* emotions and reactionary social ideas.

If we conceive of being revolutionary as the rational rebellion against intolerable conditions in human society, the rational will "to get to the root of all things" ("radical" = "radic" = "root") and to improve them, then fascism is *never* revolutionary. It can of course appear in the guise of revolutionary emotions. But it is not the physician who tackles a disease with reckless invectives whom we call revolutionary, but the one who examines the causes of the disease quietly, courageously, and painstakingly, and fights it. Fascist rebelliousness always accrues where a revolutionary emotion, out of fear of the truth, is distorted into illusion.

In its pure form fascism is the sum total of all the *irrational* reactions of the average human character. To the obtuse sociologist who lacks the mettle to recognize the supreme role played by irrationality in the history of man, the fascist racial theory appears to be nothing more than an imperialistic interest, or, more mildly speaking, a "prejudice." The same holds true for the irresponsible glib politician. The scope and widespread dissemination of these "racial prejudices" are evidence of their origin in the irrational part of the human character. The racial theory is not a product of fascism. On the contrary: it is fascism that is a product of racial hatred and is its politically organized expression. It follows from this that there is a German, Italian, Spanish, Anglo-Saxon, Jewish, and Arabian fascism. *Race ideology is a pure biopathic expression of the character structure of the orgastically impotent man.*

The sadistically perverse character of race ideology is also betrayed in its attitude toward religion. Fascism is supposed to be a reversion to paganism and an archenemy of religion. Far from it—fascism is the supreme expression of religious mysticism. As such, it comes into being in a peculiar social form. Fascism countenances that religiosity that stems from sexual perversion, and it transforms the masochistic character of the old patriarchal religion of suffering into a sadistic religion. In short, it transposes religion from the "other-worldliness" of the philosophy of suffering to the "this worldliness" of sadistic murder.

Fascist mentality is the mentality of the "little man," who is enslaved and craves authority and is at the same time rebellious. It is no coincidence that all fascist dictators stem from the reactionary milieu of the little man. The industrial magnate and the feudal militarist exploit this social fact for their own purposes, after it has evolved within the framework of the general suppression of life-impulses. In the form of fascism, mechanistic, authoritarian civilization reaps from the suppressed little man only what it has sown in the masses of subjugated human beings in the way of mysticism, militarism, automatism, over the centuries. This little man has studied the big man's behavior all too well, and he reproduces it in a distorted and grotesque fashion. The fascist is the drill sergeant in the colossal army of our deeply sick, highly industrialized civilization. It is not with impunity that the hullabaloo of high politics is made a show of in front of the little man. The little sergeant has surpassed the imperialistic general in everything: in martial music; in goose-stepping; in commanding and obeying; in cowering before ideas; in diplomacy, strategy, and tactic; in dressing and parading; in decorating and "honorating." A Kaiser Wilhelm was a miserable duffer in all these things compared with the famished civil servant's son, Hitler. When a "proletarian" general pins his chest full of medals, he gives a demonstration of the little man who will not be "outclassed" by the "genuine" big general.

An extensive and thorough study of the suppressed little man's character, an intimate knowledge of his backstage life, are indispensable prerequisites to an understanding of the forces fascism builds upon.

In the rebellion of vast numbers of abused human animals against the hollow civilities of *false* liberalism (not to be mistaken with *genuine* liberalism and *genuine* tolerance), it was the character layer, consisting of secondary drives, that appeared.

The fascist madman cannot be made innocuous if he is sought, according to the prevailing political circumstances, only in the German or the Italian and not in the American and the Chinese man as well; if he is not tracked down *in oneself*; if we are not conversant with the social institutions that hatch him daily.

Fascism can be crushed only if it is countered *objectively* and *practically*, with a well-grounded knowledge of life's processes. In political maneuver, acts of diplomacy and making a show, it is without peer. But it has no answer to the *practical* questions of life, for it sees everything merely in the speculum of ideology or in the shape of the national uniform.

When a fascist character, regardless of hue, is heard sermonizing about the "honor of the nation" (instead of talking about the honor of man) or the "salvation of the sacred family and the race" (instead of the community of toiling mankind); when he is seen puffing himself up and has his chops full of slogans, let him be asked quietly and simply in public:

"What are you doing in a practical way to feed the nation, without murdering other nations? What are you doing as a physician to combat chronic diseases, what as an educator to intensify the child's joy of living, what as an economist to erase poverty, what as a social worker to alleviate the weariness of mothers having too many children, what as an architect to promote hygienic conditions in living quarters? Let's have no more of your chatter. Give us a straightforward, concrete answer or shut up!"

It follows from this that international fascism will never be overcome by political maneuver. It will fall victim to the natural organization of work, love, and knowledge on an international scale.

In our society, love and knowledge still do not have the power at their disposal to regulate human existence. In fact, these great forces of the positive principle of life are not conscious of their enormity, their indispensability, their overwhelming importance for social existence. It is for this reason that human society today, one year after the military victory over party fascism, still finds itself on the brink of the abyss. The fall of our civilization is inevitable if those who work, the natural scientists of all living (not dead) branches of knowledge and the givers and receivers of natural love, should not become conscious of their enormous responsibility quickly enough.

The life-impulse can exist without fascism, but fascism cannot exist without the life-impulse. Fascism is the vampire leeched to the body of the living, the impulse to murder given free rein, when love calls for fulfillment in spring.

Will individual and social freedom, will the self-regulation of our lives and of the lives of our offspring, advance peacefully or violently? It is a fearful question. No one knows the answer.

Yet, he who understands the living functions in an animal and in a newborn babe, he who knows the meaning of devoted work, be he a mechanic, researcher, or artist, knows. He ceases to think with the concepts that party manipulators have spread in this world. The life-impulse cannot "seize power violently," for it would not know what to do with power. Does this conclusion mean that the life-impulse will always be at the mercy of political gangsterism, will always be its victim, its martyr? Does it mean that the would-be politician will always suck life's blood? This would be a false conclusion.

As a physician it is my job to heal diseases. As a researcher I must shed light upon unknown relationships in nature. Now if a political windbag should come along and try to force me to leave my patients in the lurch and to put aside my microscope, I would not let myself be inconvenienced. I would simpiy throw him out, if he refused to leave voluntarily. Whether I have to use force against intruders to protect my work on life does not depend on me or on my work, but on the in-truders' degree of insolence. But just imagine now that all those who are engaged in vital living work could recognize the political windbag *in time*. They would act in the same way. Perhaps this simplified example con-tains some intimation of the answer to the question how the life-impulse will have to defend itself sooner or later against intruders and destroyers.

The Mass Psychology of Fascism was thought out during the Ger-man crisis years, 1930–33. It was written in 1933; the first edition appeared in September of 1933 and the second edition in April of 1934, in Denmark.

Ten years have elapsed since then. The book's exposure of the irrational nature of the fascist ideology often received a far too enthusi-astic acclaim from all political camps, an acclaim that was not based on accurate knowledge and did not lead to appropriate action. Copies of the book—sometimes pseudonymously—crossed the German border in large numbers. The illegal revolutionary movement in Germany accorded it a happy reception. For years it served as a source of contact with the German anti-fascist movement.

The fascists banned the book in 1935, together with all literature on political psychology.[1] Excerpts from it were printed in France, America, Czechoslovakia, Scandinavia, and other countries, and it was discussed in detailed articles. Only the party Socialists, who viewed everything from an economic point of view, and the salaried party officials, who were in control of the organs of political power, did not and still do not know what to make of it. In Denmark and in Norway, for instance, it was severely attacked and denounced as "counterrevolutionary" by the leadership of the Communist party. It is significant, on the other hand, that the revolution-oriented youth from fascist groups understood the sex-economic explanation of the irrational nature of the racial theory.

In 1942 an English source suggested that the book be translated into English. Thus I was confronted with the task of examining the validity of the book ten years after it was written. The result of this examination exactly reflects the stupendous revolution in thinking that had taken place over the course of the last decade. It is also a test of the

---

[1] *Deutsches Reichsgesetzblatt* (an official gazette announcing new laws), No. 213, April 13, 1935. According to the VO* of February 4, 1933, the publication "What Is Class Consciousness" by Ernst Parell**; "Dialectical Materialism and Psychoanalysis" by Wilhelm Reich; No. 1 and No. 2 of the politico-psychological series of the publishers for sexual politics, Copenhagen-Prague-Zurich, as well as all other publications scheduled to appear in this series, are to be confiscated and withdrawn from circulation by the Prussian police, as they constitute a danger to public security and order.

41230/35   II 2 B 1 Berlin
9/4/35   Gestapo

No. 2146, May 7, 1935. According to the VO of the President of the State issued on February 28, 1933, the distribution of all foreign publications of the politico-psychological series of the publishers for sexual politics (Publishers for Sexual Politics, Copenhagen, Denmark, also Prague, Czechoslovakia, and Zurich, Switzerland) is prohibited in the State until further notice.

III P. 3952 53. Berlin
6/5/35 R.M.d.I.

* VO = Verordnung = decree.
** A fictitious name used by Reich.

tenableness of sex-economic sociology and its bearing on the social revolutions of our century. I had not had this book in my hands for a number of years. As I began to correct and enlarge it, I was stunned by the errors in thinking that I had made fifteen years before, by the revolutions in thought that had taken place, and by the great strain the overcoming of fascism had put on science.

To begin with, I could well afford to celebrate a great triumph. The sex-economic analysis of fascist ideology had not only held its own against the criticism of the time—its essential points were more than confirmed by the events of the past ten years. It outlived the downfall of the purely economic, vulgar conception of Marxism, with which the German Marxist parties had tried to cope with fascism. That a new edition is called for some ten years after its initial publication speaks *in favor of Mass Psychology*. None of the Marxist writings of the 1930's, whose authors had denounced sex-economy, could make such a claim.

My revision of the second edition reflects the revolution that had taken place in my thinking.

Around 1930 I had no idea of the *natural work-democratic relations* of working men and women. The inchoate sex-economic insights into the formation of the human structure were inserted into the intellectual framework of Marxist parties. At that time I was active in liberal, socialist, and communist cultural organizations and was regularly forced to make use of the conventional Marxist sociologic concepts in my expositions on sex-economy. Even then the enormous contradiction between sex-economic sociology and vulgar economism was brought out in embarrassing disputes with various party functionaries. As I still believed in the fundamental scientific nature of the Marxist parties, it was difficult for me to understand why the party members attacked the social effects of my medical work most sharply precisely when masses of employees, industrial workers, small businessmen, students, etc., thronged to the sex-economic organizations to obtain knowledge of living life. I shall never forget the "Red professor" from Moscow who was ordered to attend one of the lectures in Vienna in 1928, to advocate the "party line" against me. Among other things, this professor declared that "the Oedipus complex was all nonsense," such a thing did not exist. Fourteen years later his Russian comrades bled to death under the tanks of the führer-enslaved German machine-men.

One should certainly have expected parties claiming to fight for human freedom to be more than happy about the effects of my political and psychological work. As the archives of our institute convincingly show, the exact opposite was the case. The greater the social effects of our work on mass psychology, the harsher were the countermeasures adopted by the party politicians. As early as 1929–30, Austrian Social Democrats barred the doors of their cultural organizations to the lecturers from our organization. In 1932, notwithstanding the strong protest of their members, the socialist as well as communist organizations prohibited the distribution of the publications of the "Publishers for Sexual Politics," which was located in Berlin. I myself was warned that I would be shot as soon as the Marxists came to power in Germany. That same year the communist organizations in Germany closed the doors of their assembly halls to physicians advocating sex-economy. This too was done against the will of the organizations' members. I was expelled from both organizations on grounds that I had introduced sexology into sociology, and shown how it affects the formation of human structure. In the years between 1934 and 1937 it was always Communist party functionaries who warned fascist circles in Europe about the "hazard" of sex-economy. This can be documentarily proven. Sex-economic publications were turned back at the Soviet Russian border, as were the throngs of refugees who were trying to save themselves from German fascism. There is no valid argument in justification of this.

These events, which seemed so senseless to me at that time, became completely clear while revising *The Mass Psychology of Fascism*. Sex-economic-biologic knowledge had been compressed into the terminology of vulgar Marxism as an elephant into a foxhole. As early as 1938, while revising my "youth" book,* I noticed that every sex-economic word had retained its meaning after eight years, whereas every party slogan I had included in the book had become meaningless. The same holds true for the third edition of *The Mass Psychology of Fascism*.

It is generally clear today that "fascism" is not the act of a Hitler or a Mussolini, but that it is the *expression of the irrational structure of mass man*. It is more clear today than it was ten years ago that *the race theory is biologic mysticism*. We also have far more knowledge at our

---

* This is a reference to *Der Sexuelle Kampf der Jugend* (The Sexual Fight of Youth).

disposal, which enables us to understand man's orgastic yearnings, and we have already begun to divine that *fascist mysticism is orgastic yearning, restricted by mystic distortion and inhibition of natural sexuality.* The *sex-economic* statements about fascism are more valid today than they were ten years ago. On the other hand the Marxist party concepts used in this book had to be completely eliminated and replaced by new concepts.

Does this mean that the Marxist economic theory is fundamentally false? I should like to answer this question with an illustration. Is the microscope of Pasteur's time or the water pump constructed by Leonardo da Vinci, "false"? Marxism is a scientific theory of economy, which originated in the social conditions at the beginning and middle of the nineteenth century. But the social process did not stop there; it continued into the totally different process of the twentieth century. In this *new* social process we find all the essential features that existed in the nineteenth century, just as we rediscover the basic construction of the Pasteurian microscope in the modern microscope, or da Vinci's basic principle in modern water supply. Yet neither the Pasteurian microscope nor Leonardo da Vinci's pump would be of any use to anybody today. They have become outdated as a result of the totally new processes and functions corresponding to a totally new conception and technology. The Marxist parties in Europe failed and came to naught (I don't derive any malicious joy from saying that!) because they tried to comprehend twentieth-century fascism, which was something completely new, with concepts belonging to the nineteenth century. They lost their impetus as social organizations because they failed to keep alive and develop the vital possibilities inherent in every scientific theory. I have no regrets about the many years I spent as a physician in Marxist organizations. My knowledge of society does not derive from books; essentially it was acquired from my practical involvement in the fight of masses of people for a dignified and free existence. In fact, my best sex-economic insights were gained from the *errors* in thinking of these same masses of people, i.e., the very errors that made them ripe for the fascist plague. As a physician I got to know the international working man and his problems in a way that no party politician could have known him. The party politician saw only "the working class," which he wanted "to infuse with class consciousness." I saw man as a creature who had come under the domination of the worst possible social conditions, conditions he himself had created and bore within himself as a part of his character and from which he sought to free himself in vain. The gap between the purely economic and bio-sociologic views became unbridgeable. The theory of "class man" on the one hand was set against the *irrational* nature of the society of the animal "man" on the other hand.

Everyone knows today that Marxist economic ideas have more or less infiltrated and influenced the thinking of modern man, yet very often individual economists and sociologists are not conscious of the source of their ideas. Such concepts as "class," "profit," "exploitation," "class conflict," "commodity," and "surplus value," have become common knowledge. For all that, today there is no party that can be regarded as the heir and living representative of the scientific wealth of Marxism, when it comes to the actual facts of sociological development and not to the slogans, which are no longer in agreement with their original import.

In the years between 1937 and 1939 the new sex-economic concept *"work-democracy"* was developed. The third edition of this book includes an exposition of the principal features of this new sociologic concept. It comprises the best, still valid, sociologic findings of Marxism. It also takes into account the social changes that have taken place in the concept "worker" in the course of the last hundred years. I know from experience that it is the "sole representatives of the working class" and the former and emerging "leaders of the international proletariat" who will oppose this extension of the social concept of the worker on grounds that it is "fascist," "Trotskyian," "counterrevolutionary," "hostile to the party," etc. Organizations of workers that exclude Negroes and practice Hitlerism do not deserve to be regarded as creators of a new and free society. Hitlerism, however, is not confined to the Nazi party or to the borders of Germany; it infiltrates workers' organizations as well as liberal and democratic circles. Fascism is not a political party but a specific concept of life and attitude toward man, love, and work. This does not alter the fact that the policies pursued by the prewar Marxist parties are played out and have no future. Just as the concept of sexual energy was lost within the psychoanalytic organization only to reappear strong and young in the discovery of the orgone, the concept of the international worker lost its meaning in the practices of Marxist parties only to be resurrected within the framework of sex-economic sociology. For the activities of sex-economists are possible only within the framework of socially necessary work and not within the framework of reactionary, mystified, nonworking life.

Sex-economic sociology was born from the effort to harmonize Freud's depth psychology with Marx's economic theory. Instinctual *and* socio-economic processes determine human existence. But we have to reject eclectic attempts to combine "instinct" and "economy" arbitrarily. Sex-economic sociology dissolves the contradiction that caused psychoanalysis to forget the social factor and Marxism to forget the animal origin of man. As I stated elsewhere: Psychoanalysis is the mother, sociology the father, of sex-economy. *But a child is more than the sum total of his parents.* He is a new, independent living creature; he is the seed of the future.

In accord with the new, sex-economic comprehension of the concept of "work," the following changes were made in the book's terminology. The concepts "communist," "socialist," "class consciousness," etc., were replaced by more specific sociologic and psychologic terms, such as "revolutionary" and "scientific." What they import is a "radical revolutionizing," "rational activity," "getting to the root of things."

This takes into account the fact that today it is not the Communist or the Socialist parties but, *in contradistinction to them,* many *nonpolitical* groups and social classes of every political hue that are becoming more and more revolutionary, i.e., are striving for a fundamentally new, rational social order. It has become part of our universal social consciousness—and even the old bourgeois politicians are saying it— that, as a result of its fight against the fascist plague, the world has become involved in the process of an enormous, international, *revolutionary* upheaval. The words "proletariat" and "proletarian" were coined more than a hundred years ago to denote a completely defrauded class of society, which was condemned to pauperization on a mass scale. To be sure, such categories still exist today, but the great grandchildren of the nineteenth-century proletariat have become specialized, technically highly developed, indispensable, responsible industrial workers who are conscious of their skills. The words "class consciousness" are replaced by *"consciousness of one's skills"* or *"social responsibility."*

In nineteenth-century Marxism "class consciousness" was restricted to *manual* laborers. Those who were employed in other vital occupations, i.e., occupations without which society could not function, were labeled "intellectuals" or "petty bourgeois" and set against the "manual labor proletariat." This schematic and no longer applicable juxtaposition played a very essential part in the victory of fascism in Germany. The concept "class consciousness" is not only too narrow, it does not at all tally with the structure of the class of manual workers. For this reason, "industrial work" and "proletariat" were replaced by the terms *"vital work"* and *"the working man."* These two terms include *all those who perform work that is vital to the existence of the society.* In addition to the industrial workers, this includes the physician, teacher, technician, laboratory worker, writer, social administrator, farmer, scientific worker, etc. This new conception closes a gap that contributed in no small way to the fragmentation of working human society and, consequently, led to fascism, both the black and red variety.

Owing to its lack of knowledge of mass psychology, Marxist sociology set "bourgeois" against "proletariat." This is incorrect from a psychological viewpoint. The character structure is not restricted to the capitalists; it is prevalent among the working men of all occupations. There are liberal capitalists and reactionary workers. *There are no "class distinctions" when it comes to character.* For that reason, the purely economic concepts "bourgeoisie" and "proletariat" were replaced by the concepts *"reactionary"* and *"revolutionary"* or "free-minded," which relate to man's character and not to his social class. These changes were forced upon us by the fascist plague.

The dialectical materialism Engels outlined in his *Anti-Dühring* went on to become an *energetic functionalism.* This *forward* development was made possible by the discovery of the biological energy, the orgone (1936–38). Sociology and psychology acquired a solid biological foundation. Such a development could not fail to exercise an influence on our thinking. Our extension of thought brings about changes in old concepts; new ones take the place of those that have ceased to be valid. The Marxist word "consciousness" was replaced by *"dynamic structure"*; *"need"* was replaced by *"orgonotic instinctual processes"*; "tradition" by "biological and characterological rigidity," etc.

The vulgar Marxist concept of "private enterprise" was totally misconstrued by man's irrationality; it was understood to mean that the liberal development of society precluded *every* private possession. Naturally, this was widely exploited by political reaction. Quite obviously, social development and individual freedom have nothing to do with the so-called abolishment of private property. Marx's concept of private property did not refer to man's shirts, pants, typewriters, toilet paper, books, beds, savings, houses, real estate, etc. This concept was used exclusively in reference to the private ownership of the *social* means of production, i.e., those means of production that determine the general course of society. In other words: railroads, waterworks, generating plants, coal mines, etc. The "socialization of the means of production" became such a bugbear precisely because it was confounded to mean the "private expropriation" of chickens, shirts, books, residences, etc., in conformity with the ideology of the expropriated. Over the course of the past century the nationalization of the social means of production has begun to make an incursion upon the latter's private availability in all capitalist countries, in some countries more, in others less.

Since the working man's structure and capacity for freedom were too inhibited to enable him to adapt to the rapid development of social organizations, it was the *"state"* that carried out those acts that were actually reserved for the *"community" of working man.* As for Soviet Russia, the alleged citadel of Marxism, it is out of the question to speak of the "socialization of the means of production." The Marxist parties simply confused "socialization" with "nationalization." It was shown in this past war that the government of the United States also has the jurisdiction and the means of nationalizing poorly functioning industries. A *socialization* of the means of production, their transfer from the private ownership of single individuals to social ownership, sounds a lot less horrible when one realizes that today, as a result of the war, only a few independent owners remain in capitalist countries, whereas there are many trusts that are responsible to the state; when one realizes, moreover, that in Soviet Russia the social industries are certainly not managed by the people who work in them, but by groups of state functionaries. *The socialization of the social means of production will not be topical or possible until the masses of working humanity have become structurally mature, i.e., conscious of their responsibility to manage them.* The overwhelming majority of the masses today is neither willing nor mature enough for it. Moreover, a socialization of large industries, which would place these industries under the sole management of the manual laborer, excluding technicians, engineers, directors, administrators, distributors, etc., is sociologically and economically senseless. Today such an idea is rejected by the manual laborers themselves. If that were not the case, Marxist parties would already have conquered power everywhere.

This is the most essential sociological explanation of the fact that more and more the private enterprise of the nineteenth century is turning into a state-capitalist planned economy. It must be clearly stated that even in Soviet Russia state socialism does not exist, but a rigid state capitalism *in the strict Marxian sense of the word.* According to Marx, the social condition of "capitalism" does not, as the vulgar Marxist believed, derive from the existence of individual capitalists, but from the existence of the specific "capitalist modes of production." It derives, in short, from *exchange economy* and not from *use economy*, from the *paid labor* of masses of people and from *surplus* production, whether this surplus accrues to the state *above* the society, or to the individual capitalists through their appropriation of social production. In this strict Marxian sense the capitalist system continues to exist in Russia. And it will continue to exist as long as masses of people are irrationally motivated and crave authority as they are and do at present.

The sex-economic psychology of structure adds to the economic view of society a new interpretation of man's character and biology. The removal of individual capitalists and the establishment of state capitalism in Russia in place of private capitalism, *did not effect the slightest change in the typical, helpless, subservient character-structure of masses of people.*

Moreover, the political ideology of the European Marxist parties was based on economic conditions that were confined to a period of some two hundred years, from about the seventeenth to the nineteenth century, during which the machine was developed. Twentieth-century fascism, on the other hand, raised the basic question of *man's character, human mysticism* and *craving for authority*, which covered a *period of some four to six thousand years*. Here, too, vulgar Marxism sought to ram an elephant into a foxhole. The human structure with which sex-economic sociology is concerned did not evolve during the past two hundred years; on the contrary, it reflects a patriarchal authoritarian civilization that goes back thousands of years. Indeed, sex-economy goes so far as to say that the abominable excesses of the capitalist era of the past three thousand years (predatory imperialism, defraudation of the working man, racial subjugation, etc.) were possible only because the human structure of the untold masses who had endured all this had become totally dependent upon authority, incapable of freedom and extremely accessible to mysticism. That this structure is not native to man but was inculcated by social conditions and indoctrination does not alter its effects one bit; but it does point to a way out, namely *restructurization*. If being radical is understood to mean "getting to the root of things," then the point of view of sex-economic biophysics is, in the strict and positive sense of the word, infinitely more radical than that of the vulgar Marxist.

It follows from all this that the social measures of the past three hundred years can no more cope with the mass pestilence of fascism than an elephant (six thousand years) can be forced into a foxhole (three hundred years).

Hence, the discovery of natural biological work-democracy in international human intercourse is to be considered the answer to fascism. This would be true, even if not a single contemporary sex-economist, orgone biophysicist, or work-democrat should live to see its complete realization and victory over irrationality in social life.

WILHELM REICH
MAINE, AUGUST 1942

GLOSSARY

BIONS. Vesicles representing transitional stages between non-living and living substance. They constantly form in nature by a process of disintegration of inorganic and organic matter, which process it has been possible to reproduce experimentally. They are charged with orgone energy and develop into protozoa and bacteria.

BIOPATHY. A disorder resulting from the disturbance of biological pulsation in the total organism. It comprises all those disease processes that occur in the autonomic life apparatus. The central mechanism is a disturbance in the discharge of biosexual excitation.

CHARACTER ANALYSIS. A modification of the customary psychoanalytic technique of symptom analysis, by the inclusion of the character and character resistance into the therapeutic process.

CHARACTER STRUCTURE. An individual's typical structure, his stereotype manner of acting and reacting. The orgonomic concept of character is functional and biological, and not a static psychological or moralistic concept.

ORGASM ANXIETY. Sexual anxiety caused by an external frustration of instinctual gratification and anchored internally by the fear of dammed up sexual excitation. It forms the basis of the general pleasure anxiety that is an integral part of the prevailing human structure.

ORGASTIC IMPOTENCE. The absence of orgastic potency, i.e., the incapacity for complete surrender to the involuntary convulsion of the organism and complete discharge of the excitation at the acme of the genital embrace. It is the most important characteristic of the average human of today, and—by damming up biological (orgone) energy in the organism—provides the source of energy for all kinds of biopathic symptoms and social irrationalism.

ORGONE ENERGY. Primordial Cosmic Energy; universally present and demonstrable visually, thermically, electroscopically, and by means of Geiger-Mueller counters. In the living organism: Bioenergy, Life Energy. Discovered by Wilhelm Reich between 1936 and 1940.

ORGONOMIC (ENERGETIC) FUNCTIONALISM. The functional thought technique that guides clinical and experimental orgone research. The guiding principle is that of the identity of variations in the common functioning principle (CFP). This thought technique grew in the course of the study of human character formation and led to the discovery of the functional organismic and cosmic orgone energy, thereby proving itself to be the correct mirroring of both living and nonliving basic natural processes.

SEX-ECONOMY. The term refers to the manner of regulation of biological energy, or, what is the same thing, of the economy of the sexual energies of the individual. Sex-economy means the manner in which an individual handles his biological energy; how much of it he dams up and how much of it he discharges orgastically. The factors that influence this manner of regulation are of a sociological, psychological, and biological nature. The science of sex-economy consisted of that body of knowledge that was derived from a study of these factors. This term was applicable to Reich's work from the time of his refutation of Freud's cultural philosophy to the discovery of the orgone when it was superseded by orgonomy, the science of the Life Energy.

SEX POLITICS. The term "sex politics" or "sex political" refers to the practical application of the concepts of sex-economy on the social scene on a mass basis. This work was done within the mental hygiene and revolutionary freedom movements in Austria and Germany from 1927 to 1933.

SEXPOL. The name of the German organization concerned with mass sex political activities.

VEGETOTHERAPY. With the discovery of the muscular armor, the character analytic therapeutic process was modified to liberate the bound up vegetative energies, thereby restoring to the patient his biophysical motility. The combining of character analysis and vegetotherapy was known as character analytic vegetotherapy. The later discovery of organismic orgone energy (bioenergy) and the concentration of atmospheric orgone energy with an orgone energy accumulator necessitated the further development of character analytic vegetotherapy into an inclusive, biophysical orgone therapy.

WORK-DEMOCRACY: Work-democracy is not an ideological system. Nor is it a "political" system, which could be imposed upon human society by the propaganda of a party, individual politicians, or any group sharing a common ideology. Natural work-democracy is the sum total of all functions of life governed by the rational interpersonal relations that have come into being, grown and developed in a natural and organic way. What is new in work-democracy is that for the first time in the history of sociology, a *possible* future regulation of human society is derived not from ideologies or conditions that must be created, but from natural processes that have been present and have been developing from the very beginning. Work-democratic "politics" is distinguished by the fact that *it rejects all politics and demagogism.* Masses of working men and women will not be relieved of their social responsibility. They will be *burdened* with it. Work-democrats have no ambition to be political führers. Work-democracy consciously develops formal democracy, which is expressed in the mere election of political representatives and does not entail any further responsibility on the part of the electorate, into a genuine, factual, and practical democracy on an international scale. This democracy is borne by the functions of love, work, and knowledge and is developed organically. It fights mysticism and the idea of the totalitarian state not through political attitudes but through practical functions of life, which obey their own laws. In short, natural work-democracy is a newly discovered bio-sociologic, natural and basic function of society. It is not a political program.

The Mass Psychology of Fascism

I

Ideology as a Material Force

The German freedom movement prior to Hitler was inspired by Karl Marx's economic and social theory. Hence, an understanding of German fascism must proceed from an understanding of Marxism.

In the months following National Socialism's seizure of power in Germany, even those individuals whose revolutionary firmness and readiness to be of service had been proven again and again, expressed doubts about the correctness of Marx's basic conception of social processes. These doubts were generated by a fact that, though irrefutable, was at first incomprehensible: Fascism, the most extreme representative of political and economic reaction in both its goals and its nature, had become an international reality and in many countries had visibly and undeniably outstripped the socialist revolutionary movement. That this reality found its strongest expression in the highly industrialized countries only heightened the problem. The rise of nationalism in all parts of the world offset the failure of the workers' movement in a phase of modern history in which, as the Marxists contended, "the capitalist mode of production had become economically ripe for explosion." Added to this was the deeply ingrained remembrance of the failure of the Workers' International at the outbreak of World War I and of the crushing of the revolutionary uprisings outside of Russia between

1918 and 1923. They were doubts, in short, which were generated by grave facts; if they were justified, then the basic Marxist conception was false and the workers' movement was in need of a decisive reorientation, provided one still wanted to achieve its goals. If, however, the doubts were not justified, and Marx's *basic* conception of sociology was correct, then not only was a thorough and extensive analysis of the reasons for the continual failure of the workers' movement called for, but also—and this above all—a complete elucidation of the unprecedented mass movement of fascism was also needed. Only from this could a new revolutionary practice result.[1]

A change in the situation was out of the question unless it could be proven that either the one or the other was the case. It was clear that neither an appeal to the "revolutionary class consciousness" of the working class nor the practice *à la Coué*—the camouflaging of defeats and the covering of important facts with illusions—a practice that was in vogue at that time, could lead to the goal. One could not content oneself with the fact that the workers' movement was also "progressing," that here and there resistance was being offered and strikes were being called. What is decisive is not that progress is being made, but at what tempo, in relation to the international strengthening and advance of political reaction.

The young work-democratic, sex-economic movement is interested in a thorough clarification of this question not only because it is a part of the social liberation fight in general but chiefly because the achievement of its goals is inextricably related to the achievement of the political and economic goals of natural work-democracy. For this reason we want to try to explain how the specific sex-economic questions are interlaced with the general social questions, seen from the perspective of the workers' movement.

In some of the German meetings around 1930 there were intel-

---

[1] Cf. Preface.

ligent, straightforward, though nationalistically and mystically oriented, revolutionaries—such as Otto Strasser, for example—who were wont to confront the Marxists as follows: "You Marxists like to quote Marx's theories in your defense. Marx taught that theory is verified by practice only, but your Marxism has proved to be a failure. You always come around with explanations for the defeat of the Workers' International. The 'defection of the Social Democrats' was your explanation for the defeat of 1914; you point to their 'treacherous politics' and their illusions to account for the defeat of 1918. And again you have ready 'explanations' to account for the fact that in the present world crisis the masses are turning to the Right instead of to the Left. But your explanations do not blot out the fact of your defeats! Eighty years have passed, and where is the concrete confirmation of the theory of social revolution? Your basic error is that you reject or ridicule soul and mind and that you don't comprehend that which moves everything." Such were their arguments, and exponents of Marxism had no answer. It became more and more clear that their political mass propaganda, dealing as it did solely with the discussion of *objective* socio-economic processes at a time of crisis (capitalist modes of production, economic anarchy, etc.), did not appeal to anyone other than the minority already enrolled in the Left front. The playing up of material needs and of hunger was not enough, for *every* political party did that much, even the church; so that in the end it was the mysticism of the National Socialists that triumphed over the economic theory of socialism, and at a time when the economic crisis and misery were at their worst. Hence, one had to admit that there was a glaring omission in the propaganda and in the overall conception of socialism and that, moreover, this omission was the source of its "political errors." It was an error in the Marxian comprehension of political reality, and yet all the prerequisites for its correction were contained in the methods of dialectical materialism. They had simply never been turned to use. In their political practice, to state it briefly at the outset, the Marxists *had failed to take into account the character structure of the masses and the social effect of mysticism.*

Those who followed, and were practically involved in the revolutionary Left's application of Marxism between 1917 and 1933, had to notice that it was restricted to the sphere of *objective* economic processes and governmental policies, but that it neither kept a close eye on nor comprehended the development and contradictions of the so-called "subjective factor" of history, i.e., the ideology of the masses. The revolutionary Left failed, above all, to make fresh use of its own method of dialectical materialism, to keep it alive, to comprehend every *new* social reality from a new perspective with this method.

The use of dialectical materialism to comprehend *new* historical realities was not cultivated, and fascism was a reality that neither Marx nor Engels was familiar with, and was caught sight of by Lenin only in its beginnings. The reactionary conception of reality shuts its eyes to fascism's contradictions and actual conditions. Reactionary politics automatically makes use of those social forces that oppose progress; it can do this successfully only as long as science neglects to unearth *those* revolutionary forces that must of necessity overpower the reactionary forces. As we shall see later, not only regressive but also very energetic progressive social forces emerged in the rebelliousness of the lower middle classes, which later constituted the *mass basis* of fascism. This contradiction was overlooked; indeed, the role of the lower middle classes was altogether in eclipse until shortly before Hitler's seizure of power.

Revolutionary activity in every area of human existence will come about by itself when the contradictions in every new process are comprehended; it will consist of an identification with those forces that are moving in the direction of genuine *progress*. To be radical, according to Karl Marx, means "getting to the root of things." If one gets to the *root* of things, if one grasps their contradictory operations, then the overcoming of political reaction is assured. If one does not get to the root of things, one ends, whether one wants to or not, in mechanism, in economism, or even in metaphysics, and inevitably loses one's footing. Hence, a critique

6

can only be significant and have a practical value if it can show where the contradictions of social reality were *overlooked*. What was revolutionary about Marx was not that he wrote this or that proclamation or pointed out revolutionary goals; his major revolutionary contribution is that he recognized the industrial productive forces as the progressive force of society and that he depicted the contradictions of capitalist economy as they relate to real life. The failure of the workers' movement must mean that our knowledge of those forces that retard social progress is very limited, indeed, that some major factors are still altogether unknown.

As so many works of great thinkers, Marxism also degenerated to hollow formulas and lost its scientific revolutionary potency in the hands of Marxist politicians. They were so entangled in everyday political struggles that they failed to develop the principles of a vital philosophy of life handed down by Marx and Engels. To confirm this, one need merely compare Sauerland's book on "Dialectical Materialism" or any of Salkind's or Pieck's books with Marx's *Das Kapital* or Engels' *The Development of Socialism from Utopia to Science*. Flexible methods were reduced to formulas; scientific empiricism to rigid orthodoxy. In the meantime the "proletariat" of Marx's time had developed into an enormous class of industrial workers, and the middle-class shopkeepers had become a colossus of industrial and public employees. Scientific Marxism degenerated to "vulgar Marxism." This is the name many outstanding Marxist politicians have given to the economism that restricts all of human existence to the problem of unemployment and pay rates.

It was this very vulgar Marxism that maintained that the economic crisis of 1929–33 was of such a magnitude that it *would of necessity* lead to an ideological Leftist orientation among the stricken masses. While there was still talk of a "revolutionary revival" in Germany, even after the defeat of January 1933, the reality of the situation showed that the economic crisis, which, according to expectations, was supposed to entail a development to the Left in the ideology of the masses, had led to an extreme development to the Right in the ideology of the proletarian strata of the population. The result was a cleavage between the economic basis, which developed to the Left, and the ideology of broad layers of society, which developed to the Right. This cleavage was overlooked; consequently, no one gave a thought to asking how broad masses living in utter poverty could become nationalistic. Explanations such as "chauvinism," "psychosis," "the consequences of Versailles," are not of much use, for they do not enable us to cope with the tendency of a distressed middle class to become radical Rightist; such explanations do not really comprehend the processes at work in this tendency. In fact, it was not only the middle class that turned to the Right, but broad and not always the worst elements of the proletariat. One failed to see that the middle classes, put on their guard by the success of the Russian Revolution, resorted to new and seemingly strange preventative measures (such as Roosevelt's "New Deal"), which were not understood at that time and which the workers' movement neglected to analyze. One also failed to see that, at the outset and during the initial stages of its development to a mass movement, fascism was directed against the upper middle class and hence could not be disposed of *"merely* as a bulwark of big finance," if only because it was a mass movement.

Where was the problem?

The basic Marxist conception grasped the facts that labor was exploited as a commodity, that capital was concentrated in the hands of the few, and that the latter entailed the progressive pauperization of the majority of working humanity. It was from this process that Marx arrived at the necessity of "expropriating the expropriators." According to this conception, the forces of production of capitalist society transcend the limits of the modes of production. The contradiction between *social* production and *private* appropriation of the products by capital can only be cleared up by the balancing of the modes of production with the level of the forces of production. Social production must be complemented by the social appropriation of the products. The first act of this assimilation is social revolution; this is the basic economic principle of Marxism. This assimilation can take place, it is said, only if the pauperized majority establishes the "dictatorship of the proletariat" as the dictatorship of the working majority over the minority of the now expropriated owners of the means of production.

According to Marx's theory the *economic* preconditions for a social revolution were given: capital was concentrated in the hands of the few, the growth of national economy to a world economy was completely at variance with the custom and tariff system of the national states; capitalist economy had achieved hardly half of its production capacity, and there could no longer be any doubt about its basic anarchy. The majority of the population of the highly industrialized countries was living in misery; some fifty million people were unemployed in Europe; hundreds of millions of workers scraped along on next to nothing. But the expropriation of the expropriators failed to take place and, contrary to expectations, at the crossroads between "socialism and barbarism," it was in the direction of barbarism that society first proceeded. For the international strengthening of fascism and the lagging behind of the workers' movement was nothing other than that. Those who still hoped for a revolution to result from the anticipated second World War, which in the meantime had become a reality—those, in other words, who counted on the masses to turn the weapons thrust into their hands against the inner enemy—had not followed the development of the new techniques of war. One could not simply reject the reasoning to the effect that the arming of the broad masses would be highly unlikely in the next war. According to this conception, the fighting would be directed against the unarmed masses of the large industrial centers and would be carried out by very reliable and selected war-technicians. Hence, a reorientation of one's thinking and one's evaluations was the precondition of a new revolutionary practice. World War II was a confirmation of these expectations.

ECONOMIC AND IDEOLOGICAL STRUCTURE OF THE GERMAN SOCIETY, 1928–1933

Rationally considered, one would expect economically wretched masses of workers to develop a keen consciousness of their social situation; one would further expect this consciousness to harden into a determination to rid themselves of their social misery. In short, one would expect the socially wretched working man to revolt against the abuses to which he is subjected and to say: "After all, I perform responsible social work. It is upon me and those like me that the weal and ill of society rests. I myself assume the responsibility for the work that must be done." In such a case, the thinking ("consciousness") of the worker would be in keeping with his social situation. The Marxist called it "class consciousness." We want to call it "consciousness of one's skills," or "consciousness of one's social responsibility." The cleavage between the social situation of the working masses and their consciousness of this situation implies that, instead of improving their social position, the working masses worsen it. It was precisely the wretched masses who helped to put fascism, extreme political reaction, into power.

It is a question of the role of ideology and the emotional attitude of these masses seen as a historical factor, a question of the *repercussion of the ideology on the economic basis*. If the material wretchedness of the broad masses did not lead to a social revolution; if, objectively considered, contrary revolutionary ideologies resulted from the crisis, then the development of the ideology of the masses in the critical years thwarted the "efflorescence of the forces of production," prevented, to use Marxist concepts, the "revolutionary resolution of the contradictions between the forces of production of monopolistic capitalism and its methods of production."

The composition of the classes in Germany appears as follows. Quoted from Kunik: "An Attempt to Establish the Social Composition of the German Population," *Die Internationale*, 1928, edited by Lenz: "Proletarian Policies," *Internationaler Arbeiterverlag*, 1931.

	wage earners	with families
	IN THOUSANDS	IN MILLIONS
Industrial workers[2]	21,789	40.7
Urban middle class	6,157	10.7
Lower- and middle-class farmers	6,598	9.0
Bourgeoisie (including property owners and big farmers)	718	2.0
Population (excluding children and wives)	34,762	total 62.4

[2] "The proletariat" according to Marx.

DISTRIBUTION OF URBAN MIDDLE CLASS

IN THOUSANDS

Lower strata of small tradesmen (Home industries, tenant farmers, shops operated by one person, shops operated by less than three persons)	1,196
Small shops having three or more employees	1,403
White-collar workers and civil servants	1,763
Professional people and students	431
People with small independent means and small property owners	644
	total 6,157

DISTRIBUTION OF THE WORKING CLASS

Workers in industry, trade, commerce, etc.	11,826
Agricultural workers	2,607
Home workers	138
Domestics	1,326
Social security recipients	1,717
Lower white-collar workers (less than 250 marks per month)	2,775
Lower civil servants (and pensioners)	1,400
	total 21,789

11

THE RURAL MIDDLE CLASS

Small farmers and tenant farmers (less than 5 hectare)	2,366
Middle-class farmers (between 5 and 50 hectare)	4,232
	total 6,598

These figures are taken from the German census of 1925.

It is necessary to point out, however, that they represent the distribution solely according to the socio-economic position; the ideological distribution is different. Thus, *socio-economically* viewed, the Germany of 1925 comprised:

	wage earners	*including families*
Workers	21,789,000	40,700,000
Middle Classes	12,755,000	19,700,000

On the other hand, a rough estimate of the *ideological* structure showed the following distribution:

Workers in industry, trade, commerce, etc. and agricultural workers		14,433,000
Lower middle class		20,111,000
Home workers (individual production)	138	
Domestics	1,326	
Social security recipients	1,717	
Lower category of white-collar workers (employed in big industries, e.g., "Nord-stern," Berlin)	2,775	
Lower category of civil servants (e.g., tax auditors, post office employees)	1,400	
	7,356	
	(of economic "proletariat")	

Urban Middle Class	6,157
Rural Middle Class	6,598
	total 20,111

No matter how many middle-class employees may have voted for left-wing parties and how many workers may have voted for right-wing parties, it is nonetheless striking that the figures of the *ideological distribution,* arrived at by us, *agree approximately with the election figures of 1932:* Taken together the Communists and the Social Democrats received twelve to thirteen million votes, while the NSDAP* and the German Nationalists received some nineteen to twenty million votes. Thus, with respect to *practical politics, it was not the economic but the ideological distribution that was decisive.* In short, the political importance of the lower middle class is greater than had been assumed.

During the rapid decline of the German economy, 1929–32, the NSDAP jumped from 800,000 votes in 1928 to 6,400,000 in the fall of 1930, to 13,000,000 in the summer of 1932 and 17,000,000 in January of 1933. According to Jäger's calculations ("Hitler" *Roter Aufbau,* October 1930) the votes cast by the workers made up approximately 3,000,000 of the 6,400,000 votes received by the National Socialists in 1930. Of these 3,000,000 votes, some 60 to 70 percent came from employees and 30 to 40 percent from workers.

To my knowledge it was Karl Radek who most clearly grasped the problematic aspect of this sociological process as early as 1930, following the NSDAP's first upsurge. He wrote:

> Nothing similar to this is known in the history of political struggle, particularly in a country with firmly established political differentiations, in which every new party has had to fight for any position held by the old parties. There is nothing more characteristic than the fact that, neither in bourgeois nor in socialist literature, has anything been said about this party, which assumes the second place in German political life. It is a party without history which suddenly emerges in German political life, just as an island suddenly emerges in the middle of the sea owing to volcanic forces.
> —"German Elections," *Roter Aufbau,* October, 1930

We have no doubt that this island also has a history and follows an inner logic.

---

* Nationalsozialistische Deutsche Arbeiterpartei.

13

The choice between the Marxist alternative: "fall to barbarism" or "rise to socialism," was a choice that, according to all previous experience, would be determined by the ideological structure of the dominated classes. Either this structure would be in keeping with the economic situation or it would be at variance with it, as, for instance, we find in large Asian societies, where exploitation is passively endured, or in present-day Germany, where a cleavage exists between economic situation and ideology.

Thus, the basic problem is this: What causes this cleavage, or to put it another way, what prevents the economic situation from coinciding with the psychic structure of the masses? It is a problem, in short, of comprehending the nature of the psychological structure of the masses and its relation to the economic basis from which it derives.

To comprehend this, we must first of all free ourselves from vulgar Marxist concepts, which only block the way to an understanding of fascism. Essentially, they are as follows:

In accordance with one of its formulas, vulgar Marxism completely separates economic existence from social existence as a whole, and states that man's "ideology" and "consciousness" are *solely* and *directly* determined by his economic existence. Thus, it sets up a mechanical antithesis between economy and ideology, between "structure" and "superstructure"; it makes ideology rigidly and one-sidedly dependent upon economy, and fails to see the dependency of economic development upon that of ideology. For this reason the problem of the so-called "repercussion of ideology" does not exist for it. Notwithstanding the fact that vulgar Marxism now speaks of the "lagging behind of the subjective factor," as Lenin understood it, it can do nothing about it in a practical way, for its former conception of ideology as the product of the economic situation was too rigid. It did not explore the contradictions of economy in ideology, and it did not comprehend ideology as a historical force.

In fact, it does everything in its power *not* to comprehend the structure and dynamics of ideology; it brushes it aside as "psychol-

14

ogy," which is not supposed to be "Marxistic," and leaves the handling of the subjective factor, the so-called "psychic life" in history, to the metaphysical idealism of political reaction, to a Gentile and a Rosenberg, who make "mind" and "soul" *solely* responsible for the progress of history and, strange to say, have enormous success with this thesis. The neglect of *this* aspect of sociology is something Marx himself criticized in the materialism of the eighteenth century. To the vulgar Marxist, psychology is a metaphysical system pure and simple, and he draws no distinction whatever between the metaphysical character of reactionary psychology and the basic elements of psychology, which were furnished by revolutionary psychological research and which it is our task to develop. The vulgar Marxist simply negates, instead of offering constructive criticism, and feels himself to be a "materialist" when he rejects facts such as "drive," "need," or "inner process," as being "idealistic." The result is that he gets into serious difficulties and meets with one failure after another, for he is continually forced to employ practical psychology in political practice, is forced to speak of the "needs of the masses," "revolutionary consciousness," "the will to strike," etc. The more the vulgar Marxist tries to gainsay psychology, the more he finds himself practicing metaphysical psychologism and worst, insipid Couéism. For example, he will try to explain a historical situation on the basis of a "Hitler psychosis," or console the masses and persuade them not to lose faith in Marxism. Despite everything, he asserts, headway is being made, the revolution will not be subdued, etc. He sinks to the point finally of pumping illusionary courage into the people, without in reality saying anything essential about the situation, without having comprehended what has happened. That political reaction is never at a loss to find a way out of a difficult situation, that an acute economic crisis can lead to barbarism as well as it can lead to social freedom, must remain for him a book with seven seals. Instead of allowing his thoughts and acts to issue from social reality, he transposes reality in his fantasy in such a way as to make it correspond to his wishes.

Our political psychology can be nothing other than an investi-

gation of this "subjective factor of history," of the character structure of man in a given epoch and of the ideological structure of
society that it forms. Unlike reactionary psychology and psychologistic economy, it does not try to lord it over Marxist sociology by
throwing "psychological conceptions" of social processes in its teeth,
but gives it its proper due as that which deduces consciousness from
existence.

The Marxist thesis to the effect that originally "that which is
materialistic" (existence) is converted into "that which is ideological" (in consciousness), and not vice versa, leaves two questions
open: (1) *how* this takes place, what happens in man's brain in this
process; and (2) how the "consciousness" (we will refer to it as
psychic structure from now on) that is formed in this way reacts
upon the economic process. Character-analytic psychology fills this
gap by revealing the process in man's psychic life, which is determined by the conditions of existence. By so doing, it puts its finger
on the "subjective factor," which the vulgar Marxist had failed to
comprehend. Hence, political psychology has a sharply delineated
task. It cannot, for instance, explain the genesis of class society or
the capitalist mode of production (whenever it attempts this, the
result is always reactionary nonsense—for instance, that capitalism is
a symptom of man's greed). Nonetheless, it is political psychology—and not social economy—that is in a position to investigate
the structure of man's character in a given epoch, to investigate how
he thinks and acts, how the contradictions of his existence work
themselves out, how he tries to cope with this existence, etc. To be
sure, it examines individual men and women only. If, however, it
specializes in the investigation of typical psychic processes *common*
to one category, class, professional group, etc., and excludes individual differences, then it becomes a *mass psychology*.

Thus it proceeds directly from Marx himself.

The presuppositions with which we begin are not arbitrary
presuppositions; they are not dogmas; they are real presuppositions
from which one can abstract only in fancy. *They are the actual*

16

individuals, their actions and the material conditions of their lives, those already existing as well as those produced by action.

—*German Ideology*

"*Man himself is the basis of his material production, as of every other production which he achieves.* In other words, all conditions affect and more or less modify all of the functions and activities of man—the subject of production & the creator of material wealth, of commodities. In this connection it can be indeed proven that *all human conditions and functions, no matter how and when they are manifested, influence material production and have a more or less determining effect on them*" [My italics, WR].

—*Theory of Surplus Value*

Hence, we are not saying anything new, and we are not revising Marx, as is so often maintained: "*All* human conditions," that is, not only the conditions that are a part of the work process, but also the most private and most personal and highest accomplishments of human instinct and thought; also, in other words, *the sexual life of women and adolescents and children, the level of the sociological investigation of these conditions and its application to new social questions.* With a certain kind of these "human conditions," Hitler was able to bring about a historical situation that is not to be ridiculed out of existence. Marx was not able to develop a sociology of sex, because at that time sexology did not exist. Hence, it now becomes a question of incorporating both the purely economic and sex-economic conditions into the framework of sociology, of destroying the hegemony of the mystics and metaphysicians in this domain.

When an "ideology has a repercussive effect upon the economic process," this means that it must have become a material force. When an ideology becomes a material force, as soon as it has the ability to arouse masses, then we must go on to ask: How does this take place? How is it possible for an ideologic factor to produce a materialistic result, that is, for a theory to produce a revolutionary effect? The answer to this question must also be the answer to the question of reactionary mass psychology; it must, in other words, elucidate the "Hitler psychosis."

The ideology of every social formation has the function not only of reflecting the economic process of this society, but also and more significantly of embedding this economic process in the *psychic structures of the people who make up the society*. Man is subject to the conditions of his existence in a twofold way: directly through the immediate influence of his economic and social position, and indirectly by means of the ideologic structure of the society. His psychic structure, in other words, is forced to develop a contradiction corresponding to the contradiction between the influence exercised by his material position and the influence exercised by the ideological structure of society. The worker, for instance, is subject to the situation of his work as well as to the general ideology of the society. Since man, however, regardless of class, is not only the object of these influences but also reproduces them in his *activities*, his thinking and acting must be just as contradictory as the society from which they derive. But, inasmuch *as a social ideology changes man's psychic structure, it has not only reproduced itself in man but, what is more significant, has become an active force, a material power in man, who in turn has become concretely changed, and, as a consequence thereof, acts in a different and contradictory fashion.* It is in this way and *only* in this way that the repercussions of a society's ideology on the economic basis from which it derives is possible. The "repercussion" loses its apparent metaphysical and psychologistic character when it can be comprehended as the functioning of the character structure of socially active man. As such, it is the object of natural scientific investigations of the character. Thus, the statement that the "ideology" changes at a slower pace than the economic basis is invested with a definite cogency. The basic traits of the character structures corresponding to a definite historical situation are formed in early childhood, and are far more conservative than the forces of technical production. It results from this that, as time goes on, *the psychic structures lag behind the rapid changes of the social conditions from which they derived, and later come into conflict with new forms of life.* This is the basic trait of the nature of so-called tradition, i.e., of the contradiction between the old and the new social situation.

HOW MASS PSYCHOLOGY SEES THE PROBLEM

We begin to see now that the economic and ideologic situations of the masses need not necessarily coincide, and that, indeed, there can be a considerable cleavage between the two. The economic situation is not directly and immediately converted into political consciousness. If this were the case, the social revolution would have been here long ago. In keeping with this dichotomy of social condition and social consciousness, the investigation of society must proceed along two different lines. Notwithstanding the fact that the psychic structure derives from the economic existence, the economic situation has to be comprehended with methods other than those used to comprehend the character structure: the former has to be comprehended socio-economically, the latter biopsychologically. Let us illustrate this with a simple example: When workers who are hungry, owing to wage-squeezing, go on strike, their act is a direct result of their economic situation. The same applies to the man who steals food because he is hungry. That a man steals because he is hungry, or that workers strike because they are being exploited, needs no further psychological clarification. In both cases ideology and action are commensurate with economic pressure. Economic situation and ideology coincide with one another. Reactionary psychology is wont to explain the theft and the strike in terms of supposed irrational motives; reactionary rationalizations are invariably the result. Social psychology sees the problem in an entirely different light: what has to be explained is not the fact that the man who is hungry steals or the fact that the man who is exploited strikes, but why the majority of those who are hungry *don't* steal and why the majority of those who are exploited *don't* strike. Thus, social economy can give a complete explanation of a social fact that serves a rational end, i.e., when it satisfies an immediate need and reflects and magnifies the economic situation. The social economic explanation does not hold up, on the other hand, when a man's thought and action *are inconsistent with* the economic situation, are *irrational,* in other words. The vulgar Marxist and the narrow-minded economist, who do not acknowledge psychology, are helpless in the face of such a contradiction. The more mechanistically and economistically oriented a sociologist is, the less he knows about man's psychic structure, the more he is apt to fall prey to superficial psychologism in the practice of mass propaganda. Instead of probing and resolving the psychic contradictions in the individuals of the masses, he has recourse to insipid Couéism or he explains the nationalistic movement on the basis of a "mass psychosis."[3] Hence, the line of questioning of mass psychology begins precisely at the point where the *immediate* socio-economic explanation hits wide of the mark. Does this mean that mass psychology and social economy serve cross purposes? No. For thinking and acting on the part of the masses contradictory to the immediate socio-economic situation, i.e., irrational thinking and acting, are themselves the result of an earlier, *older* socio-economic situation. One is wont to explain the repression of social consciousness by so-called tradition. But no investigation has been made as yet to determine just what "tradition" is, to determine which psychic elements are molded by it. Narrow-minded economy has repeatedly failed to see that the most essential question does not relate to the workers' consciousness of social responsibility (this is self-evident!) but to what it is that *inhibits the development of this consciousness of responsibility.*

Ignorance of the character structure of masses of people invariably leads to fruitless questioning. The Communists, for example, said that it was the misdirected policies of the Social Democrats that made it possible for the fascists to seize power. Actually this explanation did not explain anything, for it was precisely the Social

---

[3] In view of the fact that the economist neither knows nor acknowledges the existence of psychic processes, the words "mass psychosis" do not mean to him what they mean to us, namely a social circumstance of enormous historical importance; to him it is a matter of no social significance whatever.

Democrats who made a point of spreading illusions. In short, it did not result in a new mode of action. That political reaction in the form of fascism had "befogged," "corrupted," and "hypnotized" the masses is an explanation that is as sterile as the others. This is and will continue to be the function of fascism as long as it exists. Such explanations are sterile because they fail to offer a way out. Experience teaches us that such disclosures, no matter how often they are repeated, do not convince the masses; that, in other words, social economic inquiry by itself is not enough. Wouldn't it be closer to the mark to ask *what was going on in the masses* that they could not and would not recognize the function of fascism? To say that "The workers *have* to realize . . ." or "We didn't understand . . ." does not serve any purpose. Why didn't the workers realize, and why didn't they understand? The questions that formed the basis of discussion between the Right and the Left in the workers' movements are also to be regarded as sterile. The Right contended that the workers were not predisposed to fight; the Left, on the other hand, refuted this and asserted that the workers were revolutionary and that the Right's statement was a betrayal of revolutionary thinking. Both assertions, because they failed to see the complexities of the issue, were rigidly mechanistic. A realistic appraisal would have had to point out that the average worker bears a contradiction in himself; that he, in other words, is neither a clear-cut revolutionary nor a clear-cut conservative, but stands divided. His psychic structure derives on the one hand from the social situation (which prepares the ground for revolutionary attitudes) and on the other hand from the entire atmosphere of authoritarian society —the two being at odds with one another.

It is of decisive importance to recognize such a contradiction and to learn precisely how that which is reactionary and that which is progressive-revolutionary in the workers are set off against one another. Naturally, the same applies to the middle-class man. That he rebels against the "system" in a crisis is readily understandable. However, notwithstanding the fact that he is already in an economically wretched position, the fact that he fears progress and becomes extremely reactionary is not to be readily understood from a socio-economic point of view. In short, he too bears a contradiction in himself between rebellious feelings and reactionary aims and contents.

We do not, for instance, give a full sociological explanation of a war when we analyze the specific economic and political factors that are its immediate cause. In other words, it is only part of the story that the German annexation ambitions prior to 1914 were focused on the ore mines of Briey and Longy, on the Belgian industrial center, on the extension of Germany's colonial possessions in the Near East; or that Hitler's imperial interests were focused on the oil wells of Baku, on the factories of Czechoslovakia, etc. To be sure, the economic interests of German imperialism were the *immediate* decisive factors, but we also have to put into proper perspective the *mass psychological* basis of world wars; we have to ask how the *psychological structure of the masses* was capable of absorbing the imperialistic ideology, to translate the imperialistic slogans into deeds that were diametrically opposed to the peaceful, politically disinterested attitude of the German population. To say that this was due to the "defection of the leaders of the Second International" is insufficient. *Why did the myriad masses of the freedom-loving and anti-imperialistic oriented workers allow themselves to be betrayed?* The fear of the consequences involved in conscientious objection accounts only for a minority of cases. Those who went through the mobilization of 1914 know that various moods were evident among the working masses. They ranged from a conscious refusal on the part of a minority to a strange resignedness to fate (or plain apathy) on the part of very broad layers of the population, to the point of clear martial enthusiasm, not only in the middle classes but among large segments of industrial workers also. The apathy of some as well as the enthusiasm of others was undoubtedly part of the foundations of war in the structure of the masses. This function on the part of the psychology of the masses in both world wars can be understood only from the sex-economic point of view, namely that the *imperialistic ideology concretely changed the structures of the working masses to suit imperialism.* To say that social catastrophes are caused by "war psychoses" or by "mass befogging" is merely to throw out phrases. Such explanations explain nothing. Besides it would be a very low estimation of the masses to suppose that they would be accessible to mere befogging. The point is that *every social order produces in the masses of its members that structure which it needs to achieve its main aims.*[4] No war would be possible without this psychological structure of the masses. An essential relation exists between the economic structure of society and the mass psychological structure of its members, not only in the sense that the ruling ideology is the ideology of the ruling class, but, what is even more important for the solving of practical questions of politics, the *contradictions* of the economic structure of a society are also embedded in the psychological structure of the subjugated masses. Otherwise it would be inconceivable that the economic laws of a society could succeed in achieving concrete results solely through the activities of the masses subjected to them.

To be sure, the freedom movements of Germany knew of the so-called "subjective factor of history" (contrary to mechanistic materialism, Marx conceived of man as the subject of history, and it was precisely this side of Marxism that Lenin built upon); what was lacking was a comprehension of *irrational, seemingly purposeless actions* or, to put it another way, of *the cleavage between economy and ideology.* We have to be able to explain how it was possible for mysticism to have triumphed over scientific sociology. This task can

---

[4] "In every epoch the ideas of the ruling class are the ruling ideas, i.e., the class which is the ruling material power of the society also constitutes that society's ideological power. The class which has the means of material production at its disposal also has the means of ideological 'production' at its disposal, so that those who lack the means of ideological production are thereby on the average subject to those who have. The ruling ideas are nothing more than the idealistic expression of the ruling material conditions, that is to say, the ruling material conditions expressed as ideas; the conditions which enabled the one class to become the ruling class or, to put it another way, the ideas of their rulership [Marx]."

be accomplished only if our line of questioning is such that a new mode of action results spontaneously from our explanation. If the working man is neither a clear-cut reactionary nor a clear-cut revolutionary, but is caught in a contradiction between reactionary and revolutionary tendencies, then if we succeed in putting our finger on this contradiction, the result must be a mode of action that offsets the conservative psychic forces with revolutionary forces. Every form of mysticism is reactionary, and the reactionary man is mystical. To ridicule mysticism, to try to pass it off as "befogging" or as "psychosis," does not lead to a program against mysticism. If mysticism is correctly comprehended, however, an antidote must of necessity result. But to accomplish this task, the relations between social situation and structural formation, especially the *irrational* ideas that are not to be explained on a purely socio-economic basis, have to be comprehended as completely as our means of cognition allow.

THE SOCIAL FUNCTION OF SEXUAL REPRESSION

Even Lenin noted a peculiar, irrational behavior on the part of the masses before and in the process of a revolt. On the soldiers' revolt in Russia in 1905, he wrote:

> The soldier had a great deal of sympathy for the cause of the peasant; at the mere mention of land, his eyes blazed with passion. Several times military power passed into the hands of the soldiers, but this power was hardly ever used resolutely. The soldiers wavered. A few hours after they had disposed of a hated superior, they released the others, entered into negotiations with the authorities, and then had themselves shot, submitted to the rod, had themselves yoked again.
>
> —*Ueber Religion* p. 65

Any mystic will explain such behavior on the basis of man's eternal moral nature, which, he would contend, prohibits a rebellion against the divine scheme and the "authority of the state" and its

24

representatives. The vulgar Marxist simply disregards such phenomena, and he would have neither an understanding nor an explanation for them because they are not to be explained from a purely economic point of view. The Freudian conception comes considerably closer to the facts of the case, for it recognizes such behavior as the effect of infantile guilt-feelings toward the father figure. Yet it fails to give us any insight into the sociological origin and function of this behavior, and for that reason does not lead to a practical solution. It also overlooks the connection between this behavior and the repression and distortion of the sexual life of the broad masses.

To help clarify our approach to the investigation of such irrational *mass* psychological phenomena, it is necessary to take a cursory glance at the line of questioning of *sex-economy*, which is treated in detail elsewhere.

Sex-economy is a field of research that grew out of the sociology of human sexual life many years ago, through the application of functionalism in this sphere, and has acquired a number of new insights. It proceeds from the following presuppositions:

Marx found social life to be governed by the conditions of economic production and by the class conflict that resulted from these conditions at a definite point of history. It is only seldom that brute force is resorted to in the domination of the oppressed classes by the owners of the social means of production; its main weapon is its ideological power over the oppressed, for it is this ideology that is the mainstay of the state apparatus. We have already mentioned that for Marx it is the living, productive man, with his psychic and physical disposition, who is the first presupposition of history and of politics. The character structure of active man, the so-called "subjective factor of history" in Marx's sense, remained uninvestigated because Marx was a sociologist and not a psychologist, and because at that time scientific psychology did not exist. Why man had allowed himself to be exploited and morally humiliated, why, in short, he had submitted to slavery for thousands of years, remained unanswered; what had been ascertained was only the economic process of society and the mechanism of economic exploitation.

Just about half a century later, using a special method he called *psychoanalysis*, Freud discovered the process that governs psychic life. His most important discoveries, which had a devastating and revolutionary effect upon a large number of existing ideas (a fact that garnered him the hate of the world in the beginning), are as follows:

Consciousness is only a small part of the psychic life; it itself is governed by psychic processes that take place unconsciously and are therefore not accessible to conscious control. Every psychic experience (no matter how meaningless it appears to be), such as a dream, a useless performance, the absurd utterances of the psychically sick and mentally deranged, etc., has a function and a "meaning" and can be completely understood if one can succeed in tracing its etiology. Thus psychology, which had been steadily deteriorating into a kind of physics of the brain ("brain mythology") or into a theory of a mysterious objective *Geist*, entered the domain of natural science.

Freud's *second* great discovery was that even the small child develops a lively sexuality, which has nothing to do with procreation; that, in other words, *sexuality* and *procreation*, and *sexual* and *genital*, are not the same. The analytic dissection of psychic processes further proved that sexuality, or rather its energy, the *libido*, which is of the body, is the prime motor of psychic life. Hence, the biologic presuppositions and social conditions of life overlap in the mind.

The *third* great discovery was that childhood sexuality, of which what is most crucial in the child-parent relationship ("the Oedipus complex") is a part, is usually repressed out of fear of punishment for sexual acts and thoughts (basically a "fear of castration"); the child's sexual activity is blocked and extinguished from memory. Thus, while repression of childhood sexuality withdraws it from the influence of consciousness, it does not weaken its force. On the contrary, the repression intensifies it and enables it to manifest itself in various pathological disturbances of the mind. As there is hardly an exception to this rule among "civilized man," Freud could say that he had all of humanity as his patient.

The *fourth* important discovery in this connection was that, far from being of divine origin, man's moral code was derived from the educational measures used by the parents and parental surrogates in earliest childhood. At bottom, those educational measures opposed to childhood sexuality are most effective. The conflict that originally takes place between the child's desires and the parent's suppression of these desires later becomes the conflict between instinct and morality *within* the person. In adults the moral code, which itself is unconscious, operates against the comprehension of the laws of sexuality and of unconscious psychic life; it supports sexual repression ("sexual resistance") and accounts for the widespread resistance to the "uncovering" of childhood sexuality.

Through their very existence, each one of these discoveries (we named only those that were most important for our subject) constitutes a severe blow to reactionary moral philosophy and especially to religious metaphysics, both of which uphold eternal moral values, conceive of the world as being under the rulership of an objective "power," and deny childhood sexuality, in addition to confining sexuality to the function of procreation. However, these discoveries could not exercise a significant influence because the psychoanalytic sociology that was based on them retarded most of what they had given in the way of progressive and revolutionary impetus. This is not the place to prove this. Psychoanalytic sociology tried to analyze society as it would analyze an individual, set up an absolute antithesis between the process of civilization and sexual gratification, conceived of destructive instincts as primary biological facts governing human destiny immutably, denied the existence of a matriarchal primeval period, and ended in a crippling skepticism, because it recoiled from the consequences of its own discoveries. Its hostility toward efforts proceeding on the basis of these discoveries goes back many years, and its representatives are unswerving in their opposition to such efforts. All of this has not the slightest effect on our determination to defend Freud's great discoveries against every attack, regardless of origin or source.

Sex-economic sociology's line of questioning, which is based on these discoveries, is not one of the typical attempts to supplement, replace, or confuse Marx with Freud or Freud with Marx. In an earlier passage we mentioned the area in historical materialism where psychoanalysis has to fulfill a scientific function, which social economy is not in a position to accomplish: the comprehension of the structure and dynamics of ideology, not of its historical basis. By incorporating the insights afforded by psychoanalysis, sociology attains a higher standard and is in a much better position to master reality; the nature of man's structure is finally grasped. It is only the narrow-minded politician who will reproach character-analytic structure-psychology for not being able to make immediate practical suggestions. And it is only a political loudmouth who will feel called upon to condemn it in total because it is afflicted with all the distortions of a conservative view of life. But it is the genuine sociologist who will reckon psychoanalysis' comprehension of childhood sexuality as a highly significant revolutionary act.

It follows of itself that the science of sex-economic sociology, which builds upon the *sociological* groundwork of Marx and the *psychological* groundwork of Freud, is essentially a mass psychological and sex-sociological science at the same time. Having rejected Freud's philosophy of civilization,[5] it begins where the clinical psychological line of questioning of psychoanalysis ends.

Psychoanalysis discloses the effects and mechanisms of sexual suppression and repression and of their pathological consequences in the individual. Sex-economic sociology goes further and asks: *For what sociological reasons is sexuality suppressed by the society and repressed by the individual?* The church says it is for the sake of salvation beyond the grave; mystical moral philosophy says that it is a direct result of man's eternal ethical and moral nature; the

---

[5] In which, despite all its idealism, more truth is found about living life than in all sociologies and some Marxist psychologies taken together.

Freudian philosophy of civilization contends that this takes place in the interest of "culture." One becomes a bit skeptical and asks how is it possible for the masturbation of small children and the sexual intercourse of adolescents to disrupt the building of gas stations and the manufacturing of airplanes. It becomes apparent that it is not cultural activity itself which demands suppression and repression of sexuality, but only the present *forms* of this activity, and so one is willing to sacrifice these forms if by so doing the terrible wretchedness of children and adolescents could be eliminated. The question, then, is no longer one relating to culture, but one relating to social order. If one studies the history of sexual suppression and the etiology of sexual repression, one finds that it cannot be traced back to the beginnings of cultural development; suppression and repression, in other words, are not the presuppositions of cultural development. It was not until relatively late, with the establishment of an authoritarian patriarchy and the beginning of the division of the classes, that suppression of sexuality begins to make its appearance. It is at this stage that sexual interests in general begin to enter the service of a minority's interest in material profit; in the patriarchal marriage and family this state of affairs assumes a solid organizational form. With the restriction and suppression of sexuality, the nature of human feeling changes; a sex-negating religion comes into being and gradually develops its own sex-political organization, the church with all its predecessors, the aim of which is nothing other than the eradication of man's sexual desires and consequently of what little happiness there is on earth. There is good reason for all this when seen from the perspective of the now-thriving exploitation of human labor.

To comprehend the relation between sexual suppression and human exploitation, it is necessary to get an insight into the basic social institution in which the economic and sex-economic situation of patriarchal authoritarian society are interwoven. Without the inclusion of this institution, it is not possible to understand the sexual economy and the ideological process of a patriarchal society. The psychoanalysis of men and women of all ages, all countries, and every social class shows that: *The interlacing of the socio-economic structure with the sexual structure of society and the structural reproduction of society take place in the first four or five years and in the authoritarian family.* The church only continues this function later. Thus, the authoritarian state gains an enormous interest in the authoritarian family: *It becomes the factory in which the state's structure and ideology are molded.*

We have found the social institution in which the sexual and the economic interests of the authoritarian system converge. Now we have to ask *how* this convergence takes place and *how* it operates. Needless to say, the analysis of the typical character structure of reactionary man (the worker included) can yield an answer only if one is at all conscious of the necessity of posing such a question. The moral inhibition of the child's natural sexuality, the last stage of which is the severe impairment of the child's *genital* sexuality, makes the child afraid, shy, fearful of authority, obedient, "good," and "docile" in the authoritarian sense of the words. It has a crippling effect on man's rebellious forces because every vital life-impulse is now burdened with severe fear; and since sex is a forbidden subject, thought in general and man's critical faculty also become inhibited. In short, morality's aim is to produce acquiescent subjects who, despite distress and humiliation, are adjusted to the authoritarian order. Thus, the family is the authoritarian state in miniature, to which the child must learn to adapt himself as a preparation for the general social adjustment required of him later. *Man's authoritarian structure*—this must be clearly established—*is basically produced by the embedding of sexual inhibitions and fear in the living substance of sexual impulses.*

We will readily grasp why sex-economy views the family as the most important source for the reproduction of the authoritarian social system when we consider the situation of the average conservative worker's wife. Economically she is just as distressed as a liberated working woman, is subject to the same economic situation, but *she* votes for the Fascist party; if we further clarify the actual difference between the sexual ideology of the average liberated woman and that of the average reactionary woman, then we recognize the decisive importance of sexual structure. Her anti-sexual, moral inhibitions prevent the conservative woman from gaining a consciousness of her social situation and bind her just as firmly to the church as they make her fear "sexual Bolshevism." Theoretically, the state of affairs is as follows: The vulgar Marxist who thinks in mechanistic terms assumes that discernment of the social situation would have to be especially keen when sexual distress is added to economic distress. If this assumption were true, the majority of adolescents and the majority of women would have to be far more rebellious than the majority of men. Reality reveals an entirely different picture, and the economist is at a complete loss to know how to deal with it. He will find it incomprehensible that the reactionary woman is not even interested in hearing his economic program. The explanation is: The suppression of one's primitive material needs compasses a different result than the suppression of one's sexual needs. The former incites to rebellion, whereas the latter—inasmuch as it causes sexual needs to be repressed, withdraws them from consciousness and anchors itself as a moral defense—prevents rebellion against *both* forms of suppression. Indeed, the inhibition of rebellion itself is unconscious. In the consciousness of the average nonpolitical man there is not even a trace of it.

The result is conservatism, fear of freedom, in a word, reactionary thinking.

It is not only by means of this process that sexual repression strengthens political reaction and makes the individual in the masses passive and nonpolitical; it creates a secondary force in man's structure—an artificial interest, which actively supports the authoritarian order. When sexuality is prevented from attaining natural gratification, owing to the process of sexual repression, what happens is that it seeks various kinds of substitute gratifications. Thus, for instance, natural aggression is distorted into brutal sadism, which constitutes an essential part of the mass-psychological basis of those imperialistic wars that are instigated by a few. To give another instance: From the point of view of mass psychology, the effect of militarism is based essentially on a libidinous mechanism. The sexual effect of a uniform, the erotically provocative effect of rhythmically executed goose-stepping, the exhibitionistic nature of militaristic procedures, have been more practically comprehended by a salesgirl or an average secretary than by our most erudite politicians. On the other hand it is political reaction that consciously exploits these sexual interests. It not only designs flashy uniforms for the men, it puts the recruiting into the hands of attractive women. In conclusion, let us but recall the recruiting posters of war-thirsty powers, which ran something as follows: "Travel to foreign countries—join the Royal Navy!" and the foreign countries were portrayed by exotic women. And why are these posters effective? Because our youth has become sexually starved owing to sexual suppression.

The sexual morality that inhibits the will to freedom, as well as those forces that comply with authoritarian interests, derive their energy from repressed sexuality. Now we have a better comprehension of an essential part of the process of the "repercussion of ideology on the economic basis": *sexual inhibition changes the structure of economically suppressed man in such a way that he acts, feels, and thinks contrary to his own material interests.*

Thus, mass psychology enables us to substantiate and interpret Lenin's observation. In their officers the soldiers of 1905 unconsciously perceived their childhood fathers (condensed in the conception of God), who denied sexuality and whom one could neither kill nor want to kill, though they shattered one's joy of life. Both their repentance and their irresolution subsequent to the seizure of power were an expression of its opposite, hate transformed into pity, which as such could not be translated into action.

Thus, the practical problem of mass psychology is to activate the passive majority of the population, which always helps political reaction to achieve victory, and to eliminate those inhibitions that run counter to the development of the will to freedom born of the socio-economic situation. Freed of its bonds and directed into the channels of the freedom movement's rational goals, the psychic energy of the average mass of people excited over a football game or laughing over a cheap musical would no longer be capable of being fettered. The sex-economic investigation that follows is conducted from this point of view.

II

The Authoritarian Ideology of the Family in the Mass Psychology of Fascism

FÜHRER AND MASS STRUCTURE

If, at some future date, the history of social processes would allow the reactionary historian time to indulge in speculations on Germany's past, he would be sure to perceive in Hitler's success in the years between 1928 and 1933 the proof that a great man makes history only inasmuch as he inflames the masses with "his idea." In fact, National Socialist propaganda was built upon this "führer ideology." To the same limited extent to which the propagandists of National Socialism understood the mechanics of their success, they were able to comprehend the historical basis of the National Socialist movement. This is very well illustrated by an article published at that time entitled, "Christianity and National Socialism," written by the National Socialist Wilhelm Stapel. He stated: "For the very reason that National Socialism is an *elementary* movement, it cannot be gotten at with 'arguments.' Arguments would be effective only if the movement had gained its power by argumentation."

In keeping with this peculiarity the rally speeches of the National Socialists were very conspicuous for their skillfulness in operating upon the *emotions* of the individuals in the masses and of *avoiding relevant arguments as much as possible*. In various passages in his book *Mein Kampf* Hitler stresses that true mass psychological tactics dispense with argumentation and keep the masses' attention fixed on the "great final goal" at all times. What the final goal looked like *after* the seizure of power can easily be shown by Italian fascism. Similarly, Göring's decrees against the economic organizations of the middle classes, the rebuff to the "second revolution," which was expected by the partisans, the failure to fulfill the promised socialist measures, etc., revealed the reactionary function of fascism. The following view shows just how little Hitler himself understood the mechanism of his success:

> This broadness of outline from which we must never depart, in combination with steady, consistent emphasis, allows our final success to mature. And then, to our amazement, we shall see what tremendous results such perseverance leads to—to results that are *almost beyond our understanding* [my italics, WR].[1]

Hitler's success, therefore, could certainly not be explained on the basis of his reactionary role in the history of capitalism, for this role, had it been openly avowed in his propaganda, would have achieved the opposite of that which was intended. The investigation of Hitler's mass psychological effect has to proceed from the presupposition that a führer, or the champion of an idea, can be successful (if not in a historical, then at least in a limited perspective) only *if his personal point of view, his ideology, or his program bears a resemblance to the average structure of a broad category of individuals.* This leads to the question: *To what historical and sociological situation do these mass structures owe their genesis?* And so the line of questioning of mass psychology is shifted from the metaphysics of the "führer idea" to the reality of social life. *Only when the structure of the führer's personality is in harmony with the structures of broad groups can a "führer" make history.* And whether he makes a *permanent* or only a *temporary* impact on history depends solely upon whether his program lies in the direction of progressive social processes or whether it stems them. Hence one is on the wrong scent when one attempts to explain Hitler's success solely on the basis of the demagogy of the National Social-

---

[1] *Mein Kampf* by Adolf Hitler, translated by Ralph Manheim, Houghton Mifflin Company, Boston, 1943, p. 185.

ists, the "befogging of the masses," their "deception," or to apply the vague, hollow term "Nazi psychosis," as the Communists and other politicians did later. For it is precisely a question of understanding why the masses *proved to be accessible to deception, befogging, and a psychotic situation.* Without a precise knowledge of what *goes on in the masses,* the problem cannot be solved. To assert that the Hitler movement was a reactionary movement is not enough. The NSDAP's mass success is inconsistent with this supposed reactionary role, for why would millions upon millions affirm their own suppression? Here is a contradiction that can be explained only by mass psychology—and not by politics or economics.

National Socialism made use of various means in dealing with various classes, and made various promises depending upon the social class it needed at a particular time. In the spring of 1933, for example, it was the *revolutionary* character of the Nazi movement that was given particular emphasis in Nazi propaganda in an effort to win over the industrial workers, and the first of May was "celebrated," but only after the aristocracy had been appeased in Potsdam. To ascribe the success solely to political swindle, however, would be to become entangled in a contradiction with the basic idea of freedom, and would practically exclude the possibility of a social revolution. What must be answered is: *Why do the masses allow themselves to be politically swindled?* The masses had every possibility of evaluating the propaganda of the various parties. Why didn't they see that, while promising the workers that the owners of the means of production would be disappropriated, Hitler promised the capitalists that their rights would be protected?

Hitler's personal structure and his life history are of no importance whatever for an understanding of National Socialism. It is interesting, however, that the lower middle-class origin of his ideas coincide in the main with the mass structures, which eagerly accepted these ideas.

As is done in every reactionary movement, Hitler relied upon the various strata of the lower middle class for his support. National Socialism exposes all the contradictions that characterize the mass psychology of the petty bourgeois. Now it is a question of (1) comprehending the contradictions themselves, and (2) getting an insight into their common origin in the conditions of imperialistic production. We will restrict ourselves to questions of *sex* ideology.

HITLER'S BACKGROUND

The führer of the German middle classes in revolt was himself the son of a civil servant. He tells of a conflict which is especially characteristic of a middle-class mass structure. His father wanted him to become a civil servant; but the son rebelled against the paternal plan, resolved "on no account" to obey, became a painter, and fell into poverty in the process. Yet alongside this rebellion against the father, a respect for and acceptance of his authority continued to exist. This ambivalent attitude toward authority—*rebellion against it coupled with acceptance and submission*—is a basic feature of every middle-class structure from the age of puberty to full adulthood and is especially pronounced in individuals stemming from materially restricted circumstances.

Hitler speaks of his mother with great sentimentality. He assures us that he cried only once in his life, namely when his mother died. His rejection of sex and his neurotic idolization of motherhood are clearly evident in his theory on race and syphilis (see next chapter).

As a young nationalist who lived in Austria, Hitler resolved to take up the fight against the Austrian dynasty, which had abandoned the "German fatherland to Slavization." In his polemics against the Hapsburgs, the reproach that there were several syphilitics among them assumes a conspicuous position. One would not pay any further attention to this factor if it were not that the idea of the "poisoning of the nation" and the whole attitude toward the question of syphilis are brought up again and again, and later, after the seizure of power, constitute a central part of his domestic policies.

In the beginning Hitler sympathized with the Social Democrats, because they led the fight for universal suffrage, and this might have brought about a weakening of the "Hapsburger regime," which he despised. But Hitler was repelled by Social Democracy's emphasis on class differences, their negation of the nation, the authority of the state, the private ownership of the social means of production, of religion and morals. What finally caused him to turn away from the Social Democrats was the invitation to join the union. He refused and justified his refusal with his first insight into the role of Social Democracy.

Bismarck becomes his idol, because it was he who had brought about the unification of the German nation and had fought against the Austrian dynasty. The anti-Semite Lueger and the German national Schönerer play a decisive role in shaping Hitler's further development. From now on his program is based on nationalistic-*imperialistic* aims, which he intends to compass with different, more suited means than those used by the old "bourgeois" nationalists. *The means he chooses are determined by his recognition of the effectiveness of organized Marxism's power, by his recognition of the importance of the masses for every political movement.*

> . . . Not until the international world view—politically led by organized Marxism—is confronted by a folkish world view, organized and led with equal unity, will success, supposing the fighting energy to be equal on both sides, fall to the side of eternal truth.
>
> —Op. cit. p. 384

> . . . What gave the international world view success was its representation by a political party organized into storm troops; what caused the defeat of the opposite world view was its lack up to now of a unified body to represent it. Not by unlimited freedom to interpret a general view, but only in the limited and hence integrating form of a political organization can a world view fight and conquer.
>
> —Op. cit. p. 385

Hitler soon recognized the inconsistency of the Social Democratic policies and the powerlessness of the old bourgeois parties, including the German National party.

All this was only the necessary consequence of the absence of a basic new anti-Marxist philosophy endowed with a stormy will to conquer.

—Op. cit. p. 173

The more I occupied myself with the idea of a necessary change in the government's attitude toward Social Democracy as the momentary embodiment of Marxism, the more I recognized the lack of a serviceable substitute for this doctrine. What would be given the masses, if, just supposing, Social Democracy had been broken? There was not one movement in existence which could have been expected to succeed in drawing into its sphere of influence the great multitudes of workers grown more or less leaderless. It is senseless and more than stupid to believe that the international fanatic who had left the class party would now at once join a bourgeois party, in other words, a new class organization.

—Op. cit. p. 173

The "bourgeois" parties, as they designated themselves, will never be able to attach the "proletarian" masses to their camp, for here two worlds oppose each other, in part naturally and in part artificially divided, whose mutual relation can only be struggle. The younger will be victorious—and this is Marxism.

—Op. cit. p. 174

National Socialism's basic anti-Soviet attitude was evident almost from the beginning.

. . . If land was desired in Europe, it could be obtained by and large only at the expense of Russia, and this meant that the new Reich must again set itself on the march along the road of the Teutonic Knights of old, to obtain by the German sword sod for the German plow and daily bread for the nation.

—Op. cit. p. 140

Hitler saw himself confronted with the following questions: How is the National Socialist idea to be carried to victory? How is Marxism to be combatted effectively? How is one to get to the masses?

39

These questions in mind, Hitler appeals to the *nationalistic* feelings of the masses, decides, however, to develop his own technique of propaganda and to employ it consistently, thus organizing on a mass basis, as Marxism had done.

Hence, what he wants—and it is openly admitted—is to implement nationalistic imperialism with methods he has borrowed from Marxism, including its technique of mass organization. *But the success of this mass organization is to be ascribed to the masses and not to Hitler.* It was man's authoritarian freedom-fearing structure that enabled his propaganda to take root. Hence, what is important about Hitler sociologically does not issue from his personality but from the importance attached to him *by the masses.* And what makes the problem all the more complex is the fact that Hitler held the masses, with whose help he wanted to carry out his imperialism, in complete contempt. Instead of giving many examples in substantiation of this, let *one* candid confession suffice: ". . . the mood of the people was always a mere discharge of what was funneled into public opinion from above [op. cit. p. 128]."

How were the structures of the masses constituted that they were still capable of imbibing Hitler's propaganda, despite all this?

ON THE MASS PSYCHOLOGY OF THE LOWER MIDDLE CLASS

We have stated that Hitler's success is to be ascribed neither to his "personality" nor to the objective role his ideology played in capitalism. Nor, for that matter, is it to be ascribed to a mere "befogging" of the masses who followed him. We put our finger on the core of the matter: *What was going on in the masses that they followed a party whose leadership was objectively as well as subjectively in diametrical opposition to the interests of the working masses?*

In answering this question, we must first of all bear in mind that, in its first successful onset, the National Socialist movement relied upon the broad layers of the so-called middle classes, i.e., the millions of private and public officials, middle-class merchants and lower and middle-class farmers. *From the point of view of its social basis, National Socialism was a lower middle-class movement, and this was the case wherever it appeared,* whether in Italy, Hungary, Argentina, or Norway. Hence, this lower middle class, which was formerly on the side of the various bourgeois democracies, must have gone through an inner transformation causing it to change its political position. The social situation and its corresponding psychological structure in the lower middle classes offer an explanation of the basic similarities as well as differences between the ideology of the liberal bourgeoisie and the fascists.

Fascism's lower middle class is the same as liberal democracy's lower middle class, only in a different historical epoch of capitalism. In the election years of 1930 to 1932, National Socialism polled its new votes almost exclusively from the German National Party and the smaller faction parties of the German Reich. Only the Catholic center maintained its position, even in the Prussian election of 1932. It wasn't until the later election that National Socialism also succeeded in making an incursion into the masses of industrial workers. The middle class was and continued to be the mainstay of the swastika. And it was this class, championing the cause of National Socialism, which stepped onto the political tribunal and halted the revolutionary reconstruction of society during the most severe economic convulsion the capitalist system had experienced (1929–32). Political reaction's assessment of the middle class's importance was absolutely correct. In a leaflet of the German National Party of April 8, 1932, we read: "The middle class is of decisive importance for the existence of a state."

After January 30, 1933, the question of the social importance of the middle class was widely discussed by the Left. Until then the middle class was given far too little attention, partly because all interests were focused on the development of political reaction and the authoritarian leadership of the state, and partly because a line of questioning based on a psychology of the masses was foreign to the politicians. From now on, the "rebellion of the middle class" was given more and more prominence in various places. In following the

41

discussion of this question, one noted two principal views: the one contended that fascism was "nothing other" than the party guard of the upper middle class; the other did not overlook this fact but stressed "the rebellion of the middle classes," with the result that the exponents of this view were accused of obliterating the reactionary role of fascism. In substantiation of this accusation, one cited the nomination of Thyssen as economic dictator, the dissolution of the middle-class economic organizations, the rebuff to the "second revolution"; in short, fascism's unadulterated reactionary character, which, from about the end of June 1933, became more and more evident and pronounced.

Certain obscurities were evident in these very heated discussions. The fact that, after the seizure of power, National Socialism showed itself more and more to be an imperialistic nationalism, which was intent upon eliminating everything "socialistic" from the movement and preparing for war with every available means, did not contradict the other fact that fascism, *viewed with respect to its mass basis, was actually a middle-class movement.* Had he not promised to take up the fight against big business, Hitler would never have won the support of the middle classes. They helped him to achieve victory because they were *against* big business. Owing to the pressure they exerted, the authorities were forced to adopt *anti-*capitalist measures, just as the authorities were later forced to abandon them under the pressure applied by big business. If the subjective interests in the mass basis of a reactionary movement are not distinguished from the objective reactionary function—the two contradict one another but were reconciled in the *totality* of the Nazi movement in the beginning—it is not possible to reach an understanding. The former pertains to the reactionary interests of the fascist masses, while the latter pertains to the reactionary role of fascism. All its contradictions originate in the antithesis of these two sides of fascism, just as their reconciliation in the *one* form, "National Socialism," characterizes the Hitler movement. Insofar as National Socialism was forced to stress its character as a middle-class movement (*before* the seizure of power and right afterward), it was

42

in fact *anti-capitalist and revolutionary*. However, since it *did not* deprive big business of its rights and had to consolidate and hold on to the power it had secured, its capitalistic function was brought more and more into the foreground until finally it became an extreme advocate and champion of imperialism and the capitalist economic order. In this respect it is wholly immaterial whether and how many of its leaders had an honest or dishonest socialist orientation (in their sense of the word!), and it is just as immaterial whether and how many were out-and-out deceivers and power-mongers. A radical anti-fascist policy cannot be based on these considerations. Everything necessary for an understanding of German fascism and its ambivalence could have been learned from the history of Italian fascism, for the latter also showed these two strictly contradictory functions reconciled in a totality.

Those who either deny the function of the mass basis of fascism or fail to give it its proper due are stupefied by the fact that the middle class, since it neither possesses the principal means of production nor works with them, cannot really be a permanent motive force in history, and for that reason must oscillate between capital and the workers. They fail to see that the middle class can be and is "a motive force in history," if not *permanently* then at least *temporarily*, as we learn from Italian and German fascism. By this we mean not only the crushing of the workers' organizations, the countless sacrifices, the eruptions of barbarism; over and above this, it prevents the economic crisis from developing into a political upheaval, into a social revolution. Clearly: The greater the extent and the importance of a nation's middle-class strata, the more decisive is their significance as an effective social force. From 1933 to 1942 we are confronted with the paradox that fascism was able to outstrip social revolutionary internationalism as an *international* movement. The Socialists and the Communists were so certain about the progress of the revolutionary movement in relation to that of political reaction that they committed outright political suicide, even if motivated by the best of intentions. This question deserves the greatest of attention. The process that has taken place in the middle-class strata of all countries during the last decade deserves far greater attention than the banal, all-too-well-known fact that fascism constitutes extreme political reaction. The mere fact of fascism's reactionary nature is no basis for an effective counter political policy, as was amply shown by the events between 1928 and 1942.

The middle class got caught up in the movement and made its appearance as a social force in the form of fascism. Therefore, it is not a question of Hitler's or Göring's reactionary purpose, but a question of the social interests of the middle-class strata. Owing to its character structure, the middle class has a social power far in excess of its economic importance. It is the class that preserves nothing less than several thousand years of patriarchy and keeps it alive with all its contradictions.

That a fascist movement exists at all is doubtlessly the social expression of nationalistic imperialism. However, that this fascist movement could become a mass movement, indeed, could seize power (only then fulfilling its imperialistic function), is to be ascribed to the full backing it received from the middle class. Only by taking these antitheses and contradictions into account, each in its turn, can the phenomena of fascism be comprehended.

The social position of the middle class is determined by (1) *its position in the capitalist production process,* (2) *its position in the authoritarian state apparatus,* (3) *its special family situation,* which is directly determined by its position in the production process and is the key to an understanding of its ideology. There are indeed differences in the economic situation of the small farmers, the bureaucrats, and the middle-class businessmen, but the basic nature of their family situation is the *same.*

The rapid development of capitalist economy in the nineteenth century, the continuous and rapid mechanization of production, the amalgamation of the various branches of production in monopolistic syndicates and trusts, form the basis of the progressive pauperization of the lower middle-class merchants and tradesmen. Not capable of competing with the cheaper and more economically operating large industries, the small enterprises go to ruin, never to recover.

"The middle class has nothing but ruthless annihilation to expect from this system. This is the issue: Whether we shall all sink into the great grey bleakness of proletarianism where we shall all have the same thing, namely nothing, or whether energy and diligence shall again put the individual in a position to acquire property by hard work. Middle class or proletarian! That is the issue!"—so the German Nationals warned before the election of the president of the republic in 1932. The National Socialists were not so blunt; they were careful not to create a wide gap between the middle class and the body of industrial workers in their propaganda, and they were more successful with their approach.

The fight against the large department stores played a large role in the propaganda of the NSDAP. The contradiction between the role played by National Socialism for big business and the interests of the middle class, from which it derived its main support, was expressed in Hitler's talk with Knickerbocker:

> "We will not make German-American relations dependent upon a haberdasher shop [the reference is to the fate of the Woolworth store in Berlin] . . . the existence of such enterprises are an encouragement of Bolshevism. . . . They destroy many small enterprises. For that reason, we will not sanction them, but you can rest assured that your enterprises of this nature in Germany will be dealt with no differently than similar German enterprises."[2]

Private business debts to foreign countries were an enormous burden to the middle class. Since his foreign policy was dependent upon the fulfillment of foreign claims, Hitler was for the payment of these private debts. His followers, however, demanded that they be annulled. Thus the lower middle class rebelled "against the system,"

---

[2] Following the seizure of power in the months of March and April, masses of people plundered the department stores, but the NSDAP leadership soon put a stop to this. (Interdiction against autocratic interference in the economy, dissolution of middle-class organizations, etc.).

by which it understood the "Marxist regime" of Social Democracy.

As much as these lower middle-class strata were urged, under the stress of the crisis, to form organizational alliances, the economic competition of the small enterprises nonetheless operated against the establishment of a feeling of solidarity corresponding to that of the industrial workers. As a consequence of his social situation the lower middle-class man could join forces neither with his social class nor, for that matter, with the industrial workers; not with his own class because competition is the rule there, not with the industrial workers because it is precisely proletarianization that he fears most of all. And yet the fascist movement brought about an alliance of the lower middle class. What was the basis of this alliance in the psychology of the masses?

The answer to this is supplied by the social position of the lower- and middle-class public and private officials. The economic position of the average official is worse than that of the average skilled industrial worker; this poorer position is partially compensated by the meager prospect of a career, and in the case of the government official by a lifelong pension. Thus dependent upon governmental authority, a competitive bearing toward one's colleagues prevails in this class, which counteracts the development of solidarity. The social consciousness of the official is not characterized by the fate he shares with his coworkers, but by his attitude to the government and to the "nation." This consists of a complete *identification with the state power;*[3] in the case of the company employee, it consists of an identification with the company. He is just as submissive as the industrial worker. Why is it that he does not develop a feeling of solidarity as the industrial worker does? This is due to his intermediate position between authority and the body of manual laborers.

---

[3] By *identification,* psychoanalysis understands the process whereby a person begins *to feel at one with* another person, adopts that person's characteristics and attitudes, and in his fantasy puts himself in the other's place; this process entails an actual change in the identifying person, inasmuch as the latter "internalizes" characteristics of his model.

While subordinate to the top, he is to those below him a representative of this authority and enjoys, as such, a privileged moral (not material) position. The arch personification of this type in the psychology of the masses is to be found in the army sergeant.

Butlers, valets, and other such employees of aristocratic families are a flagrant example of the power of this identification. By adopting the attitudes, way of thinking, and demeanor of the ruling class, they undergo a complete change and, in an effort to minimize their lowly origin, often appear as caricatures of the people whom they serve.

This identification with authority, firm, state, nation, etc., which can be formulated "*I* am the state, the authority, the firm, the nation," constitutes a psychic reality and is one of the best illustrations of an ideology that has become a material force. At first it is only the idea of being like one's superior that stirs the mind of the employee or the official, but gradually, owing to his pressing material dependence, his whole person is refashioned in line with the ruling class. Always ready to accommodate himself to authority, the lower middle-class man develops *a cleavage between his economic situation and his ideology*. He lives in materially restricted circumstances, but assumes gentlemanly postures on the surface, often to a ridiculous degree. He eats poorly and insufficiently, but attaches great importance to a "decent suit of clothes." A silk hat and dress coat become the material symbol of this character structure. And nothing is more suited for a first-impression appraisal of the mass psychology of a people than its dress. It is its accommodating attitude that specifically distinguishes the structure of the lower middle-class man from the structure of the industrial worker.[4]

How deep does this identification with authority go? We know already that such an identification exists. The question, however, is how—apart from economic existential conditions, which affect him

---

[4] This applies only to Europe. The adaptation of lower middle-class habits by the industrial worker in America obliterates the boundary between the two.

directly—emotional factors reinforce and consolidate the lower middle-class man's attitude to such an extent that his structure does not waver in times of crisis or even in times in which unemployment destroys the immediate economic base.

We stated above that the economic positions of the various strata of the lower middle class are different but that the basic features of their family situation are the same. *It is in this family situation that we have the key to the emotional foundation of the structure that we described earlier.*

FAMILY TIES AND NATIONALISTIC FEELINGS

In the beginning the family situation of the various strata of the lower middle class is not differentiated from the immediate economic position. The family—those of officials excluded—also constitutes an economic enterprise on a small scale. The members of a small merchant's family work in his business, thus eliminating the expense of outside help. On small and medium farmsteads the coinciding of family and mode of production is even more pronounced. The economy of the great patriarchs (the Zagruda, for instance) is essentially built upon this practice. In the close interlacing of family and economy lies the key to the question why the peasantry is "bound to the earth," "traditional," and for that reason so accessible to the influence of political reaction. This does not mean to say that it is solely the economic mode of existence that determines the attachment to the earth and tradition, but that the farmer's mode of production entails a strict family tie of all members of the family and that this tie presupposes a far-reaching sexual suppression and repression. It is from this double base, then, that the typical peasant way of looking at things arises. Its core is formed by patriarchal sexual morality. Elsewhere I described the difficulties encountered by the Soviet government in the collectivization of agriculture; it was not only the "love of the soil," but first and foremost the family tie conditioned by the soil that created such difficulties.

48

For one thing, the possibility of preserving a healthy peasant class as a foundation for a whole nation can never be valued highly enough. Many of our present-day sufferings are only the consequence of the unhealthy relationship between rural and city population. A solid stock of small and middle peasants has at all times been the best defense against social ills such as we possess today. And, moreover, this is the only solution which enables a nation to earn its daily bread within the inner circuit of its economy. Industry and commerce recede from their unhealthy leading position and adjust themselves to the general framework of a national economy of balanced supply and demand.

—*Mein Kampf*, p. 138

That was the position taken by Hitler. As senseless as it was economically speaking, as little as political reaction could ever succeed in checking the mechanization of big agriculture and the dissolution of agriculture on a small scale, this propaganda was nonetheless significant from the standpoint of mass psychology, for it had an effect on the close-knit family structure of the lower middle-class strata.

The close interrelation between family tie and rural forms of economy was finally expressed by the NSDAP after the seizure of power. Since, with respect to its mass basis and ideological structure, the Hitler movement was a lower middle-class movement, one of its first measures—intended to secure the middle classes—was the edict issued on May 12, 1933, on the "New Order of Agriculture Ownership," which reverted to age-old legal codes based on the "indissoluble unity of blood and soil."

A few characteristic passages are appended here:

This indissoluble unity of blood and soil is the indispensable presupposition for a nation's health. In Germany rural legislation of past centuries also gave legal guarantees to this tie born of a nation's natural feelings of life. The farmstead was the *unsaleable* inheritance of the ancestral peasant family. Later non-native legislation was imposed and destroyed the legal basis of this rural constitution. In many parts of the country, nonetheless, the German peasant, having a healthy sense of his people's basic conception of life, persevered in the old custom, handing down the farmstead from generation to generation.

It is the imperative duty of the government of an awakened people to guarantee the national awakening by legal regulation of the indissoluble unity of blood and soil preserved by German custom through the law of entail.

The owner of a farmstead or forestry who is registered as the heir to entailed property in the competent district court must pass on his property in accordance with the law of entail. The owner of this inherited farm is called a farmer. A farmer cannot own more than one farm inherited under this law. Only one of the farmer's children is allowed to take over the inherited farm. He is the legal *inheritor*. The co-inheritors will be provided for by the farmstead until they are economically independent. If through no fault of their own they fall into straitened circumstances, they also have the right to seek refuge at the farmstead in later years. The transfer of a non-registered farmstead, which is nonetheless qualified for registration, is governed by the law of entail.

An entail-inherited farmstead can be owned only by a farmer who is a *German citizen* and of *German blood*. Only he who has no one among his male ancestry or other ancestry of Jewish or colored origin for four generations is of German blood. Clearly, however, every Teuton is of German blood according to the letter of this law. A marriage with a person of non-German blood permanently excludes the offspring of this marriage from being the owner of a farmstead inherited under this law.

The purpose of this law is to protect the farmsteads against heavy indebtedness and harmful fragmentation in the process of inheritance, and to preserve it as the permanent inheritance of the families of free farmers. At the same time the law aims at a healthy distribution of the agricultural land. A large number of self-sufficient small and medium farmsteads spread throughout the country as evenly as possible is necessary for the preservation of a state's and people's health.

What tendencies are expressed in this law? It was at variance with the interests of big agriculture, which was intent upon absorbing the medium and small farmsteads and creating an ever widening division between landowner and propertyless rural proletariat. But the frustration of this intent was amply compensated by the preservation of the rural middle class, in which big agriculture had a considerable interest in view of the fact that it represented the mass basis of its power. It is not only as a *private owner of property* that the small landowner is identified with the large landowner. By itself this would not mean very much. What is important here is the preservation of the ideologic atmosphere of the small and medium property owners, that atmosphere, namely, that exists in small enterprises operated by a family unit. It is this atmosphere that is known to produce the best nationalistic fighters and to imbue the women with nationalistic fervor. And this explains why political reaction is always prattling about the "morality-preserving influence of the peasantry." However, this is a sex-economic question.

This interlacing of individualistic modes of production and authoritarian family in the lower middle class is one of the many sources of the fascist ideology of the "large family." This question will return later in another context.

The economic pitting of the small businesses against one another corresponds to the family encapsulation and competition typical of the lower middle class, notwithstanding the fascist ideology "common welfare comes before personal welfare" and "corporate idea." The basic elements of fascist ideology, "führer principle," family policy, etc., have an individualistic character. What is collective in fascism stems from the socialistic tendencies in the mass basis, as the individualistic elements stem from the interests of big business and the fascist leadership.

In view of man's natural organization, this economic and family situation would break down, if it were not secured by a specific relationship between man and woman, a relationship we designate as patriarchal, and a mode of sexuality derived from this specific relationship.

Economically, the urban middle-class man is not in a better position than the manual laborer. Thus, in his efforts to differentiate himself from the laborer, he must rely essentially on his family and sexual modes of life. His economic deprivations have to be compensated for in a sexual moralistic way. In the case of the official, this motive is the most effective element of his identification with the ruling power. Since one is not on a plane with the upper middle class but is nonetheless identified with it, the sex-moralistic ideologies have to compensate for the economic limitations. Essentially, the sexual modes of life and the cultural modes of life dependent upon them serve to differentiate him from the lower classes.

The sum total of these moralistic attitudes, which cluster around one's attitude toward sex and are commonly designated as "philistine," culminate in notions of—we say notions of, not acts of—*honor* and *duty*. The effect of these two words on the lower middle class must be correctly assessed, otherwise it will not serve much purpose to concern ourselves with them. They appear again and again in the fascist dictator-ideology and race theory. Actually it is precisely the lower middle class's way of life, its business practices, that impose a completely opposite behavior. A touch of dishonesty is part of the very existence of private merchandizing. When a peasant buys a horse, he runs it down in every possible way. If he sells the same horse a year later, it will have become younger, better, and stronger. One's sense of "duty" is molded by business interests and not by national character traits. One's own commodity will always be the best—the other person's always the worst. Deprecation of one's competitors—a deprecation that is usually devoid of all honesty—is an essential tool of one's "business." The small businessman's obsequious and deferential behavior toward his customers, testifies to the fierce pressure of economic existence, which has to warp the best character in the long run. Nevertheless the concepts of "honor" and "duty" play a very decisive role in the life of the lower middle class. This cannot be explained solely on the basis of efforts to conceal one's crude materialistic background. For, despite all hypocrisy, the ecstasy derived from the notions of "honor" and "duty" is genuine. It is merely a question of its source.

This ecstasy stems from sources of unconscious emotional life. One does not pay much attention to these sources at first, and one is only too happy to overlook their relation to the above ideology. However, an analysis of lower middle-class people leaves no doubt about the importance of the relation between sexual life and the ideology of "duty" and "honor."

For one thing, the political and economic position of the father is reflected in his patriarchal relationship to the remainder of the family. In the figure of the father the authoritarian state has its representative in every family, so that the family becomes its most important instrument of power.

The authoritarian position of the father reflects his political role and discloses the relation of the family to the authoritarian state. Within the family the father holds the same position that his boss holds toward him in the production process. And he reproduces his subservient attitude toward authority in his children, particularly in his sons. Lower middle-class man's passive and servile attitude toward the führer-figure issues from these conditions. Without really divining it, Hitler was building upon this lower middle-class attitude when he wrote:

> The people in their overwhelming majority are so feminine by nature and attitude that sober reasoning determines their thoughts and actions far less than emotion and feeling.
>
> And this sentiment is not complicated, but very simple and all of a piece. It does not have multiple shadings; it has a positive and a negative; love or hate, right or wrong, truth or lie, never half this way and half that way, never partially, or that kind of thing.
>
> —Op. cit. p. 183

This is not a question of an "inherent disposition," but of a typical example of the reproduction of an authoritarian social system in the structures of its members.

What this position of the father actually necessitates is the strictest sexual suppression of the women and the children. While women develop a resigned attitude under lower middle-class influence—an attitude reinforced by repressed sexual rebellion—the sons, apart from a subservient attitude toward authority, develop a strong identification with the father, which forms the basis of the emotional identification with every kind of authority. How it comes about that the psychic structures of the supporting strata of a society are so constructed that they fit the economic framework and serve the purposes of the ruling powers as precisely as the parts of a precision machine will long remain an unsolved riddle. At any rate, what we describe as the structural reproduction of a society's economic system in the psychology of the masses is the basic mechanism in the process of the formation of political ideas.

It is only much later that the attitude of economic and social competition contributes to the development of the structure of the lower middle class. The reactionary thinking that is shaped at this stage is a secondary continuation of psychic processes that reach back into the first years of a child raised in an authoritarian family atmosphere. For one thing there is the competition between the children and the grown-ups, but of more far-reaching consequence, there is the competition among children of the same family in their relationship to the parents. In childhood this competition, which later in adulthood and in the life outside the family is predominantly an economic one, is mainly operative in the strong emotional love-hate relationships among members of the same family. This is not the place to pursue these relationships in detail. This is a field of study by itself. Let it suffice to say here: the sexual inhibitions and debilitations that constitute the most important prerequisites for the existence of the authoritarian family and are the most essential groundwork of the structural formation of the lower middle-class man are compassed with the help of religious fears, which are infused with sexual guilt-feelings and deeply embedded in the emotions. Thus we arrive at the problem of the relation of religion to the negation of sexual desire. Sexual debility results in a lowering of self-confidence. In one case it is compensated by the brutalization of sexuality, in the other by rigid character traits. The compulsion to control one's sexuality, to maintain sexual repression, leads to the development of pathologic, emotionally tinged notions of honor and duty, bravery and self-control.[5] But the pathology and emotionality of these psychic attitudes are strongly at variance with the reality of one's personal behavior. The man who attains genital satisfaction, is honorable, responsible, brave, and controlled, without making much of a fuss about it. These attitudes are an organic part of his personality. The man whose genitals are weakened, whose sexual structure is full of contradictions, must continually remind himself to control his sexuality, to preserve his sexual dignity, to be brave in the face of temptations, etc. The struggle to resist the temptation to masturbate is a struggle that is experienced by every adolescent and every child, without exception. All the elements of the reactionary man's structure are developed in this struggle. It is in the lower middle classes that this structure is reinforced most strongly and embedded most deeply. Every form of mysticism derives its most active energy and, in part, also its content from this compulsory suppression of sexuality. Insofar as the various categories of industrial workers are subject to the same social influences, they too develop corresponding attitudes; yet, owing to the distinct difference in their way of life compared with the lower middle class, sex-affirming forces are far more pronounced in them and also more conscious. The affective anchoring of these structures by means of unconscious anxiety, their concealment by character traits that appear completely asexual, are responsible for the fact that these deep layers of the personality cannot be reached with rational arguments alone. What importance this statement has for practical sex-politics will be discussed in the last chapter.

To what extent the *unconscious* struggle against one's own sexual needs gives rise to metaphysical and mystical thinking cannot be discussed in detail here. We will mention only one example, which is typical of the National Socialist ideology. Again and again we run across series such as this: *personal honor, family honor,*

---

[5] *Die Moral der Kraft* by the National Socialist Ernst Mann is an especially informative book for the recognition of these relationships.

racial honor, national honor. This sequence is consistent with the various layers in the individual structure. However, it fails to include the socio-economic basis: *capitalism, or rather patriarchy; the institution of compulsive marriage; sexual suppression; personal struggle against one's own sexuality; personal compensatory feeling of honor; etc.* The highest position in the series is assumed by the ideology of "national honor," which is identical with the irrational core of nationalism. To understand this, however, it is necessary to turn aside from our main theme again.

Authoritarian society's fight against the sexuality of children and adolescents, and the consequent struggle in one's own ego, takes place within the framework of the authoritarian family, which has thus far proven to be the best institution to carry out this fight successfully. Sexual desires naturally urge a person to enter into all kinds of relations with the world, to enter into close contact with it in a vast variety of forms. If they are suppressed, they have but one possibility: to vent themselves within the narrow framework of the family. Sexual inhibition is the basis of the familial encapsulation of the individual as well as the basis of individual self-consciousness. One must give strict heed to the fact that metaphysical, individual, and familial sentimental behavior are only various aspects of one and the same basic process of sexual negation, whereas reality-oriented, nonmystical thinking moves along with a loose attitude toward the family and is at the very least indifferent to ascetic sexual ideology. What is important in this connection is that the tie to the authoritarian family is established by means of sexual inhibition; that it is the original biological tie of the child to the mother and also of the mother to the child that forms the barricade to sexual reality and leads to an indissoluble sexual fixation and to an incapacity to enter into other relations.[6] The tie to the mother is the

---

[6] Hence, the "Oedipus complex," which Freud discovered, is not so much a cause as it is a result of the sexual restrictions imposed upon the child by society. Yet, wholly unconscious of what they are doing, the parents carry out the intentions of authoritarian society.

basis of all family ties. In their *subjective emotional core* the notions of *homeland and nation are notions of mother and family.* Among the middle classes the mother is the homeland of the child, just as the family is the "nation in miniature." This will enable us to understand why the National Socialist Goebbels chose the following words as the motto for his ten commandments in the National Socialist almanac of 1932, doubtlessly without knowledge of its deeper connotation: "Never forget that your country is the mother of your life." On the occasion of "Mother's Day," 1933, *Angriff* stated:

> *Mother's Day.* The national revolution has swept away every-thing petty! Ideas lead again and lead together—family, society, nation. The idea of Mother's Day is perfectly suited to honor that which the German idea symbolizes: The German Mother! Nowhere does this importance devolve upon the wife and the mother as it does in new Germany. She is the protectress of the family life from which sprout the forces which will again lead our nation forward. She—the German mother—is the sole bearer of the idea of the German nation. *The idea of "Mother" is inseparable* from the idea of "being German." Is there anything which can lead us closer together than our mutual honoring of the mother?

No matter how false these sentences are economically and so-cially speaking, they are true from the point of view of the human structure. Thus, nationalistic sentiments are the direct continuation of the family tie and are likewise rooted in the fixated[7] tie to the mother. This cannot be explained biologically. For this tie to the mother, insofar as it develops into a familial and nationalistic tie, is itself a *social* product. In puberty it would make room for other attachments, i.e., natural sexual relations, if sexual restrictions would not cause it to be eternalized. It is as this socially motivated eternalization that it becomes the basis of nationalist feelings in the adult; it is only at this stage that it becomes a reactionary social

---

[7] I.e., unresolved, unconsciously rooted.

force. If the nationalist sentiments of the industrial worker are far less pronounced than those of the lower middle-class worker, it is to be ascribed to the different social life and consequent looser family ties of the former.

Now I hope no one will get upset and reproach us with wanting to "biologize" sociology, for we know perfectly well that the difference in the industrial worker's family life is also determined by his position in the production process. The question must be asked, nonetheless, why it is that the industrial worker is clearly accessible to internationalism, whereas the lower middle-class worker has such a strong leaning toward nationalism. In the objective economic situation this factor of diversity can be ascertained only when the above-described connection between the industrial worker's economic and familial situation is taken into account. It cannot be ascertained in any other way. The strange refusal on the part of Marxist theorists to regard family life as a factor of *equal importance* as far as the anchoring of the social system is concerned, indeed to regard it as the *decisive* factor in the formation of the human structure, is to be traced back to their family ties. The fact that the family tie is the most intense and the most emotional, cannot be overrated.[8]

---

[8] He who has not freed himself from his own tie to his family and to his mother, or who has not at least clarified and excluded their influence from his judgments, should not seek to investigate the formation of ideology. He who would want to dismiss these facts as "Freudian" would only give proof of his scientific cretinism. One should argue and not chatter, without possessing special knowledge. Freud discovered the Oedipus complex. Revolutionary family politics would be impossible without this discovery. But Freud is just as far from such an assessment and sociological interpretation of the family formation as the mechanistic economist is from a comprehension of sexuality as a social factor. Let it be proven that dialectical materialism has been incorrectly used, but facts that every worker knew before Freud discovered the Oedipus complex, would not be refuted. And fascism is to be destroyed, not with slogans but with knowledge. Errors are possible and can be corrected, but scientific obtuseness is reactionary.

The essential connection between familial and nationalistic ideology can be pursued further. Families are just as cut off from and opposed to one another as nations are. In both cases the ultimate basis for this separation and opposition is an economic one. The lower middle-class family (those of officials, lower-income white-collar workers, etc.) is continually harassed by food and other material worries. Hence the large lower middle-class family's expansion tendencies also reproduce an imperialistic ideology: "The nation needs space and food." It is for this reason that the lower middle-class man is especially accessible to imperialistic ideology. He is capable of fully identifying with the personified conception of the nation. It is in this way that familial imperialism is ideologically reproduced in national imperialism.

Goebbels' statement printed in the brochure *Die verfluchten Hakenkreuzler* (Eher Verlag, Munich, p. 16 and 18) is of interest in this connection. It was written in answer to the question whether a Jew is a man.

> If someone cracks a whip across your mother's face, would you say to him, Thank you! Is he a man too!? One who does such a thing is not a man—he is a brute! How many worse things has the Jew inflicted upon *our mother Germany* [italics mine, WR] and still inflicts upon her! He [the Jew] has debauched our race, sapped our energy, undermined our customs and broken our strength. . . . The Jew is the graphic demon of decay . . . begins his criminal butchery of people.

One has to know the importance of the idea of castration as punishment for sexual pleasure; one has to comprehend the sexual-psychological background of fantasies of ritual murder as well as the background of anti-Semitism as such; and moreover, one has to appraise correctly the sexual guilt-feelings and sexual anxieties of the reactionary man, to be able to judge just how such unconsciously written sentences impinge upon the unconscious emotionality of the average reader. It is in such statements and their unconscious emotional impact that we find the psychological roots of National Socialism's anti-Semitism. They were supposed to be nothing but "befogging." Certainly, befogging also. But it was overlooked that, ideologically, fascism was the resistance of a sexually as well as economically deadly sick society to the painful but resolute revolutionary tendencies toward sexual as well as economic freedom, a freedom the very thought of which instills the reactionary man with mortal terror. That is to say: the establishment of economic freedom goes hand in hand with the dissolution of old institutions (particularly those governing sexual policies), to which the reactionary man and also the industrial worker, insofar as he is a reactionary, are not immediately equal. More than anything else it is the fear of "sexual freedom," conceived of as sexual chaos and sexual dissipation in the mind of the reactionary thinker, which has a retarding effect upon the yearning to be free of the yoke of economic exploitation. This will be the case only as long as this misconception of sexual freedom prevails. And it can continue to prevail only in consequence of the lack of clarity surrounding these very decisive questions in masses of people. It is precisely for this reason that sex-economy must play an essential role in the ordering of social relations. The more extensively and deeply the reactionary structure has taken hold of the toiling masses, the more decisive is the importance of the sex-economic work of educating the masses of the people to assume social responsibility.

In this interplay between economic and structural factors, it is the authoritarian family that represents the foremost and most essential source of reproduction of every kind of reactionary thinking; it is a factory where reactionary ideology and reactionary structures are produced. Hence, the "safeguarding of the family," i.e., of the authoritarian and large family, is the first cultural precept of every reactionary policy. This is what is essentially concealed behind the phrase "safeguarding of the state, culture, and civilization."

An NSDAP election proclamation for the presidential election of 1932 (Adolf Hitler: *Mein Programm*) stated:

By virtue of her nature and destiny, woman is man's mate. Thus both man and woman are companions in life as well as companions in work. Just as the economic development over the centuries has changed man's sphere of work, it is only logical that it has also changed woman's sphere. Over and above the necessity of working together, it is man's and woman's duty to preserve man himself. In this most noble mission of the sexes, we also discover the basis of their individual talents, which Providence, in its eternal wisdom, gave to both of them immutably. Thus, it is the highest task to make the *founding of a family* possible to the mates in life and companions in work. *Its final destruction would mean the end of every form of higher humanity.* No matter how far woman's sphere of activity can be stretched, *the ultimate aim of a truly organic and logical development must always be the creation of a family.* It is the smallest but *most valuable unit in the complete structure of the state.* Work honors both man and woman. But the child exalts the woman.

Under the heading "Preservation of the Peasantry Means the Preservation of the German Nation," the same proclamation states: "In the preservation and encouragement of a healthy peasantry, I further see the best safeguard against social woes as well as against the racial decay of our people."

In this respect the traditional family tie of the peasantry must not be forgotten if one does not want to make an error. It continues:

> It is my belief that, to build up its resistance, a people must not live solely in accordance with rational principles; it also needs spiritual and religious support. The poisoning and disintegration of the national body by the events of our cultural Bolshevism are almost more disastrous than the effect of political and economic communism.

As a party that, as Italian fascism, owed its initial success to the interests of big landowners, the NSDAP had to win over the small and medium farmers, had to establish a social basis for itself in them. In this, naturally, it could not openly promote the interests of big landowners in its propaganda, but had to direct its appeal to the small farmers, specifically to the structures produced in them by the overlapping of the family and economic situation. Only with respect to this element of the lower middle class is the sentence valid that man and woman are companions in work. It does not apply to the body of industrial workers. Even to the peasant it applies only formally, for in reality the peasant's wife is the peasant's servant. The prototype and realization of the fascist ideology of the hierarchic organization of the state is to be found in the hierarchic organization of the peasant family. The peasant family is a nation in miniature, and every member of this family is identified with this miniature nation. Thus, the groundwork for the absorption of a grand imperialistic ideology is present in the peasantry and in the lower middle class where an entire family is engaged in a small enterprise. The idolization of motherhood is conspicuous in both cases. How is this idolization related to reactionary sexual politics?

NATIONALISTIC SELF-CONFIDENCE

In the individual structures of the masses of the lower middle class, national and familial ties coincide. These ties are especially intensified by a process that not only runs parallel to it but is actually derived from it. From the standpoint of the masses, the nationalistic führer is the personification of the nation. Only insofar as this führer actually personifies the nation in conformity with the national sentiments of the masses does a personal tie to him develop. Insofar as he knows how to arouse emotional family ties in the individuals of the masses, he is also an authoritarian father figure. He attracts all the emotional attitudes that at one time were meant for the strict but also protecting and impressive father (impressive in the child's eyes). In discussions with National Socialist enthusiasts about the untenability and contradictoriness of the NSDAP program, one often heard it said that Hitler understood all of that much better—"he would manage everything all right." Here we have a clear expression of the child's need for the protective attitude of the father. In terms of social reality it is this need for protection on the part of the masses of the people that enables the dictator "to manage everything." This attitude on the part of masses of people impedes social self-administration, i.e., rational independence and cooperation. No genuine democracy can or should build upon it.

Even more essential, however, is the *identification* of the individuals in the masses with the "führer." The more helpless the "mass-individual" has become, owing to his upbringing, the more pronounced is his identification with the führer, and the more the childish need for protection is disguised in the form of a feeling at one with the führer. This inclination to identify is the psychological basis of national narcissism, i.e., of the self-confidence that individual man derives from the "greatness of the nation." The reactionary lower middle-class man perceives *himself* in the führer, in the authoritarian state. On the basis of this identification he feels himself to be a defender of the "national heritage," of the "nation," which does not prevent him, likewise on the basis of this identification, from simultaneously despising "the masses" and confronting them as an individual. The wretchedness of his material and sexual situation is so overshadowed by the exalting idea of belonging to a master race and having a brilliant führer that, as time goes on, he ceases to realize how completely he has sunk to a position of insignificant, blind allegiance.

The worker who is conscious of his skills—he, in short, who has rid himself of his submissive structure, who identifies with his work and not with the führer, with the international working masses and not with the national homeland—represents the opposite of this. *He feels himself to be a leader*, not on the basis of his identification with the führer, but on the basis of his consciousness of performing work that is vitally necessary for society's existence.

What are the emotional forces that are at work here? This is not difficult to answer. The *emotions* by which this fundamentally different mass-psychological type is motivated are the same as those that are to be found in the nationalists. It is merely the content of that which excites the emotions that is different. The need to identify is the same, but the objects of identification are different, namely fellow workers and not the führer, one's own work and not an illusion, the working men of the earth and not the family. In short, international consciousness of one's skills is opposed to mysticism and nationalism. But this certainly does not imply a neglect of the liberated worker's self-confidence; it is the reactionary man who begins to rave about "service to the community," and "general welfare comes before personal welfare," at a time of crisis. It merely implies that the self-confidence of the liberated worker is derived from the consciousness of his skills.

During the past fifteen years we have been confronted with a fact which is difficult to comprehend: Economically, society is divided into sharply defined social classes and occupations. According to the purely economic point of view, the social ideology is derived from the specific social situation. It follows from this that the specific ideology of a class would more or less have to correspond to the socio-economic situation of that class. In keeping with their collective working habits, the industrial workers would have to develop a stronger collective feeling, while the small businessmen would have to develop a stronger individualism. The employees of large concerns would have to have a collective feeling similar to that of the industrial workers. But we have already seen that psychic structure and social situation seldom coincide. We draw a distinction between the responsible worker who is conscious of his skills and the mystical-nationalistic reactionary subject. We meet with both types in every social and professional class. There are millions of reactionary industrial workers and there are just as many teachers and physicians who are conscious of their skills and champion the cause of freedom. Hence, there is no simple mechanistic connection between social situation and character structure.

The social situation is only the external condition that has an influence on the ideological process in the individual. The *instinctual drives* through which the various social influences gain *exclusive*

64

control over the emotions are now to be investigated. To begin with, this much is clear: Hunger is not one of them; at least, it is not the decisive factor. If it were, the international revolution would have followed upon the world crisis of 1929–33. This is a sound statement, no matter how dangerous it may be to antiquated, purely economic points of view.

When psychoanalysts unversed in sociology try to explain social revolution as an "infantile revolt against the father," they have in mind the "revolutionary," who comes from intellectual circles. This is indeed the case there. But it does not apply to the industrial workers. The paternal suppression of children among the working class is not less severe, indeed, it is sometimes more brutal than it is among the lower middle class. This is not the issue. That which specifically distinguishes these two classes is found in their modes of production and the attitude toward sex which derives from these modes. The point is this: Sexuality is suppressed by the parents among the industrial workers also. But the contradictions to which the children of industrial workers are subjected don't exist in the lower middle class. Among the lower middle class it is *only* sexuality that is suppressed. The sexual activity of this class is a pure expression of the contradiction between sexual drive and sexual inhibition. This is not the case among the industrial workers. Along with their moralistic ideology the industrial workers have their own—in some cases more and in others less pronounced—sexual views, which are diametrically opposed to the moralistic ideology. Moreover, there is the influence exercised by their living conditions and their close association in their work. All of this runs counter to their moralistic sexual ideology.

Accordingly, the average industrial worker differs from the average lower middle-class worker by his open and untrammeled attitude toward sexuality, no matter how muddled and conservative he might be otherwise. He is incomparably more accessible to sex-economic views than the typical lower middle-class worker is. And it is precisely the absence of those attitudes that are central to national socialistic and clerical ideology that makes him more accessible: identification with the authoritarian state-power, with the "supreme führer," with the nation. This, too, is proof of the fact that the basic elements of National Socialist ideology have a sex-economic origin.

Owing to his individualistic economy and to the extreme isolation of his family situation, the small farmer is very accessible to the ideology of political reaction. This is the reason for the cleavage between social situation and ideology. Characterized by the strictest practice of patriarchy and the morality corresponding to it, the small farmer nonetheless develops natural—even if distorted— forms in his sexuality. Just as in the case of the industrial workers— in contrast to the lower middle-class workers—farm youths begin to have sexual intercourse at an early age; owing to the strict patri- archal education, however, the youth is sexually very disturbed or even brutal; sexuality is practiced in secret; sexual frigidity is the rule among girls; sexual murder and brutal jealousy, as well as enslave- ment of the women, are typical sexual occurrences among the peasantry. Hysteria is nowhere so rampant as it is in the country. Patriarchal marriage is the final aim of rural upbringing, rigidly dictated by rural economy.

An ideologic process has begun to take shape among the indus- trial workers during the last decades. The material manifestations of this process are most evident in the pure culture of the workers' aristocracy, but they are also to be noted among the average indus- trial worker. The industrial workers of the twentieth century are not the nineteenth-century proletariat of Karl Marx's time. To a very large extent they have accepted the conventions and views of the bourgeois layers of society. To be sure, formal bourgeois democracy did not eliminate economic class distinctions any more than it did away with racial prejudices. Yet the social tendencies that are gaining ground within its compass have obliterated the structural and ideologic boundaries among the various social classes. The industrial workers of England, America, Scandinavia, Germany, are becoming more and more bourgeois. To understand how fascism infiltrates the working classes, this process has to be traced from bourgeois democracy to the "emergency powers act" to the suspension of parliament to open fascist dictatorship.

THE "DOMESTICATION" OF THE INDUSTRIAL WORKERS

Fascism infiltrates workers' groups from two sides: the so-called "lumpen proletariat" (an expression to which everyone takes exception) by means of direct material corruption and from the "workers' aristocracy," also by means of material corruption, as well as ideological influencing. In its political unscrupulousness, German fascism promised everybody everything. In an article by Dr. Jarmer, "Capitalism" (*Angriff*, Sept. 24, 1931), we find:

> At the German National Party rally in Stettin, Hugenberg spoke out against international capitalism with refreshing distinctness. At the same time, however, he stressed the necessity of a national capitalism.
>
> In so doing he once again clearly demarcated the German Nationals from the National Socialists; for the latter know only too well that the capitalist economic order which is in the process of breaking down throughout the world has to be replaced by a different order, because even in national capitalism there can be no justice.

That sounds almost communistic. Here we have an example of fascist propaganda appealing directly and with a consciously fraudulent intention to the revolutionary ardor of the industrial workers. But the crucial question was why the National Socialist industrial workers failed to see that fascism promised everybody everything. It was known that Hitler negotiated with industrial magnates, received financial support from them and promised an injunction against striking. Thus, it must have been due to the psychological structure of the average worker that such contradictions were not squarely faced, despite the intensive work on the part of revolutionary organizations to make him conscious of them. In his interview with the American journalist Knickerbocker, Hitler had this to say about the recognition of private debts to foreign countries:

> I am convinced that international bankers will soon realize that, under a National Socialist government, Germany will be a secure place of investment, that a rate of interest of about 3% will be most willingly paid for credit.
> —*Deutschland so oder so* p. 211

If it were revolutionary propaganda's cardinal task "to undeceive the proletariat," this could not have been done solely by appealing to their "class consciousness," nor solely by constantly impressing upon them the objective economic and political situation, and certainly not by constantly exposing the frauds that had been practiced on them. The first and foremost task of revolutionary propaganda should have been to give the *contradictions in the workers* the most sympathetic consideration, to grasp the fact that it was not a clear revolutionary will that was concealed or befogged, but that the revolutionary impulse in the psychic structure of the proletariat was partially undeveloped and partially interfused with contrary reactionary structural elements. The distillation of the revolutionary sentiments of the broad masses is undoubtedly the basic task in the process of awakening their social responsibility.

In times of "quiet" bourgeois democracy two fundamental possibilities are open to the industrial worker: identification with the bourgeoisie, which holds a higher position in the social scale, or identification with his own social class, which produces its own antireactionary way of life. To pursue the first possibility means to envy the reactionary man, to imitate him, and, if the opportunity arises, to assimilate his habits of life. To pursue the second of these possibilities means to reject the reactionary man's ideologies and habits of life. Due to the simultaneous influence exercised by both social and class habits, these two possibilities are equally strong. The revolutionary movement also failed to appreciate the importance of the seemingly irrelevant everyday habits, indeed, very often turned them to bad account. The lower middle-class bedroom suite, which the "rabble" buys as soon as he has the means, even if he is otherwise revolutionary minded; the consequent suppression of the wife, even if he is a Communist; the "decent" suit of clothes for Sunday; "proper" dance steps and a thousand other "banalities," have an incomparably greater reactionary influence when repeated day after day than thousands of revolutionary rallies and leaflets can ever hope to counterbalance. Narrow conservative life exercises a continuous influence, penetrates every facet of everyday life; whereas factory work and revolutionary leaflets have only a brief effect. Thus, it was a grave mistake to cater to the conservative tendencies in the workers by giving banquets "as a means of getting at the masses." Reactionary fascism was much more expert at this. The budding revolutionary modes of life were not cultivated. There was more truth about the reactionary structure of the workers in the "evening dress" bought by the wife of a worker for such a "banquet" than in a hundred articles. The evening dress or at-home beer parties were, of course, only external manifestations of a process in the worker, a testimony of the fact that the groundwork for the reception of National Socialist propaganda was already there. When, added to this, the fascist promised the "abolition of the proletariat" and was successful with this promise, it was the evening dress and not the economic program that accounted for success in ninety of one hundred cases. We must pay more, much more, attention to these details of everyday life. It is around these details that social progress or its opposite assume concrete forms, not around the political slogans that arouse temporary enthusiasm only. There is important and fruitful work waiting here. In Germany the revolutionary work for the masses was restricted almost exclusively to propaganda "against hunger." The basis of this propaganda, as *important* as it was, proved to be too narrow. There are thousands of different things taking place behind the scenes in the life of the individuals of the masses. For instance, the young worker has a thousand sexual and cultural problems, which plague him as soon as he has appeased his hunger to a small degree. The fight against hunger is of primary importance, but the hidden processes of human life must also be placed under the fierce light of this monkey show, in which we are spectator and actor at one and the same time; and this must be done without restraint and without fear of consequences.

The working man would undoubtedly show himself to be infinitely creative in his attempts to develop his own conceptions of life and natural way of viewing things. The mastering of everyday social problems would give invincible impetus to the reactionary-infested masses. A detailed, concrete, and germane study of these problems is indispensable. It will accelerate and secure the victory of the revolution. And please don't raise the threadbare objection that such proposals are utopian. Only by stressing all possibilities of a work-democratic way of life, by taking a militant stance toward reactionary thinking and militantly developing the seed of a living culture of masses of people, can lasting peace be secured. As long as reactionary social irresponsibility predominates over social responsibility, the worker will also be fairly closed to revolutionary, i.e., rational behavior. This is also another reason psychological work among the masses is so imperative.

The degradation of manual labor (which is a basic element of the inclination to imitate the reactionary white-collar worker) constitutes the psychological basis upon which fascism relies as soon as it begins to infiltrate the working classes. Fascism promises the abolition of the classes, that is to say, the abolition of proletarian status, and in this way it plays upon the social inferiority felt by the manual laborer. As long as peasants were still migrating to the city to become workers, they brought along a fresh rural family ideology, which, as we have already shown, is the best soil for the fostering of an imperialistic-nationalistic ideology. In addition to this, there is an ideological process in the workers' movement, which, in the assessment of the chances of a revolutionary movement in countries having a highly developed industry as well as in those countries whose industry was still undeveloped, has been accorded much too little attention.

Kautsky noted that, politically, the worker in highly industrialized England was less developed than the worker in industrially
undeveloped Russia (*Soziale Revolution*, 2nd edition, pp. 59–60).
The political events in the various countries of the world during the
past thirty years have clearly shown that revolutionary revolts take
place more readily in industrially undeveloped countries, such as
China, Mexico, and India, than in countries such as England,
America, and Germany. And this is the case, notwithstanding the
existence of disciplined, well-organized workers' movements rooted
in old traditions in the latter countries. If bureaucratization, which
is itself a pathological symptom, is abstracted from the workers'
movement, the question arises as to the exceptional entrenchment
of conservatism in Social Democracy and in the trade unions in
Western countries. *From the standpoint of the psychology of the
masses, Social Democracy is based on the conservative structures of
its followers.* As in the case of fascism, the problem here lies not so
much in the policies pursued by the party leadership as it does in
the psychological basis in the workers. I want to point out only a
few relevant facts, which, however, may well solve a riddle or two.
Here are the facts:

In early capitalism, besides the sharp economic division between bourgeoisie and proletariat, there was an equally sharp ideologic division, and particularly a structural division. The absence of
any kind of social policy, the emasculating sixteen-, indeed eighteen-
hour workday, the low standard of living of the industrial workers—
classically described in Engels' "Condition of the Working Classes
in England"—precluded any structural assimilation of the proletariat to the bourgeoisie. The structure of the nineteenth-century
proletariat was characterized by a meek submission to fate. The
psychological mood of this proletariat, including the peasantry, was
one of indifference and apathy. Bourgeois thinking was lacking;
consequently, this apathy did not hinder the sudden outbreak of
revolutionary sentiments, if suitable occasions arose and did not
prevent these sentiments from developing to an unexpected intensity and resoluteness. In later stages of capitalism, on the other
hand, it was different. If an organized workers' movement had

71

succeeded in winning socio-political improvements—as shorter working hours, franchise, social security—this had the effect of strengthening the working class; but at the same time a contrary process set in: With the raising of the standard of living, there was a structural assimilation to the middle class. With the elevation of one's social position, "one's eyes turned upward." In times of prosperity this adaptation of middle-class habits was intensified, but the subsequent effect of this adaptation, in times of economic crisis, was to obstruct the full unfolding of revolutionary sentiments.

The strength of the Social Democracies during the crisis years shows just how completely the workers had been infected with this conservatism. Thus, this strength was not to be explained on purely political grounds. It is now important to comprehend its basic elements. Two facts stand out: the emotional tie to the führer, that is to say, the unshakableness of the faith in the infallibility of the political leadership[9] (notwithstanding all the criticism, which never materialized into action), and the sex-moralistic assimilation to the conservatism of the lower middle class. This assimilation to the middle class was energetically encouraged by the upper middle class everywhere. The Social Democrats should have literally swung

---

[9] Following a congress in Leipzig, in 1932, I spoke with Social Democrat workers who had attended the congress about the political crisis. They were in accord with all the arguments against the "way to socialism" propagandized by Social Democracy, but otherwise hardly drew a distinction between themselves and the Communist. I asked one of them why they did not proceed accordingly and detach themselves from their leaders. His answer staggered me— that's how inconsistent it was with his previously expressed views: *"Our leaders surely know what they are doing."* This was an all-too-clear expression of the contradiction in which the Social Democrat worker found himself: the tie to the leader, which prevented criticism of his policies from materializing into action. In view of this it is easier to understand the grave error that was committed when attempting to win over the Social Democrat worker by reviling his leaders. Since he identified with his leaders, he could only be repelled by such insults. The inner rottenness of German Social Democracy was clearly brought out in the arrest of Severing, the Social Democrat minister of the interior, by a few armed men, shortly before Hitler's seizure of power. Twelve million Social Democrats did not prevent it.

their cudgels, in the beginning, at a time when fascism had not yet attained victory. Instead, they held them in reserve and used them only against the revolutionary workers. For the masses who were Social Democrats, they had a far more dangerous expedient: conservative ideology in all areas.

When, then, the Social Democrat worker found himself in the economic crisis which degraded him to the status of a coolie, the development of his revolutionary sentiments was severely retarded by the conservative structuralization that had been taking shape in him for decades. Either he remained in the camp of the Social Democrats, notwithstanding his criticism and rejection of their policies, or he went over to the NSDAP in search of a better replacement. Irresolute and indecisive, owing to the deep contradiction between revolutionary and conservative sentiments, disappointed by his own leadership, he followed the line of least resistance. Whether he would give up his conservative tendencies and arrive at a complete consciousness of his actual responsibility in the production process, i.e., at a revolutionary consciousness, depended solely on the correct or incorrect leadership of the revolutionary party. Thus the communist assertion that it was the Social Democrat policies that put fascism in the saddle was correct from a psychological viewpoint. *Disappointment in Social Democracy, accompanied by the contradiction between wretchedness and conservative thinking, must lead to fascism* if there are no revolutionary organizations. For example, following the fiasco of the Labor party's policies in England, in 1930–31, fascism began to infiltrate the workers who, then, in the election of 1931, cut away to the Right, instead of going over to communism. Democratic Scandinavia was also severely threatened by such a development.[10]

---

[10] To a large extent, the breakdown of the Norwegian government in 1940 was to be traced back to the same influence exercised by Social Democrat conservatism. For example, the Social Democrat government had prohibited military units from holding parades. But in 1939 the Norwegian fascists were the only ones who still marched through the streets and held exercises. Quisling's betrayal was greatly encouraged by such "liberalism."

Rosa Luxemburg took the view that a revolutionary fight was not possible with "coolies," (Ges. W. Bd. 4, p. 647). What kind of a coolie are we dealing with: the coolie *before* or *after* he has gone through conservative structuralization? Beforehand we are dealing with a coolie who has an almost impenetrable dullness, but also a great capacity for revolutionary action. Afterward we are dealing with *disappointed* coolies. Would it not be more difficult to rouse their revolutionary inclinations? How long can fascism exploit the masses' disappointment in Social Democracy and their "rebellion against the system" for its own narrow purposes? As difficult as it may be to answer this momentous question, one thing is certain: the international revolutionary movement will have to tackle it, if it wants to deal fascism its death blow.

III

The Race Theory

The race theory is German fascism's theoretical axis. In fascist ideology the economic program of the so-called twenty-five points figures solely as an expedient intended "to improve the Germanic race genetically and to protect it against racial interbreeding" which, according to the National Socialists, always entails the decline of the "higher race." Indeed, it is their contention that even the decline of a culture is to be traced back to miscegenation. Hence, "keeping the blood and the race pure" is a nation's noblest task, in the fulfillment of which one must be prepared to make any sacrifice. In Germany and the German-occupied countries, no means were spared in putting this theory into practice in the form of the persecution of the Jews.

The race theory proceeds from the presupposition that the exclusive mating of every animal with its own species is an "iron law" in nature. Only exceptional circumstances, such as captivity, are capable of causing a violation of this law and of leading to racial interbreeding. When this occurs, however, nature revenges itself and uses every means at its disposal to oppose such infringements, either by making the bastard sterile or by limiting the fertility of later offspring. In every crossbreeding of two living creatures of different "levels," the offspring will of necessity represent something intermediate. But nature aims at a higher breeding of life; hence

75

bastardization is contrary to the will of nature. Natural selection also takes place in the daily struggle for survival, in which the weaker, i.e., racially inferior, perish. This is consistent with the "will of nature," for every improvement and higher breeding would cease if the weak, who are in the majority, could crowd out the strong, who are in the minority. Hence, nature subjects the weaker specimens to more severe conditions of life as a means of limiting their number; on the other hand, it does not allow the rest to multiply indiscriminately; they are subjected to a ruthless selection on the basis of energy and health.

The National Socialist went on to apply this supposed law in nature to peoples. Their line of reasoning was something as follows: Historical experience teaches that the "intermixing of Aryan blood" with "inferior" peoples always results in the degeneration of the founders of civilization. The level of the superior race is lowered, followed by physical and mental retrogression; this marks the beginning of a progressive "decline."

The North American continent would remain strong, Hitler states, "as long as he [the German inhabitant] does not fall a victim to defilement of the blood,"[1] that is to say, as long as he does not interbreed with non-Germanic peoples.

"To bring about such a development is, then, nothing else but to sin against the will of the eternal creator."[2] These views are unmistakably mystical; nature "regulates" and "wills" "according to reason." They are the logical culmination of biological metaphysics.

According to Hitler, humanity is to be divided into three races: the founders of civilization, the upholders of civilization, and the destroyers of civilization. Only the Aryan race is considered as the founder of civilization, for it built the "foundation and walls of human creation." The Asian peoples, the Japanese[3] and the Chi-

---

[1] *Mein Kampf*, op. cit., p. 286.

[2] Op. cit. 286.

[3] Political irrationalism was clearly expressed in the later military alliance between a superior race and an inferior race.

nese, for example, merely took over the Aryan civilization and translated it into their own form. Thus, they are upholders of civilization. The Jewish race, however, is a destroyer of civilization. The existence of "inferior human beings" is the chief prerequisite for the establishment of a higher civilization. Man's first civilization rested upon the use of inferior human races. In olden times it was the vanquished who were made to pull the plow, which only much later was pulled by the horse. As conqueror, the Aryan subjugated the inferior masses and regulated their activity in accordance with Aryan needs to compass Aryan ends. However, as soon as the subjugated peoples began to learn the language and to adopt the customs of the "masters," and the clear-cut demarcation between master and slave was obliterated, the Aryan relinquished the purity of his blood and lost "his sojourn in paradise." Through this, he also lost his cultural genius. We are not forgetting that Adolf Hitler represents the flowering of civilization.

> Blood mixture and the resultant drop in the racial level is the sole cause of the dying out of old cultures; for men do not perish as a result of lost wars, but by the loss of that force of resistance which is contained only in pure blood.
>
> —Op. cit. 296

An objective and technical refutation of this basic idea is out of the question here. It borrows an argument from Darwin's hypothesis of natural selection, some elements of which are as reactionary as his proof of the origin of species from lower organisms is revolutionary. Moreover, this idea conceals the imperialist function of fascist ideology. For if the Aryans are the sole founders of civilization, then, by virture of their divine destiny, they can lay claim to world dominion. And, in fact, one of Hitler's principal claims was the expansion of the borders of the German empire, especially "toward the East," i.e., into Soviet Russian territory. Thus, we can see that the glorification of an imperialist war lay wholly within the compass of this ideology.

> . . . The aim for which we were fighting the War was the loftiest, the most overpowering, that man can conceive: it was the

freedom and independence of our nation, the security of our future food supply, and—our national honor;

—Op. cit. 177

Here we are solely interested in the irrational origin of these ideologies, which, objectively viewed, were in conformity with the interests of German imperialism; most of all we are interested in the contradictions and incongruities existing in the race theory. Race theorists who refer to a biological law in support of their theory overlook the fact that racial breeding of animals is an artifact. It is not a question whether dog and cat have an "instinctive aversion" to interbreeding, but whether collie and greyhound, German and Slav, have the same aversion.

Race theorists, who are as old as imperialism itself, want to achieve racial purity in peoples whose interbreeding, as a result of the expansion of world economy, is so far advanced that racial purity can have a meaning only to a numbskull. We do not want to enter into the other absurdities here—as if racial circumscription and not its opposite, promiscuous mating within the same species, were the rule in nature. In the present examination we are not concerned with the rational content of the race theory, a theory that, instead of proceeding from facts to valuations, proceeded from valuations to a distortion of the facts. Nor will arguments be of any use against a fascist who is narcissistically convinced of the supreme superiority of his Teutonism, if only because he operates with irrational feelings and not with arguments. Hence, it would be hopeless to try to prove to a fascist that black people and Italians are not racially "inferior" to the Teutons. He feels himself to be "superior," and that's the end of it. The race theory can be refuted only by exposing its irrational functions, of which there are essentially two: that of giving expression to certain *unconscious* and *emotional* currents prevalent in the nationalistically disposed man and of concealing certain psychic tendencies. Only the latter function will be discussed here. We are especially interested in the fact that Hitler speaks of "incest" when an Aryan interbreeds with a non-Aryan, whereas it is usually sexual intercourse among those who are related by blood that is designated as incest. How are such stupidities to be explained in a "theory" that presumed to be the basis of a new world, a "third Reich"? When we bear in mind that in the final analysis the irrational, emotional basis of such a hypothesis owes its existence to definite existential factors; when we free ourselves of the notion that the discovery of such irrational sources of views of life, which have come into being on a rational basis, means a shifting of the question into the sphere of metaphysics, then we open the way to the source of metaphysics itself. We comprehend not only the historical conditions under which metaphysical thinking arises, but also its material substance. Let the results speak for themselves.

THE OBJECTIVE AND SUBJECTIVE FUNCTIONS OF IDEOLOGY

The failure to differentiate between the objective and subjective functions of an ideology frequently results in a misunderstanding of the relation of an ideology to its *historical* function. At the outset, a dictator's views are to be understood solely in terms of the economic basis from which they originated. Thus the fascist race theory and nationalistic ideology in general have a concrete relation to the imperialistic aims of a ruling class that is attempting to solve difficulties of an economic nature. The German and the French nationalism of World War I appealed to the "Greatness of the Nation," behind which were concealed the economic expansion tendencies of German and French big business. These economic factors do not constitute what is substantial in the corresponding ideology, but only the social soil in which they germinate; in short, they constitute the conditions that are indispensable to the genesis of such ideologies. At times nationalism is not at all socially represented with respect to its substance; nor for that matter can it be brought into line with racial points of view. In Austria-Hungary of former days, a nationalism did not coincide with race, but with the "homeland" Austria-Hungary. In 1914, when Bethmann-Hollweg invoked "Teutonism against Slavism," if he had wanted to be consistent, he would have had to proceed against Austria, this predominantly Slavic state. Thus we see that, while the economic conditions of an ideology give us an insight into its material basis, they offer us no immediate knowledge of its irrational core. It is man's character structure that directly constitutes this core. Subject to the specific economic conditions of a society, man reproduces the historical economic process in his ideology. *By forming ideologies, man reshapes himself; man's material core is to be sought in the process by which he forms ideologies.* Thus, ideology appears to have a twofold material basis: the economic structure of society and the typical structure of the people who produce it, a structure that is itself determined by the economic structure of society. Thus it is clear that the irrational formation of an ideology also makes man's structure irrational.

The structure of fascism is characterized by metaphysical thinking, unorthodox faith, obsession with abstract ethical ideals, and belief in the divine predestination of the führer. These basic features are linked with a deeper layer, which is characterized by a strong authoritarian tie to the führer-ideal or the nation. The belief in a "master race" became the principal mainspring of the tie to the "führer" on the part of the National Socialist masses, as well as the foundation of their voluntary acceptance of slavish submission. In addition to this, however, the intensive identification with the führer had a decisive effect, for it concealed one's real status as an insignificant member of the masses. Notwithstanding his vassalage, every National Socialist felt himself to be a "little Hitler." Now, however, we want to turn our attention to the characterological basis of these attitudes. We must seek out the dynamic functions that, while they themselves are determined by education and the social atmosphere as a whole, remold human structures to such an extent that tendencies of a reactionary-irrational nature are capable of taking shape in them; to such an extent that, completely enveloped in their identification with the "führer," the masses are immune to the insult heaped upon them by the label "inferior."

If we shut our eyes to the dazzling effect of ideologic phraseology, if we focus our attention on its irrational content, and if we know how to show its proper bearing upon the sex-economic aspects of the process of ideologic formation, then the stereotype equating of *"racial poisoning"* and *"blood poisoning"* is immediately conspicuous. What does this mean?

RACIAL PURITY, BLOOD POISONING, AND MYSTICISM

". . . running parallel to the political, ethical, and moral contamination of the people, there had been for many years a no less terrible poisoning of the health of the national body . . . [through] syphilis. . . ."[4] The principal cause of this was to be sought in the prostitution of love:

> . . . The cause lies, primarily, in our prostitution of love. Even if its results were not this frightful plague, it would nonetheless be profoundly injurious to man, since the moral devastations which accompany this degeneracy suffice to destroy a people slowly but surely. This Jewification of our spiritual life and mammonization of our mating instinct will sooner or later destroy our entire offspring. . . .
>
> —*Mein Kampf*, p. 247

Hitler sums up his position as follows:

> *Blood sin and desecration of the race are the original sin in this world and the end of a humanity which surrenders to it.*
>
> —*Mein Kampf*, p. 249

Thus, according to this view, racial interbreeding leads to blood interbreeding and in turn to the "blood poisoning of the national body."

> . . . The most visible results of this mass contamination [by syphilis] can be found . . . in our—children. They in particular are the sad product of the irresistibly spreading contamination of

---

[4] Op. cit., p. 246.

our sexual life; the vices of the parents are revealed in the sicknesses of the children.

—*Mein Kampf*, p. 248

In this connection, "vices of the parents" can only refer to their interbreeding with racially alien blood, i.e., especially with Jewish blood, whereby the Jewish "world plague" finds ingress into "pure" Aryan blood. It is remarkable how closely this theory of blood poisoning is related to the political thesis of the poisoning of Teutonism by the "world Jew, Karl Marx." The irrational fear of syphilis constitutes one of the major sources of National Socialism's political views and its anti-Semitism. It follows, then, that racial *purity*, that is to say, *purity of blood*[5] is something worth striving for and fighting for with every available means.

---

[5] The following story appeared in the London *Times* on August 23, 1933: "The son and daughter of the United States Ambassador in Berlin were among the foreigners who were in Nuremberg on Sunday, August 13, and saw a girl led through the streets with her head shaved and her shorn plaits pinned to a placard suspended from her shoulders which bore the words 'I have offered myself to a Jew.' "

Several other foreigners were eye-witnesses of this spectacle. There are at all times foreign tourists in Nuremberg, and the parade of the girl was carried out in such a manner that few people in the center of the town could have failed to see it. The girl who is described by one of them as being small, fragile, and, in spite of her shaven head and condition, obviously pretty, was marched in and out of the ring of international hotels by the station, through the main streets, where the traffic was blocked by the crowds, and from cabaret to cabaret. Her escort was formed of storm troopers, and a crowd estimated by a trustworthy observer at some 2,000 people followed her about. She occasionally stumbled and was replaced on her feet by the stalwart brownshirts, who sometimes held her aloft in order that more distant onlookers might see her, and on these occasions she was hooted and derided by the crowd and jocularly invited to make a speech.

For not rising when the Horst Wessel song was played a girl at Neu-Ruppin, near Berlin, was led through the streets of the town flanked by storm troopers and wearing two placards hung from her neck. The inscription read: "I, shameless creature that I am, dared to remain seated when the Horst Wessel song was sung, thus mocking the victims of the National Socialist revolution."

Later in the day the girl was again led through the streets. The time of the "spectacle" had been announced in the local newspaper so that large crowds should gather.

Hitler repeatedly stressed that one could not get at the masses with arguments, proofs, and knowledge, but only with feelings and beliefs. In the language of National Socialism, in that of Keyserling, Driesch, Rosenberg, Stapel, etc., the nebulous and the mystical are so conspicuous that an analysis of this peculiarity will certainly prove profitable.

What was it in the mysticism of fascism that so fascinated the masses?

The answer is supplied by the analysis of the "proofs" that Rosenberg (*Mythus des 20. Jahrhunderts*) offers in substantiation of the fascist race theory. Right at the outset Rosenberg writes:

> The values of a race's soul, i.e., those values which are the motor forces of the new conception of the world, have not yet become a part of living consciousness. Soul, however, means race seen from within. Conversely, race is the outer world of the soul.
>
> —*Mythus*, p. 22

Here we have an example of one of the many typical National Socialist phrases, which, on first impression, doesn't seem to mean anything, indeed, seems intentionally to disguise its meaning, perhaps from the author himself. To understand the political-irrational impact of precisely such statements, one has to be familiar with and recognize the importance of the effect they have on the structure of the masses. Rosenberg goes on to say:

> Hence, the history of race is the history of nature and soul mysticism at one and the same time; but the history of the religion of the blood is, conversely, the great world history of the rise and fall of peoples, of their heroes and thinkers, their inventors and artists.

The recognition of this fact leads to the realization that the "fight of the blood" and the "intuitive mysticism of existential phenomena" are not two separate things, but one and the same thing represented in different ways. "Fight of the blood," "intuitive mysticism of existential phenomena," "rise and fall of peoples," "blood poisoning," "Jewish world plague," are all part and parcel of the same line, which begins with "fight of the blood" and ends with the bloody terror against the "Jewish materialism" of Marx and the genocide of the Jews.

The cause of freedom is not advanced by merely ridiculing this mysticism; it must be unmasked and reduced to its basic irrational content. The greater part of this mysticism and what is most important about it is a biological energy process, an extreme expression of reactionary sexual ideology, irrationally and mystically conceived. *The creed of the "soul" and its "purity" is the creed of asexuality,* of "sexual purity." Basically, it is a symptom of the sexual repression and sexual shyness brought about by a patriarchal authoritarian society.

"Coming to grips with blood and environment, with blood and blood, is for us the last attainable reality, behind which it is no longer granted us to search and to investigate," Rosenberg states. He errs. We are immodest enough to want to investigate and not only to expose, without sentimentality, the living process "between blood and blood," but also to demolish a pillar of the National Socialist creed.

We shall let Rosenberg himself prove that the core of the fascist race theory is a mortal fear of natural sexuality and of its orgasm function. Using the ancient Greeks as an example, Rosenberg seeks to prove the validity of the thesis that the rise and fall of peoples is to be traced back to racial interbreeding and "blood poisoning." According to his theory the Greeks were originally the representatives of Nordic racial purity. The gods Zeus and Apollo and the goddess Athene were "symbols of the most devout piety," guardians and protectors of "the noble and the joyous," "keepers of order, teachers of the harmony of inner power and of artistic values." Homer, he claims, had not the least interest in the "ecstatic." Of Athene, he writes that she was:

> . . . the symbol of life-consuming lightning, the wise and thoughtful virgin, sprung from the head of Zeus: protectress of the Hellenic people and faithful shield of its battles.
>
> These very pious creations of the Greek soul are proof of the pure, untrammeled inner life of the Nordic people; in the highest

sense of the word, they are religious confessions and expressions of confidence in their own species.

—*Mythus*, p. 41 ff

These gods, which are said to symbolize purity, sublimity, and religiosity, are then contrasted to the gods of the Near-Eastern peoples:

> While the Greek gods were heroes of light and heaven, the gods of the non-Aryan Near Easterners are imbued with earthly characteristics.

Rosenberg contends that Demeter and Hermes were the organic offspring of these "souls of race." *Dionysus, the god of ecstasy, sensual pleasure, unbridled maenadism, constituted the "intrusion of the foreign race of the Etruscans and marked the beginning of the decline of Hellenism."*

In a far-fetched effort to support his thesis of the soul of a race, Rosenberg quite arbitrarily separates the gods into two categories: those that represent the "positive" process of Hellenistic cultural development, he labels Greek; while the others, which also originated in Hellenism, are described as *foreign* gods. Rosenberg asserts that historical research, which "racially falsifies" and erroneously interprets Hellenism, is responsible for our misunderstanding of Greek history.

> In awe and veneration, the great German romantics sense how ever darker veils enshroud the bright gods of heaven, and they plunge ever deeper into the instinctual, amorphous, demonic, sexual, ecstatic, chthonic, into a *veneration of the mother* [my italics WR]. And all of this was still supposed to be characteristic of the Greeks.

—*Mythus*, p. 43

All forms of idealistic philosophy fail to investigate the conditions under which the "ecstatic" and "instinctual" come into existence in certain cultural epochs; instead they get entangled in the abstract evaluation of these phenomena from the point of view of that cultural outlook that, elevating itself so far above the "earthly" (natural), comes to naught as a result of that very elevation. We, too, arrive at an evaluation of such phenomena, but it is an evaluation based on the conditions of a social process that appear as the symptoms of "decline" of a civilization. In this way we are able to recognize the forces that impel forward and those that retard, and to comprehend the phenomenon of decline as a historical event, and, last but not least, to seek out the seed of the new cultural form and to assist its germination. When Rosenberg—in view of the decline of twentieth-century authoritarian civilization—reminds us of the fate of the Greeks, he puts himself on the side of conservative historical tendencies, despite his protestations of a "revival" of Teutonism. If we can succeed in understanding the standpoint of political reaction, we shall have gained a significant insight into the attitude toward cultural revolution and its sex-economic core. For the reactionary cultural philosopher there are only two possibilities: resignation and skepticism, or the turning back of the wheel of history by "revolutionary" means. But if one has shifted the focal point of one's cultural outlook, has recognized in the collapse of an ancient civilization, not the fall of civilization altogether but merely the fall of a *certain* civilization, namely the authoritarian, then a natural shifting also takes place in one's assessment of those cultural elements previously appraised as positive or negative. One realizes that the old form is "laboring with" the new form of civilization, one based on genuine freedom. It is mainly a question of understanding the attitude that the revolution takes toward those phenomena regarded as symptoms of decline by political reaction. It is indicative, for example, that the latter declares itself in favor of the patriarchal theory in ethnology, whereas the former declares itself in favor of the matriarchal theory. Apart from the objective historical factors, there are interests at work in these two contrary sociological currents, interests that correspond to the previously unknown processes of sex-economy. Matriarchy, which is a historically demonstrated system, is not only in accord with the organization of natural work-democracy, but also with the

86

society organized on a natural, sex-economic basis.[6] Patriarchy, on the other hand, not only has an authoritarian economy, its sex-economic organization is catastrophic.

Long after the Church lost its hold on scientific research, it continued to promulgate the metaphysical doctrine of "man's moral nature," and of his monogamous disposition, etc. It was for this reason that Bachofen's findings threatened to make hay of tradition. The amazing thing about matriarchy is not so much its wholly different consanguinity, but the natural self-regulation of sexuality that it entails. The social means of production are not privately owned in a matriarchy, as Morgan and Engels recognized. As a fascist ideologist, Rosenberg had no other choice than to deny the descent of ancient Greek culture from matriarchal beginnings (a *proven* fact) and to seize upon the hypothesis that "in this phase [the Dionysian] the Greeks assumed characteristics which were both physically and spiritually alien to their culture."

In contrast to Christian ideology (as we shall see later), fascist ideology separates man's orgastic yearning from the human structure produced under authoritarian patriarchy and relates it to various races: *Nordic is equated to bright, majestic, heavenly, asexual, pure,* whereas *"Near Eastern" is equated to instinctual, demonic, sexual, ecstatic, orgastic.* This explains why Bachofen's "intuitive and romantic" investigations were rejected as the theory of that which only "appears to be" ancient Greek life. In the fascist race theory the orgasm anxiety of the man subjugated to authority appears in an absolute form, eternalized as the "pure" and contrasted with the animal-like and orgastic. Thus, "what is Greek" and "what is racial" become an emanation of "what is pure," what is "asexual"; while "what is racially alien," "the Etruscan," is related to "what is animal" and therefore "inferior." In keeping with this line of reasoning, patriarchy is taken as the source of the human history of the Aryans:

---

[6] See Morgan's *Ancient Society;* Engels' *Origin of the Family;* Malinowsky's *The Sexual Life of Savages* and Reich's *Der Einbruch der Sexualmoral.*

The first great historically decisive battle between *racial* values was carried out on Greek soil, a battle decided in favor of the Nordic nature. From this point on man approaches life from *daylight*, from *life itself*; everything which we call Greek culture and our great heritage from antiquity, originated from the law of light and of heaven, from the spirit and nature of the father.

—Rosenberg

The patriarchal authoritarian sexual order that resulted from the revolutionary processes of latter-day matriarchy (economic independence of the chief's family from the maternal gens, a growing exchange of goods between the tribes, development of the means of production, etc.) becomes the primary basis of authoritarian ideology by depriving the women, children, and adolescents of their sexual freedom, making a commodity of sex and placing sexual interests in the service of economic subjugation. From now on, sexuality is indeed distorted; it becomes diabolical and demonic and has to be curbed. In terms of patriarchal demands, the innocent sensuousness of matriarchy appears as the lascivious unchaining of dark powers. The Dionysian becomes "sinful yearning," which patriarchal culture can conceive of only as something chaotic and "dirty." Surrounded by and imbued with human sexual structures that have become distorted and lascivious, patriarchal man is shackled for the first time in an ideology in which sexual and dirty, sexual and vulgar or demonic, become inseparable associations.

Secondarily, however, this evaluation also has a *rational* justification.

With the imposition of chastity, women become unchaste under the pressure of their sexual demands; the sexual brutality on the part of the male, and the corresponding conception on the part of the female that for her the sexual act is something disgraceful, takes the place of natural orgastic sensuousness. Extramarital sexual intercourse, to be sure, is not done away with anywhere. With the shifting of the valuation and the abolition of the institutions that previously protected and sanctioned it in a matriarchal society, it becomes involved in a conflict with official morality and is forced to lead a clandestine existence. The change in the social attitude toward sexual intercourse also effects a change in the inner experience of sexuality. The conflict that is now created between the natural and "sublime morality" disturbs the individual's ability to gratify his needs. The feeling of guilt now associated with sexuality cleaves the natural, orgastic course of sexual coalescence and produces a damming up of sexual energy, which later breaks out in various ways. Neuroses, sexual aberrations, and antisocial sexuality become permanent social phenomena. Childhood and adolescent sexuality, which were given a positive value in the original matriarchal work-democracy, fall prey to systematic suppression, which differs only in form. As time goes on, this sexuality, which is so distorted, disturbed, brutalized, and prostituted, advocates the very ideology to which it owes its origin. Those who negate sexuality can now justifiably point to it as something brutal and dirty. That this dirty sexuality is not natural sexuality but merely patriarchal sexuality is simply overlooked. And the sexology of latter-day capitalistic patriarchy is no less affected by this evaluation than the vulgar views. This condemns it to complete sterility.

Later we shall see how religious mysticism becomes the organized center of these evaluations and ideologies. For the present we must merely bear in mind that religious mysticism denies the sex-economic principle altogether and condemns sexuality as a sinful phenomenon of humanity, from which only the Hereafter can deliver us. Nationalistic fascism, on the other hand, transfers sexual sensuality to the "alien race," which is relegated to an inferior status in this way. From now on, the depreciation of the "alien race" coincides organically with latter-day patriarchal imperialism.

In Christian mythology, God never appears without his counterpart the Devil, as the "God of the Underworld," and the victory of the divine God over the infernal God becomes the symbol of human elevation. This confrontation is also depicted in Greek mythology by the struggle between orgastic biosexuality and strivings that demand chastity. To the abstract moralist and to the mystifying philosopher, this confrontation appears as the wrestling of two essences or "human ideas," one of which is regarded as vulgar from the outset, while the other is looked upon as the "truly human" or "superhuman." However, if this "struggle of essences" as well as the valuations attached to them are traced to their material fountainhead, if they are arranged in their proper place in the sociological fabric and sexuality is given its due as a historical factor, we arrive at the following facts: every tribe that developed from a matriarchal to a patriarchal organization had to change the sexual structure of its members to produce a sexuality in keeping with its new form of life. This was a necessary change because the shifting of power and of wealth from the democratic gens to the authoritarian family of the chief was mainly implemented with the help of the suppression of the sexual strivings of the people. It was in this way that sexual suppression became an essential factor in the division of society into classes.

Marriage, and the lawful dowry it entailed, became the axis of the transformation of the one organization into the other.[7] In view of the fact that the marriage tribute of the wife's gens to the man's family strengthened the male's, especially the chief's, position of power, the male members of the higher ranking gens and families developed a keen interest in making the nuptial ties permanent. At this stage, in other words, only the man had an interest in marriage. In this way natural work-democracy's simple alliance, which could be easily dissolved at any time, was transformed into the permanent and monogamous marital relationship of patriarchy. The permanent monogamous marriage became the basic institution of patriarchal society—which it still is today. To safeguard these marriages, however, it was necessary to impose greater and greater restrictions upon and to depreciate natural genital strivings. This applied not only to the "lower" class, which was subjected to greater and greater exploitation. It was precisely those classes that until then had not

---

[7] Proof of this is to be found in: *Der Einbruch der Sexualmoral.*

known any cleavage between morality and sexuality that were now forced to experience this ever deepening conflict. But let it not be assumed that this compulsive morality had an external effect only; its full force is not felt until it has become *internalized,* until it has become a sexual inhibition anchored in the structure. Different aspects of the conflict will predominate during different stages of this process. In the initial stages, it is sexual need that wins the upper hand; later it is the compulsive moral inhibition that prevails. When the entire social organization is plunged into a state of political upheaval, the conflict between sexuality and compulsive morality will of necessity reach an acute peak. Some will view this state of affairs as moral degeneration, while others will see it as a "sexual revolution." In any event, it is the breakthrough of natural sexuality that is looked upon as "cultural degeneration." This breakthrough is felt to be a "degeneration" only because it constitutes a threat to compulsive morality. Viewed objectively, it is only the system of sexual dictatorship that breaks down, a system devised to preserve compulsive moralistic values in the individual in the interest of authoritarian marriage and family. Among the ancient Greeks, whose written history does not begin until patriarchy had reached a state of full development, we find the following sexual organization: male supremacy, hetaerae for the upper classes and prostitution for the middle and lower classes; and along with this the wives leading an enslaved and wretched existence and figuring solely as birth machines. The male supremacy of the Platonic era is entirely homosexual.[8]

The sex-economic contradictions of latter-day Greece appeared at a time when the affairs of the Greek state were politically and economically on the downgrade. To the fascist Rosenberg, the "chthonian" becomes intermixed with the "apollonian" in the Dionysian era, and they perish together. The phallus, Rosenberg

---

[8] The same principle governs the fascist ideology of the male strata of leaders (Blüher, Roehm, etc.).

writes, becomes the symbol of the latter-day Greek conception of the world. For the fascists, therefore, the return of natural sexuality is viewed as a sign of decadence, lasciviousness, lechery, and sexual filth. This, however, is not merely fascist fantasy; it corresponds to the actual situation created by the burning contradiction in the mode of experience of the people of such an epoch. The "Dionysian feasts" correspond to the masquerades and costume balls of our reactionary classes. However, one must know exactly what occurs at such feasts not to fall prey to the common deception of seeing in this "Dionysian" happening the epitome of sexual experience. Nowhere are the indissoluble contradictions between dissolute sexual yearnings and a capacity for experience debilitated by morality more glaringly exposed than at such feasts. "Dionysos' law of limitless sexual gratification means uninhibited racial interbreeding between Greeks and Asiatics of all tribes and varieties [*Mythus*, p. 52]." Just imagine a historian of the year 4000 representing the sexual feasts of the twentieth century as the uninhibited interbreeding of the Germans with the blacks and the Jews "of all tribes and varieties"!

In this we clearly recognize the meaning of the idea of racial interbreeding. It is a defense against the Dionysian, a defense rooted in patriarchal society's economic interest in marriage. Hence, even in the story of Jason, compulsive marriage figures as the bulwark against hetaerism.

"Hetaerae" are women who refuse to submit to the yoke of compulsive marriage and insist on their right to determine their own sex life. However, this demand gets involved in a conflict with early childhood education, which incapacitated the organism's capacity for sexual experience.

Hence, the hetaera plunges herself into one adventure after the other to escape her homosexuality, or she lives a disturbed and disintegrated existence in both directions at once. Hetaerism is supplemented by male homosexuality. Owing to their compulsive marital life, the men flee to the hetaerae and voluptuaries in an effort to restore their capacity for sexual experience. Understandably, the sexual structure of the fascists, who affirm the most severe form of patriarchy and actually reactivate the sexual life of the Platonic era in their familial mode of living—i.e., "purity" in ideology, disintegration and pathology in actual practice—must bear a resemblance to the sexual conditions of the Platonic era. Rosenberg and Blüher recognize the state solely as a male state organized on a homosexual basis. It is very curious to see how the view of the worthlessness of democracy emerges from this ideology. Pythagoras is rejected because he came out as the prophet of the equality of all people, as the "herald of democratic Tellurism, of the community of goods and females." This idea of the inner association of the "community of goods and females" plays a central role in the antirevolutionary fight. The democratization of Roman patrician rule, which provided three hundred senators from three hundred aristocratic families until the fifth century, is traced back to the fact that intermarriages between patricians and plebeians were permitted from the fifth century on, and that this led to a "racial deterioration." Thus, even the democratization of a political system brought about through intermarriages is interpreted as a sign of racial decline. It is here that the reactionary character of the race theory is thoroughly exposed, for now sexual intercourse between Greeks and Romans belonging to different *classes* is looked upon as ruinous racial interbreeding. *Members of the suppressed class are equated with those who are racially alien.* At another point Rosenberg speaks of the workers' movement as the "ascending of the asphalt-humanity of the big cities with all the refuse of Asianism [*Mythus*, p. 66]." *Thus, behind the idea of the interbreeding with alien races lies the idea of sexual intercourse with members of the suppressed class.* And operating at an even deeper level is the tendency of political reaction to draw lines of demarcation, which are rigid from an economic viewpoint, but are completely nonexistent from a sexual-moralistic viewpoint owing to the sexual restrictions imposed upon middle-class women. At the same time, however, sexual interbreeding between classes means an undermining of class rule; it creates the possibility of a "democratization," that is to say, the possibility of the proletarianization of the "aristocratic" youth. For the lower social strata of every social order develop sexual conceptions and habits that constitute a serious threat to the rulers of every authoritarian order.[9]

If, in the final analysis, it is the idea of the interbreeding of members of the ruling class with members of the ruled class that lies at the root of the idea of racial interbreeding, then we obviously have here the key to the question as to the role played by sexual suppression in class society. In this connection we can differentiate several functions. We know, for instance, that material suppression relates solely to the lower classes; but on no account can we assume that the same holds true for sexual suppression. The relations of sexual suppression to class society are much more complicated. At this time we want to single out only two of these functions:

1. Since sexual suppression has its origin in the economic interest of marriage and the law of inheritance, it begins within the ruling class itself. At first the morality of chastity applies most rigidly to the female members of the ruling class. This is intended to safeguard those possessions that were acquired through the exploitation of the lower classes.

2. In early capitalism and in the large feudal societies of Asia the ruling class is *not yet* interested in a sexual suppression of the enslaved classes. It is when the materially suppressed classes begin to organize themselves, begin to fight for socio-political improvements and to raise the cultural level of the broad masses, that sexual-moralistic inhibitions set in. Only then does the ruling caste begin to show an interest in the "morality" of the suppressed classes. Thus, parallel to the rise of the organized working class, a contrary process sets in, namely the ideological assimilation to the ruling class.

Their own sexual habits are not relinquished in this process,

---

[9] Cf. the appraisal of the "impure caste" in the Indian patriarchal society.

however; they continue to exist alongside the moralistic ideologies, which, from now on, become more and more entrenched. This results in the previously described contradiction in the human structure between reactionary and freedom-aspiring tendencies. Historically, the development of this contradiction in the structure of the masses coincides with the loosening of feudal absolutism through bourgeois democracy. To be sure, exploitation has merely undergone a change in form; but this change entails a change in the character structure of the masses. These are the facts to which Rosenberg gives a mystical interpretation when he writes that the primordial god of the earth, Poseidon, repelled by Athene the goddess of asexuality, rules in the form of a serpent in the ground beneath her temple, in the same way as the "Pelasgic python dragon" rules beneath the temple of Apollo in Delphi. "But the Nordic Theseus did not kill the Asiatic brutes everywhere; as soon as Aryan blood begins to slumber, the foreign monster springs up again and again— that Asiatic mongrelism and physical robustness of Eastern man."

It is clear what is meant by "physical robustness." It is that remnant of sexual spontaneity that distinguishes the members of the suppressed classes from the ruling class, that same spontaneity, namely, that is gradually blunted in the course of "democratization" but is never completely lost. Psychologically, the serpent Poseidon and the Python dragon represent genital sensuality symbolized as the phallus. Genital sensuality has been suppressed, has become subterranean in both society's and man's structure, but it is still alive. The feudal upper class, which has a direct interest in the renunciation of natural sexuality (cf. Japan), feels itself threatened by the more elemental sexual habits of the suppressed classes, all the more so because it itself has not only not mastered its own sensuality, but sees it, on the contrary, reappearing in its own class in a distorted and perverse form. Thus, the sexual customs of the masses constitute not only a psychological but also a social danger to the ruling class; above all, the latter senses a threat to its institution of the family. As long as the ruling castes are economically strong and in the ascendancy, it is not difficult for them to maintain a total sexual-moralistic separation from the masses. An example of this was the English bourgeoisie around the middle of the nineteenth century. In periods when their rulership is shaken, and particularly when there is an outright crisis (as has existed, for example, in Central Europe and England since the beginning of the twentieth century), the moral restrictions imposed on sexuality are loosened within the ruling class itself. The disintegration of sexual moralism begins with the liquidation of family ties. At first the middle and lower middle classes, in complete identification with the upper class and its morals, become the real champions of the official, strongly defended anti-sexual morality. It is precisely when the economy of the lower middle classes shows signs of breaking down that natural sexuality must appear as a particular threat to the continued existence of sexual institutions. Since the lower middle class is the mainstay of the authoritarian order, the latter attaches special importance to its "morality" and to its "remaining uncontaminated" by the "influence of inferior races." If the lower middle class would lose its moralistic attitude toward sex to the same extent that it loses its intermediate economic position between the industrial worker and the upper class, this would constitute a very grave threat to any dictator. For the "python dragon" is also lurking among the lower middle class, ever ready to shatter its shackles and, consequently, its reactionary tendencies. It is for this reason that, in times of crisis, a dictatorial power always steps up its propaganda for "morality" and the "strengthening of the bonds of marriage and the family." For it is the authoritarian family that constitutes the bridge from the wretched social situation of the lower middle class to reactionary ideology. If the compulsive family is undermined by economic crises, proletarianization of the middle class and wars, then the authoritarian system, which is so firmly entrenched in the structure of the masses, is also seriously threatened. We shall have to enter into this question more thoroughly. Thus, we have to agree with Leng, the National Socialist biologist and race theorist from

Munich, who asserted that the authoritarian family was the core of cultural politics. He made this statement at a meeting of the National Socialist society "Deutscher Staat" in 1932. We can add that it is the core of reactionary as well as of revolutionary cultural politics, for these observations have far-reaching social consequences.

IV

The Symbolism of the Swastika

We have satisfied ourselves that fascism is to be regarded as a problem of the masses and not as a problem of Hitler as a person or the politics of the National Socialist party. We have demonstrated how it is possible for an impoverished mass of people to turn to an arch reactionary party in such a tumultuous way. In order now to proceed step by step to the practical consequences that derive from this investigation for sexual political work, it is first of all necessary to turn our attention to the *symbolism* that the fascists made use of to put the comparatively uninhibited structures of the masses into reactionary fetters. The fascists were not conscious of their technique.

It did not take National Socialism long to rally workers, most of whom were either unemployed or still very young, into the SA.* To a large extent, however, these workers were revolutionary in a dull sort of way and still maintained an authoritarian attitude. For this reason National Socialist propaganda was contradictory; its content was determined by the class for which it was intended. Only in its manipulation of the mystical feelings of the masses was it clear and consistent.

In talks with followers of the National Socialist party and especially with members of the SA, it was clearly brought out that the

---

* Sturm-Angriff (Stormtrooper).

revolutionary phraseology of National Socialism was the decisive factor in the winning over of these masses. One heard National Socialists deny that Hitler represented capital. One heard SA men warn Hitler that he must not betray the cause of the "revolution." One heard SA men say that Hitler was the German Lenin. Those who went over to National Socialism from Social Democracy and the liberal central parties were, without exception, revolutionary minded masses who were either nonpolitical or politically undecided prior to this. Those who went over from the Communist party were often revolutionary elements who simply could not make any sense of many of the German Communist party's contradictory political slogans. In part they were men upon whom the external features of Hitler's party, its military character, its assertiveness, etc., made a big impression.

To begin with, it is the symbol of the flag that stands out among the symbols used for purposes of propaganda.

> Wir sind das Heer vom Hakenkreuz
> Hebt hoch die roten Fahnen,
> Der deutschen Arbeit wollen wir
> Den Weg zur Freiheit bahnen.[1]

With respect to its emotional content, this text is clearly revolutionary. National Socialists made conscious use of revolutionary melodies, to which they sang reactionary lyrics. The hundreds of political formulations appearing in Hitler's newspapers were also constructed along these lines. For example:

> The political bourgeoisie is about to make its exit from the stage of historical dramatization. It is the hitherto suppressed class, the producing people of fist and brow, the working class, which now enters upon the stage to fulfil its historical mission.

---

[1] We are the army of the swastika
Raise the red banners high,
For the German worker
The way to freedom we shall pave.

This is a clear echo of communist propaganda. The revolutionary character of the National Socialist masses clearly stands out in the clever design of the flag, about which Hitler wrote:

> . . . As National Socialists, we see our program in our flag. In *red* we see the social idea of the movement, in *white* the nationalistic idea, in the *swastika* the mission of the struggle for the victory of the Aryan man, and, by the same token, the victory of the idea of creative work, which as such always has been and always will be anti-Semitic.
>
> —*Mein Kampf*, p. 496f

The red and the white are suggestive of man's contradictory structure. What is still not clear is the role played by the *swastika* in the emotional life. Why is this symbol so suitable to evoke mystical feelings? Hitler contended that it was a symbol of anti-Semitism. But the swastika took on this meaning only much later. And, as far as that goes, the question as to the irrational content of anti-Semitism is still open. It is the misrepresentation of natural sexuality as something which is "dirty and sensual" that explains the irrational content of the race theory. In this regard the Jew and the black man are not differentiated in the mind of the fascist. This holds true for the American fascist also. In America the racial fight against the black man takes place predominantly in the sphere of sexual defense. The black man is thought of as a sensuous pig who rapes white women. With reference to the occupation of the Rheinland by black troops, Hitler wrote:

> Only in France does there exist today more than ever an inner *unanimity* between the intentions of the Jew-controlled stock exchange and the desire of the *chauvinist-minded national statesmen*. But in this very identity there lies an immense danger for Germany. For this very reason, France is and remains by far the most terrible enemy. *This people, which is basically becoming more and more negrified, constitutes in its tie with the aims of Jewish world domination an enduring danger for the existence of the white race in Europe.* For the contamination by Negro blood on the Rhine in

the heart of Europe is just as much in keeping with the perverted sadistic thirst for vengeance of this hereditary enemy of our people as the ice-cold calculation of the Jew thus to begin bastardizing the European continent at its core and to deprive the white race of the foundations for a sovereign existence through infection with lower humanity.

—Op. cit. p. 624

We must get into the habit of paying strict attention to precisely what the fascist has to say and not to dismiss it as nonsense or hogwash. Now we have a better understanding of the emotional content of this theory, which sounds like a persecution mania when it is considered together with the theory of the poisoning of the nation. The swastika also has a content capable of stirring the deepest reaches of one's emotions, but in a way completely different from what Hitler could ever have dreamed.

To begin with, the swastika was also found among the Semites, namely, in the Myrtle court of the Alhambra at Granada. Herta Heinrich found it in the synagogue ruins of Edd-Dikke in East Jordania on the Lake of Gennesaret. Here it had the following form:[2]

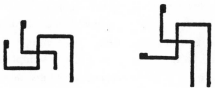

The swastika is often found together with a facet, the former being the symbol of the male principle, the latter of the female principle. Percy Gardner found it in Greece, where it was called *Hemera* and was the symbol of the sun, again representing the male principle. Löwenthal describes a fourteenth-century swastika, which he discovered in the altar cloth of Maria zur Wiese in Soest; here

---

[2] Herta Heinrich: *Hakenkreuz, Vierklee und Granatapfel* (Zeitschrift fuer Sexualwissenschaft, 1930, p. 42).

the swastika is embellished with vulva and a double cross. In this instance the swastika appears as the symbol of a stormy sky, the facet as the symbol of the fertile earth. Smigorski discovered a swastika in the form of the Indian swastika-cross, a four-pronged lightning with three dots at the end of each prong:[3]

Lichtenberg found swastikas with a skull in place of the three dots. *Thus the swastika was originally a sexual symbol.* In the course of time it assumed various meanings including that of a millwheel, the symbol of work. From an emotional point of view, work and sexuality were originally the same. This explains the inscription on the swastika discovered by Bilmans and Pengerots on the miter of St. Thomas à Becket, dating back to Indo-Germanic times:

"Hail to thee earth, O mother of man. May you thrive in God's embrace. Overflow with fruit for man's benefit."

Here fertility is sexually represented as the sexual act of Mother-Earth with God-Father. According to Zelenin, old Indian lexicographers referred to both the cock and the voluptuary as swastikas, i.e., the hooked cross as the symbol of sexual instinct.

If we now have another look at the swastikas on the preceding page, we see that they are the schematic but nonetheless clearly recognizable representations of two interlocked human figures. The swastika on the left represents a *sexual act* lying down; the one on the right, a sexual act in standing position. Thus, the swastika represents a basic living function.

The effect of the swastika on one's unconscious emotionality

---

[3] From John Löwenthal's *Zur Hakenkreuzsymbolik* (Zeitschrift fuer Sexual-wissenschaft, 1930, p. 44).

does not account for the success of fascism's mass propaganda, but it certainly contributes to it. Random tests with men and women of different ages and social positions show that very few people fail to recognize the meaning of the swastika; most people divine its meaning sooner or later if they look at it for awhile. Thus we can assume that this symbol depicting two interlocked figures acts as a powerful stimulus on deep layers of the organism, a stimulus that proves to be that much more powerful, the more dissatisfied, the more burning with sexual desire, a person is. If, in addition, the symbol is presented as the emblem of honorableness and faithfulness, it can be accepted more readily. In this way allowances are made for the defensive strivings of the moralistic ego. Let it not be assumed, however, that by exposing its sexual meaning we want to depreciate the effect of this symbol. First, we certainly do not want to depreciate the sexual act; and second, we would meet with strong opposition, for the moralistic disguise would operate as a resistance to the acceptance of our attempts. Sex-economic mental hygiene has something else in mind.

V

The Sex-Economic Presuppositions
of the Authoritarian Family

Since authoritarian society reproduces itself in the individual structures of the masses with the help of the authoritarian family, it follows that political reaction has to regard and defend the authoritarian family as *the* basis of the "state, culture, and civilization." In this propaganda it can count on deep irrational factors in the masses. The reactionary politician cannot divulge his real intentions in his propaganda. The German masses would not have responded to a slogan calling for the "conquest of the world." In political propaganda, which is a question of producing a psychological effect on the masses, one is not dealing directly with economic processes but with human structures. This consideration dictates a definite approach in the work of mental hygiene, and failure to make use of this approach can lead to errors in mass psychology. Consequently, revolutionary sexual politics must do more than just point out the objective basis of the authoritarian family. If it is to have an effect on the psychology of the masses, it must appeal to man's yearning for happiness in both life and love.

From the point of view of social development, the family cannot be regarded as the basis of the authoritarian state, but only as one of the most important institutions that supports it. We, however, have to look upon it as *political reaction's germ cell*, the most important center for the production of reactionary men and women. Originating and developing from definite social processes, it becomes the most essential institution for the preservation of the authoritarian system that shapes it. In this regard, the findings of Morgan and Engels are as valid today as they were then. However, we are not interested in the history of the family. What concerns us is an important contemporary sex-political question, namely: How can sex-economy most effectively counter reactionary sexual and cultural politics in which the authoritarian family plays such a decisive role? A precise discussion of the basis and effects of the authoritarian family is vitally necessary, especially in view of the lack of clarity on this question that exists even in revolutionary circles.

The authoritarian family contains a contradiction which must be understood in all of its details if we are to have an effective sex-economic mass hygiene.

More than the economic dependency of the wife and children on the husband and father is needed to preserve the institution of the authoritarian family. For the suppressed classes, this dependency is endurable only on condition that the consciousness of being a sexual being is suspended as completely as possible in women and in children. *The wife must not figure as a sexual being, but solely as a child-bearer.* Essentially, the idealization and deification of motherhood, which are so flagrantly at variance with the brutality with which the mothers of the toiling masses are actually treated, serve as means of preventing women from gaining a sexual consciousness, of preventing the imposed sexual repression from breaking through and of preventing sexual anxiety and sexual guilt-feelings from losing their hold. *Sexually awakened women, affirmed and recognized as such, would mean the complete collapse of the authoritarian ideology.* Conservative sexual reform has always made the mistake of merely making a slogan of "the right of woman to her own body," and not clearly and unmistakably regarding and defending woman as a *sexual* being, at least as much as it regards and defends her as a mother. Furthermore, conservative sexual reform based its sexual policies predominantly on the function of procreation, instead of undermining the reactionary view that equates sexuality and procreation. It is for this reason that it was not able to counter mysticism with sufficient force.

The ideology extolling the "blessings of large families" is necessary for the preservation of the authoritarian family. It is necessary not only in the interest of warlike imperialism; its most essential purpose is to *obscure woman's sexual function as opposed to her function as a child-bearer.* The drawing of a clear-cut distinction between "mother" and "prostitute" as we find, for example, in the writings of the philosopher Weininger, corresponds to the distinction that the reactionary man draws between sexual desire and procreation. According to this view, *to have sex for the pleasure of it* degrades the woman and mother; a "prostitute" is a woman who affirms pleasure and lives for it. The notion that sexuality is moral only in the service of procreation, that what lies outside the pale of procreation is immoral, is the most important feature of reactionary sexual politics. This notion is no less reactionary when represented by Communists such as Salkind and Stoliarov.

Aggressive imperialism dictates that women be nothing but child-bearing machines and it brooks no rebellion against this function. In short, this means that *sexual gratification must not interfere with her function of reproduction.* Apart from this, however, a woman who is conscious of her sexuality would never willingly heed the reactionary slogans, which have her enslavement in mind. This antithesis between sexual gratification and procreation applies only to authoritarian society, not to work-democracy. It is a question of the social conditions under which women are to bear children: under favorable, socially guaranteed conditions, or conditions that do not provide adequate protection for the mother and child. In other words, if women are to bear children without any kind of social protection, without social guarantees for the rearing of their offspring; if, moreover, they are not allowed to determine for themselves how many children they will have and are to accept this function willingly and unquestionably—then motherhood, as opposed to woman's sexual function, has to be idealized.

If we are to comprehend the fact that Hitler's party, just as the center parties, relied chiefly upon women's votes, we must comprehend irrationalism. The irrational mechanism at work here is the setting up of an antithesis between woman as child-bearer and woman as a sexual being. With this in mind we shall be in a better position to understand fascist attitudes such as the following:

> The preservation of the already existing large families is a matter of social feeling; the preservation of the form of the large family is a matter of biologic conception and national character. The large family is to be preserved not because it is hungry; it is to be preserved as a valuable, indispensable part of the German people. Valuable and indispensable not only because it alone guarantees the preservation of the population in the future [objectively speaking, this is its imperialistic function, WR], but because *national morality and national culture find their strongest support in it.* . . . . The preservation of the existing large families amalgamated with the preservation of the form of the large family, for these two problems are inseparable. . . . The preservation of the form of the large family is a matter of national, cultural and political necessity. . . . This view is also strictly opposed to the repeal of paragraph 218, and it holds pregnancy to be inviolable. The termination of pregnancy is at variance with the meaning of the family, whose task is precisely the education of the coming generation—apart from the fact that the termination of pregnancy would mean the final destruction of the large family.

This is how the *Völkischer Beobachter* put it on October 14, 1931. Thus, political reactions's family politics are the key to the question of the termination of pregnancy also, far more so than the factors that had previously been pushed into the foreground—industrial reserve army and cannon fodder for imperialist wars. The argument in support of an industrial reserve army almost completely lost its relevance in the years of the economic crisis, when there were many millions of unemployed workers in Germany, and some forty million throughout the world in 1932. When political reaction tells us again and again that the preservation of the abortion law is necessary in the interest of the family and "moral order," when the social hygienist Grothjan, who was a Social Democrat, argues along the same lines as the National Socialists in this regard, then we must agree with them that "authoritarian family" and "moralistic ethics" are decisively important reactionary forces. We must not brush them aside as unimportant. It is a matter of binding the women to the authoritarian family by means of suppressing their sexual needs; it is a matter of the reactionary influence exercised by these women on their husbands; it is a matter of safeguarding the effect that reactionary sexual propaganda has on millions of women who are suppressed and who tolerate their suppression. From a revolutionary point of view it is imperative to follow political reaction wherever its effects are felt. It must be routed wherever it defends its system. Thus, the interest in the authoritarian family as an institution intended to "preserve the state" takes priority in all questions of reactionary sexual politics. It coincides with the similar interests of all members of the middle class who operate small businesses, for whom the family constitutes, or at least used to constitute, an economic unity. It is from this point of view that fascist ideology sees state and society, economics and politics. It is also from this point of view, determined as it is by the old mode of economy of the lower middle class, which prompts reactionary sexology to promulgate the state as an "organic whole." For the wage earner of modern civilization there is no longer any direct correlation between family and social mode of existence. The family is not economically anchored. Hence, the modern wage earner is in a position to look upon the state as a coercive institution of society; the "biologic" view that the state is an "organic whole" is not valid for his sexology and sex-economy. If the working man proves to be accessible to this reactionary view, it is to be ascribed to the authoritarian family education that he received. And the small farmer and the lower middle-class man would be more accessible to an insight into their social responsibility if their family situation were not organically bound up with their economic situation.

In the economic world crisis it was shown that this connection between family and economy was loosened as a result of the economic ruin of small enterprises. Subsequently, the essential features of the oft-mentioned tradition of the lower middle class, namely its authoritarian familial tie, still had an effect. Hence it was much more accessible to the fascist ideology of the "large family" than it was to the revolutionary ideology of birth control, mainly because the revolutionary movement failed to elucidate this question and to give it top priority.

As clear as all this is, we would err if we failed to assess it in relation to other factors which are contradictory to it. Our assessment would of necessity be false if we failed to take into account the contradictions that exist in the life of the sexually inhibited man. To begin with, the contradiction between sexual moralistic thinking and feeling on the one hand and the concrete sexual mode of existence on the other hand is decisive. An example: in Western Germany there were a large number of birth control groups of a predominantly "socialist" nature. In the Wolf-Kienle campaign of 1931 the abortion law was put to a vote. It turned out that the same women who cast their vote for the center parties or the NSDAP were *for the repeal of this law*, while their parties were passionately opposed to its repeal. These women voted for sex-economic birth control in an effort to secure sexual gratification. At the same time they voted for the center and NSDAP parties, not because they had no knowledge of the reactionary intentions of these parties, but because they were still imbued with the reactionary ideology of "pure motherhood," of the antithesis between motherhood and sexuality; but most of all they were still under the influence of authoritarian ideology itself. While these women knew nothing of the sociological role of the authoritarian family in a dictatorship, they were nonetheless under the influence of political reaction's sexual politics: They affirmed birth control, but they feared the responsibility imposed upon them by the revolutionary world.

Sexual reaction made no bones about using any means whatever to exploit sexual anxiety for its own purposes. Since there was no corresponding sex-economic counterpropaganda from the revolutionary side, the wife of the average worker or lower middle-class woman who held Christian or nationalistic views, had to be impressed by the following kind of propaganda.

In 1918 the *Vereinigung zur Bekämpfung des Bolschewismus* (Alliance for the Fight against Bolshevism) printed posters having the following text:

> German Women!
> Have you any idea what Bolshevism has in store for you?
> Bolshevism wants the socialization of women:

1. The right of possession of women between 17 and 32 years of age is being abolished.
2. All women are the property of the people.
3. The former owners retain a priority on their wives.
4. Every man who wants to use a specimen of the people's property must have a permit from the workers' committee.
5. No man has the right to avail himself of a woman more than three times per week and longer than three hours.
6. Every man is required to report a woman who resists him.
7. Every man who does not belong to the working class has to pay a monthly fee of 100 rubles for the right to use this public property.

The sordidness of such propaganda is as evident as its mendacity, but the first reaction of the average woman is to shrink back in horror, while the reaction of a progressive woman will be something as follows:

> I admit that for us, the workers, there is only one way out of the present misery, and that way is socialism. But it has to remain within certain moderate limits, and not reject everything that was as wrong and unnecessary. Otherwise this will lead to a brutalization of customs, which would be even worse than the present sad material situation. And unfortunately, it is a very important and a high ideal that is attacked by socialism: marriage. Complete freedom, complete licentiousness, is being demanded, to a certain extent sexual Bolshevism. Every one is supposed to live one's life to the full, to have one's fling—freely, without inhibitions. Man and wife are no longer to belong together, instead one is together with this woman

today and tomorrow with that one, just as one's mood happens to be. This is called freedom, free love, the new sex morality. But these beautiful names cannot gloss over the fact that grave dangers are lurking here. Man's highest and noblest feelings would be degraded by such practices: love, faithfulness, sacrifice. That a man or woman can love many other men or women at the same time is wholly impossible—it is contrary to nature. The result would be a terrible brutalization which would destroy culture. I have no idea how these things look in the Soviet Union, but either the Russians are peculiar people or they really haven't allowed this absolute freedom and certain sanctions still exist there. . . . Thus, as beautiful as the socialist theory is, and as much as I am in agreement with you on all economic questions, I don't follow you when it comes to sexual matters, and because of this I often have doubts about the whole thing.

—Letter to the editor from a working woman

This letter clearly reflects the conflict with which the average person is faced: *He is made to believe that he must choose between compulsive sexual morality on the one hand and sexual anarchy on the other hand. The average person has no knowledge of the sex-economic regulation of sexuality, which is as far from compulsive morality as it is from anarchy.* He reacts to the imposed severe compulsion with promiscuous impulses; he defends himself against both. Morality is a burden, and instinct appears as a tremendous danger. The man reared under and bound by authority has no knowledge of the natural law of self-regulation; he has no confidence in himself. He is afraid of his sexuality because he never learned to live it naturally. Thus, he declines all responsibility for his acts and decisions, and he demands direction and guidance.

The revolutionary movement has not yet had any success with its sexual politics—gauged against the success that consistent revolutionary sexual politics could have achieved—because it failed to react with appropriate weapons against political reaction's successful attempts to exploit man's suppressed sexual powers. If sexual reaction had publicized only its political thesis on population, it

111

would not have poked a single cat from under the bed. But it exploited the sexual anxiety in women and girls, and to this it owes its success. It was skillful in linking its population aims with the compulsive moralistic inhibitions of the people, at all levels of society as a matter of fact. The hundreds of thousands of organized Christian workers are proof of this.

Here is another example of the propaganda methods used by political reaction:[1]

> In their devastating campaign against the entire bourgeois world, the Bolsheviks were from the very beginning particularly fixed on the family, "this especially strong remnant of the confounded old regime." As early as June 10, 1924, the plenary assembly of the Comintern declared: "The revolution is powerless as long as the old idea of the family and family relationships continues to exist." In consequence of this attitude, a violent fight against the family broke out immediately. Bigamy and polygamy were not prohibited and therefore permissible. The Bolsheviks' attitude toward marriage is characterized by the following definition of the marital tie, proposed by Professor Goichbarg: "Marriage is an institution for the gratification of sexual needs in a less dangerous and more convenient way." How far family and marriage disintegrated under such conditions is indicated by the statistics of the general census of 1927. *Izvestia* writes: "In Moscow, the census revealed numerous cases of polygamy and polyandry. Frequently, two or even three women designated the same man as their spouse." There is no need for surprise when the German Professor Selheim describes family relationships in Russia in the following way: "It is a complete regression to the sexual order of prehistoric times, from which marriage and a usable sexual order was developed in the course of time."

Compulsive marital and familial life are also attacked; complete freedom of sexual intercourse has been proclaimed. The well-known

---

[1] *Welt vor dem Abgrund, Der Einfluss des russischen Kulturbolschewismus auf die anderen Völker. Deutscher Volkskalender*, p. 47, 1932.

female Communist Smidowitsch worked out a scheme of sexual morality,[2] according to which most boys and girls act. The scheme runs something as follows:

1. Every student of the workers' faculty, even if he is a minor, is entitled and obliged to gratify his sexual needs.

2. When a young girl, whether she is a university student, a worker, or just a schoolgirl, is desired by a man, she is obliged to yield to this desire, otherwise she will be looked upon as a bourgeois girl who cannot pretend to be a genuine Communist.

Pravda wrote quite openly: "Among us there are only sexual relations between man and woman. We do not recognize the existence of love. Love is to be looked down upon as something psychological. Among us only physiology has a right to exist." In consequence of this communist attitude, every woman and every girl is obliged to gratify the sexual drive of the male. In view of the fact that this certainly does not always happen in an entirely voluntary way, the rape of women in Soviet Russia has become a veritable plague.

Such lies on the part of political reaction cannot be set aside simply by exposing them for what they are, lies; nor, for that matter, by protestations to the effect that one is just as "moral" as they are, or that the revolution does not destroy the authoritarian family and moralism, etc. The truth of the matter is that sexuality changes in the course of the revolution, that the old compulsive regimentation is loosened. This cannot be disavowed. Nor can the correct sex-economic position be ascertained, if ascetic attitudes on these questions are tolerated in one's own camp and are allowed to be operative. We will have to inquire into this matter very carefully later.

The sexual politics of those who strive to achieve a genuine freedom in this sphere failed to explain—not once, twice, but again and again—and to establish a sex-economic regulation of sexual life. They failed to comprehend and to allay woman's fear of sexual

---

[2] Smidowitsch's remarks were actually meant to be ironical, and were intended as a criticism of adolescent sexuality.

health. More than anything else, however, they failed to establish clarity in their own ranks by constantly and consistently pointing out the disparity between the reactionary and the sex-economic conception of sexuality. Experience shows that the average person accepts sex-economic regulation of sexuality if it is made sufficiently clear to him.

The anti-revolutionary movement originates from political reaction's creeds, which are held together by the lower middle class's economic mode of existence and by ideologic mysticism. The core of political reaction's cultural politics is the sexual question. Accordingly, the core of revolutionary cultural politics must also be the sexual question.

It is sex-economy that gives the political answer to the chaos that was created by the contradiction between compulsive morality and sexual libertinism.

VI

Organized Mysticism as an International
Anti-Sexual Organization

THE INTEREST IN THE CHURCH

To clarify the tasks of sex-economic mental hygiene, we have to pay close attention to the way political reaction attacks and defends itself on the cultural political front. We decline to dismiss political reaction's mystical figures of speech as "red herrings." As we have already pointed out, when political reaction is successful with a certain ideological propaganda, this cannot be ascribed solely to befogging. It is our contention that a problem of mass psychology must lie at the root of each instance of its success. Something that we still haven't grasped is going on in the masses, and it is that "something" that enables them to think and to act against their own vital interests. The question is decisive, for without this attitude on the part of the masses, political reaction would be wholly powerless. It is the willingness of the masses to absorb these ideas—what we call a dictator's *"soil of mass psychology"*—that constitutes fascism's strength. Thus, it is imperative to seek a complete understanding of this.

As the economic pressure on the toiling masses increases, compulsive moralistic pressure is also wont to become more rigid. This can only have the function of precluding a rebellion on the part of the working masses against the social pressure by intensifying their sexual guilt-feelings and their moral dependency on the existing order. How does this come about?

Since mystical contagion is the most important psychological precondition for the assimilation of fascist ideology by the masses, an understanding of the psychological effect of mysticism in general is an indispensable part of an investigation of fascist ideology.

When the Papen government[1] came into power in the spring of 1932, following the ousting of Brüning, one of its first acts was to proclaim its intention to carry out a "more strict moral education of the nation." The Hitler government stepped up this program.[2] An edict relating to the education of the youth stated:

> Youth will be able to cope with its difficult lot and with the high demands of the future only when it has learned to be ruled by the principles of the people and of the state . . . that, however, means to learn to be responsible to and to be capable of making sacrifices for the whole. *Softness and exaggerated consideration of every individual inclination are misplaced in dealing with a youth* which must be prepared to face many hardships in life. Youth will be fully prepared for its service to the people and to the state only when it has learned to work objectively, to think clearly, to fulfill its obligation; when it has become accustomed to *conforming to the regulations of the educational community in a disciplined and obedient way and of voluntarily submitting to its authority*. . . . The teaching of the youth to have a genuine feeling for the state must be supplemented and deepened by a German education based on the historical and cultural values of the German people . . . *by submersion in our epic national heritage*. . . . The teaching of the youth to appreciate the value of the state and of the community, derives its strongest inner power from the truths of Christianity.

---

[1] Papen paved the way for Hitler and later played a significant role as a fascist diplomat.

[2] The following is a news item, dated Hamburg, August 1933: *Concentration Camp for "Immoral" Aquatic Athletes.* Hamburg. "The Hamburg police department has instructed its force to keep a sharp eye on the behavior of aquatic athletes who often 'fail to observe the simple rules of public morals.' The police department gives public notice to the fact that it intends to take drastic steps against rowboaters who violate its regulations, and to put them in concentration camps so that they can learn decency and morality."

. . . Loyalty and responsibility toward the people and the fatherland are *most deeply anchored in Christian faith.* For this reason it will always be my special duty to safeguard the right and free development of the *Christian school and the Christian fundamentals of all education.*

What is the source of this glorification of the strength of mystical belief? That is what we want to know now. Political reaction is absolutely correct in asserting that the teaching of "loyalty to the state" derives its strongest inner power from the "truths of Christianity." Before we give proof of this, however, we must briefly summarize the differences existing within the political reactionary camp regarding the conception of Christianity.

The basis of National Socialism's mass psychology differs from that of Wilhelmian imperialism in that the former had a pauperized middle class, whereas the German empire had a *prosperous* middle class as its mass basis. Thus, the Christianity of Wilhelmian imperialism had to be different from the Christianity of National Socialism. For all that, the ideological modifications did not undermine the fundamentals of the mystical world view in the least; rather they intensified its function.

To begin with, National Socialism rejected the Old Testament as being "Jewish"—that, at least, was the position of its well-known exponent, Rosenberg, who belonged to the right wing. In the same way the internationalism of the Roman Catholic Church was regarded as "Jewish." The international church was to be replaced by the "German national church." Following the seizure of power, the church was indeed brought into line. This limited its political scope, but very much extended its ideological sphere of power.

> Surely, some day the German people also will find a form for its perception and experience of God, a form dictated by its Nordic blood. Surely, only then will the trinity of *blood, faith* and *state* be complete.
>
> —Gottfried Feder: *Das Programm der NSDAP und seine weltanschaulichen Grundlagen,* p. 49

An identification of the Jewish God with the Holy Trinity had to be avoided at all cost. The fact that Jesus himself was a Jew caused some embarrassment, but Stapel quickly found a way out of this dilemma: Since Jesus was a son of *God*, he could not be considered a Jew. Jewish dogmas and traditions were to be replaced by the "experience of one's own conscience"; indulgence was to be replaced by the "idea of personal honor."

The belief in the transmutation of the soul after death is rejected as the "hocus-pocus of the South Sea Islanders." The Virgin Mary's immaculate conception is rejected on the same basis. On this subject, Scharnagel writes:

> He [Rosenberg] confuses the dogma of the immaculate conception of the Blessed Virgin, i.e., her freedom from original sin, with the dogma of the virginal birth of Jesus ("who was conceived by the Holy Spirit") . . .

The extensive success of religious mysticism is to be ascribed to the fact that it is centrally rooted in the doctrine of *original sin as a sexual act for the sake of pleasure*. National Socialism retains this motif and makes full use of it with the help of another ideology, one in keeping with its own purpose:

> The crucifix is the allegory of the doctrine of the sacrificial lamb, an image which impresses upon us the breakdown of all forces, and through its . . . horrific representation of pain, distresses and makes us humble, as the power-thirsty churches intend. . . . A German church would replace little by little the symbol of the crucifixion in the churches assigned to it by the instructive spirit of fire, personifying the hero in the highest sense.
>
> —*Mythus*, p. 577

In short, it is a matter of substituting one fetter for another: The sadistic-narcissistic mysticism of nationalism is to take the place of masochistic, international, religious mysticism. From now on it is a question of

> . . . recognizing German national honor as the supreme standard of behavior in order to live for it. . . . It [the state] will

118

allow every religious conviction free scope; it will allow moral teachings of various forms to have their say, on condition that they do not get in the way of the assertion of national honor.

We have already seen how the ideology of national honor derives from authoritarian ideology and the latter from the sex-negating regulation of sexuality. Neither Christianity nor National Socialism attacks the institution of compulsive marriage: for the former, apart from its function of procreation, marriage is a "complete, life-long union"; for the National Socialists it is a biologically rooted institution for the preservation of racial purity. Outside of compulsive marriage, there is no sexuality for either of them.

Furthermore, National Socialism does not want to maintain religion on a historical basis, but on a "topical" basis. This change is to be explained in terms of the disintegration of Christian sexual morality, which can no longer be upheld solely on the basis of historical demands.

> The ethnical racial state must one day still discover its deepest roots in religion. Not until our belief in God ceases to be related to a specific event in the past, but is again and again, through everlasting experience, intricately interwoven with the native activity and life of a people and of a state, as well as of the individual, will our world be firmly reestablished.
> —Ludwig Haase: *Nationalsozialistische Monatshefte* I, Nr. 5,
> p. 213

Let us not forget that "native activity and life" mean "moral" life, i.e., sexual negation.

It is precisely in that which prompted the National Socialists to differentiate themselves from the Church and in that which represents their common points of reference that what is unessential for the reactionary function of religion can be distinguished from what is actually effective.[3]

---

[3] It is true that the National Socialists rejected the Bavarian concordat of July 15, 1930, and the Prussian concordat of July 1, 1929. However, this rejection pertained merely to the endowment of 1931, which amounted to 4,122,370

The historical factors, the dogmas, some violently defended articles of faith become, as is shown, meaningless, if one can succeed in replacing them in their function by something else that is

---

RM. The increase of the priests' salary in Bavaria from 5.87 million RM in 1914 to 19.7 million in 1931 (severe crisis year!), was not attacked. We extract the following data on the Bavarian concordat from an article by Robert Boeck: *Konkordate sehen Dich an.* According to the concordat of January 25, 1925, the Church was granted the following rights:

1. The priests are *state officials*.
2. The state admits that the secularization of 1817 (disappropriation of Church property) inflicted a severe injustice upon the Church and the state puts it into the hands of the Church to reclaim its property, or its money-value of 60 million goldmarks.
3. The state must spend almost 50% of its revenue from the Bavarian state forestry to be able to pay a part of its *assessment to the church*; therefore, it has mortgaged, as it were, the revenues of the forestry to the Church.
4. The Church is entitled, on the basis of civil tax registers, to levy taxes (*church taxes*).
5. The Church is entitled to acquire *new property* and to have it as its possession; this property is imprescriptible and will be protected by the state.
6. The state is obliged to provide Church dignitaries with *"living quarters in keeping with their dignity and rank."*
7. The Church, its priests and 28,000 monks shall enjoy *unlimited freedom* in the exercise of their religious industrial activities (the manufacture of books, beer, and schnaps).
8. A *professor of philosophy and a professor of history* must be appointed to the universities of Munich and of Würzburg; these professors must enjoy the confidence of the Church, and their lectures must bear out ecclesiastical teachings.
9. The state guarantees the *teaching of religion* in primary schools, and the bishop or one whom he appoints has the right to take exception to and to demand redress from the state authorities for grievances in the public religious life of Catholic pupils and their detrimental or improper (!) influence.

According to conservative estimates, the Catholic Church in Bavaria was guaranteed, by the concordat, funds—i.e., *cash remittances*, commodity values, exemption from real estate and commercial taxation and individual earnings— amounting to one billion marks.

The Bavarian state paid the Catholic Church 13 million marks in 1916; 28,468,400 marks in 1929; and 26,050,250 marks in 1931.

Obviously, the Church's service to the state must be profitable. The conclusion of the concordat between the German Reich and the Vatican in July of 1933 did not bring about any basically new relationships between church and state (nothing that was decisive for mass psychology). The basic economic functions of the Church remained inviolable.

equally effective. National Socialism wants "religious experience." In fact, that is its sole concern; it merely wants to give it a different basis. What is this "everlasting experience"?

THE FIGHT AGAINST "CULTURAL BOLSHEVISM"

Nationalistic and familial sentiments are intimately interlaced with religious feelings, which are vague and mystical to a lesser or greater extent. There is no end to the literature on this subject. A detailed academic critique of this field is out of the question—for the time being at least. We want to pick up the thread of our main problem. If fascism relies so successfully on the mystical thinking and sentiments of the masses, then a fight against it can be effective only if mysticism is comprehended and if the mystical contagion of the masses is tackled through education and hygiene. It is not enough that the scientific view of the world gains ground, for it moves much too slowly to keep pace with the rapid spread of mystical contagion. The reason for this can lie only in our incomplete comprehension of mysticism itself. Scientific enlightenment of the masses was mainly concerned with the exposing of the corrupt practices of church dignitaries and church officials. The overwhelming majority of the masses was left in the dark. Scientific elucidation appealed only to the intellect of the masses—not to their feelings. If, however, a man has mystical feelings, he is impervious to the unmasking of a church dignitary, no matter how artfully done. He is no more impressed by the detailed exposure of how the state uses the workers' pennies to support the church than he is by Marx's and Engels' historical analysis of religion.

To be sure, atheist movements also tried to employ emotional means in their efforts to enlighten the masses. For example, the youth initiation festivals of the German free thinkers were dedicated to this kind of work. Despite all this the Christian youth organizations had approximately thirty times as many members as the Communist and Social Democrat parties taken together. In the years 1930–32, Christian youth organizations had approximately one and a half million members as opposed to the fifty thousand members of the Communist party and the sixty thousand members of the Socialist party. According to its own statistics, National Socialism had some forty thousand youth in its organization in 1931. We extract detailed figures from the *Proletarische Freidenkerstimme* of April, 1932. According to this newspaper the distribution ran as follows:

The Catholic Young Men's Association of Germany	386,879
The Central Association of Catholic maidens	800,000
The Association of Catholic bachelors	93,000
The South German Youth Alliance of Catholic females	25,000
The Association of Bavarian Catholic Book Clubs ..	35,220
The Association of Catholic Students of Institutions of Higher Learning ("New Germany")	15,290
Catholic Youth Alliance of Germany's Working Girls	8,000
National Association of German *Windhorst* Clubs ..	10,000

[These figures are taken from the *Handbuch der Jugendverbände,* 1931]

The social composition is what is important. The Catholic Young Men's Association of Germany had the following distribution:

Workers	45.6%
Skilled workers	21.6%
Rural youth	18.7%
Business men	5.9%
Students	4.8%
Officials	3.3%

The proletarian element constituted the overwhelming majority. In 1929 the composition according to age was:

14–17 years	51.0%
17–21 years	28.3%
21–25 years	13.5%
over 25	7.1%

122

Thus, four-fifths of the members were at the age of puberty or post-puberty!

While the Communists, in their efforts to win over these young people, gave prominence to the question of class, as opposed to the question of creed, the Catholic organization took up its position precisely on the cultural and philosophic front. The Communist wrote:

> If our work is clear and consistent, the question of class membership will prove to be stronger than the impeding questions of creed, among the young Catholics also. . . . We must not give prominence to the question of creed, but to the question of class membership, to the misery which binds us and is our common lot.

The leadership of the Catholic youth, on the other hand, wrote in *Jungarbeiter* No. 17, 1931:

> The greatest and most likely the gravest danger of the Communist Party is the fact that it gets its hands on the young workers and the children of workers at a very early age. We are very pleased that the government . . . is strongly opposed to the subversive Communist Party. Above all, however, we expect the German government to deal sharply with the fight of the communists against church and religion.

Representatives of eight Catholic organizations held positions on the Berlin examining board for the "Protection of Youth against Filth and Obscenity." In 1932 a proclamation of the Center Youth stated:

> We demand that the state use every available means to protect our Christian heritage against the poisonous influence of a filthy press, obscene literature, and erotic films—all of which degrade and falsify national sentiments. . . .

Thus, the church defended its mystical function, not where it was attacked by the communist movement, but at an entirely different place.

"It is the task of the non-orthodox proletarian youth," the

aforementioned *Freidenkerstimme* states, to show "the young work-ing Christians the role of the church and of their organizations in the implementation of fascist measures and their advocation of crisis bills and economic measures." Why, as it turned out, did the *masses* of the young Christian workers offer resistance to this attack on the church? The Communists expected the Christian youth to see for *themselves* that the church was serving a capitalist function. Why did they fail to see this? Evidently, it was because this function had been concealed from them and because their authori-tarian upbringing had made them credulous and incapable of criticism. Nor could it escape one's notice that the representatives of the church in the youth organizations spoke out *against* capital-ism, so that the antithesis between the social positions assumed by the Communists and the priests was not readily perceptible to the youth. At first it appeared as if a clear-cut demarcation existed only in the sphere of sexuality. It seemed as if the Communists, as opposed to the church, had taken a positive attitude toward adoles-cent sexuality. However, it soon turned out that the Communist organizations not only allowed this decisive area to lie fallow, but even felt themselves to be in accord with the church in their con-demnation and inhibition of adolescent sexuality. The measures adopted by the Communists against the German *Sexpol*, which never hesitated to raise the question of adolescent sexuality and to attempt to solve it, were no less severe than those of some clerical representatives. The fact that the Communist pastor Salkind, who was also a psychoanalyst, was an authority in the field of sexual negation in Soviet Russia, speaks for itself.

It was not enough to point out that the authoritarian state was in control of and could exploit the parental home, the church, and the school as a means of binding the youth to its system and its world of ideas. The state used its entire power apparatus to keep these institutions intact. Hence, nothing short of a social revolution would have been capable of abolishing them. And yet, an under-mining of their reactionary influence was one of the most essential preconditions of the social revolution and therefore the presupposition of their abolition. Many Communists considered this the main task of the "Red cultural front." To accomplish this task, it was of *decisive* importance to comprehend the ways and means with the help of which the authoritarian parental home, the school, and the church could exercise so much influence, and to discover the process that took hold of the youth as a result of these influences. Generalizations such as "enslavement" or "brutalization" did not offer an adequate explanation. "Brutalization" and "enslavement" were the results. What we wanted to know were the processes that enable dictatorial interests to gain a foothold in the structure of the masses.

Der sexuelle Kampf der Jugend was an attempt to show the role played by the suppression of adolescent sexuality in this process. In the present work we want to investigate the basic elements of political reaction's cultural aims, and to ascertain the emotional factors on which revolutionary work has to be based. Here, too, we have to adhere to the principle of paying strict attention to everything to which cultural reaction gives prominence; for that to which it gives prominence is not incidental, nor is it a means of "distracting" one's attention. It is the central arena in which the fight between revolutionary and reactionary world philosophy and politics is to take place.

We are forced to avert an encounter in the philosophic and cultural sphere, *the center of which is the sexual question,* as long as we do not possess the necessary knowledge and the required training to engage in such a clash successfully. However, if we can succeed in gaining a firm foothold in the cultural question, we have everything necessary to pave the way for work-democracy. For let it be stated once again: *Sexual inhibition prevents the average adolescent from thinking and feeling in a rational way.* We must see to it that mysticism is countered with appropriate means. To this end a knowledge of its mechanism is urgently necessary.

Let us quote from one of the many typical works on this subject: *Der Bolschewismus als Todfeind und Wegbereiter der Revolution,* 1931, written by the pastor Braumann. We could quote from any other work just as well. The essential points of their arguments

125

are the same, and minor differences in detail are of no importance here.

> Every religion is liberation from the world and its powers through unification with Godhood. Therefore, Bolshevism will never be able to enchain man completely as long as there is still something of religion in him.
>
> —Braumann, p. 12

Here, to be sure, mysticism's function is clearly articulated: to divert attention from daily misery, "to liberate from the world," the purpose of which is to prevent a revolt against the real causes of one's misery. But scientific findings on the sociological function of mysticism will not take us very far. First and foremost, it is the rich experience gained from discussions between scientifically and mystically oriented youth that has a practical value for our work against mysticism. Such discussions give us a clue to an understanding of mysticism, and hence to the mystical feelings of the individuals in the masses.

A workers' youth organization invited a Protestant pastor to a discussion on the economic crisis. He came, followed and sheltered by some twenty Christian youths between eighteen and twenty-five years of age. In his talk he made the following points, although it was his shifting from partially correct statements to mystical points of view that was most striking: The causes of the existing misery, he explained, were the war and the Young plan. The world war was an expression of man's depravity and of his meanness, an injustice and a sin. Capitalistic exploitation was also a grave sin. (By assuming an anti-capitalist attitude and thus anticipating the anti-capitalist feelings of the Christian youth, he made it difficult to undo his influence.) Capitalism and socialism, he went on to say, were essentially the same. The socialism of the Soviet Union was also a form of capitalism. Socialism entailed disadvantages for some classes just as capitalism entailed disadvantages for other classes. Every form of capitalism should "be given a good kick in the pants." Bolshevism's fight against religion was a criminal act; religion was not responsible for misery. It was capitalism's abuse of religion that was at fault. (This was a decidedly progressive pastor.) What were the conclusions to be drawn from this presentation? Since man was vile and wicked, *the wretchedness of his situation was not at all to be done away with; it had to be endured, coped with.* The capitalist was not happy either. Man's *inner* anguish, which lay at the root of all anguish, would not disappear even after the fulfillment of the third five-year plan of the Soviet Union.

A number of revolutionary youths tried to represent their point of view. They pointed out that it was not a question of individual capitalists, but a question of "the system." It was a question of whether the majority or a dwindling minority was suppressed. To say that wretchedness had to be endured did not help matters at all and only benefited political reaction. And so on and so forth. In the end it was agreed that a reconciliation of the opposing views was not possible, that no one went away with a conviction different from the one with which he had come. The young attendants of the pastor hung on the words of their leader. Their material situation appeared to be just as indigent as that of the Communists, and yet each one of them acquiesced in the opinion that there was no escape from misery and that one had to make the best of it and "have faith in God."

Following the discussion, I asked a number of communist youths why they had not entered into the main issue, namely the church's insistence on sexual abstinence. They replied that this subject would have been too ticklish and too difficult, that it would have had the effect of a bomb, and finally that it was not customary to speak about such matters at political discussions.

Some time prior to this a mass rally had been held in one of Berlin's western districts, at which representatives of the church and representatives of the Communist party explained their respective viewpoints. A good half of the 1,800 people attending the rally were Christians and lower middle-class people. As the principal speaker, I summarized the sex-economic position in several questions:

127

1. The church contends that the use of contraceptives is contrary to nature, as is any interference with natural procreation. If nature is so strict and so wise, why did it produce a sexual apparatus that does not impel one to engage in coitus only as often as one wants to procreate children, but on the average of two to three thousand times in a lifetime?

2. Would the representatives of the church who were present state openly if they engaged in sexual intercourse only when they wanted to procreate children? (They were Protestant pastors.)

3. Why had God produced two kinds of glands in one's sexual apparatus: one for sexual excitation and one for procreation?

4. How did they explain the fact that even small children developed a sexuality, long before the procreation function begins?

The clerical representatives' embarrassed answers evoked peals of laughter. When I began to explain the role played within the framework of authoritarian society by the church's and reactionary science's denial of the pleasure function, that the suppression of sexual gratification was intended to produce humility and general resignation in economic areas also, I had the entire audience on my side. The mystics had been beaten.

Extensive experience at mass rallies shows that the political reactionary role of mysticism in connection with the suppression of sexuality is readily comprehended when the right to sexual gratification is medically and socially explained in a clear and direct fashion. This fact requires thorough elucidation.

THE APPEAL TO MYSTICAL FEELINGS

"Bolshevism," so we hear it stated by "anti-Bolshevik" propaganda, is supposed to be the "arch enemy of every religion," especially of "spiritually valuable" religion. In consequence of its "materialism," Bolshevism recognizes only material goods and is only interested in producing material goods. It has not the least understanding for spiritual values and psychic riches.

What are these spiritual values and psychic riches anyhow?

Faithfulness and faith are often named; as for the rest, the phraseology is lost in a vague concept of "individuality."

> Because Bolshevism wants to stifle everything individual, it destroys the family which has always given man an individual character. For that reason it hates all national strivings. All peoples are to become as homogeneous as possible and be submissive to Bolshevism. . . . But all efforts to stifle one's personal life will be futile as long as there is still a trace of religion in man, because in religion personal freedom from the outside world breaks through again and again.

When the mystic speaks of "Bolshevism," he does not mean the political party founded by Lenin. He has no notion of the sociological controversies that took place at the turn of the century. "Communist," "Bolshevist," "Red," etc., became reactionary slogans, which have nothing to do with politics, parties, economics, etc. These words are just as irrational as the word "Jew" in the mouth of the fascists. They are expressive of the anti-sexual attitude that relates to the mystical-reactionary structure of authoritarian man. Thus, Roosevelt was labeled a "Jew" and a "Red" by the fascists. The irrational content of these slogans always refers to what is sexually alive, even when the person who is so labeled is far removed from any kind of affirmation of childhood and adolescent sexuality. The Russian Communists were even less affirmative to sexuality than many middle-class Americans. One will have to learn to comprehend the irrationalism of slogans if one wants to counter mysticism, the primary cause of all political reaction. Wherever we read "Bolshevism" in what follows, "orgasm anxiety" is also to be thought of.

The reactionary man who is also a fascist assumes an intimate relation between family, nation, and religion. This fact had been wholly neglected by sociological research. To begin with, the sex-economic diagnosis is confirmed: what religion calls freedom from the outside world really means fantasized substitute gratification for actual gratification. This fits in perfectly with the Marxist theory that religion is the opium of the people. This is more than just a metaphor. Vegetotherapy was able to prove that mystical experience actually sets the same process going in the autonomic living apparatus as a narcotic does. These processes *are excitations in the sexual apparatus that cause narcoticlike conditions and that crave for orgastic gratification.*

First of all, however, we have to obtain more exact information on the relationship between mystical and familial sentiments. Braumann writes in a way that is typical for reactionary ideology:

> But Bolshevism has still another way of annihilating religion, namely, through the systematic destruction of marital and familial life. It knows only too well that the great forces of religion stem from the family. It is for this reason that marriage and divorce are facilitated to such a degree that Russian marriages border on free love.

With reference to the "culture-destroying" effect of the Soviet Russian five-day week, we read:

> This serves to destroy familial life as well as religion. . . . What is most disturbing is the havoc which Bolshevism spreads in the sexual sphere. By its destruction of marital and familial life, it fosters every kind of immoral dissipation to the extent of allowing unnatural intercourse between brothers and sisters, parents and children. [This is a reference to the abolition of punishment for acts of incest in the Soviet Union.] Bolshevism recognizes no moral inhibitions whatever.

Instead of countering such reactionary attacks with an exact presentation of natural sexual processes, Soviet literature often made the attempt to defend itself. It is not at all true, it contended, that sexual life in the Soviet Union is "immoral"; marriages are becoming consolidated again. Such attempts at defense were not only ineffective politically; they did not correspond to the facts. *From a Christian point of view,* sexuality in the Soviet Union was indeed immoral. It was out of the question to speak of a consolidation of marriages, for the institution of marriage in the authoritarian and mystical connotation of the word had been abolished. Until about 1928 the most popular form of marriage in the Soviet Union was something equivalent to what we call common-law marriage in the United States; it was both legal and practical. Thus Russian communism had loosened compulsive marital and familial ties and had done away with moralism.* It was merely a matter of making masses of people conscious of their contradiction, namely that while they secretly and urgently yearned for precisely that which the social revolution had accomplished, they also consented to moralism. To accomplish this task, however, clarity on the relationship between compulsive family, mysticism, and sexuality is necessary.

We showed earlier that nationalistic sentiments are a direct continuation of the sentiments of the authoritarian family. But mystical feelings are also a source of nationalistic ideology. Hence, patriarchal family attitudes *and* a mystical frame of mind are the basic psychological elements of fascism and imperialistic national-ism in the masses. In short, it is psychologically confirmed on a mass basis that a mystical upbringing becomes the foundation of fascism when a social catastrophe sets the masses in motion.

In *The New York Times* of August 14, 1942, Otto D. Tolischus wrote as follows on the imperialistic ideology of the Japanese. (One could almost have the feeling that he had studied our *Mass Psychology of Fascism.*)

> A startling revelation of the Japanese war mind, as well as the ambitions prevalent not only in the military and ultra-nationalist cliques now dominating the Japanese Government but also among the intelligentsia, is contained in a booklet issued in Tokyo in February of this year by Professor Chikao Fujisawa, one of the leading exponents of Japan's political thought and philosophy.

---

* However, since about 1934, old anti-sexual and moralistic concepts have re-appeared indicative of the failure of the sexual revolution in Russia, including the reversion to compulsive marriage and reactionary sexual legislation. Cf. *The Sexual Revolution.*

According to this booklet, which was made up for widest distribution, Japan, as the original motherland of the human race and world civilization, is fighting a holy war to reunite warring mankind into one universal family household in which each nation will take its proper place under the divine sovereignty of the Japanese Emperor, who is a direct descendant of the Sun Goddess in the "absolute cosmic life-center," from which the nations have strayed and to which they must return.

In its general argument the booklet merely summarizes, systematizes and applies to the present war the ideas derived from Shinto mythology that Japanese politicians under the leadership of Yosuke Matsuoka developed into an imperialistic dogma to justify Japan's expansion policy. But for that very reason it appeals to all the religious, racial and national ideas and emotions most deeply ingrained in the Japanese nature. In that sense Professor Fujisawa is a sort of Japanese Nietzsche and Wagner and his pamphlet becomes the Japanese equivalent of Adolf Hitler's *Mein Kampf*.

As was the case with *Mein Kampf*, the outside world has paid little attention to this trend in Japanese thought, which is either regarded as pure phantasy or relegated to the field of theology. But for years it has furnished the ideological background for Japan's expansion policy, which led to the present war, and the last Japanese notes to the United States cannot be understood without reference to it.

The authoritative nature of the booklet is indicated by the fact Professor Fujisawa has been a permanent representative on the secretariat of the League of Nations and professor of political science in Kyushu Imperial University and has published numerous works in various languages on Japanese political science. He is now director of the research department of the Imperial Rule Association, created to organize the Japanese people for war, and is charged with making such ideas effective throughout the world.

The flavor of the booklet is amply illustrated by the first few paragraphs, which read:

"Japan is often called in our poetic language 'Sumera Mikuni,' which conveys somewhat the meaning of divine clime, all-integrating and all-embracing. By keeping in mind its philosophic implications one will be able to grasp the keynote of the imperial rescript issued Sept. 27, 1939, at the time of the conclusion of the Tripartite pact. Therein our gracious Tenno proclaimed solemnly that the cause of great justice should be extended to the far ends of the earth so as to turn the world into one household and thus enable all nations to secure their due places. This significant passage in the rescript will clarify the very character of our august sovereign, ever anxious to act as head of an all-embracing universal family, in the bosom of which to all nations shall be allotted their respective posts in a dynamic order of harmony and cooperation.

"It is incumbent upon our Tenno to do his best to restore the 'absolute cosmic life-center' and reconstruct the fundamental vertical order once prevalent among nations in remote antiquity; by so doing he wishes to transform the present-day lawless and chaotic world, where the weak are left to fall prey to the strong, into one large family community in which perfect concord and consummate harmony shall prevail.

"This is the objective of the divine mission that Japan has been called on to fulfill from time immemorial. In a word, it is to permeate the whole world and earth with the cosmic vitality embodied in our divine sovereign, so that all segregated national units may be led to reunite themselves spiritually with the sincere feeling of brothers sharing the same blood.

"Only in this way will all nations of the world be induced to abandon their individualistic attitude, which finds expression first of all in current international law."

This, says Professor Fujisawa, is "the way of the gods," and, after explaining this in mystical terms, he continues:

"In this light one can well understand that capitalistic individualism prevalent in the United States runs counter to the cosmic truth, for it ignores the all-embracing life-center and deals exclusively with rampancy and unbridled ego. Dictatorial communism, elevated to an official doctrine by Soviet Russia, proves likewise irreconcilable with the cosmic truth, since it tends to disregard personal initiative and merely exercises drastic bureaucratic control of the State.

"It is noteworthy that the guiding principle of National Socialist Germany and Fascist Italy have much in common with Musubi principle, one of many distinguishing these Axis powers from the democracies and the Soviet Union. It is because of this spiritual solidarity that Japan, Germany and Italy have been prompted to present a common front against . . . those powers defending the old order."

Sumera Mikuni, Professor Fujisawa explains, is at war with the administrations of President Roosevelt and Prime Minister Churchill, which have been eager for realization of their "inordinate ambition" to dominate the Orient. But thanks to the earnest prayers offered by Sumera Mikoto (the Japanese Emperor) day and night to the spirit of the Sun Goddess, divine power has at last mobilized to deal a thoroughgoing blow to those revolting against the inviolable cosmic law.

In fact, Professor Fujisawa writes, "the present Greater East Asia is virtually a second descent of the grandchild [of the Sun Goddess, the mythological ancestor of the Japanese dynasty], who perpetuates himself in the everlasting life of Sumera Mikoto."

Wherefore, Professor Fujisawa concludes:

"The holy war launched by Sumera Mikuni will sooner or later awaken all nations to the cosmic truth that their respective national lives issued forth from one absolute life-center embodied by Sumera Mikoto and that peace and harmony cannot be realized otherwise than by reorganizing them into one all-embracing family system under the guidance of Sumera Mikoto."

Piously Professor Fujisawa adds:

"This noble idea should not be considered in any sense in the light of imperialism, under which weak nations are mercilessly subjugated."

Startling as these ideas may appear, even more startling is Professor Fujisawa's "scientific" basis for them. Although all Japanese chronicles and histories admit that at the foundation of the Japanese Empire, which the Japanese Government has put at 2600 B.C. but which historians date around the beginning of the Christian era, the inhabitants of the Japanese isles were still primitive savages, some of whom were "men with tails" living in trees, Professor Fujisawa blandly advances the claim that Japan is the motherland of the entire human race and its civilization.

Recent discoveries and rare archives in Japan, supplemented by the writings of some Western authorities, Professor Fujisawa explains, prove "the wonderful fact that in the prehistoric age mankind formed a single worldwide family system with Sumera Mikoto as its head, and Japan was highly respected as the land of parents while all other lands were called lands of children or branch lands."

As proof of this the professor cites a world map prepared by "a certain Hilliford in 1280" on which "East is located on top and the space occupied by the Japanese is named 'Kingdom of Heaven.' "

Professor Fujisawa continues:

"Eminent scholars preoccupied with thoroughgoing researches regarding the prehistoric chronicles of Japan are unanimous in concluding that the cradle of mankind was neither the Pamir Plateau nor the banks of the Tigris and the Euphrates, but the middle mountainous region of the Japanese mainland. This new theory concerning the origins of humanity is attracting the keen attention of those who confidently look to Japan's divine mission for the salvation of disoriented mankind."

According to this professorial thesis, the Sumerians, who are believed to have founded Babylonian civilization, from which all other civilizations, including those of Egypt, Greece and Rome, blossomed, are identical with the early Japanese settlers at Erdu, and this, says Professor Fujisawa, explains the correspondence between the prehistoric accounts of Japan and the Old Testament. The same, he says, is true of the Chinese, who, he insists, were civilized by Japan, instead of the other way around. Yet Japanese histories record that the Japanese did not learn to read or write till the Koreans and Chinese taught them, around 400 A.D.

Unfortunately, says the professor, "the world order, with Japan functioning as its absolute unifying center, collapsed in consequence of repeated earthquakes, volcanic eruptions, floods, tidal waves and glaciers, and due to these tremendous cataclysms all mankind became estranged geographically and spiritually from the parent land of Japan."

But, it seems, Sumera Mikuni "was immune miraculously from all these natural catastrophes, and its divine sovereigns, Sumera Mikoto, enjoying lineage unbroken for ages eternal, have appointed to themselves the sacred mission of remolding this floating dismembered mankind into a large family community such as existed in prehistoric ages."

"Obviously," Professor Fujisawa adds, "none is better qualified than Sumera Mikoto to accomplish this divine work of saving humanity."

Tolischus does not comprehend the phenomena that he describes. He believes that it is a conscious mystical veiling of rational imperialism. However, his report clearly demonstrates that sex-economy is correct in its judgment that all forms of fascistic, imperialistic, and dictatorial mysticism can be traced back to the mystical distortion of the vegetative sensations of life, a distortion that results from a patriarchal and authoritarian organization of the family and the state.

While national feeling is derived from the maternal tie (home feeling), mystical sentiments originate in the anti-sexual atmosphere that is inseparably bound to this familial tie. The authoritarian familial tie presupposes the inhibition of sensuous sexuality. Without exception, all children brought up in a patriarchal society are subject to this sensuous inhibition. No sexual activity, no matter how showy and "free" it appears to be, can delude the expert as to this deeply rooted inhibition. In fact, it is precisely this *inhibition* of the capacity for orgastic experience that lies at the bases of many pathological manifestations that occur in later sexual life, such as indiscriminate choice of partners, sexual restlessness, proclivity to pathological extravagances, etc. The inevitable result of this inhibition ("orgastic impotence") characteristic of every authoritarian upbringing and experienced as unconscious guilt-feelings and sexual anxiety, is an insatiable unconscious *intense orgastic longing,* which is accompanied by physical sensations of tension in the region of the solar plexus. The proverbial localization of sensual yearning in the breast and abdomen has its physiological meaning.[4]

To begin with, the continuous tension in the psychophysical organism constitutes the basis of daydreaming in small children and

---

[4] See my clinical presentation in *The Function of the Orgasm,* 1942.

young adolescents. This daydreaming is very easily converted into and developed as sentiments of a mystical, sentimental, and religious nature. The atmosphere of the mystical authoritarian man is infused with all these sentiments. Thus, the average child acquires a structure that is practically compelled to absorb the mystical influences of nationalism, mysticism, and superstitions of all kinds. The gruesome fairy tales of early childhood, the detective stories that follow later, the mysterious atmosphere of the church, only prepare the ground for the later susceptibility of the biopsychic apparatus to military and fatherland consecrations. Whether the mystical man appears rough or even brutal on the surface, is not of importance in assessing the effect of mysticism. The processes that take place far beneath the surface are of importance. The sentimentality and religious mysticism of a Matuschka, Haarmann, or Kürten are intimately related to their sadistic cruelty. These contrary sentiments owe their origin to one and the same source: The insatiable *vegetative yearning* produced by sexual inhibition and barred from natural gratification. On the one hand, therefore, this intense yearning is very accessible to muscular sadistic discharges, and on the other hand (owing to the existing guilt-feelings) finds expression in mystical religious experiences. The fact that the child-murderer Kürten was sexually disturbed was made clear by the testimony of his wife; that this was the case had not occurred to our psychiatric clinical "experts." The cohesion of sadistic brutality and mystical sentiments is usually to be met with wherever the normal capacity to experience orgasm is disturbed. And this is true of a mass murderer of our time as it was of the inquisitors of the Middle Ages or the brutality and mysticism of Philip II of Spain.[5] If a hysteria does not stifle unresolved excitation in nervous impotence, or a compulsive neurosis does not stifle the same excitation in futile and grotesque compulsive symptoms, the patriarchal-authoritarian

---

[5] In this connection see De Coster's *Till Eulenspiegel,* a masterpiece, which, as far as I am concerned, has remained without peer in its liberal humanity.

compulsive order offers sufficient opportunity for sadistic-mystical discharges.[6] The social rationalization of such behavior effaces its pathological character. It would be worthwhile to make a thorough study of the various mystical sects in America, the Buddhist ideology in India, the various theosophic and anthroposophical trends, etc., as socially important manifestations of patriarchal sexual economy. Let it suffice to say here that mystical groups merely represent a concentration of facts that we find in a more diffuse, less tangible, but, for all that, no less clear form, in all layers of the population. There is a direct correlation between mystical, sentimental, and sadistic sentiments on the one hand and the average disturbance of the natural orgastic experience on the other hand. There is more to be learned about this problem by observing the behavior of the audience at a third-rate musical than by reading a hundred textbooks on sexology. As different and as diverse as the contents and directions of this mystical experience are, their sex-economic basis is universal and typical. Compare this with the realistic, unsentimental, vital experience of the genuine revolutionary, the dedicated natural scientist, healthy adolescents, etc.

At this point the obvious objection makes itself heard, namely, that the primitive who led a natural life in a matriarchal order also had mystical feelings. A very thorough proof is needed to show that there is a fundamental difference between the matriarchal man and the patriarchal man. Above all, this can be proven by the fact that religion's attitude toward sexuality underwent a change in patriarchal society. Originally, it was a religion of sexuality; later it became an anti-sexual religion. The "mysticism" of the primitives who were members of a sexually affirmative society is partially direct orgastic experience and partially animistic interpretation of natural processes.

---

[6] Morphia addicts are always orgastically impotent; therefore they attempt to get rid of their excitations artificially, but they are never completely successful. Usually, they are sadistic, mystical, vain, homosexual, and tortured by consuming anxiety, which they attempt to work off by brutal behavior.

THE GOAL OF THE CULTURAL REVOLUTION
IN THE LIGHT OF FASCIST REACTION

The social revolution concentrates all of its forces on the elimination of the social basis of human suffering. The priority given to the necessity of revolutionizing the social order obscures the sex-economic goals and intentions. The revolutionary is compelled to put off the solution of very urgent questions until the most urgent task, the establishment of the *preconditions* for the practical solution of these questions, is accomplished. The reactionary, on the other hand, spares no effort in assailing precisely the ultimate cultural goals of the revolution, which are obscured by the preliminary and immediate tasks.

> Cultural Bolshevism aims at the destruction of our existing culture and wants to so reconstruct it as to serve man's earthly happiness. . . . [*Sic!*]

That's how Kurt Hutten put it in his call to arms, *Kulturbolschewismus*, published by the V*olksbundes*, 1931. Does political reaction's accusation relate to that which the cultural revolution really has in mind, or does it, for demagogic reasons, impute goals to the revolution that definitely do not lie within its compass? In the former case a defense and clear elucidation of the necessity of these goals would be indispensable. In the latter, the proof of false imputation would be sufficient, that is to say, a denial of that which political reaction imputes to the revolution.

How does political reaction itself appraise the antithesis between earthly happiness and religion? Kurt Hutten writes:

> To begin with: Cultural Bolshevism's most fierce fight is directed against religion. For religion, as long as it is alive, constitutes the strongest bulwark against its goals. . . . Religion subordinates all of human life to something supernatural, and eternal authority. It demands denial, sacrifice, renunciation of one's own wishes. *It imbues human life with responsibility, guilt, judgment, eternity.* It inhibits an unbridled exhaustion of human drives. *The revolution of*

139

culture is the cultural revolution of man, is the subjugation of all spheres of life to the pleasure principle [my italics, WR].

Here we have a clear articulation of the reactionary rejection of earthly happiness. The reactionary leader senses a threat to the anchoring of imperialistic mysticism ("culture"). He is much more keenly aware of this threat than the revolutionary is aware of his goal, for the latter must first concentrate his energy and knowledge on the changing of the social order. The reactionary leader recognizes the danger that the revolution constitutes to the authoritarian family and mystical moralism, long before the average revolutionary has the least notion that the revolution will entail such consequences. In this respect, indeed, the social revolutionary himself is very often prepossessed. The reactionary leader stands for heroism, the acceptance of affliction, the abiding of privation, absolutely and eternally; hence, he represents the interests of imperialism, whether he wants to or not (cf. Japan). To this end, however, he needs mysticism, that is to say, he needs sexual abstinence. To him happiness is essentially sexual gratification, and he is *right* in this appraisal. The revolutionary also demands a great deal of restraint, duty, renunciation, for the possibilities of happiness must first be fought for. In his practical work for the masses, the revolutionary easily forgets—*and sometimes likes to forget*—that the real goal is not work (social freedom brings about a continuous reduction of the working day), but sexual play and life in all of its forms, from orgasm to the highest accomplishments. Work is and remains the basis of life, but within the social framework, work is transferred from man to the machine. That is the essence of the economy of work.

Sentences such as the following are to be found in many mystical and reactionary writings, even if they are not always so clearly formulated as in the case of Kurt Hutten:

> Cultural Bolshevism is not a recent thing. It takes as its basis a striving that was planted in man's breast in primeval times: *The intense longing for happiness*. It is the primordial nostalgia for

140

paradise on earth. . . . The religion of faith is replaced by the religion of pleasure.

We, however, want to know: *Why shouldn't we have happiness on earth? Why shouldn't pleasure be the substance of life?*

Let the masses vote on *this* question! No reactionary conception of life would stand the test.

To be sure, the reactionary leader perceives the relation of mysticism to compulsive marriage and compulsive family in a mystical way, but he perceives it correctly.

> To fulfill this responsibility (for the consequences of pleasure), human society has founded the institution of marriage which, as a life-long partnership, is intended to represent the protective framework for the sexual relationship.

And the complete register of "cultural values," which fits into the fabric of reactionary ideology as parts into a machine, is immediately appended:

> Marriage as a tie, family as a duty, fatherland as a value in itself, morality as authority, religion as an obligation deriving from eternity.

The rigidity of the human plasma could not be more accurately described!

All reactionary types condemn sexual pleasure (not without impunity, however) because it attracts and repulses them at one and the same time. They cannot resolve the contradiction between sexual demands and moralistic inhibitions in themselves. The revolutionary negates perverse and pathological pleasure because it is not *his* pleasure, is not the sexuality of the *future*, but *the pleasure born of the contradiction between morality and instinct*; it is the pleasure of a dictatorial society, *debased, sordid, pathological pleasure*. Only when he himself is not clear, he makes the mistake of condemning pathological pleasure, instead of opposing it with his own positive sex-economy. If, as a result of his own sexual inhibitions, he does not fully comprehend the goal of a social organization founded on

141

freedom, he is apt to repudiate pleasure altogether, become an ascetic and thereby lose all possibility of establishing contact with the youth. In the otherwise excellent film *The Road to Life*, the sexual practices of disreputable people (in the tavern scene) are contrasted not with the sexual practices of people who are free but with ascetism and anti-sexuality. The sexual problem of adolescents is completely set aside. This is wrong and confuses the issue instead of solving it. The disintegration of moralistic codes in the sexual sphere is initially expressed as sexual *rebellion;* but at the outset it remains pathological sexual rebellion, from which the sex-economist rightly flees. The task, however, is to give a rational form to this rebellion, to lead it into a sex-economic channel, just as freedom of life was once born of convulsions of life.

142

VII

Sex-Economy in the Fight
Against Mysticism

At a mass rally in Berlin in January of 1933, the National Socialist Otto Strasser asked his opponent, the sociologist and sinolo-
gist Wittfogel, a question which was so penetrating that it had a
disconcerting effect. Those who were present were given the impression that Wittfogel's reply could have meant mysticism's doom.
Strasser accused the Marxists of underestimating the importance of
psychic life and religious feeling. His argument ran as follows: If
religion, according to Marx, were really only the flower on the chain
of the exploitation of toiling humanity, then how was it to be explained that religion had held up for thousands of years—the Christian religion, indeed, almost unchanged for two thousand years—
especially in view of the fact that in the beginning its survival had
demanded more sacrific than all revolutions taken together. The
question was not answered, but it fits in very well with the material
under discussion. It had to be admitted that the question was
justified. It was time for natural science to take stock of itself to
determine whether its comprehension of mysticism and the means
of its anchoring in the human structure was as thorough and as
complete as it could be. The answer had to be in the negative:
natural science had not yet succeeded in comprehending the powerful emotional content of mysticism. The exponents of mysticism
had dealt with all sides of the question and given practical answers
in their writings and sermons. The sex-political nature of every form

of mysticism is evident. Yet it was as completely overlooked by the freethinkers as the equally evident sexuality of children had been overlooked by the most famous educators. It is clear that mysticism has a hidden bulwark at its disposal and that it has been defending this bulwark against natural science with every means at its command. Science is only beginning to divine its existence.

THE THREE BASIC ELEMENTS OF RELIGIOUS FEELING

I do not want at this point to make a thorough investigation of religious feeling. I would like merely to summarize what is already known. At a certain point there is a correlation between the phenomena of orgastic excitation and the phenomena of religious excitation, ranging from the simplest pious surrender to total religious ecstasy. The idea of religious excitation is not to be confined to the sensations that are wont to arise in deeply religious people while attending a religious service. We have to include all excitations that are characterized by a definite psychic and somatic state of excitation. In other words, we also have to include the excitation experienced by submissive masses when they open themselves to a beloved leader's speech, and the excitation one experiences when one allows oneself to be overwhelmed by impressive natural phenomena. Let us begin by summarizing what was known about religious phenomena before sex-economic research.

Sociological research was able to show that religious *forms* and also the contents of various religions were dependent upon the stage of development of socio-economic conditions. For example, animal religions correspond to the mode of life of primitive peoples who lived from hunting. The way in which people conceive of a divine supernatural being is always determined by the level of the economy and of the culture. Another very important sociological factor in determining religious conceptions is man's ability to master natural and social difficulties. Helplessness in the face of natural forces and elemental social catastrophes is conducive to the development of religious ideologies in cultural crises. Thus, the sociological explanation of religion refers to the *socio-economic* soil from which religious cults spring. It has nothing to say about the dynamics of religious ideology, nor does it give us any clue as to the psychic process that takes place in the people who come under the influence of this ideology.

Thus, the formation of religious cults is not dependent upon the will of the individual. They are sociological formations, which originate from the interrelations between man and man and the relation of man to nature.

The psychology of the unconscious added a *psychological* interpretation to the *sociological* interpretation of religion. The dependency of religious cults upon socio-economic factors was understood. Now one began to study the psychological process *in the people* who came under the influence of these objective religious cults. Thus, psychoanalysis was able to show that our idea of *God* is identical with our idea of *father*, that the idea of the *Mother of God* is identical with the *mother* of every religious individual. The triangle of father, mother, and child is directly reflected in the *trinity* of the Christian religion. The psychic content of religion is drawn from early childhood familial relationships.

Thus, psychological research enabled us to interpret the content of religious cults, but it gave us no insight into the energy process by means of which this content became embedded in man's structure. Above all, no insight was given into the fanaticism and the high degree of emotionality of religious conceptions. Why the ideas of the all-powerful father and the benevolent mother became mystical ideas, and what relation they have to the sexual life of the individual, was also vague.

Many sociologists have established that some patriarchal religions have an orgastic character. It has also been established that patriarchal religions are always of a political reactionary nature. They always serve the interests of the ruling power of every class society and preclude, *to all intents and purposes,* the elimination of mass misery by ascribing it to God's will and by putting off claims to happiness with fine words about the Beyond.

To the existing knowledge on religion, sex-economic research now adds the following questions:

1. *How* do the idea of God, the ideology of sin, and the ideology of punishment—which are produced by society and reproduced in the family—become embedded in the individual? In other words: Why is it that man does not feel these basic conceptions of religion as a burden? What is it that compels him not only to accept them but to affirm them fervently, indeed, compels him to defend and preserve them at the sacrifice of his most fundamental interests of life?

2. *When* do these religious conceptions become embedded in man?

3. What *energy* is used to accomplish this?

It is clear that until these three questions are answered, it may indeed be possible to give a sociological and psychological interpretation of religion, but it will not be possible to effect a real change in man's structure. For if religious feelings are not imposed on man, but are embedded and retained in his structure, opposed as they are to his own vital interests, then what is needed is an energetic change in man's structure.

The basic religious idea of all patriarchal religions is the negation of sexual need. There are no exceptions, if we disregard the sexually affirmative primordial religions, in which the religious and the sexual experience were still a unity. In the transition of society from a matriarchal organization based on natural law to a patriarchal organization based on the division of classes, the unity of the religious and sexual cult was split. The religious cult became the antithesis of the sexual cult. At this juncture the sexual cult ceases to exist and is replaced by the barbarism of brothels, pornography, and clandestine sexuality. No additional proof is required to show that at that moment when sexual experience ceased to constitute a unity with the religious cult and indeed became its antithesis, religious excitation also had to become a substitute for the socially affirmed sensuality that was lost. It is only on the basis of this contradiction in religious excitation, which is anti-sexual *and* a *substitution* for sexuality at one and the same time, that the strength and tenacity of religions can be comprehended.

The emotional structure of the genuinely religious man can be briefly described as follows: biologically, he is subject to sexual tensions just as all other human beings and creatures. Owing, however, to his assimilation of sex-negating religious conceptions, and especially to the fear of punishment that he has acquired, he has completely lost his ability to experience natural sexual tension and release. Consequently, he suffers from a chronic state of physical excitation, which he is continuously compelled to master. He is not only shut off from earthly happiness—it does not even appear desirable. Since he expects to be rewarded in the Beyond, he succumbs to a feeling of being *incapable of happiness* in this world. In view of the fact that he is a biologic creature and *cannot* under any circumstances forego happiness, release, and gratification, he seeks *illusionary* happiness. This he can obtain from the *forepleasure* of religious tensions, i.e., the vegetative somatic currents and excitations with which we are familiar. Together with his fellow believers, he will arrange entertainments and create institutions that alleviate this state of physical excitation and are also capable of disguising the real nature of this excitation. His biologic organism prompts him to construct a musical instrument, an organ, the sound of which is capable of evoking such currents in the body. The mystical darkness of the church intensifies the effect of a superpersonal sensibility to one's own inner life and to the sounds of a sermon, a chorale, etc., intended to achieve this effect.

In reality, the religious man has become completely helpless. As a result of the suppression of his sexual energy, he has lost his capacity for happiness as well as the aggressiveness necessary to deal with life's difficulties. The more helpless he becomes, the more he is forced to believe in supernatural forces that support and shelter him. Thus, it is not difficult to understand that in some situations he is also capable of developing an incredible power of conviction, indeed, a passive indifference toward death. He draws this power from his love of his own religious conviction, which, as we said, is

borne by highly pleasurable physical excitations. Naturally, he believes that this power stems from "God." In reality, therefore, his
intense longing for God is the longing that derives from his excitations of sexual forepleasure and clamors for release. Deliverance is
and can be nothing other than the deliverance from the unbearable
physical tensions, which can be pleasurable only as long as they are
lost in a fantasized unification with God, i.e., with gratification and
release. The tendency of fanatically religious people to injure themselves and to behave masochistically, etc., confirms what we have
said. Clinical experience in sex-economy shows that the desire to be
beaten or to castigate oneself corresponds to the instinctual desire
for *release without incurring guilt*. There is no physical tension that
will not evoke fantasies of being beaten or of being tortured as soon
as the person concerned feels that he himself is incapable of bringing about the release. Here we have the root of the passive ideology
of suffering of all genuine religions.

The need to be consoled, supported, and helped by others,
especially in the struggle against one's own evil impulses—"sins of
the flesh," as they are called—stems from one's actual helplessness
and intense physical suffering. If a religious person becomes more
and more excited under the influence of religious conceptions, the
state of vegetative irritation increases with the physical excitation
and reaches a point of near gratification without, however, bringing
about an actual physical release. It is known from the treatment of
mentally sick priests that an involuntary ejaculation often occurs at
the height of religious ecstasy. Normal orgastic gratification is replaced by a general condition of physical excitation, which excludes
the genitals and, as if by accident, brings about a partial release
against one's will.

Originally and naturally, sexual pleasure was the good, the beautiful, the happy, that which united man with nature in general.
When sexual feelings and religious feelings became separated from
one another, that which is sexual was forced to become the bad, the
infernal, the diabolical.

Elsewhere I attempted to show the etiology and mechanism of

the *pleasure* anxiety, i.e., the fear of sexual excitation. Let me briefly summarize: As time goes on, people who are incapable of release must begin to sense sexual excitations as torturous, burdensome, destructive. In fact, sexual excitation is destructive and torturous if it is not allowed to achieve release. Thus, we see that the religious conception of sex as an annihilating, diabolical force, predisposing one for final doom, is rooted in actual physical processes. As a result the attitude toward sexuality is forced to become divided: The typical religious and moralistic valuations "good"–"bad," "heavenly"—"earthly," "divine"—"diabolical," etc., become the symbols of sexual gratification on the one hand and the punishment thereof on the other hand.

The deep longing for redemption and release—*consciously* from "sins," *unconsciously* from sexual tensions—is warded off. States of religious ecstasy are nothing other than conditions of sexual excitation of the vegetative nervous system, which can never be released. Religious excitation cannot be comprehended and therefore cannot be mastered, without first understanding the contradiction by which it is ruled. It is not only anti-sexual, but to a large extent sexual as well. It is not only moralistic; it is altogether unnatural. From a sex-economic point of view, it is unhygienic.

In no social class do hysteria and perversions flourish to such an extent as they do in the ascetic circles of the church. One should not conclude from this, however, that these ascetics should be treated as perverse criminals. In talking with religious people it is often found that they have a very good understanding of their own condition. As everyone else, their personalities are divided into a public and a private side. Officially, they regard sexuality as a sin; privately, they know only too well that they cannot exist without their substitute gratifications. Indeed, many of them are accessible to the sex-economic resolution of the contradiction between sexual excitation and morality. If one does not reject them as human beings and succeeds in winning their confidence, one finds they understand very well that that which they describe as union with God is the feeling of relatedness to the process of nature as a whole, that their selfhood is a part of nature. As all human beings, they too feel themselves to be a microcosm in a macrocosm. It has to be admitted that their deep conviction has a true core. What they believe is really true, namely the vegetative currents of their bodies and the states of ecstasy to which they can rise. Especially in the case of men and women who come from poor social strata, religious feeling is absolutely genuine. It loses its genuineness only insofar as it rejects and veils from itself its origin and the unconscious desire for gratification. It is in this way that that attitude of priests and religious people that has a *contrived* goodness about it comes into being.

This presentation is incomplete. Summarizing the basic points, however, we can say:

1. Religious excitation is vegetative excitation whose sexual nature is disguised.

2. Through the mystification of the excitation, the religious individual negates his sexuality.

3. Religious ecstasy is a substitute for orgastic vegetative excitation.

4. Religious ecstasy does not produce a sexual release; at best, it produces a muscular and mental fatigue.

5. Religious feeling is subjectively genuine and has a physiological basis.

6. The negation of the sexual nature of this excitation causes one's character to lose its genuineness.

Children do not believe in God. It is when they have to learn to suppress the sexual excitation that goes hand in hand with masturbation that the belief in God generally becomes embedded in them. Owing to this suppression, they acquire a fear of pleasure. Now they begin to believe in God in earnest and to develop a fear of him. On the one hand they fear him as an omniscient and omnipotent being, and on the other hand they invoke his protection against their own sexual excitation. All of this has the function of avoiding masturbation. Thus, it is in early childhood that religious ideas become embedded. However, the idea of God would not be able to bind the child's sexual energy if it were not also associated with the actual figures of father and mother. He who does not honor the father is sinful. In other words, he who does not fear the father and indulges in sexual pleasure is punished. The strict father, who denies the fulfillment of the child's desires, is God's representative on earth and, in the fantasy of the child, is the executioner of God's will. If the respect for the father is shaken by a clear insight into his weaknesses and human inadequacies, this does not lead to his rejection by the child. He continues to exist in the figure of the abstract mystical conception of God. In a patriarchal social organization an appeal to God is really an appeal to the actual authority of the father. When a child invokes "God," he is really invoking his actual father. In the structure of the child, sexual excitation, idea of *father*, and idea of *God* constitute a unity. In treatment we meet this unity as a palpable condition of genital muscular spasm. With the elimination of the spastic condition in the genital musculature, the idea of God and the fear of the father always lose ground. Hence, the genital spasm not only represents the physiological anchoring of religious fear in the human structure, but at the same time it also produces the pleasure anxiety that becomes the core of every religious morality.

I have to leave it to later investigations to work out the very complicated and detailed interrelations among the different kinds of cults, socio-economic social organization, and human structure. *Genital shyness* and *pleasure anxiety* remain the energetic core of all anti-sexual patriarchal religions.

ANCHORING OF RELIGION BY MEANS OF SEXUAL ANXIETY

Religiosity that is hostile to sex is the product of patriarchal authoritarian society. The son-father relationship, which we find in every patriarchal religion, is only the inevitable socially determined content of religious experience. The experience itself, however, derives from the patriarchal suppression of sexuality. The function that religion comes to serve in the course of time, the bearing of obedience toward authority and renunciation, is also only a secondary function of religion. It can build upon a solid foundation: *the structure of patriarchal man molded by means of sexual suppression.* It is the negation of the pleasures of the body that serves as the living source of the religious view, and is the axis of every religious dogma. This is especially evident in the religions of Christianity and Buddhism.

Anchoring of Mysticism in Childhood

> Lieber Gott, nun schlaf ich ein,
> Schicke mir ein Engelein.
> Vater, lass die Augen Dein,
> Ueber meinem Bette sein.
> Hab ich Unrecht heut getan,
> Sieh es, lieber Gott, nicht an.
> Vater, hab mit mir Geduld
> Und vergib mir meine Schuld.
> Alle Menschen, gross und klein
> Mögen Dir befohlen sein.

> [Dear God, now I go to sleep,
> Send me a little angel.
> Father, may your eyes
> Rest upon my bed.
> If today I have transgressed
> Overlook it, dear God.
> Father, be patient with me
> And forgive my trespasses.
> May all men, big and small,
> Be recommended to your Mercy.]

This is one of the many typical prayers that children have to recite before going to sleep. The content of such texts is ignored. And yet these texts are a concentrated form of the substance and emotional content of mysticism. In the first couplet, we have a plea for protection; in the second, a repetition of this plea made directly to the "father"; in the third, a plea for forgiveness for a committed sin: may the God-Father *overlook* our trespasses. What does this guilt-feeling refer to? What is it that God is supposed to overlook? *The guilt experienced from the playing with one's sexual organs stands at the top of the list of forbidden deeds.*

The forbidding of the child to play with his sexual organs would be ineffective if it were not reinforced by the idea that God sees *everything*, and therefore the child has to be "*good*" even when the parents are away. Those who feel inclined to dismiss this association as a stretch of the imagination may be convinced by the following impressive story. It gives a very clear picture of the anchoring of the mystical idea of God by means of sexual anxiety.

A girl of some seven years of age who was consciously brought up without any idea of God suddenly developed a compulsion to pray. It was compulsive because she really didn't want to pray and felt it to be against her better judgment. The background of this compulsion to pray is as follows: The child was in the habit of masturbating before going to sleep every night. One night, for some reason, she was afraid to do so; instead she had the impulse to kneel down in front of her bed and to recite a prayer similar to the one quoted above. "If I pray, I won't be afraid." *It was on the day she renounced masturbation for the first time that fear appeared.* Whence this self-renunciation? She told her father, who had her complete confidence, that a few months earlier she had had an unpleasant experience while on vacation. As so many children, she and a boy had played at having sexual intercourse ("had played Mommy and Daddy"). Another boy had suddenly come upon them and had shouted "shame" at them. Though she had been told by her parents that there was nothing wrong with such games, she felt ashamed and, in place of the game, masturbated before going to sleep. One evening, shortly before the appearance of the compulsion to pray, she had walked home from a house party with several other children. Along the way they had sung revolutionary songs. An old woman passed them who reminded her of the witch in *Hänsel and Gretel*. This old woman had called out to them: "May the Devil take you—you band of atheists!" That evening, when she wanted to masturbate again, it struck her for the first time that perhaps there really was a God who sees and punishes. Unconsciously, she had associated the old woman's threat with the experience with the boy. Now she too began to struggle against masturbation, became afraid, and to allay her fear began to pray compulsively. *Prayer had taken the place of sexual gratification.* Nonetheless, the fear did not give way completely. She began to have frightful nocturnal fantasies. From that time on she was afraid of a supernatural being who could punish her for her sexual offenses. Hence, she recommended herself to His care. This constituted a reinforcement of her struggle against the temptation to masturbate.

This is not to be looked upon as an isolated occurrence. It is typical of the process whereby the idea of God becomes embedded in the overwhelming majority of the children of religious cultural circles. As we have learned from the analytic study of fairy tales, the same function is served by such fairy tales as *Hänsel and Gretel,* in which there is a concealed—but for the unconscious of the child unambiguous—threat of punishment for masturbation. We cannot at this point enter into the details of the genesis of the child's mystical thinking from such fairy tales and the relation between mystical thinking and sexual inhibition. In all cases treated by character analysis, it was clearly shown that mystical sentiments develop from the fear of masturbation in the form of a general feeling of guilt. It is difficult to understand how this fact could have been overlooked by analytic research until now. One's own conscience, the internalized admonitions and threats of the parents and teachers, are objectified in the idea of God. Scientific research has made this clear. It is less clear that faith and fear of God are energetic sexual excitations that have exchanged their goal and content. Accordingly, the religious feeling is the same as the sexual feeling, except that it is imbued with a mystical, psychic content. This explains the frequency with which sexual elements appear in many

154

ascetic practices, e.g., the delusion of some nuns that they are the brides of Christ. It is not very likely that such ideas attain to genital consciousness. In most cases they revert to other sexual paths, e.g., masochistic martyrdom.

Let us return to our little girl. The compulsion to pray disappeared when she was made aware of the origin of her fear; this awareness made it possible for her to masturbate again without feelings of guilt. As improbable as this incident may appear, it is pregnant with meaning for sex-economy. It shows how the mystical contagion of our youth could be prevented. Several months after the disappearance of the compulsion to pray, the little girl wrote a letter to her father from a summer camp:

> Lieber Karli, there is a cornfield here and we have set up our hospital on the edge of it (only pretending of course). We always play doctor there (we are five girls). If one of us has a hurt on our ding-dong, then he goes there, where we have salves and creams and cotton. We swiped all that.

Who will deny that *this is sexual cultural revolution.* Sexual revolution, yes—but cultural revolution? The girl is in the same class with children who are an average of one to two years older than she, and her teachers bear witness to her diligence and talents. In politics and general knowledge she is far ahead of other girls her age, and she has a very lively interest in reality. Twelve years later, she was sexually healthy, intellectually outstanding, and socially liked.

The Anchoring of Mysticism in Adolescents

Using the little girl as an example, I attempted to show how religious fear becomes anchored in a small child. Sexual anxiety is the main vehicle in the anchoring of the authoritarian social order in the child's structure. Now we want to pursue this function of sexual anxiety into the puberty period. Let us have a look at one of the typical anti-sexual pamphlets.

To Land or to Strand

Nietzsche: Their souls are steeped in mire, and woe unto us if
the mire is imbued with intellect.

Kirkegaard: If Reason alone is baptized, the passions remain pagan.

Two rocks are placed in the life of each man. He can land on
them or be stranded on them, set himself right or be dashed to
pieces: God and—the opposite sex. Countless young men are
stranded or fail in life, not because they did not learn enough, but
because they fail to gain clarity about God and because they cannot
cope with *the* instinct which can bring man ineffable happiness, but
also unfathomable misery: the *sexual instinct.*

There are so many men who never achieve full manhood because they are dominated by their instincts. Actually, strong instincts alone are no reason to be grieved. On the contrary, they
constitute wealth and intensity of life. They are the rousing cry to a
strong personality. But the instinct becomes a burden to itself and a
sin against the Creator, when man ceases to keep it under control,
loses his authority over it and becomes its slave. In man, it is either
the spiritual or the instinctual, i.e., bestial that predominates. The
two are incompatible with one another. Thus, every thoughtful man
is one day faced with the imponderable question: Do you want to
know the real meaning of your life, to illuminate it, or do you want
to be consumed in the fiery furnace of your unbridled drives?

Do you want to live your life as an animal or as a man of God?

The process of attaining manhood—which is what we are
concerned with here—is the problem of the hearth-fire. Tempered
and controlled, the fire illuminates and warms the room, but—
mercy upon us, if the fire leaps forth from the hearth! Mercy upon
us if the sexual instinct so dominates the whole man that it becomes the master of all his thoughts, acts and endeavors!

We live in sick times. In earlier times, one demanded that eros
be disciplined and made responsible. Today we are of the opinion
that modern man no longer has need of discipline. In this regard,
however, we fail to see that present-day man living in the big city is
much more nervous and weaker of will and therefore requires more
discipline.

Cast your eyes around you: It is not mind that rules in our fatherland. Unbridled drives have the upperhand, and among our youth it is chiefly the undisciplined sexual drive, which degenerates into immorality. In the factory and in the office, on the stage and in public life, it is the spirit of the half-world that holds sway; obscenity is the order of the day. And who can say how much joyous youthful pleasure goes to ruin in the plague-palaces of the big city, in the dance-halls and cabarets, pin-ball galleries and obscene movies! The young man of today considers himself pretty clever when he adheres to the hedonist theory. In truth, however, the words of Goethe's Mephistopheles apply to him:

"He calls it Reason, using light celestial
Just to outdo the beasts in being bestial."

Two things, yes, two things render difficult the process of attaining manhood: the metropolis with its abnormal conditions and the demon in ourselves. The young man who comes to the metropolis alone for the first time, perhaps from a well-sheltered home, sees himself surrounded by a wealth of new impressions. Unceasing noise, exciting sights, erotic books and magazines, bad air, alcohol, movies, theaters, and provocatively dressed females everywhere he turns. Who can stand up to such a concentrated onslaught? And to the external temptation, the internal demon is only too happy to give his assent. For Nietzsche was right, "the soul is steeped in mire." In all men "the wild hounds are howling in the cellar," waiting to be set free.

Many fall prey to the compulsion of immorality because the dangers were not explained to them at the proper time. Such men will be grateful for an open word of warning and advice enabling them to escape and turn back.

Usually, one is first exposed to immorality in the form of *masturbation*. Scientific investigations show that this is usually begun at a frightfully early age. It is true, the consequences of this bad habit are often exaggerated. Yet, the judgment of respected physicians must give everyone pause for thought. Professor Dr. Hartung, long time senior physician of dermatology at the Aller-heiligen-Hospital in Breslau, has this to say on this matter: "There is no doubt that an excessive indulgence of this propensity is severely harmful to the body, and that it is precisely in later life that disturbances result from the indulgence of this vice. They are usually manifested in form of general nervousness, mental incapacity for work and physical prostration."

He also stresses the fact that the young man who practices masturbation does something dirty in his consciousness; he also loses his self-respect and his clear brow. The continual consciousness of a loathsome secret which has to be concealed from others, morally degrades him in his own eyes. He goes on to say that those young people who indulge in this vice become indolent and sloppy, lose their desire to work, and that all kinds of nervous and irritable conditions weaken their memory and their efficiency. Other respected physicians who have written on this subject agree with Dr. Hartung.

But masturbation not only fouls the blood, it does away with spiritual forces and inhibitions which are necessary for the process of attaining manhood. It deprives the soul of its resoluteness. *If it becomes habitual,* it has the effect of a gnawing worm.

However, the consequences of *immorality with the opposite sex* are much worse. It is certainly not by chance that man's most terrible scourge—venereal disease—is a result of this transgression. It is only astounding how incredibly foolish people are in this area, people who otherwise tend to be sensible.

Dr. Paul Lazarus, Professor at the University of Berlin, painted a shocking picture of the deep psychic and physical illness of our people caused by venereal disease.

Syphilis must be designated as one of the most effective gravediggers of our national energy.

But also gonorrhea, which many young men are foolish enough to take lightly, is a serious and dangerous disease. And the very fact that it is not possible for medical science to cure it with certainty should be enough to banish all levity on the subject.

Professor Binswanger had this to say about venereal disease: "It is remarkable that cases of infection which appear to be very minor lead to severe suffering, that often many years elapse between the original infection and the outbreak of an incurable nervous complaint, and that more than 60% of the cases of that disease, which occurs so frequently today and is called a softening of the brain by laymen, can be traced back to earlier sexual infections."

Is it not a thought which shakes us to our innermost core that, owing to such sins of our youth, those who will one day be closest to us—wife and child—may have to suffer such terrible illnesses?

But I have to mention one other aberration, which is far more rife today than some would imagine: *homosexuality*. Let us make this much clear at the outset: We want to extend our warmest sympathy and understanding to all those who, owing to inclination or heredity in this area, wage a quiet and often desperate struggle in an effort to maintain their purity. Hail to those who achieve a victory, for they wrestle with God on their side. But just as Jesus loved the individual sinner and helped everyone who wanted to be helped, yet countered sin itself with holy earnestness, so we too have to counter the phenomenon of homosexuality which corrupts our youth and our people as a whole. There was already a time in which the world was on the verge of drowning in a flood of perversity. At that time it was the gospel that vanquished the culture so engulfed in the putrefaction of these repulsive offenses and lewdness, and established a new culture. Speaking of the slaves and victims of these sins, Paul wrote to the Romans: ". . . and the men likewise gave up natural relations with women and were consumed with passion for one another. Men committed shameless acts with men. . . . *For this reason God gave them up.* . . ." Romans 1:27 & 26. Homosexuality is the mark of Cain, of a godless and soulless culture which is sick to the core. It is the consequence of the prevailing view of the world and of life, the highest aim of which is love of pleasure. Professor Foerster has rightfully stated in his *Sexualethik:* "Where spiritual heroism is made fun of and the sowing of one's wild oats is glorified, everything which is perverse, demonic and vile plucks up courage to manifest itself openly; indeed, it scoffs at the healthy as an illness and sets itself up as the standard of life."

We see today things which man fears to admit in his most hidden depravity. Completely different things will come to light, and then one will understand that only a great spiritual power—the gospel of Jesus Christ—can be of help here.

However, some will raise objections to what has been said. "Are we not dealing," you will say perhaps, "with a natural instinct which has to be satisfied?"—Unchained passions are not something natural, but something highly unnatural. *In almost all cases it is only through one's own guilt or through the guilt of others that the wicked desire is sowed, ignited and fed.* Take an alcoholic or a drug addict: Is his craving for alcohol or morphine something natural? Only by indulging this vice repeatedly does it become an unnatural craving. The instinct implanted in us by God for marriage and the preservation of mankind is in itself good and not at all too difficult to curb. Thousands of men are successful in controlling it in the right way.

"But isn't it harmful for a mature man to abstain from these things?" Professor Dr. Hartung, whom we should like to quote again, says literally: "I will answer you short and clear: No, it is not. *If anyone ever told you that a healthy man could get sick from chastity and abstinence in the broad sense of the words, he put you on the wrong track altogether. And if that person had really thought over what he told you, then he was either an ignorant or wicked man.*"

One must be urgently warned against the use of contraceptives. The only sure protection is abstinence until marriage.

I have made an honest and truthful attempt to open your eyes to the consequences of immorality. You have seen the ruin of both body and spirit of those who indulge in these sins. Added to this, however, is also the harm which results to the soul from this vice. I swear to you in holy earnestness: *Unchastity is a crime against God. It deprives one of one's peace of mind and prevents one from obtaining true joy and serenity.* It is written: "For he who sows to his own flesh will from the flesh reap corruption . . ." Gal. 6:8.

The spirit of the half-world moves in with inevitable necessity wherever the connection to the over-world is lost.

For all those, however, who do not want to be or do not want to remain the victims of immorality, I want to add a few words of advice and encouragement. One must make a complete break with the sins of immorality *in thought, word and deed.* This is what must be heeded by those who do not want to become its slave. Obviously, *places of corruption* and sin must not be sought out, indeed, everything must be avoided as much as possible which would in any way assist corruption. Thus, association and intercourse with immoral young men and women are to be avoided at all cost; the reading of obscene books, the viewing of vile pictures and the visiting of dubious performances must also be avoided. In short, you have to seek out good associates, through whom you will be preserved and elevated. Everything is to be recommended which hardens the body and eases the fight against immorality, such as *gymnastics, sports, swimming,* hikes and getting up *as soon as* one wakes up. *Moderation* in the consumption of food and above all of beverages. *Alcohol is to be avoided.* All this, however, is not enough, for many men, even when they follow this advice, are forced to make the painful discovery that the unchained instinct is much too strong.

Where are we to find the firmness so necessary to resistance: the energy needed for victory, if we are not to lose what is best in us, our personality? When temptation comes to us in glowing allurement, when the blazing fire of sensual pleasure shoots forth, we find that education alone does not help. Energy, vital energy—that is what we need to master our drives and to subdue the vile forces in us and outside of us. There is only one who gives us this energy: Jesus. Through his bloody expiatory death, he not only procured remission for us—so that we can find peace from the indictment of our conscience—he is also the vital energy of a new, pure life for us, through his very spirit. *Through him, even a will paralyzed in the service of sin can become firm again and be resurrected to freedom and to life,* and successfully stand the test in the difficult struggle with sin.

Let him who wants to achieve real freedom come to the *living savior, who has deprived sin of its power and has abounding energy and help for everyone. This is not Christian theory, but a fact which many sorely troubled young men have tried and experience daily.* Whenever possible, *unbosom yourself to a sincere Christian and true friend,* who can counsel and help you in your struggle. *For there will be a struggle, but a struggle which promises victory.*

And now, in conclusion, let me address this question to you personally: How are things with you, my friend, and what do you intend to do with this admonition?

Do you want to ruin yourself to please frivolous and unprincipled people? Or do you want to join forces with pure, noble men, whose company will elevate your soul and harden your will to struggle against everything vile? Do you want to be a man who, through his words, his example and his being, is a curse to himself and others, or do you want always more intensely to be a man who is a blessing to his fellowman?

Do you want, for the sake of a few moments of transitory pleasure, to ruin your body, character and soul—now and forever— or be saved, as long as there is still time?

I beg you—answer these questions honestly and have the courage to do what God has made clear to your conscience!

Choose honestly! Half-world or Over-world? Animal or Man of Spirit? Land or Strand?

In this pamphlet, youth is given the alternative: God or sexuality. To be sure, "full manhood" as well as "super-manhood" requires more than asexuality, but this is its first prerequisite. The setting up of "animal" and "man of spirit" as opposites, follows from the setting up of "sexual" and "spiritual" as opposites. It is the antithesis that always forms the basis of every theosophical moral philosophy. It has been unassailable until now because its basis, the negation of sex, was not impugned.

From early childhood on, the average youth is faced with the acute conflict between sexuality and fear, the heritage of the authoritative parental home. A pamphlet such as the one quoted above forces the youth in the direction of mysticism without, however, getting rid of the difficulties. The Catholic church circumvents this difficulty by periodically absolving the youth's masturbation in confession. By so doing, however, it entangles itself in another difficulty. The church maintains its basis in the masses by two kinds of measures: It binds the masses to itself by means of sexual anxiety, and it stresses its anti-capitalistic position. It condemns the life of the big city with its many opportunities of leading young men and women astray, for it must fight against the revolutionary sexual force that is awakened in the youth by big-city life. On the other hand, the sexual life of the masses concentrated in big cities is characterized by an acute contradiction between a pressing sexual need and minimal material and structural possibilities for gratification. Essentially, the nature of this contradiction is that the very family authority that has been destroyed by the economic crises and by sexual anguish is again defended by every available means. The recognition of such contradictions is very important, for it opens broad possibilities of assailing political reaction's ideological apparatus in its weakest spot.

Where is it that the youth is to seek the energy to subdue his genital titillations? In faith in Jesus! As a matter of fact, he does derive an enormous power against his sexuality from his faith in Jesus. What is the basis of its mechanism? The mystical experience puts him in a state of vegetative excitation, which never culminates in natural orgastic gratification. The youth's sexual drive develops in a passive homosexual direction. In terms of the drive's energy, passive homosexuality is the most effective counterpart of natural masculine sexuality, for it replaces activity and aggression by passivity and masochistic attitudes, that is to say, by precisely those attitudes that determine the mass basis of patriarchal authoritarian mysticism in the human structure. At the same time, however, this implies unquestioning loyalty, faith in authority, and ability to adapt to the institution of patriarchal compulsive marriage. In short, religious mysticism pits one sexual drive against another. It even avails itself of sexual mechanisms to achieve its goals. These nongenital sexual stimuli, which it has partially set in motion and partially brought to a peak, determine in turn the mass psychology of the followers: moralistic masochism (often with distinct physical manifestations) and passive subordination. Religion draws its power from the suppression of genital sexuality, which, on a secondary level, entails a regression along the line of passive and masochistic homosexuality. Thus, in terms of the dynamics of the drive, religion is based on genital anxiety and on the substitution of genitality by secondary impulses that are no longer natural to the adolescent. Sex-economy's task among religious-mystical adolescents is to pit the natural genital demands against the secondary (homosexual) and mystical drives. It is in complete accord with the objective line of development of social progress in the sex-economic sphere: *elimination of genital negation and affirmation of adolescent genital sexuality*.

However, the question is not exhausted solely by disclosing the mechanism by which the masses are infected. The cult of the Virgin Mary assumes an especially important position in this. Let us have a look at another typical pamphlet.

> *Veneration of the Virgin Mary and the Young Man*
> by Gerhard Kremer, Dr. of Theol.

Catholic youths who are genuinely pious will always feel a sincere affection for the ideal of the Virgin Mary. It is not as if the veneration of the Virgin Mary would detract from a warm and strong devotion to Christ. On the contrary, a true veneration of the Virgin Mary must lead to Christ and a moral code of life. We do not want to dispense with the ideal of the Virgin Mary for the moral and religious education of our youth.

Youth is the age of becoming, of external and internal struggle. Passions awaken, there is a fermenting and wrestling in man, a turbulent urging and awakening. To meet this distress, the youth must have an ideal, strong and powerful, an illuminating shining ideal, which will not be shaken by the urging and fermenting. This ideal must elevate the wavering mind and rouse the wavering heart. Its radiance will eclipse the ignoble and vile. *Such an ideal is the Virgin Mary, for it is she who embodies an all-radiant purity and beauty.* "It is said that there are women whose very presence educates us; whose very behavior banishes sordid thoughts, prevents all questionable words from crossing our lips. The Virgin Mary is the epitome of such a woman. A young knight devoted to her service is incapable of vulgarity. But if—forgetting her presence—he should nonetheless slip, the remembrance of her will cause inconsolable anguish of soul and at the same time help the noble mind to regain its authority [P. Schilgen S. J.]."

To the young man, the Virgin Mary stands out as unrivaled grace, loftiness and dignity, the like of whom is not to be found in nature, art and the world of man. Why have artists and painters devoted their skill and creativity to the Madonna again and again? It is because they perceive in her the most sublime beauty and dignity. It is a dignity and beauty which never disappoints. Here we have a mistress and queen, "to serve whom, for whom to exist, must be the highest honor for the young man. Here we have an exalted woman and bride of the spirit, to whom you can give yourself with the full power of the love which gushes from your youthful heart, without having to fear degradation and desecration."

The ideal of the Virgin Mary should inspire young men. Especially in an age which takes pleasure in darkening the radiant and dragging what is lofty into the mire, the ideal of the Virgin Mary should shine forth as a salvation and power. In this ideal the young man will perceive that there is indeed something great and elevated in beauty and chastity. Here he will find the strength to walk the steep path, even if all the others lose their best in the depths. The ideal of the Virgin Mary will fortify him who wavers, lift up and strengthen him who stumbles. Indeed, it will so overwhelm him who has fallen that he will be rehabilitated with new courage. The Virgin Mary is that radiant star which will illuminate the passion of the young individual in the dark night, that star which calls forth what is noble in him when everything appears to be shattered in him.

Look up, O young men, you who have your ideal meaning and wrestle for holy virtues, *look up to your mistress and queen.* How can a young man look up to her without being filled with holy idealism? How can he address her in Ave Maria, without feeling a keen longing for chastity? How can he sing the glorious songs about the Virgin Mary without feeling the courage to fight? How could a young man who has grasped the ideal of the Virgin Mary, deprive a woman of her chastity? How can he call her mother and queen and then acquire a taste for female indignity? *When the ideal of the Virgin Mary is taken seriously, it becomes a strong incentive for every young man, a mighty summons to chastity and manliness.* "Gazing upon her, her image locked in your heart, must you not become chaste, no matter how hard you must wrestle?"

The young man's attitude toward girls and toward women is decisive for his moral behavior.

"In former days when knights were dubbed, the knight had to give his solemn promise to protect defenseless women. That was when cathedrals were built in honor of the queen of heaven [P. Gemmel S. J.]." There is an intimate relation between courtship of the Virgin Mary and true chivalry toward the female sex. The man who is inspired by the ideal of the Virgin Mary must of necessity bear within himself that knightly dub which stems from reverent respect for female dignity and majesty. Therefore, the dubbing of the knight in the Middle Ages bound the young man to holy Minnedienst, as well as to the protection of a woman's honor. The symbols of this knighthood no longer exist: but what is worse is that, more and more, *shy reverence for woman is dying out* among the male youth and is giving way to *a frivolous and vile robber-knighthood.* Just as the knights of old in armor and arms protect and shelter frail femininity and innocence, so should and must the true man of today feel himself to be in the debt of the honor and innocence of woman. True manliness and real nobility of heart will become known to the female sex most easily and most beautifully. Lucky the young man who has girded his passion with this armor! Lucky the girl who has found the love of such a young man! *"Inflict no wrong on a girl and remember that your mother too was once a girl."*

The young man of today is the husband of tomorrow. How will the husband and man be able to protect womanhood and assure female respect, if the young man and fiancé has desecrated love and engagement! Engagement is to be a time of *undesecrated love.* How many men's fate would be happier, if the ideal of the Virgin Mary were more keenly alive in the world of youth. How much suffering and grief could be avoided, if young men would not play shameless games with the love of a girl's soul. *Hear me, O young people, let the radiant light of the ideal of the Virgin Mary illuminate your love, so that you don't trip and fall.*

The ideal of the Virgin Mary can mean a great deal to our young men. It is precisely for this reason that we have unfurled the banner of the Virgin Mary in our youth clubs and congregations. O, that our young Catholic men would rally around this banner!

—Katholisches Kirchenblatt, No. 18, May 3, 1931

The cult of the Virgin Mary is drawn upon very successfully as a means of inculcating chastity. Again we must inquire into the psychological mechanism that is capable of assuring the success of these intentions. It is a problem of the masses of young men and women who are subjected to this influence. It is chiefly a matter of overpowering genital drives. Just as the Jesus cult mobilizes passive homosexual forces against the genitals, the cult of the Virgin Mary also mobilizes sexual forces, this time from the heterosexual sphere itself. "Inflict no wrong on a girl and remember that your mother too was once a girl." Thus, in the emotional life of Christian youths, the Mother of God assumes the role of one's own mother, and the Christian youth showers upon her all the love that he had for his own mother at one time, that very ardent love of his first genital desires. But the *incest prohibition* cleaves his genital desires into an intense longing for orgasm on the one hand and asexual tenderness on the other hand. The intense longing for orgasm has to be repressed, and its energy intensifies one's tender strivings and molds them into an almost indissoluble tie to the mystical experience. This intense longing offers violent resistance, not only to the incestuous desire, but to *every* natural genital relationship with a woman. The same vital energy and enormous love that a healthy young man puts forth in an orgastic experience with his loved one is used by the mystical man to support the mystical cult of the Virgin Mary, *after* genital sensuality has been suppressed. This is the source from which mysticism draws its forces. Being *unsatisfied* forces, they should not be underestimated. They make intelligible the age-old power of mysticism over man and the inhibitions that operate against the responsibility of the masses.

In this regard it is not a matter of the veneration of the Virgin Mary or of any other idol. It is a matter of *producing a mystical structure in the masses* in every new generation. But mysticism is nothing other than unconscious longing for orgasm (cosmic plasmatic sensations). The orgastically potent, healthy man is capable of great veneration of historical figures. But there is no correlation between his appreciation of man's primordial history and his sexual happiness. He does not have to become mystical, reactionary, or a slave to metaphysics to appreciate historical phenomena. Healthy adolescent sexuality would not necessarily have to stifle a veneration for the Jesus legend. The Old and the New Testament can be appreciated as stupendous achievements of the human mind, but this appreciation should not be used to suppress sexuality. My medical experience has taught me that adolescents who are sexually sick have an unhealthy appreciation of the legend of Jesus.

HEALTHY AND NEUROTIC SELF-CONFIDENCE

For the sexually mature young man who has a sex-economic structure, the orgastic experience with a woman constitutes a gratifying bond; it elevates the partner and effaces any tendency to degrade the woman who has shared the experience. In the case of orgastic impotence, only the psychic forces of defense can come into play, nausea and disgust at genital sensuality. These defense forces draw their energy from several sources. To begin with, the defensive force is at least as strong as the genital yearning that is being resisted. And the fact that it has not been satisfied has only intensified it, nor does it make the least difference that it is unconscious. In addition, the actual brutalization of sexuality in modern man offers some justification for the disgust at sexual intercourse. This *brutalized* sexuality becomes the prototype of sexuality in general. Thus, compulsive morality produces precisely that to which it later appeals to justify its existence ("sexuality is asocial"). A third emotional source of the defense forces is the sadistic conception of sexuality that the children of all patriarchal cultural circles acquire in early childhood. Since every inhibition of genital gratification intensifies the sadistic impulse, the entire sexual structure becomes sadistic. Since, moreover, genital claims are replaced by anal claims, the reactionary sexual slogan that a woman is degraded by sexual intercourse strikes a chord in the adolescent structure. In short, it is owing to the already existing perversity in the adolescent structure that the slogan can be effective. It is from his own per-

sonal experience that the adolescent has developed a sadistic conception of sexual intercourse. Thus, here too we find a confirmation
of the fact that man's compulsive moralistic defense forces constitute the basis of political reaction's power. Ever more sharply, the
relation between mystical sentiments and sexual "morality" is
brought into focus. Regardless of the content of the mystical experience, it is essentially the negation of genital strivings. It is essentially
sexual defense, and it takes place with the help of nongenital sexual
excitations. The difference between the sexual response and the
mystical response is that the latter does not allow the perception of
sexual excitation and precludes orgastic *release*, even in cases of so-
called religious ecstasy.

Perception of sexual desire excluded and orgasm precluded,
mystical excitation is forced to effect a permanent change in the biopsychic apparatus. The sexual act itself is experienced as something
degrading. There is never a complete natural experience. The ward-
ing off of orgastic desire forces the ego to form compulsive conceptions of "purity" and "perfection." Healthy sensuousness and the
ability to gratify one's desires produces natural self-confidence. The
defensive formations in the mystical man result in a pathological
self-confidence that is rotten at the core. Just as the self-confidence
of the nationalist, the self-confidence of the mystical man is drawn
from the defensive attitudes. Even on the surface, however, the self-
confidence of the mystical man differs from the self-confidence that
derives from natural genital gratification. The former is exaggerated,
lacks naturalness in behavior, and is characterized by feelings of
sexual inferiority. This explains why the man who has been inculcated with mystical or nationalistic "ethics" is so accessible to
political reactionary catchwords, such as *honor, purity*, etc. He is
continually forced to remind himself to be honorable and pure. The
genital character is spontaneously pure and honorable—he does not
have to be constantly reminded.

VIII

Some Questions of Sex-Political Practice

Reactionary academic research postulates a "separation between that which is and that which should be," between "cognition and execution." Therefore, it imagines itself to be "nonpolitical," to be divorced from politics. Logic, indeed, contends that what should be, can never be deduced from what is. We recognize a restriction here, the purpose of which is to enable the academician to devote himself to research, without obligating himself to draw the consequences that are inherent in every serious scientific insight. Such consequences are always progressive, very often revolutionary. For us, the development of theoretical views is dictated by the necessities of vital life, by the need to solve *practical* problems. Our theoretical views must lead to new, better, more suitable action and the mastering of practical tasks. Our theory is of value only insofar as it is confirmed in and by practice. Everything else, we leave to the intellectual jugglers, to the guardians of the hierarchy of "values." First of all, we have to correct the basic error of theology, which stagnates in academic expositions and therefore cannot show us a rational way out. We concur with the opinion of many researchers that all forms of religious mysticism mean mental darkness and narrow-mindedness. We know that over the centuries man's religiousness has become an instrument of power. In this, too, we are in agreement with some academic researchers. We differ from them only in terms of our serious determination to combat mysticism and superstition successfully, and to convert our knowledge into hard practice. In the struggle between natural science and mysticism, we wonder whether natural science has exhausted all the possibilities at its disposal. We have to answer in the negative. Mysticism, on the other hand, keeps the masses of the people blindly imprisoned. Yet, before we continue, let us briefly summarize the history of this struggle.

THE STRUGGLE AGAINST MYSTICISM UNTIL NOW

Four general phases can be distinguished in the development of mysticism and the struggle against it. The first phase is character-ized by a complete lack of natural scientific views; animistic views rule in their place. Fearing that which appears incomprehensible, the primitive has a strong urge to find an explanation for natural phenomena. On the one hand he must give his life a sense of security, and on the other hand he seeks protection against the overpowering forces of nature. He acquires the one as well as the other (subjectively, not objectively) through mysticism, supersti-tion, and animistic views of natural processes, his inner and psychic processes included. He believes, for example, that he can increase the fertility of the soil by erecting phallic sculptures or that he can get rid of a period of drought by urinating. The principal features of this situation remain unchanged among all peoples of the earth, until at the close of the Middle Ages rudimentary efforts toward a scientific comprehension of nature, efforts prompted by several technical discoveries, assume a serious character. These efforts con-stitute more and more of a threat to mysticism. In the process of the great bourgeois revolution, an intense struggle breaks out against religion and for enlightenment. The period approaches in which science would be able to replace mysticism's explanation of nature, and technology would be able to assume a much more significant role in dealing with the human needs for protection (second phase). But now that the revolutionaries are in power, they are no longer revolutionary. They make an about-face and create a contradiction in the cultural process. On the one hand they promote scientific research with every available means, because it helps economic development. On the other hand, however, they encourage mysticism and turn it into the most powerful instrument for the purpose of suppressing millions of wage earners (third phase). This contradiction finds tragicomic expression in scientific films such as *Nature and Love*, in which each part carries two headings. The first heading reads something like this: "The earth was developed over millions of years as a result of cosmic mechanical and chemical processes." Below it, we read something like this: "On the first day God created Heaven and Earth." And highly respected scholars, astronomers, and chemists sit in the stalls and quietly look at this ironic union, convinced that "religion too has its good side." Could the separation between theory and practice be depicted more graphically! The methodical withholding of scientific findings from the masses of the population, and "monkey trials" such as we find in the United States, encourage humility, lack of discrimination, voluntary renunciation and hope for happiness in the Beyond, belief in authority, recognition of the sacredness of asceticism, and the unimpeachableness of the authoritarian family. The workers and the bourgeois elements that are intimately connected with them constitute the freethinkers' movement, which the liberal bourgeoisie allows to go its own way as long as it does not transgress certain limits. Whereas the resources of the freethinkers are confined to intellectual arguments, the church enjoys the help of the state power-apparatus and plays upon the strongest emotional forces in the psychology of the masses, sexual anxiety, and sexual repression. This great power in the emotional sphere is not countered by a commensurate emotional force. Insofar as the freethinkers employ sex policies at all, they are either intellectualized or confined to questions of population politics. At best they include the demand for economic equality for women. This, however, cannot have any mass effect on the powers of mysticism, for in most women the will to economic independence is unconsciously checked by the fear of

172

sexual responsibility, which goes hand in hand with economic independence.

The difficulties involved in overcoming these emotional factors force the revolutionary freethinkers' movement to push the so-called philosophic questions into the background, for one often achieves the opposite of what one intends in this regard. Since mysticism cannot be countered by a commensurate emotional power, this point of view is certainly justified.

The Russian Revolution raises the struggle against religion to an unprecedentedly high level (fourth phase).[1] The power apparatus is no longer in the hands of the church and big business, but in the hands of the executive committees of the Soviets. The anti-religious movement obtains a firm foundation, the reorganization of the economy on a collective basis. For the first time it becomes possible to replace religion with natural science on a mass scale, to replace the feeling of protection offered by superstition with an ever growing technology, to destroy mysticism itself with sociological elucidation of the functions of mysticism. Essentially, there are three ways in which the fight against religion takes place in the USSR: by the elimination of the economic basis, i.e., in a direct economic way; by anti-religious propaganda, i.e., in a direct ideological way; and by the raising of the cultural level of the masses, i.e., in an indirect ideological way.

The enormous importance of the power apparatus of the church can be seen from some statistics, which shed light upon the

---

[1] Literature on the religious question in the Soviet Union. "Schule und Kirche in Sowjetrussland," *Süddeutsche Arbeiterzeitung* of Sept. 9, 1927; "Kirche und Staat in der Sowjetrepublik" by Stepanow, *Jhrb. f. P. u. W.* 23–24; "Kirche und Staat" by Jaroslawski, ibid., 1925–26; "Die Freidenkerbewegung in Russland," by Muzak, *Der Freidenker*, No. 6; "Das Verhältnis von Kirche und Staat im neuen Russland" by Jakoby Weimar, *Neue Bahnen*, 1928; "Uber die Religion" by Lenin, *Bd IV der kleinen Lenin-Bibl.*; "Die Kulturrevolution in der Sowjetunion" by A. Elgers, *Verlagsanstalt proletarischer Freidenker*, 1931; "Die sozialistische Kulturrevolution im 5-Jahresplan" by A. Kurella, *Internationaler Arbeiterverlag*; "Antireligiöse Propaganda im Dorf" by Deodorow; "Sozialistischer Aufbau des Dorfes und die Religion" by Wogan.

conditions that existed in old Russia. In 1905 the Russian church possessed 2,611,000 desjatines of land, i.e., about 2 million hectares. In 1903, 908 houses belonged to the parish churches in Moscow; 146 belonged to the monasteries. The annual income of the metropolitans amounted to 84,000 rubles in Kiev; 259,000 rubles in Petersburg; 81,000 rubles in Moscow; 307,000 rubles in Nishni-Novgorod. The earnings in kind and fees received for every individual religious performance cannot even be estimated. Two hundred thousand persons were in the service of the church, at the expense of mass taxation. The Troitskaya Lavra monastery, which is visited by an average of a hundred thousand pilgrims annually, possesses sacred vessels valued at some 650 million rubles.

Backed by its economic power, the church was able to exercise considerable ideologic influence. Needless to say, all schools were denominational and subject to the control and domination of the priesthood. The first article of the constitution of czarist Russia stated: "The sovereign of all Russians is an autocratic and absolute monarch and God Himself enjoins voluntary subordination to his supreme power." We already know what "God" represents, and on which infantile feelings in the human structure such claims to power can rest. Hitler refashioned the church in Germany in precisely the same way. He extended its absolute power and granted it the pernicious right to make the school children's emotions ripe for the reception of reactionary ideologies. The task of raising "moral standards" holds top priority for Hitler, who executes the will of our most holy God. Let us return to old Russia.

In the theological seminaries and academies there were special academic chairs for the fight against the revolutionary movement. On January 9, 1905, a clerical proclamation appeared in which the rebelling workers were accused of having been bribed by the Japanese. The February Revolution of 1917 brought about only minor changes. All churches were put on an equal footing, but the long-awaited separation of church and state failed to materialize. The large landowner Prince Lvov became head of the church administration. At a church council in October of 1917 the Bolsheviks were excommunicated; the patriarch Tikhon declared war on them.

On January 23, 1918, the Soviet government issued the following decree:

> With respect to religion, the Russian Communist Party is not content to accept the already decreed separation of the church from the state and the school. In short, it is not content with measures which also appear in the programs of bourgeois democracies, which have never been able to carry them through to the end anywhere in the world owing to the numerous factual connections between capital and religious propaganda.

> It is the conviction of the Russian Communist Party that only the realization of methodicalness and consciousness in the entire social and economic life of the masses will effect the complete withering away of religious prejudices. The Party is working toward a complete elimination of all the connections between the exploiting classes and the organization of religious propaganda. It has organized a comprehensive scientific propaganda of an instructive and anti-religious nature. This propaganda contributes in a factual way toward the liberation of the working masses from religious prejudices. However, every effort must be made not to offend the feelings of the faithful, for this would only lead to an intensification of religious fanaticism.

> It follows from this that local ordinances which would restrict the freedom of conscience or create privileges for members of a particular confession on the territory of the Republic are prohibited [paragraph 2 of the decree].

> *Every citizen can profess whichever religion he chooses or no religion whatever.* All previous curtailments of rights in this regard are annulled.

> Any reference to a citizen's religious denomination or absence of denomination is to be removed from all official documents [paragraph 3 of the decree].

> The activities of all public and other official and social institutions will take place without any religious customs and ceremonies [paragraph 4].

> The free exercise of religious customs is guaranteed, provided

175

they do not entail any disturbance of the public order and do not infringe upon the rights of citizens of the Soviet Union. In such cases where disturbances occur or rights are infringed upon, the local authorities are entitled to take all measures necessary to restore peace and order.

No one has the right to evade his civic obligations on the basis of his religious views.

Exceptions to this are allowed only on the basis of a decision of the people's court in each individual case, and on condition that one civic duty is replaced by another [paragraph 6].

The religious oath is abolished. If need be, a formal declaration can be made [paragraph 7].

Civil status records will be kept solely by civil authorities, namely, by the registration office for marriages and births [paragraph 8].

The school is separated from the church.

The propagation of religious confession is prohibited at all state and public as well as private institutions of learning which follow a curriculum of general education [paragraph 9].

All clerical and religious societies are subject to the general regulations which govern private societies and associations, and they shall not enjoy any privileges or subsidies from the state or an autonomous local self-administrative organ [paragraph 10].

The exaction of taxes from members for the benefit of clerical or religious societies is prohibited [paragraph 11].

Clerical and religious societies have no private property rights, nor do they have the rights of a corporate body [paragraph 12].

All property of clerical and religious societies in Russia is declared to be the property of the people.

Edifices and objects necessary for divine services are put at the disposal of the various religious societies free of charge on the basis of special regulations of the local and central authorities [paragraph 13].

Priests, monks and nuns enjoy neither an active nor a passive right to vote because they do not perform productive work.

As early as December 18, 1917, the keeping of the civil status records was handed over to the Soviet authorities. In the Commissariat for Justice, a liquidation department was established, which began with the liquidation of church possessions. In the Troitski Lavra monastery, for example, an academy for the electro-technical division of the Red army and a training school for teachers were established. Workers' pools and communes were set up on the grounds of the monastery. The churches themselves were gradually converted into workers' clubs and reading rooms. The anti-religious propaganda began with the exposure of the clerical hierarchy's direct deception of the people. The holy fountain in the Sergius Church turned out to be a simple pump. The brow of many a saint proved to be nothing other than a cleverly arranged piece of leather. Permission to kiss a saint's brow had to be bought. The effect of this exposure in the presence of masses of people was prompt and radical. It goes without saying that the godless propaganda flooded city and country with millions of elucidative brochures and newspapers. The establishment of anti-religious natural science museums made it possible to contrast the scientific and superstitious views of the world.

Notwithstanding all this, I was told in Moscow in 1929 that the only organized and firmly rooted counterrevolutionary groups were the religious sects. *The relationship of the religious sects to the sexual life of the sect members,* as well as to the sexual structure of the society as a whole, was grievously neglected in the Soviet Union, both theoretically and practically. This neglect had serious consequences.

Thus, the assertion that the church in Soviet Russia was "annihilated" is incorrect. One was free to profess and practice the religion of one's choice. It was only its social and economic hegemony that the church lost. It was no longer possible for it to force people outside its circle of adherents to believe in God. Science and atheism had finally succeeded in acquiring the same social rights as mysticism. No clerical hierarchy could any longer decide that a natural scientist should be exiled. That is all. But the church was not satisfied. Later, when the sexual revolution disintegrated (from 1934 on), it won masses of people back into its fold.

SEXUAL HAPPINESS CONTRA MYSTICISM

The undermining of the church's power over and above its immediate sphere of influence only meant that the church's worst encroachments were done away with. This measure has no effect whatever on its ideological power, which rests upon the sympathetic feelings and superstitious structure of the average individual in the masses. For this reason the Soviets began to exercise scientific influence. However, natural scientific enlightenment and the unmasking of religion merely place an intellectual, though very powerful, force alongside religious feelings and leave the rest to the struggle between man's intellect and mystical sentiments. This struggle succeeds in favor of science only in men and women who have already begun to mature on a different basis. That it can fail even in such persons is shown by the not infrequent cases in which clear-cut materialists yield to their religious sentiments in this or that form, i.e., are compelled to pray. From this a clever advocate of religion will seek to win an argument in his favor; he will assert that this is proof of the everlastingness and ineradicableness of religious feeling. He is nonetheless in the wrong, for this only proves that, while the power of the intellect is pitted against religious feelings, the source of religious feelings is not touched. One could rightfully conclude that the foundation of mystical sentiments would be completely undermined if the social hegemony of the church were not only eliminated and an intellectual force were pitted against them but over and above this the feelings that nourish mystical sentiments were made conscious and given free rein. Clinical experience shows incontestably that religious sentiments result from inhibited sexuality, that the source of mystical excitation is to be sought in inhibited sexual excitation. The inescapable conclusion of all this is that a *clear sexual consciousness* and a *natural regulation of sexual life must foredoom every form of mysticism*; that, in other words, *natural sexuality is the arch enemy of mystical religion*. By carrying on an anti-sexual fight wherever it can, making it the core of its dogmas and putting it in the foreground of its mass propaganda, the church only attests to the correctness of this interpretation.

To begin with, I am only attempting to reduce very complicated facts to their simplest formula when I say that *sexual consciousness is the end of mysticism.* We will soon see that, as simple as this formula is, its actual basis and the conditions for its practical implementation are extremely complicated, and that we shall need the entire scientific apparatus at our disposal and the deepest conviction of the necessity of carrying out an inexorable fight against mysticism, if we are to counter successfully the cunning apparatus of superstition. But the final result will one day repay all our efforts.

To form an accurate estimation of the difficulties to be encountered in the practical implementation of this simple formula, a number of fundamental facts in the psychic structure of people who have been subjected to a sexually repressive upbringing have to be thoroughly comprehended. When a number of cultural organizations in the western part of Germany, which is predominantly Catholic, rejected the sex-economic fight against mystical contagion because they had allegedly not had any success with it, this did not invalidate my contention, but only testified to the timidity, fear of sexuality, and sex-economic inexperience of those who undertook the fight. More than anything else it testified to a lack of patience and willingness to adapt to the complicated state of affairs, to understand and master it. If I were to tell a Christian woman who is sexually frustrated that her suffering is of a sexual nature and that only through sexual happiness can her psychic suffering be relieved, she would be right in throwing me out. We are faced with two difficulties: (1) Every individual bears contradictions in himself, which have to be individually understood; and (2) the practical aspects of the problem differ from locality to locality and country to country and therefore have to be solved in a different way. But surely, the more extensive our sex-economic experience becomes, the more easily we will be able to deal with the obstacles. However, it is solely through practice that these difficulties can be eliminated. Before any headway can be made, we must agree on the correctness of our basic formula, and we must comprehend the true nature of the difficulties. In view of the fact that mysticism has ruled humanity for thousands of years, the least it can ask of novices like us is that we do not underestimate it and that we grasp it correctly. It will be up to us to prove ourselves wiser, more subtle, and more knowledgeable than its advocates.

THE INDIVIDUAL UPROOTING OF THE RELIGIOUS FEELING

Guidelines for mass mental hygiene can be obtained from the comprehension of the bio-psychic anchoring of mysticism. The changes that take place in the mystical man in the course of character-analytic treatment are of decisive importance. The insights we gain from character-analytic treatment cannot be applied directly to the masses, but they reveal the contradictions, forces, and counterforces in the average individual.

I have already described how mystical ideas and feelings become anchored in the human structure. Let us now attempt to trace the principal features in the process of the *uprooting* of mysticism.

As might be expected, the mystical attitude operates as a powerful resistance to the uncovering of unconscious psychic life, especially to repressed genitality. It is significant that mysticism tends to ward off natural genital impulses, especially childhood masturbation, more so than it tends to ward off pregenital infantile impulses. The patient clings to his ascetic, moralistic, and mystical views and sharpens the philosophically unbridgeable antithesis between "the moral element" and "the animal element" in man, i.e., natural sexuality. He defends himself against his genital sexuality with the help of moralistic deprecation. He accuses those around him of not having an understanding for "spiritual values" and of being "crude, vulgar, and materialistic." In short, to one who knows the argumentation of the mystics and fascists in political discussions, and of the characterologists and "scholars" in natural scientific discussions, all this sounds all too familiar. It is one and the same thing. Characteristically, the fear of God and the moralistic defense are immediately strengthened when one succeeds in loosening an element of sexual repression. If one succeeds in getting rid of the childhood fear of masturbation and as a result thereof genitality demands gratification, then intellectual insight and sexual gratification are wont to prevail. To the same extent to which the fear of sexuality or the fear of the old parental sexual prohibition disappears, mystical sentiments also vanish. What has taken place? Prior to this the patient had made use of mysticism to hold his sexual desires in suppression. His ego was too deeply steeped in fear, his own sexuality too deeply estranged, to enable him to master and to regulate the powerful natural forces. On the contrary, the more he resisted his sexuality, the more imperative his desires became. Hence, his moralistic and mystical inhibitions had to be applied more rigidly. In the course of treatment the ego was strengthened and the infantile dependencies on parents and teachers were loosened. The patient recognized the naturalness of genitality and learned to distinguish between what was infantile and no longer usable in the instincts and what was suited to the demands of life. The Christian youth will soon realize that his intensive exhibitionistic and perverse inclinations refer partly to a regression to early infantile forms of sexuality and partly to an *inhibition* of genital sexuality. He will also realize that his desires for union with a woman are wholly in keeping with his age and his nature, that indeed it is necessary to gratify them. From now on he no longer has need of the support offered by the belief in an all-powerful God, nor does he have need of moralistic inhibition. He becomes master of his own house and learns to regulate his own sexual economy. Character-analysis liberates the patient from the infantile and slavish dependency upon the authority of the father and father surrogates. The strengthening of the ego dissolves the infantile attachment to God, which is a continuation of the infantile attachment to the father. These attachments lose their force. If vegetotherapy subsequently enables the patient to take up a satisfying love life, then mysticism loses its last hold. The case of clerics is especially difficult, for a convincing continuation of their profession, whose physical consequences they have felt on their own body, has become impossible. The only course open to many of them is to replace their priesthood with religious research or teaching.

It is only the analyst who does not understand the genital disturbance of his patients who will not be able to confirm these processes in the mystical man. Nor, however, will they be confirmed by the well-known psychoanalyst and pastor who is of the opinion that one "may sink the plummet of psychoanalysis into the unconscious only so far as ethics permit." We want to have as little to do with such "nonpolitical," "objective" science as with that science that not only goes all out in its fight against the revolutionary consequences of sex-economy as "politics," but even advises mothers to fight the erections of small boys by teaching them exercises in holding their breath. In such cases the problem lies in the process that allows the physician's conscience to accept this line of reasoning and to become a pastor, without however rehabilitating him in the eyes of political reaction. He acts very much as the German SPD members of parliament, who sang the German national anthem at the last sitting of parliament enthusiastically and pleadingly, and still ended up in concentration camps as "Socialists."

We do not discuss the existence or nonexistence of God—we merely eliminate the sexual repressions and dissolve the infantile ties to the parents. The destruction of mysticism is not at all a part of the therapeutic intention. It is merely treated as every other psychic fact that functions as a support of sexual repression and saps one's natural energies. Thus, the sex-economic process does not consist of a contrasting of the mystical view of life with the "materialistic," "anti-religious" view. This is intentionally avoided, for it would not effect any change whatever in the biopathic structure. The process consists rather in the unmasking of the mystical attitude as an anti-sexual force; the energy that nourishes it is utilized for other purposes. The man whose ideology is moralistic to an exaggerated degree, while perverse, lascivious, and neurotic in reality, is freed of this contradiction. Along with his moralism, he also loses the antisocial character and immorality of his sexuality in the sex-economic sense of the words. *Inadequate moralistic and mystical inhibition is replaced by sex-economic regulation of sexual needs.*

From its point of view, therefore, mysticism is right when, to preserve and reproduce itself in man, it takes such a strong stand against sexuality. It merely errs in one of its premises and in its most important justification: *It is its "morality" that produces that sensuality, the moral mastery of which it feels itself called upon to accomplish. It is the abolition of this "morality" that is the precondition of the abolition of immorality, which it seeks to eliminate in vain.* This is the harsh tragedy of every form of morality and mysticism. The uncovering of the sex-economic processes, which nourish religious mysticism, will lead sooner or later to its practical elimination, no matter how often the mystics run for tar and feathers.

Sexual consciousness and mystical sentiments cannot coexist. Natural sexuality and mystical sentiments are the same in terms of their energy, so long as the former is repressed and can be easily transformed into mystical excitation.

These sex-economic facts necessarily yield a number of consequences for mass mental hygiene. These we will set forth after we have answered some obvious objections.

THE PRACTICE OF SEX-ECONOMY AND OBJECTIONS TO IT

In sex-economic practice one is used to seeing the political economist appear as the opponent of the so-called "overemphasis and exaggeration of the sexual question." At the slightest difficulty, which is to be expected in this new area, he immediately tries to dismiss the whole field. To begin with, these opponents of sex-economy must be told that their jealousy is unfounded. Sex-economic cultural work does not constitute an encroachment upon their own domain of economy or a restriction of their sphere of work. It aims at a comprehension of an extremely important area of the cultural process, an area that has been totally neglected until now. The sex-economic fight is a part of the total fight of those who are exploited and suppressed against those who exploit and suppress. At present, to decide just how important this fight is and what place it assumes within the workers' movement would be to engage in scholastic hair-splitting. In discussing the role and importance of sex-economy, instead of basing one's appraisal on what has been accomplished in a practical way, one has been inclined to set up a rivalry between economic and sexual policies. We must not waste any time with such discussions. If all the experts of the various branches of knowledge would do their utmost to subdue dictatorial forms, if each of them would completely master his own field, then all discussions about rank and role would be superfluous. The social importance of the individual branches would follow of itself. It is merely important to stick to the basic conception, namely that the economic form also determines the sexual form and that the sexual form cannot be changed unless the economic and social forms are changed.

There are many slogans that stick fast like lice; they can be removed only by the use of radical means. One often meets with the dull objection that sex-economy is "individualistic" and therefore of no use socially. To be sure, the method that is used to obtain knowledge about sex-economy is "individualistic." But doesn't social suppression of sexuality concern all the members of our society? *Isn't sexual distress a collective thing?* Is the social fight against tuberculosis individualistic because the study of tuberculosis is carried out on individual patients? The revolutionary movement has always committed the grave error of regarding sexuality as a "private matter." It is not a private matter for political reaction, which always rides on two tracks at the same time: on that of *economic policies* and that of *"moral renewal."* Until now, the freedom movement has traveled on one track only. What is needed, therefore, is to master the sexual question on a social scale, to *transform* the shadowy side of personal life into social mental hygiene, to make the sexual question a part of the total campaign, instead of

confining oneself to the question of population politics. The freedom movement has always made the mistake of mechanically
transferring the political slogans from the area of trade-unionism
and political struggle to all the other areas of social life, instead *of
developing a view for each area of human life and activity appropriate to that area and that area alone.* Among other things it was this
mistake that contributed to its defeat. Thus, in 1932 leading
functionaries of the German sex-political organization wanted to
exclude the sexual question and "to mobilize" the masses in the
sexual area with the slogan "against hunger and cold." They contrasted the sexual question with the "social question," as if the
sexual question were not a part of the whole complex of social
questions!

The population politics to which sexual reform restricts itself do
not in the strict sense of the word have a sex-political nature. They
are not concerned with the regulation of sexual needs, but only with
the increase of the population, to which naturally the sexual act is
related. Apart from this, however, it has nothing to do with sexuality in the social and biologic sense. Nor do the masses have the
slightest interest in questions of population politics; they don't care
a hoot about them. The abortion law is of interest to them, not for
political reasons, but because of the *personal distress* that hinges
upon it. Insofar as the abortion law causes distress, death, and grief,
it is a question of general social politics. Not until, and only when,
it is clearly and explicitly understood that people violate the law
because they have to *have intercourse even if they don't want to
have children* will the question of abortion become a sex-political
question. This has passed unnoticed until now, despite the fact
that it is emotionally the *most important* point of the question.
If a reactionary social politician should take it upon himself to
tell the people: "You complain that the abortion law demands
so many sacrifices in health and human life! You don't *have*
to have sexual intercourse," then there would be an end to the
approach that is concerned solely with population politics. *The
question is meaningful only when one clearly and openly speaks up*

for the necessity of a satisfactory sex life. To give prominence to the sexual needs that continually beset the men and women of all social classes would have far more relevance than to enumerate the deaths caused by the abortion law. Everyone has a personal interest in sexual needs, but an interest in the abortion law presupposes a certain level of social conscience and fellow-feeling, which cannot always be assumed in modern man. In propaganda about the provision of food, it is personal need and not unrelated social and political facts that are appealed to. The same should hold true for propaganda in the sex-economic field. In short, the sexual question is a question that applies to all of us, a top-priority question of social life and mass mental hygiene.

The objection that could be raised by a psychoanalyst is more serious. His objection might run something like this: It is altogether utopian to suppose that man's *sexual misery* could be used "politically" in the same way that his material distress is used. In psychoanalytic treatment it takes months and years of arduous work to make a patient conscious of his sexual desires. The moralistic inhibitions are just as deeply anchored as the sexual demands, and they have the upper hand. How do you propose to overcome sexual repression in the masses in view of the fact that a technique *comparable* to the one used in *individual analysis* does not exist? This objection has to be taken seriously. In the beginning, if I had allowed such objections to deter me from engaging in practical sex-economic work among the masses and gathering experience, then I too would have to agree with those who push aside sex-economy as an individualistic question and wait for the coming of a second Jesus to solve it. A very close associate once told me that my attempts constituted only a superficial elucidation, which failed to grasp the deeply-rooted sex-repressive forces. If a psychiatrist could make such an accusation, it might prove of value to discuss the difficulty in more detail. In the beginning of my work, I would not have known an answer to this question. However, practical experience revealed it.

To begin with, we have to make it clear that in sex-economic mass hygiene, we are faced with a task different from the one we are faced with in individual vegetotherapeutic treatment. In the latter we have to eliminate repression and to restore biologic health. This is not the task of sex-economic sociology; here it is a matter of *making conscious* the *contradiction* and suffering in subjugated man. One knows that one is moralistic; but that one has a sexual drive that has to be gratified is either not conscious or one's consciousness of it is so weak that it cannot operate properly. Here the additional objection could be raised that the making conscious of sexual needs also entails individual analytic work. Again practical experience gives the answer. When I talk to a sexually inhibited woman in my office about her sexual needs, I am confronted with her entire moralistic apparatus. It is difficult for me to get through to her and to convince her of anything. If, however, the same woman is exposed to a *mass* atmosphere, is present, for instance, at a rally at which sexual needs are discussed clearly and openly in medical and social terms, then she doesn't feel herself to be alone. After all, the others are also listening to "forbidden things." Her individual moralistic inhibition is offset by a *collective atmosphere of sexual affirmation*, a new sex-economic morality, which can paralyze (not eliminate!) her sexual negation because she herself has had similar thoughts when she was alone. Secretly, she herself has mourned her lost joy of life or yearned for sexual happiness. The sexual need is given confidence by the mass situation; it assumes a socially accepted status. When the subject is broached correctly, the sexual demand proves to have far more appeal than the demand for asceticism and renunciation; it is more human, more closely related to the personality, unreservedly affirmed by everyone. Thus, it is not a question of helping, but of *making suppression conscious, of dragging the fight between sexuality and mysticism into the light of consciousness, of bringing it to a head under the pressure of a mass ideology and translating it into social action.* At this point the objection might be raised that this would be a diabolical attempt, for it would precipitate people into a state of dire distress, would really make them sick if they were not already sick, without being able to help them. One is reminded of Pallenberg's witty saying in *Der brave Sunder:* "What a poor wretch man is. Fortunately he doesn't know it. If he did, what a poor wretch he'd be!" The answer is that political reaction and mysticism are infinitely more diabolical. Basically speaking, of course, the same objection applies to the distress of hunger. The Indian or Chinese coolie who bears the burden of his fate unconsciously, resigned and unquestioning, suffers less than the coolie who is aware of the hideous order of things, who, in short, consciously rebels against slavery. Who would try to make us believe that the real cause of his suffering should be concealed from the coolie for humanitarian reasons? Only a mystic, the coolie's fascist employer or some Chinese professor for social hygiene would try to make us believe such nonsense. This "humanity" is the perpetuation of inhumanity and its simultaneous concealment. Our "inhumanity" is the fight for that about which the good and the righteous prattle so much, and then allow themselves to be immediately snared in the trap of fascist reaction. Hence, we admit: Consistent sex-economic work gives a tongue to silent suffering and creates new contradictions while intensifying the contradictions that exist already. It puts man in a position where he is no longer able to tolerate his situation. At the same time, however, it provides a means of liberation, namely the possibility of a fight against the social causes of suffering. It is true that sex-economic work touches the most sensitive, most exciting, most personal area of human life. *But isn't it also true that the mystical contagion of the masses does the same thing?* What is important is the purpose that is served by the one and the purpose that is served by the other. He who has once seen the intense eyes and faces at sex-economic assemblies; he who has heard and has had to answer the hundreds of questions relating to the most personal sphere of human existence—that man has also arrived at the unshakable conviction that social dynamite lies buried here, dynamite capable of bringing this self-destructive world to its senses. However, if this work is to be carried out by revolutionaries who vie with the church in the asseveration and advocacy of moralistic mysticism, who view the answering of the sexual question as being beneath the "dignity of revolutionary ideology," who dismiss childhood masturbation as a "bourgeois invention," who, in short—for all their "Leninism" and "Marxism"—are reactionary in an important corner of their personalities, then it would be easy to offer proof that my experiences cannot be right. For in the hands of such revolutionaries, the masses would immediately react negatively toward sex.

We must still persist for awhile in our discussion of the role of moralistic resistance which we encounter in our work. I stated that the individual moralistic inhibition, which, in contrast to sexual demands, is reinforced by the entire sex-negating atmosphere of authoritarian society, can be made ineffective by the creation of a counter sex-affirmative ideology. People could become receptive to sex-economic knowledge and thereby be made immune to the influence of mysticism and reactionary forces. It is clear that such an atmosphere of sexual affirmation can be created only by a powerful international sex-economic organization. It was impossible to convince the leaders of political parties that this was one of their main tasks. In the meantime, politics as such has been exposed as reactionary irrationalism. We can no longer rely on any political party. The task lies within the framework of natural work-democratic development.

Until now we have mentioned only the quiet and mute needs of the individuals in the masses, those needs upon which we could base our work. However, they would not be enough. From the turn of the century until World War I these needs and their suppression were also present, yet at that time a sex-economic movement would have had little prospect of success. Since then a number of objective social preconditions for sex-economic work have come into being. These must be thoroughly known if one wants to set to work correctly. The very fact that so many sex-economic groups having various forms and directions came into being in Germany between 1931–33 indicates that a new social view is taking hold in the social process. One of the most important social preconditions of social sex-economy was the creation of gigantic industries employing armies of workers and officials. The two central pillars of the moralistic and anti-sexual atmosphere, the small enterprise and the family, were shaken. World War II accelerated this process appreciably. The women and girls working in factories developed freer conceptions of sexual life than they would have developed if they had remained confined to the authoritarian households of their parents. Since the industrial workers were accessible to sexual affirmation at all times, the disintegration process of authoritarian moralism began to spread among the lower middle classes also. If the lower middle-class youth of today is compared with the lower middle-class youth of 1910, it will be readily seen that the gap between real sexuality and the social ideology still prevailing has become wide and unbridgeable. The ideal of an ascetic girl has become a thing of shame, and certainly the same holds true for the ideal of the sexually weak, ascetic man. Even among the lower middle class, more open attitudes toward compulsive faithfulness in marriage have begun to appear more and more frequently. The mode of production of big industry made it possible for the contradiction of reactionary sexual policies to come out into the open. There can no longer be any talk of a return to the old consonance between real life and ascetic ideology, as was still pretty much the case before the turn of the century. As a sex-economist, one gains deep insights into the secrets of human existence and can ascertain a total disintegration of the moralistic ascetic modes of life, which are still so loudly advocated. The collectivization of adolescent life has not only undermined—even if it has not eliminated—the restrictive power of the authoritarian household but has also awakened a desire in modern youth, a desire for a new philosophy and for scientific knowledge about the fight for sexual health, sexual consciousness, and freedom. Around the turn of the century it would have been out of the question for a Christian woman to belong to a birth-control group. Today it is more and more the rule. This process was not interrupted by the fascist seizure of power in Germany, but merely forced to go underground. What remains questionable is how the process will continue to take shape, if fascist murder and barbarism last longer than we fear.

An additional objective factor, which is closely related to the above, is the rapid increase of neurotic and biopathic illnesses as an expression of disturbed sexual economy, and the intensification of the contradiction between real sexual demands on the one hand and old moralistic inhibitions and child education on the other hand. The increase of biopathies means that one is more prepared to acknowledge the sexual cause of so many sicknesses.

Political reaction's powerlessness in the face of practical sex-economic work is the strongest point in sex-economy's favor. It is well known that, owing to the lack of scientific literature on sex, it is mostly sexual tripe that is read in the public libraries. If sex-economic work could succeed in directing this enormous interest into scientific and rational channels, this would provide a measure of the importance of the sex-economic question. The fascists are able to deceive the submissive and mystically contaminated masses for a long time by pretending to represent the rights of work and the worker. It is different in the sex-economic sphere. Political reaction could never succeed in opposing revolutionary sex-economy with a reactionary sex-political program that would be anything other than complete suppression and negation of sexuality. Such a program would immediately alienate the masses, with the exception of a politically unimportant circle of old women and hopelessly dense creatures. *It is the youth that matters!* And they—this much is certain—are no longer accessible to a sex-negating ideology on a mass scale. This is our strong point. In 1932 sex-economic groups in Germany succeeded in winning over industries that were and had been completely closed to the subject of "Red trade-unionism." It is clear that, when all is said and done, sex-economic mental hygiene must join forces with the general social freedom movement. And in actual practice this is precisely what it did. However, we have to have a clear eye for facts such as this: Fascist workers and employees, indeed students, are in complete accord with the revolutionary affirmation of sexuality, an affirmation that brings them into conflict with their leadership. And what could this leadership do if one could succeed in resolving this conflict altogether? It would be forced to use terror. But to the same extent to which it used terror, it would lose its influence. Let me stress once more that the objective loosening of the reactionary shackles placed on sexuality cannot under any circumstances be retightened. This is our greatest strength. If revolutionary work fails to make headway in this area, the result will be that the youth will continue as before to live a restricted life in secret, without being conscious of the causes and consequences of such a life. However, if sex-economic work is carried out consistently, political reaction would have no answer and no counterideology. Its ascetic teachings are tenable only as long as sexual affirmation in the masses is secret and fragmentary, only as long as it is not collectively organized and directed against political reaction's asceticism.

German fascism made an all-out effort to anchor itself in the psychic structures of the masses and therefore placed the greatest emphasis upon the inculcation of the adolescents and children. It had no other means at its disposal than the rousing and cultivation of slavery to authority, the basic precondition of which is ascetic, sex-negating education. The natural sexual strivings toward the other sex, which seek gratification from childhood on, were replaced in the main by distorted and diverted homosexual and sadistic feelings, and in part also by asceticism. This applies, for instance, to the so-called esprit de corps that was cultivated in the Labor Conscription Camps as well as to the so-called "spirit of discipline and obedience," which was preached everywhere. The hidden motive behind these slogans was to unleash brutality and make it ready for use in imperialistic wars. *Sadism originates from ungratified orgastic yearnings.* The facade is inscribed with such names as "comradeship," "honor," "voluntary discipline." Concealed behind the facade, we find secret revolt, depression to the point of rebellion, owing to the hindrance of every expression of personal life, especially of sexuality. A consistent sex-economy must cast a dazzling light on the great sexual privation. If it does, it will be able to reckon with the most lively echo on the part of youth. At first this will produce bewilderment and perplexity among the fascist leaders. It is not difficult to see that the average boy or girl can easily be made conscious of his or her sexual privation. Contrary to the assertions of such youth leaders who have never attempted it practically, the experience gained from working with young people shows that the average adolescent, especially the adolescent female, takes to his or her social responsibility much more quickly, more effectively, and more willingly, when it is made intelligible by means of bringing sexual suppression into consciousness. It is merely a question of correctly comprehending the sexual question and of showing its application to the general social situation. There are a thousand proofs in support of the above statement. One should not allow oneself to be scared off by threadbare objections, but ought to be guided solely by sex-economic practice.

What answers would political reaction have to some questions posed by German adolescents?

> The conscription of German boys and girls in labor camps has seriously impinged upon their private and sexual life. Urgent questions await an explanation and solution, for serious and menacing abuses have resulted. The situation is complicated by the general shyness and timidity of the adolescents to open a discussion on their personal, burning questions, added to which is the fact that the camp authorities forbid all talk on such questions. *But it is a matter of the physical and psychic health of boys and girls!!!*
>
> *What is the sexual life of the boys and girls in the Conscription Labor Camps?*
>
> On the average, the boys and girls in Conscription Labor Camps are at the age of budding sexuality. Most of the boys were previously in the habit of gratifying their natural sexual needs with their girlfriends. To be sure, the sexual life of these boys and girls was hindered even before they entered the labor camps by the absence of suitable possibilities of engaging in a healthy love life (housing problem of the youth), by a lack of money to buy contraceptives, by the hostility of the state authorities and reactionary

circles to a healthy adolescent love life, one in accordance with their needs. This lamentable situation was made even worse by the Labor Conscription! For instance:

No possibility of coming together with girls or of preserving and cultivating former liaisons.

Being forced to choose between abstinence and self-gratification.

This leads to the brutalization and dissipation of erotic life, the proliferation of sexual obscenity and dirty jokes, disintegrating fantasies (rape, lascivious greed, beatings), which also paralyze one's will and energy.

Nocturnal involuntary emissions, which undermine one's health and offer no gratification.

Development of homosexual tendencies and the forming of relationships between boys who had never thought of such things; severe annoyances from homosexual comrades.

Increase of nervousness, irritability, physical complaints, and various psychic disturbances.

Ominous consequences for the future.

All adolescents, especially those between 17 and 25, who do not have a gratifying sexual life are threatened with a future disturbance of their potency and severe psychic depression, which always entails a disturbance of one's work capacity. If an organ or a natural function is not used over a period, it later fails to operate. Nervous and psychic illnesses, perversions (sexual aberrations) are usually the result.

What is our position with regard to the measures and regulations adopted by our leaders on these questions?

Until now, the leaders have called for a "moral strengthening of the youth" in very general statements. To us it is still not clear what is meant by this. Over the past years the German youth have engaged in a hard struggle with their parental homes and the big wheels of the system and were gradually beginning to win their right to a healthy sexual life, despite the fact that they were not able to reach their goal under the existing social conditions. But their idea was clear in broad circles: The youth had to carry on a bitter fight against sexual bigotry, sexual obscenity and hypocrisy, the consequences of the youth's sexual subjugation. It was their idea that boys and girls should have a happy intellectual and sexual relationship with one another. Their idea was that it was society's responsibility to regulate and alleviate the conditions of their lives. What is the government's position toward this?

The ordinances it has issued so far are in sharp contradiction to the views of youth. The purchase of contraceptives has been made impossible by prohibiting their public sale. The measures employed by the Hamburg police against the aquatic athletes on moral grounds, the threat that those who "offend customs and decency" will be put into concentration camps, are backed up by the law. Is it an offense to decency if a boy sleeps with his girlfriend in a tent camp?

We ask the leadership of the German youth: *What is to be the sexual life of the youth?*

There are only four possibilities.

1. *Abstinence:* Shall the youth live an abstinent life, i.e., contain every form of sexual activity until marriage?

2. *Self-gratification:* Shall the youth gratify its sexual needs by masturbation?

3. *Homosexual gratification:* Shall the German youth engage in sexual activity with members of the same sex? If so, how? By mutual masturbation or anal intercourse?

4. *Natural love and sexual intercourse between boys and girls*: Shall the German youth affirm and encourage natural sexuality? If so:

Where is intercourse to take place (housing problem)?

How and *with what* is conception to be prevented?

When is this intercourse to take place?

Is the adolescent allowed to do the same thing as the führer?

Similar questions concern work with children. It may sound strange—to some incomprehensible—but the fact remains: *In the main, revolutionary work with children can only be sex-economic work.* Overcome your astonishment and listen patiently. Why is it that children in the pre-pubertal stage can be directed by sexual education in the best and easiest way?

1. Childhood in all social classes, even in those in which hunger and privations are suffered, is filled with sexual interests, more so

than later stages of life. In addition, we have to bear in mind that hunger to the point of physical deterioration concerns only a number of children, whereas sexual suppression concerns *every child of every class without exception*. This extends the social field of attack enormously.

2. The usual methods employed by the freedom movement to organize children are the same as those employed by the reactionaries in their work with children: marching, singing, dressing up, group games, etc. Unless he stems from exceptionally liberated parents—which of course is not very often the case—the child does not distinguish between the content of reactionary and revolutionary forms of propaganda. To see to it that reality is not glossed over is only the first commandment of anti-fascist education. It is our contention that children and adolescents will march just as happily to fascist music tomorrow as they march to liberal music today. Moreover, political reaction can mold the forms of group propaganda among children incomparably better than the anti-fascist movement. In this regard the latter was always behind. In Germany, for instance, the socialist movement, in contrast to the reactionary movement, was extremely weak in its work with children.

3. While it is true that political reaction is far superior in its organizational work with children, *there is one thing that it cannot do: It cannot impart sexual knowledge to children; it cannot give them sexual clarity, nor can it dispel their sexual confusion.* Only the revolutionary movement can do this. First of all because it has no interest in the sexual suppression of children. (On the contrary, it is precisely the sexual freedom of children that it has in mind.) Second of all because the revolutionary camp has always been the advocate of a consistent and natural education of children. This powerful weapon was never put to use in Germany. And it was those in charge of child organizations who offered the strongest resistance to the proposal that the usual individual treatment of sex education be turned into sex education on a mass scale. It was both tragic and comical that these opponents of sex-economic work

among children called upon Marx and Lenin in their defense. Naturally, neither in Marx's nor in Lenin's writings do we find anything about sex-economy. And yet the fact remained that children fell to political reaction's share en masse. Notwithstanding the enormous difficulties involved, unexpected possibilities arise of developing child education on a sex-economic basis. The most important of these possibilities is the ardent interest of the children themselves. If we could once succeed in engaging the sexual interests of children and adolescents *on a mass scale,* then reactionary contamination would be faced with a tremendous counterforce—and political reaction would be powerless.

To those who doubt, resist, and are otherwise worried about the "purity" of the children, we will cite only two examples from our practical experience. They are typical of many others.

First: The church is not so squeamish. A fifteen-year-old boy who transferred to a communist youth group from a fascist organization told us that in his former organization the priest was in the habit of calling the boys aside one by one and asking them about their sexual behavior. They were always asked whether they had masturbated, which was naturally always the case and shamefully admitted. "That is a great sin, my boy; but you can atone for it if you work diligently for the church and distribute these leaflets tomorrow." That's how mysticism practices politics with sex. We, however, are "modest"; we are "pure"; we want nothing to do "with such things." And then we are surprised that mysticism is in control of the majority of the adolescents.

Second: The sex-economic work-group in Berlin had resolved to make its first attempt at sex-economic education of children, and had collectively put together a story for this purpose: *The Chalk Triangle, Group for the Study of Adult Secrets.* Before having it printed, this little story was first discussed with leaders of child groups. It was resolved to read the booklet to a group of children and to see how they reacted to it. One wished that all those who shrugged their shoulders derogatively at the mention of social sex-economy would have been present. To begin with, seventy children were present, instead of the usual twenty or so. Contrary to the usual indifferent attentiveness following the reports of the functionaries—it was always difficult to establish quiet—the children hung on the speaker's words, their eyes glowed, their faces formed one single bright spot in the auditorium. At some points, the reading was interrupted by bursts of enthusiasm. At the end the children were asked to express their opinions and criticism. Many raised their hand for permission to speak. One had to blush at one's own prudery and embarrassment in front of these children. The teachers who had edited this story had decided not to include the question of contraception and also to omit the subject of childhood masturbation. Promptly the question was asked: "Why don't you say anything about how not to get children?" "We know that anyhow," a boy interjected laughing. "What's that, a tart?" a third boy asked, "there was nothing said about that in the story." "Tomorrow we'll go to the Christians," they stated enthusiastically. "They always talk about such things—we'll get them!" "When is the book coming out? How much will it cost? Will it be cheap enough for us to buy it and also to sell it?" The first part that had been read dealt almost exclusively with sex education. It was the group's intention, however, to supplement the first volume with a second volume, which was supposed to show the social implications of these questions. The children were told this. "When is the second volume coming out? Will it also be so funny?" When has a group of children ever asked for a social booklet so enthusiastically? Shouldn't this be a lesson to us? Yes, it should. *By affirming their sexual interests and gratifying their thirst for knowledge, children must be educated to take an interest in social matters. They have to become firmly convinced that this is something political reaction cannot give them.* And they will be won over in large numbers, be immunized against reactionary influence in all countries and—what is most important—they will be firmly bound to the revolutionary freedom movement. At present, however, it is not only political reaction that obstructs the realization of this goal, but also the "moralists" in the camp of the freedom movement.

An additional important area of sex-economic work is the elucidation of the sexual situation that recently resulted in Germany from the fact that women were pushed from industry back into the kitchen. This work can be accomplished only by imbuing the concept of woman's freedom with the contents of *sexual* freedom. It must be pointed out that it is not her material dependency on the man in the family that is a nuisance to a woman. Essentially, it is the sexual restriction that goes with this dependency that is a burden. The proof of this is that those women who have succeeded in completely suppressing their sexuality not only endure this economic dependency easily and unresistingly, but even affirm it. To make these women conscious of their suppressed sexuality and to stress the unpleasant consequences of an ascetic life are the most important preconditions for the political fertilization of the material dependency on man. If sex-economic organizations fail to accomplish this work, then the new wave of sexual suppression of women in fascism will immure the consciousness of her material enslavement. In Germany and other highly industrialized countries, all the objective social preconditions are present for a forceful rebellion of the women and the adolescents against sexual reaction. If inexorable, consistent, unflinching sexual policies were applied to this area, we would be rid once and for all of a question that has occupied freethinkers and politicians time and again, without yielding an answer: Why is it that women and adolescents are always far more willing to listen to political reaction? No other field exposes so clearly the social function of sexual suppression, the intimate connection between sexual repression and political reactionary views.

In conclusion, let me mention one further objection made by a psychiatrist after reading this section. It is not easily countered. There is no doubt, he said, that the broad masses have the keenest interest in the sexual question. They are well nigh obsessed with it, but does this necessarily lead to the conclusion that their interest can be exploited politically to further the social revolution, which demands so many privations and sacrifices? Once they have grasped the idea of sex-economy, what will keep the masses from wanting to cash in on sexual freedom immediately? When we are engaged in difficult work, we have to listen to every objection very attentively, consider its validity and express our view on it. We have to be on our guard against allowing our wishful revolutionary thinking to get the best of us and regarding as a realistic possibility that which is only right "as such." The success or failure of the fight against hunger will not be decided by the fact that one wants to eliminate it at all cost, but by the presence or absence of the objective preconditions necessary for its elimination. Can, in other words, the sexual interest and sexual distress of the masses of all countries be translated into social action against the social system that causes this distress, as is done with primitive material interest? We have cited the practical experiences and the theoretical considerations that indicate that what succeeds in individual groups and in individual meetings must also be possible on a mass scale. We have merely neglected to mention several additional preconditions, which are *indispensable*. To accomplish the task of putting social sex-economy into effective operation, it is first of all necessary to have a united workers' movement. Without this precondition sex-economic work can only be of a preparatory nature. Furthermore, it is absolutely necessary to establish a tight *international* sex-economic organization, which would have the task of carrying out and securing the actual work. The final indispensable precondition is a cadre of thoroughly disciplined leaders of the movement. For the rest, it is not advisable to try to solve every individual problem in advance. That would be confusing and stagnating. It is practice itself that will yield new and more detailed practice. This book will not be burdened with such details.

THE NONPOLITICAL MAN

Finally, we arrive at the question of the so-called nonpolitical man. Hitler not only established his power from the very beginning with masses of people who were until then essentially nonpolitical; he also accomplished his last step to victory in March of 1933 in a "legal" manner, by mobilizing no less than five million nonvoters, that is to say, nonpolitical people. The Left parties had made every effort to win over the indifferent masses, without posing the question as to what it means "to be indifferent or nonpolitical."

If an industrialist and large estate owner champions a rightist party, this is easily understood in terms of his immediate economic interests. In his case a leftist orientation would be at variance with his social situation and would, for that reason, point to irrational motives. If an industrial worker has a leftist orientation, this too is by all means rationally consistent—it derives from his economic and social position in industry. If, however, a worker, an employee, or an official has a rightest orientation, this must be ascribed to a lack of political clarity, i.e., he is ignorant of his social position. The more a man who belongs to the broad working masses is nonpolitical, the more susceptible he is to the ideology of political reaction. To be nonpolitical is not, as one might suppose, evidence of a passive psychic condition, but of a highly active attitude, a *defense* against the awareness of social responsibility. The analysis of this defense against consciousness of one's social responsibility yields clear insights into a number of dark questions concerning the behavior of the broad nonpolitical strata. In the case of the average intellectual "who wants nothing to do with politics," it can easily be shown that immediate economic interests and fears related to his social position, which is dependent upon public opinion, lie at the basis of his noninvolvement. These fears cause him to make the most grotesque sacrifices with respect to his knowledge and convictions. Those people who are engaged in the production process in one way or another and are nonetheless socially irresponsible can be divided into two major groups. In the case of the one group the concept of politics is unconsciously associated with the idea of violence and physical danger, i.e., with an intense fear, which prevents them from facing life realistically. In the case of the other group, which undoubtedly constitutes the majority, social irresponsibility is based on personal conflicts and anxieties, of which the sexual anxiety is the predominant one. When a young female employee who would have sufficient economic reason to be conscious of her social responsibility is socially irresponsible, then in ninety-nine out of one hundred cases it is due to her so-called love story, or, to be more specific, it is due to her sexual conflicts. The same holds true for the lower middle-class woman who has to muster all her psychic forces to master her sexual situation so as not to fall to pieces altogether. Until now the revolutionary movement has misunderstood this situation. It attempted to awaken the "nonpolitical" man by making him conscious solely of his unfulfilled economic interests. Experience teaches that the majority of these "nonpolitical" people can hardly be made to listen to anything about their socio-economic situation, whereas they are very accessible to the mystical claptrap of a National Socialist, despite the fact that the latter makes very little mention of economic interests. How is this to be explained? It is explained by the fact that severe sexual conflicts (in the broadest sense of the word), whether conscious or unconscious, inhibit rational thinking and the development of social responsibility. They make a person afraid and force him into a shell. If, now, such a self-encapsulated person meets a propagandist who works with faith and mysticism, meets, in other words, a fascist who works with sexual, libidinous methods, he turns his complete attention to him. This is not because the fascist program makes a greater impression on him than the liberal program, but because in his devotion to the führer and the führer's ideology, he experiences a momentary release from his unrelenting inner tension. Unconsciously, he is able to give his conflicts a different form and in this way to "solve" them. Finally, this orientation enables him on occasion to see the fascists as revolutionaries and Hitler as the German Lenin. One does not have to be a psychologist to understand why the erotically provocative form of fascism offers a kind of gratification, however distorted, to a sexually frustrated lower middle-class woman who has never thought about social responsibility, or to a young salesgirl who could not arrive at social consciousness owing to an intellectual deficiency caused by sexual conflicts. One has to know the hidden life of these five million indecisive, "nonpolitical," socially-suppressed men and women to understand the role that private life, that is to say essentially sexual life, plays quietly and subterraneanly in the hubbub of social life. This is not to be grasped statistically; nor, for that matter, are we partisans of the sham exactness offered by statistics, which bypass the real facts of life, while Hitler conquers power with his negation of statistics and by making use of the dregs of sexual misery.

The socially irresponsible man is the man absorbed in sexual conflicts. To want to make him conscious of his social responsibility by excluding sexuality, as was the case until now, is absolutely hopeless. Moreover, it is the surest way of delivering him into the hands of political reaction, which makes no bones about exploiting the consequences of his sexual misery. Upon simple calculation we see that one and only one approach is possible: the comprehension of his sexual life from a social point of view. At one time I myself would have shied away from such a conclusion, considering how banal it seems. I can understand, therefore, that the seasoned political economist will look upon such an interpretation as the brainchild of a dry, politically inexperienced, sedentary scholar. However, one who has attended sex-economic meetings knows that the overwhelming majority are people who had never attended a political meeting before. Nonaffiliated and nonpolitical men and women make up the overwhelming majority of the sex-economic organizations in western Germany. Just how presumptuous the seasoned political economists are in their judgment is most graphically proven by the fact that the international organization of mysticism has held an impressive sex-political meeting in *its* sense of the word in every small nest of the world at least once a week for the past thousands of years. For the Sunday meetings and rituals of the Mohammedans, Jews, etc., are nothing other than sex-political meetings. In view of the experience with sex-economic work and knowledge on the relationship between mysticism and sexual suppression that we already have, a neglect or denial of these facts constitutes an inexcusable reactionary support of the domination of Middle Ages' mentality and economic slavery.

Finally, I want to deal with a fact that extends far beyond the everyday task: *the biologic rigidity of the human organism* and its relationship to the fight for social and individual freedom.

IX

The Masses and the State

When groups of settlers got lost in the American backwoods, they tried to find the path on which they had come in order once again to push forward into unknown terrain from known terrain. They did not form political parties to do this, nor did they engage in endless disputes about the unknown terrain. They did not knock one another's heads off or ceaselessly bother one another to draft a program on settlements. They acted in a natural work-democratic way on the basis of the given situation. They made a united effort to regain known terrain and then made a fresh effort to push on from there.

When a vegetotherapist loses himself in a maze of irrational reactions while treating a patient, he does not begin to argue with his patient on the "existence or nonexistence of God." He does not become neurotic and irrational, but reviews the situation and attempts to form a lucid picture of the previous course of the treatment. He goes back to the last point of development at which he was still clear about the course of the treatment.

Every living creature will naturally attempt to discover and eliminate the cause of a catastrophe in which it finds itself involved. It will not repeat actions that brought about the catastrophe in the first place. This is how difficulties are surmounted by experience. Our politicians are far removed from such natural reactions. It would not be farfetched to say that it is in the nature of a politician that he does not learn anything from experience. The Austrian monarchy triggered the first world war in 1914. At that time, it fought against American democrats with weapons in its hands. In 1942, during World War II, it entered a claim, which was backed by American diplomats, to reestablish the Habsburg dynasty "to avert" new wars. This is irrational political nonsense.

In World War I "the Italians" were the friends and allies of the Americans. In 1942, during World War II, they were arch enemies, and in 1943, friends again. In World War I, 1914, "the Italians" were the arch enemies of "the Germans," "hereditary enemies" from way back, as it were. In World War II, 1940, "the Italians" and "the Germans" were *blood brothers*, "again on grounds of heredity." In the next world war, let's say in 1963, "the Germans" and "the French" will have switched from "racial hereditary enemies" to "racial hereditary friends."

This is the emotional plague. It's something like this: A Copernicus comes along in the sixteenth century and asserts that the earth revolves around the sun; in the seventeenth century one of his pupils comes along and asserts that the earth *does not* revolve around the sun, and in the eighteenth century this man's pupil again asserts that it does revolve around the sun. In the twentieth century, however, the astronomers assert that both Copernicus and his pupils were right, for the earth revolves around the sun and remains still at the same time. When dealing with a Copernicus, we are ready with the stake. When dealing with a politician, however, a politician who tells a people that the most incredible nonsense is true, who in 1940 holds up to be true precisely the opposite of what be held up to be true in 1939, then millions of people lose all bounds and assert that a miracle has taken place.

It is a rule of good science not to put forth a new theory as long as the old theories work well. If, however, the old theories prove to be inadequate or erroneous, then one proceeds to ferret out their errors, to subject them to a critique and to develop new views on the basis of fresh data. Such natural procedures are alien to the politician. No matter how many new facts are added to the old; no matter how many errors are exposed; the old theories continue to exist as *slogans,* and the new facts are concealed or passed off as illusions. The democratic formalities have disappointed millions of people in Europe, and thus opened the road to fascist dictatorship. The democratic politicians fail to go back to the starting points of democratic principles, to correct them in keeping with the radical changes that have taken place in social life and to give them a useful direction. Fresh votes are held on formalities, on precisely those formalities that were dethroned so ingloriously in Europe.

One wants to think out and to plan a system of peace and to put it to a vote. It is clear that one shrinks back from this system even before the planning begins. The basic elements of peace and of human cooperation are physically present in man's natural work relationships, and they provide the basis for the development of guarantees of peaceableness. They must not be "introduced"—they are already there. A good physician does not "introduce" a "new health" into a critically sick organism. He finds out which elements of health are spontaneously present in the sick organism. When he finds them, he plays them off against the process of sickness. The same holds true for the sick social organism when one approaches it through *social science* and not with political programs and ideas. It is only possible to develop the actual conditions of freedom that are present and to eliminate the obstacles that thwart this development. But this must be done organically. One cannot impose legally guaranteed freedoms on a sick social organism.

The relationship of the masses to the state can be best illustrated by using the Soviet Union as an example. The reasons for this are as follows: The groundwork for the social revolution of 1917 was prepared by a sociological theory that had been tested over a period of ten years. The Russian Revolution made use of this theory. Millions of people took part in the social upheaval, endured it, rejoiced in it and passed it on. What became of the sociological theory and of the masses in the "proletarian state" in the course of twenty years?

The development of the Soviet Union cannot be ignored if one is seriously concerned with the question of democracy. What is its nature, can it be realized, and how? The difference between work-democratic *mastering of difficulties* on the one hand and formal democratic politicizing on the other hand was very clearly shown in the attitude of the various political and economic organizations to the Soviet Union.

1936: SPEAK THE TRUTH—BUT HOW AND WHEN?

The Italian-Abyssinian war had broken out; one event followed another precipitately. No one knew or could know how the world would change in the following months and years. The organized workers' movement did not intervene in the events. It was internationally split. It was mute, to all intents and purposes, or it followed this or that political view in a very desultory manner. It has to be admitted that the Soviet Union did fight for peace in Geneva through Litvinov, but it was a total failure as a social pioneer. New, undreamed-of catastrophes were to be expected. One had to prepare oneself for them. A new solution to the social chaos could result from them; but they could also slip past without anything being made of them, as in 1918 and 1933 in Germany. One had to make sure that one was structurally prepared for social upheavals. One had to be especially careful not to get entangled in the drag rope of the many confusing and contradictory political everyday views. It was necessary to isolate oneself from the daily political tumult and yet to maintain a close contact with the social processes. It seemed more important than ever to stick to one's work on the problem of human structure. Most of all it was necessary to establish clarity on the development of the Soviet Union. Millions upon millions of working men and women in Germany, England, America, China, and elsewhere anxiously followed every step taken by the Soviet Union. Those versed in mass psychology knew that if a disappointment in the Soviet Union were added to the catastrophe in Germany, then a hard struggle for clarity would be the first precondition to survive a new war scientifically.

The European war, i.e., the second world war in *one* generation, was impending. There was still time to reflect upon what changes this second world war might bring about. It was still possible for human thought—even if no longer possible for human action—to come to grips with the new massacre and to arrive at an understanding of the war psychosis, an understanding that would be deadly to the warmongers. Those who knew this had a hard time keeping their heads clear and their blood calm. But it had to be accomplished, for this Second World War, which had begun in Africa, and was soon to encompass the whole planet, would also have to end someday. Then the answer would have to be: "Death to the warmongers" and "Annihilation of the causes of war." But no one had any idea how this answer would look in practice.

In 1935 it was clear that the development of the Soviet Union was about to be stricken with a severe misfortune. The democratic politicians in Germany, Scandinavia, and other countries did not try to trace this misfortune to its source, though they spoke about it a great deal. They failed to go back to the genuinely democratic efforts of Engels and Lenin, to refresh their knowledge on the sociological points of departure of the Soviet society, and to proceed from there to an understanding of its later development. In Europe it was not possible to ignore these pioneers of genuine democracy, any more than it is possible for a genuinely democratic American to ignore the American constitution and the basic ideas of American pioneers, such as Jefferson, Lincoln, and others. Engels was the most outstanding exponent of German democracy, as Lenin was of Russian democracy. They had not got stuck in formalities; they had gone to the core of democracy. They were avoided. It makes no difference whether they were avoided because one was afraid of being labeled a Communist or because one was afraid of losing one's academic or political position. Engels was a well-to-do factory owner and Lenin was a well-to-do son of an official. They were descendents of the "ruling class," who sought to develop a system of genuine democracy from Marxist social economy (which, incidentally, was also born in "bourgeois circles").

Engels' and Lenin's democratic framework of ideas fell into neglect. Its demands on the conscientiousness of the Europeans were too high and, as it was later shown, on the Russian politicians and sociologists as well. It was too much for them.

Today [1944] natural work-democracy cannot be described without reviewing the forms that it assumed in the socio-political ideas of Engels and Lenin from 1850 to 1920. We must also review the forms it assumed in the early developmental process in the Soviet Union from 1917 to around 1923. The Russian Revolution was an act of extraordinary social significance. For that very reason the importance of its retardation is enormous from a sociological point of view; it is a tremendous lesson for every genuinely democratic effort. Practically speaking, there is not much to hope for from the purely emotional enthusiasm for Russia's deeds of heroism in her war against Hitler. In 1943 the motives of this enthusiasm, which was absent between 1917 and 1923, are of a very dubious nature. They are dictated far more by egoistic war interests than by the will to achieve genuine democracy.

The following examination of the development of the Soviet Union was first written in 1935. One will ask why it was not published at that time. This requires a brief explanation. In Europe, where it was impossible to engage in practical work on mass psychology outside of the parties, one who carried out scientific investigations undeterred by political interests and made predictions that were at variance with party politics, was very apt to be excluded from the organizations and thereby deprived of one's contact with the masses. All parties were of one opinion on this point. It is in the nature of a political party that it does not orient itself in terms of truth, but in terms of illusions, which usually correspond to the irrational structure of the masses. Scientific truths merely interfere with the party politician's habit of wriggling himself out of difficulties with the help of illusions. To be sure, the illusions are of no use in the long run, as was demonstrated so graphically in Europe itself from 1938 on. In the long run, scientific truths are the only reliable guidelines for social life, but these truths pertaining to the

Soviet Union were still nothing more than germs, which would have been incapable of stirring public opinion, let alone mass enthusiasm. They were nothing more than pricks of conscience. It was reserved for the Second World War to intensify on a broad scale the receptiveness for facts and above all to reveal to broad circles of working humanity the basic irrational nature of all politics.

When one establishes a fact, one is not concerned whether it is welcome or not, but only whether it applies. Thus, one always gets involved in a sharp conflict with politics, which is not concerned whether a fact is applicable or not, but solely whether it interferes with this or that political group. Hence, the scientific sociologist has no easy time of it. On the one hand it is his task to discover and to describe the actual process; on the other hand he has to remain in contact with the vital social movement. In publishing embarrassing factual material, therefore, he must consider very carefully what effect his correct statements will have on the masses of people who are predominantly under the influence of political irrationalism. A social scientific view having some intellectual range can push through and become social practice only if it is spontaneously absorbed by the masses in life itself. Outdated political systems of thought and institutions inimical to freedom must be totally exhausted politically before rational views on the vital necessities of society can be generally and spontaneously assimilated. But the exhaustion of these systems and institutions must be *perceptible to everyone*. In the United States, for example, the fuming and fussing of the politicos has popularized the general, not at all very scientifically comprehended knowledge that the politician constitutes a cancerous growth on the social body. In the Europe of 1935 one was far removed from this knowledge. It was the politician who determined what was to be regarded as true and what as false.

Usually an important social awareness begins to assume a more or less clear form among the population long before it is expressed and represented in an organized way. Today, 1944, the hatred of politics, a hatred based on concrete facts, has undoubtedly become general. If, now, a group of social scientists has made correct observations and formulations, i.e., observations and formulations that clearly reflect the objective social processes, then the "theory" must of necessity be in agreement with the vital feelings of the masses of people. It is as if two independent processes moved in a convergent direction and came together at *one* point, a point at which the social process and the will of the masses *became one* with sociological knowledge. This seems to hold true for important social processes everywhere. The American emancipation from England in 1776 followed this process, just as the emancipation of the Russian society from the czarist state followed it in 1917. The absence of correct sociological work can have a catastrophic effect. In such a case, the objective process and the will of the masses have reached a point of maturity; but if there is no simple scientific principle to consolidate them, this maturity is lost again. That is what happened in Germany in 1918 when the kaiserdom was overthrown but no genuine democracy developed.

The fusion of the scientific and social processes into the unity of a fundamentally new social order fails to result if the process of scientific awareness does not grow out of the old views just as organically as the social process grows out of the misery of practical life. I say, *to grow out of, organically*, because it is not possible to "contrive," "think out," or "plan" a *new* order. *It has to grow organically*, in close connection with the practical and theoretical facts of the human animal's life. It is for this reason that all attempts "to get at the masses politically," to impose "revolutionary ideas" on them, fail and lead only to noisy and harmful fuming and fussing.

The awareness of the peculiar nature of fascism, which could not be explained by any purely economic view of social life, and the awareness of the authoritarian and nationalistic structure of the Soviet Union of 1940 developed spontaneously everywhere; no political party had anything to do with it. It was general, latent knowledge that fascism had as little to do with the class rule of the "bourgeoisie" as the "Soviet democracy" of Stalin had to do with the social democracy of Lenin. It was noted everywhere that the old concepts were no longer applicable to the new processes. Those who were directly involved with man's vital life, those who—as physicians and educators—had acquired an exact knowledge of men and women of all walks of life and various nationalities were not easily taken in by political slogans. Those who had always been nonpolitical and had lived solely for their work were in an especially good position. It was precisely these "nonpolitical" circles in Europe, men and women who were totally absorbed by their work, who were accessible to important social insights; whereas those who had been economically and ideologically identified with this or that party apparatus at one time or another were rigid and inaccessible to every new insight. As a rule, they defended themselves with irrational hatred against every attempt to elucidate the fundamentally new phenomenon of the authoritarian, "totalitarian," dictatorial regime. When one also takes into consideration that all the party organizations, regardless of their tendencies, had a purely economic orientation, whereas the dictators based their policies not on economic processes but on the irrational attitudes of the masses, then it is easily understood that a social scientist working in the field of mass psychology was forced to proceed with the utmost caution and circumspection. All he could do was to register conscientiously whether the social development was confirming or refuting his biopsychic insights. *It confirmed them!* Many physicians, educators, writers, social workers, adolescents, industrial workers, and others became more and more convinced that political irrationalism would one day gallop itself to death, and that the demands of natural work, love, and knowledge would become part of mass consciousness and mass action. There would be no need to carry out a propaganda campaign to sell the theory. However, it was impossible to know just how great a catastrophe political irrationalism would have to cause before it was arrested by the natural feelings for life of the toiling masses, to know how long it would take before it was choked by it own acts.

Following the German catastrophe in 1933, the Soviet Union regressed rapidly to authoritarian and nationalistic forms of social leadership. It was clear to a large number of scientists, journalists, and workers' functionaries that it was a regression to "nationalism." It was not clear whether it was nationalism *patterned after fascism.*

The word fascism is not a word of abuse any more than the word capitalism is. It is a concept denoting a very definite kind of mass leadership and mass influence: authoritarian, one-party system, hence totalitarian, a system in which power takes priority over objective interests, and facts are distorted for political purposes. Hence, there are "fascist Jews," just as there are "fascist Democrats."

If one had published such observations at that time, the Soviet government would have cited them as an example of "counter-revolutionary tendencies" and "Trotskian fascism." The masses of the Soviet population were still enjoying the impetus of the 1917 Revolution. Their material situation was still improving, and there was no unemployment to speak of. The population enjoyed the reintroduction of sports for everybody, the theater, literature, and other things. Those who had experienced the German catastrophe knew that these so-called cultural enjoyments of a people do not tell us much about the nature and development of its society. In short, they did not tell us anything about the Soviet society. Going to the movies, visiting the theater, reading books, playing sports, brushing one's teeth, and attending school are of course important, but they do not constitute a difference between a dictatorial state and a genuinely democratic society. "Culture is enjoyed" in the one as well as in the other. It has been a typical and basic error on the part of Socialists and Communists to extol an apartment building, a public transportation system, or a new school as "socialistic" achievements. Apartment houses, public transportation, and schools tell us something about the technical development of a society. *They do not tell us whether the members of that society are suppressed subjects or free workers, whether they are rational or irrational men and women.*

Since the Soviet Russians extolled every technical innovation as a "specifically communist" achievement, the Soviet population got the impression that such things did not exist in the capitalist countries. Therefore, it was not to be expected that the population would understand the deterioration of Soviet democracy to nationalism, or become aware of this deterioration on its own. It is one of mass psychology's basic tenets that it does not proclaim an "objective truth" simply because it is a truth. It first asks itself how the average person of the working population will react to an objective process.

This approach automatically precludes political abuse. If, namely, someone feels that he has discovered a truth, he is obliged to wait until it has been objectively and independently manifested. If this manifestation does not take place, then his truth was not a truth after all, and it is better remaining as a possibility in the background.

The catastrophic regression in the Soviet Union was anxiously followed in Europe and elsewhere. Thus, only about one hundred copies of this examination of the relationship between "the masses and the state" were sent to various friends of sex-economy and mass psychology in Europe, Russia, and America. The prediction in 1929 that Soviet democracy would deteriorate into a totalitarian dictatorship was based on the fact that the sexual revolution in the Soviet Union had not only been checked, but almost intentionally suppressed.[1] *Sexual suppression serves, as we know, to mechanize and enslave the masses.* Thus, wherever we encounter authoritarian and moralistic suppression of childhood and adolescent sexuality, a suppression backed up by the law, we can infer with certainty that there are strong authoritarian-dictatorial tendencies in the social development, regardless of which slogans the ruling politicians use. On the other hand we can infer genuine democratic social tendencies wherever we encounter a sympathetic, life-affirmative attitude on the part of the important social institutions toward the sexuality of children and adolescents; but only to the extent to which such attitudes are present. Thus, as early as

---

[1] Cf. Reich, *The Sexual Revolution.*

1929, when reactionary sexual attitudes became more and more prevalent in the Soviet Union, one was justified in drawing the conclusion that an authoritarian, dictatorial development in the social leadership was in progress. I went into this very thoroughly in *The Sexual Revolution*. My predictions were confirmed by the official legislation passed from 1934 on, i.e., by the reintroduction of reactionary sexual laws.

At that time I did not know that a new attitude toward sex-economic questions had developed in the United States, an attitude that would later facilitate the acceptance of sex-economy.

We requested the friends to whom we had sent copies of this unofficial pamphlet to think it over carefully and, if they agreed with it on the whole, to pass it on to other sociologists in their immediate vicinity who were in a position to understand the contradiction in the development of the Soviet Union. In no case whatever were the contents of this pamphlet to be printed in any newspaper or read at a mass meeting. The events themselves would determine when it was to be discussed in public. Between 1935 and 1939 the cause of the regression to authoritarian forms in the Soviet Union was understood from the point of view of mass psychology by an increasing number of leading sociological circles. This understanding replaced the fruitless indignation one felt about the "regression"; one learned to understand that the Soviet Union's *further development foundered on the authority-craving structures of the masses of people, a fact that was not discerned by the Soviet leadership*. This was an enormously important insight.

"WHAT TAKES PLACE IN THE MASSES OF PEOPLE?"

The question as to *"how"* a new social order is to be implemented wholly coincides with the question as to the character structure of the *broad* masses, the nonpolitical, irrationally influenced working segment of the population. Thus, at the bottom of the failure to achieve a genuine social revolution lies the failure of the masses of people: They reproduce the ideology and forms of life of political reaction in their own structures and thereby in every new generation, despite the fact that they sometimes succeed in shattering this ideology and these forms within the social framework. At that time the question *"How do the broad masses of the nonpolitical segment of the population think, feel, and react?"* was neither raised nor understood. Hence, there was little possibility of mastering it in a practical way. A great deal of confusion existed. On the occasion of the plebiscite held in the Saar in 1935, the Vienna sociologist Willi Schlamm wrote the following:

> In truth, the epoch is gone in which we had the impression that the masses of society could be guided by reason and by insights into their situation of life to achieve social improvement with their own strength. In truth, the days are gone in which the masses have a function in shaping society. It has been shown that the masses can be completely molded, that they are unconscious and capable of adapting themselves to any kind of power or infamy. They have no historical mission. In the 20th century, in the century of tanks and radios, they have no mission—the masses have been excluded from the process of social formation.

Schlamm was right, but in a sterile way. He failed to ask how such an attitude on the part of the masses could arise, whether it was innate or capable of being changed. If I have understood him correctly, he had no hope, not even as a general principle.

It has to be clearly understood that such observations were not only unpopular but often mortally dangerous, because the Social Democratic and Liberal parties in the countries that were still not fascist lived precisely in the illusion that the masses as such, just as they are, were capable of freedom and liberalism, and that paradise on earth would be assured if only those wicked Hitlers were not around. As was shown again and again in both personal and public discussions, the democratic politicians and, quite particularly, the Social Democratic and Communist politicians had not the least understanding of the simple fact that the masses—owing to their century-long suppression—could not be other than incapable of freedom. They were not only unwilling to admit this fact, but often reacted in a restless and threatening way when it was mentioned. In reality, however, everything that had taken place in the sphere of international politics since the Russian Revolution of 1917 confirmed the correctness of the assertion that the masses were incapable of freedom. Without this insight it was altogether impossible to understand the fascist deluge.

In the years between 1930 and 1933 my perception of the true state of affairs became more and more crystallized, and I found myself involved in serious conflicts with well-disposed liberal, socialist, and Communist politicians. Nonetheless, the time seemed right for publication, so in 1933 I wrote the first edition of the present volume. In a pamphlet entitled *Was ist Klassenbewusstsein?*, Ernst Parell showed the implications of my insights for socialist politics.

Actually, my diagnosis could easily have led to a state of hopelessness, for if all social events are dependent upon the structure and behavior of the masses, and if it is true that the masses are incapable of freedom, then the victory of the fascist dictatorship would have to be definitive. But this diagnosis was not absolute and not without implications. It is fundamentally altered by two additional considerations:

1. *The incapacity for freedom on the part of masses of people is not innate. People were not always incapable of freedom. Hence, fundamentally speaking, they can become capable of freedom.*

2. As was thoroughly demonstrated by sex-economic sociology, with the help of clinical experience, *the mechanism that makes masses of people incapable of freedom is the social suppression of genital sexuality in small children, adolescents, and adults.* This social suppression is not part of the natural order of things. It developed as a part of patriarchy and, therefore, is capable of being eliminated, fundamentally speaking. If, however, social suppression of natural sexuality in the masses is capable of being eliminated, and if it is the central mechanism of a character structure incapable of freedom, then—and this is the conclusion—it is not hopeless. The

road is clear for society to master all the social conditions we call the "emotional plague."

Schlamm's error, and the error of many other sociologists as well was that while he confirmed the fact of the incapacity for freedom on the part of masses of people, he failed to draw the practical consequences from sex-economic sociology, with which he was well familiar, and to advocate them. More than any of the others, it was Erich Fromm[2] who later managed to disregard completely the sexual problem of masses of people and its relationship to the fear of freedom and craving for authority.[3] I was never able to understand this, for I had no reason to doubt the basic honesty of Fromm's position. But sexual negation in both social and personal life plays many a trick that is inaccessible to rational understanding.

The reader will have noticed just how much the emphasis has shifted from sociological investigations of political and economic factors to the investigation of factors pertaining to mass psychology, sex-economy, and character structure. The diagnosis that the masses of people are incapable of freedom, that the suppression of natural sexuality is the chief mechanism that is used to produce the imprisonment of the character and, above all, the shifting of the responsibility from individual organizations or politicians to the freedom-incapacitated masses themselves were enormous readjustments in thinking and, consequently, also in the practical handling of social problems. One was in a better position to understand the ceaseless complaints of the various political parties that "one still had not succeeded in reaching the working masses." One understood *why* the masses "can be completely molded, that they are unconscious and capable of adapting themselves to any kind of power or

---

[2] In his publications *Authority and Family* and *Escape from Freedom*.

[3] Earlier he had written a favorable review of *Der Einbruch der Sexualmoral* in the *Zeitschrift für Sozialforschung*. This book deals with the incursion of sexual morality in primitive societies and therewith the incursion of characterological slavery.

infamy." Above all, one understood the fascist intoxication of the masses with racism. One understood the helplessness and powerlessness of those sociologists and politicians whose orientation was purely economic, understood their helplessness in the face of the catastrophic events of the first half of the twentieth century. Now it was possible to trace back every form of political reaction to the emotional plague, which had become more and more anchored in the structures of the masses of people since the incursion of authoritarian patriarchy.

Now the genuine democratic revolutionary movement can have no other task than to guide (*not* "lead" from the top!) the human masses that have become apathetic, incapable of discrimination, biopathic and slavish as the result of the suppression of their vital life over thousands of years; to guide them in such a way that they sense every suppression immediately and learn to shake it off *promptly, finally,* and *irrevocably.* It is easier to prevent a neurosis than it is to cure it. It is easier to keep an organism healthy than it is to rid it of an infirmity. It is also easier to keep a social organism free of dictatorial institutions than it is to eliminate such institutions. It is the task of genuine democratic guidance to make the masses leap over themselves, as it were. But a mass of people can surpass itself only when it develops in its own ranks social organizations that do not compete with diplomats in political algebra, but think out and articulate for the masses of people that which they cannot think out and articulate for themselves, owing to their distress, lack of training, bondage to the führer idea and the plague of irrationalism. *In short, we hold the masses of people responsible for every social process.* We demand that they be responsible and we fight against their irresponsibility. We impute the fault to them, but we do not accuse them as one would accuse a criminal.

There is more to a new and genuine social order than the elimination of dictatorial-authoritarian social institutions. There is also more to it than the establishment of new institutions, for these new institutions will also inevitably degenerate into a dictatorial-authoritarian form if the authoritarian absolutism anchored in the character structures of the *masses of the people* is not also eliminated through education and social hygiene. It is not as if we had revolutionary angels on the one side and reactionary devils on the other side, avaricious capitalists as opposed to generous workers. If sociology and mass psychology are to have a practical function as genuine sciences, then every effort must be made to free them of the political way of seeing everything as either black or white. They have to go to the core of the contradictory nature of the man raised in an authoritarian manner and help to search out, articulate, and remove political reaction in the behavior and in the structure of the working masses of people. It should not have to be particularly stressed that these genuine sociologists and mass psychologists must not *exclude themselves* from this process. By now it will have become clear that *a nationalization or socialization of production cannot by itself effect the slightest change in human slavery.* The piece of ground one buys to build a house in which to live and work is only a precondition of life and work; it is not this life and work itself. To regard the economic process of a society as the essence of the bio-social process of the human animal's society is the same as equating the piece of ground and the house with the rearing of children, or of equating hygiene and work with dancing and music. But it was precisely this purely economic view of life (a view that Lenin had strongly opposed even in his time) that forced the Soviet Union to regress to an authoritarian form.

The economic process introduced by the Soviets was also supposed to change the people—that was the expectation around 1920. The elimination of illiteracy and the transformation of an agrarian country into an industrial country are, to be sure, tremendous achievements, but they cannot be passed off as specifically socialistic achievements, for they had been attained in the same way and often more extensively by ultra-capitalistic governments.

Since 1917 the basic question of mass psychology has been: Will the culture that originated from the social upheaval in Russia in 1917 develop a human community that is *fundamentally* and essentially different from the overthrown czarist-authoritarian social order? Will the new socio-economic order of the Russian society reproduce itself in man's character structure, and *how* will it reproduce itself? Would the new "Soviet man" be free, nonauthoritarian, rational, self-governing, and would he transmit these capacities to his children? Would the freedom developed in such a way in the human structure make every form of authoritarian social leadership unnecessary, indeed impossible? The existence or nonexistence of authoritarian dictatorial institutions in the Soviet Union would have to become clear-cut standards for the nature of the development of the Soviet man.

It is understandable that the entire world followed the Soviet Union's development with tense expectation—in some parts of the world, apprehensively; in other parts, elatedly. But the attitude toward the Soviet Union was none too rational on the whole. Some defended the Soviet system just as uncritically as others attacked it. There were groups of intellectuals who took the position that "the Soviet Union had a thing or two to boast of, too." This sounded just like the Hitlerite who said that "there are also decent Jews." Such emotional judgments were both senseless and valueless. In a word, they were sterile. And the leaders of the Soviet Union rightfully complained that people did not really do anything in a practical way for the Russian society, but merely caviled about it.

The struggle continued between the rational and progressive forces of social development on the one hand and the reactionary forces of obstruction and regression on the other hand. Thanks to Marx, Engels, and Lenin, the economic conditions of forward development were appreciably better understood than those forces that acted as a brake. No one thought to raise the question of *the irrationalism of the masses*. Hence, the development toward freedom, which was so promising in the beginning, came to a standstill and then regressed to an authoritarian form.

It was more fruitful to understand the mechanism of this regression than to deny it, as was done by the European Communist parties. By piously, religiously, and fanatically defending everything that took place in the Soviet Union, they deprived themselves of every practical possibility *of solving* the social difficulties. And yet it is certain that the natural scientific elucidation of the irrational contradictions of the human character structure will, in the long run, do more for the development of the Soviet Union than any stupid hullabaloo about salvation. Such a scientific approach may be unpleasant and painful, but in reality it is prompted by far deeper feelings of friendship than political slogans are. The Soviet Russians who are engaged in everyday practical work know this very well. I can only affirm that at that time the sex-economic physicians and educators were as concerned as the champions of Sovietism were.

This concern was certainly justified. In the industrial plants, the original "triumviral directorship" and the democratic economic production advisers were replaced by authoritarian "responsible" management.

In the schools, the first attempts at self-government (Dalton plan, etc.) had failed; and the old authoritarian school regulations, however disguised by formal student organizations, were reintroduced.

In the army the original, straightforward, and democratic officer-system was replaced by a rigid order of rank. At first the "Marshal of the Soviet Union" was an incomprehensible innovation. Then it seemed dangerous. It had overtones of "czar" and "kaiser."

Indications of a regression to authoritarian and moralistic views and laws accumulated in the field of sex-economic sociology. This is thoroughly described in Part II of my book *Die Sexualität im Kulturkampf*, 1936.*

In human intercourse, suspicion, cynicism, contrivance, and byzantine obedience became more and more rife. If in 1929 the mood of the average Soviet Russian was still imbued with heroic sacrifice for the five-year plan and full of high hopes for the success of the Revolution, around 1935 one sensed an evasive, unsteady, and embarrassed oscillation in the feelings and thinking of the

---

* Published in English under the title *The Sexual Revolution.*

population. One sensed cynicism, disappointment, and that certain kind of "worldly wiseness," which is incompatible with serious social aims.

It was not only that the cultural revolution in the Soviet Union had failed. In the course of a few years the regression in the cultural process stifled the enthusiasm and hope of an entire world.

It is not the fault of a social leadership if a social regression takes place. But this social leadership consolidates regression if it: (1) tries to pass off the regression as progress, (2) proclaims itself to be the savior of the world, and (3) shoots those who remind it of its duties.

Sooner or later it will have to give way to a different social leadership, one that adheres to the generally valid principles of social development.

THE "SOCIALIST YEARNING"

There were socialist movements and a socialist yearning long before there was scientific knowledge on the social preconditions of socialism. The fight of the disappropriated against their oppressors has been raging for thousands of years. It was these fights that provided the scientific knowledge of the freedom aspirations of the suppressed and not vice versa, as the fascist character believes. It cannot be denied that it was precisely between 1918 and 1938, i.e., years of enormous social magnitude, that the socialists suffered very serious defeats. Precisely at a time that should have offered living proof of the maturity and rationality of the socialist freedom movement, the workers' movement split up and became bureaucratic, became more and more separated from the thirst for freedom and truth from which it had originally sprung.

The socialist yearning of the millions was an intense desire for freedom from *every* form of suppression. But this *intense desire for freedom was coupled with a fear of responsibility and thus appeared in the form of a compromise.* The fear of social responsibility on the part of the masses of people brought the socialist movement into the *political* sphere. However, in the scientific sociology of Karl Marx, who worked out the economic conditions of social independence, we find no mention of the *state* as the goal of socialist freedom. The "socialist" *state* is an invention of party bureaucrats. And now, *it*, "the state," was supposed to introduce freedom: *not the masses of the people*, you see, *but the state*. It will be my object in what follows to show that the socialist idea of the state not only had nothing to do with the theory of the early socialists, but, on the contrary, represented a distortion of the socialist movement. However unconsciously it may have been brought about, this distortion is to be imputed to the *structural helplessness* of the masses of people, who were nonetheless imbued with an intense desire for freedom. An intense desire for freedom on the one hand, coupled with a structural fear of the responsibility of self-government on the other hand, produced in the Soviet Union a form of state that was less and less in accord with the original program of the Communists and eventually assumed an authoritarian, totalitarian, and dictatorial form.

Let us attempt to sketch the basic socialist character of the most important social movements toward freedom.

The early Christian movement is often and rightfully designated as "socialist." The founders of socialism also regarded the slave revolts of antiquity and the peasant wars of the Middle Ages as precursors of the socialist movement of the nineteenth and twentieth centuries. It was the lack of development of the industrial conditions and the international means of communication, as well as the lack of a sociological theory, that precluded their success. According to the sociology of its founders, "socialism" was conceivable only on an *international* scale. A national or even nationalistic socialism (National Socialism = fascism) is sociological nonsense. In the strictest sense of the word it is mass deception. Imagine that a physician discovers a medicine to fight a certain disease and calls it "serum." Now a clever profiteer comes along who wants to make money on people's illnesses. He concocts a poison that produces this sickness, which in turn evokes an intense desire in man to get

225

well again, and he calls this poisonous agent a "healing agent." He would be the national socialist heir of this physician, just as Hitler, Mussolini, and Stalin became the national socialist heirs of Karl Marx's international socialism.

To be correct, the profiteer who wants to get rich on illnesses should call his poison a "toxin." However, he calls it a "serum," because he knows very well that he would not be able to sell toxin as a medicine. The very same thing applies to the words "social" and "socialist."

Words that have been stamped with a very definite meaning cannot be used arbitrarily without causing hopeless confusion. The concept "socialism" was inextricably related to the concept "international." The theory of socialism presupposed a definite degree of maturity in international economy. The imperialistic struggle for markets, natural resources, and centers of power will have to have assumed the character of rapacious wars. Economic anarchy will have to have become the chief obstacle to the further development of social productivity. The chaos of economy will have to have become clear to everyone, for example: the destruction of excess goods to check a sudden drop in prices, while masses of people are hungry and starving. The private appropriation of collectively produced goods will have to have come into sharp conflict with the needs of the society. International trade will have to have begun to feel that the tariff boundaries of the national states and the market principle are insurmountable barriers.

The objective socio-economic preconditions of an international attitude and orientation on the part of the inhabitants of the earth have developed enormously since 1918. The airplane lessened the distances between peoples and bridged the expanses that formerly preserved differences in degrees of civilization that were equivalent to thousands of years. With ever-increasing rapidity, international traffic has begun to obliterate the civilization gaps of earlier centuries. There was an infinitely greater gap between the Arab of the nineteenth century and the Englishman of the nineteenth century than there is between the Arab and Englishman of the middle of the twentieth century. More and more curbs were placed upon capitalistic adventurers. In short, the socio-economic preconditions of internationalism increased by leaps and bounds.[4] However, *this economic ripening of internationalism was not accompanied by a corresponding development in man's structure and ideology.* While the idea of internationalism continued to develop along economic lines, it made little headway in man's structure and ideology. This was shown not only in the workers' movement, but also in the development of *nationalistic* dictators in Europe: Hitler in Germany, Mussolini in Italy, Doriot and Laval in France, Stalin in Russia, Mannerheim in Finland, Horthy in Hungary, etc. No one could have anticipated this cleavage between socio-economic progress and a regression in man's structure. The degeneration of the Workers' International to a chauvinistic national socialism was more than a collapse of the old freedom movement, which had always been nothing but *international.* It was an unprecedented outbreak of the emotional plague on an enormous scale in the very midst of the suppressed social strata, in which great minds had placed hopes that they would one day create a new order in the world. A nadir of this "national socialist" degeneration was the racial hatred felt by the white workers against the black workers in the United States and the loss of all socio-political initiative and perspective in many a large union. When the freedom idea is seized upon by the mentality of sergeants, then freedom is in a bad plight. Old and brutal injustice revenged itself upon those masses who had nothing to sell but their working power. Unscrupulous exploitation and irresponsibility on the part of powerful capitalists struck back like a boomerang. Since the idea of internationalism had failed to take root in man's structure, the national socialist movements took the wind out of its sails by exploiting the intense desire for international socialism. Under the leadership of "sergeants" who had risen from the ranks of the suppressed, the international socialist

---

[4] This process was tremendously accelerated by World War II.

movement split up into nationally confined, isolated, mutually hostile mass movements, which merely *gave the appearance* of being revolutionary. To make matters worse, a number of these rigidly nationalistic mass movements became international movements, no doubt owing to the effect of the old international orientation of their followers. Italian and German National Socialism became international fascism. In the strict sense of the word it attracted masses on an international scale in the form of a perverse "nationalistic internationalism." In this form it crushed genuine democratic revolts in Spain and in Austria. The heroic fight of the genuine revolutionaries who had been isolated by the masses of the people (1934–36), was another Thermopylae.

In all of this the irrationalism of the mass structure, as well as politics in general, was clearly expressed. For years the German working masses had resisted the program of a revolutionary internationalism. And yet, from 1933 on, they endured all the suffering that a genuine social revolution would have entailed, without, however, enjoying a single fruit that a genuine social revolution would have brought them. They had grossly deceived themselves and were defeated by their own irrationalism, i.e., their fear of social responsibility.

These facts were hardly comprehensible. Yet, let us make an honest endeavor to understand them, despite their seeming incomprehensibility.

Since the entry of the United States into World War II an international and generally human orientation has gained more and more ground. Yet it is to be feared that even more fantastic irrational mass reactions and even more deadly social catastrophes will result someday, if the responsible sociologists and psychologists fail to put off their grandiloquent academicism *before it is too late*, take an active part in the course of events and make an honest effort to help clarify them. There has been a fundamental shift in the line of questioning of sociology from economics to the *structure of the masses of people*. We no longer ask if the economic preconditions of work-democratic internationalism have reached maturity. Now we are faced with a question of greater magnitude: *Assuming fully matured international socio-economic conditions, what obstacles could again prevent the idea of internationalism from taking root and developing in man's structure and ideology? How can the social irresponsibility and propensity for authority on the part of the masses be overcome before it is too late?* How can this second international war, which is rightfully referred to as a war in which ideological rather than economic issues are at stake, be prevented from decaying into a new, even more brutal, even more deadly nationalistic, chauvinistic, fascistic-dictatorial nationalism? Political reaction lives and operates within the human structure and in the thinking and acting of the suppressed masses in the form of character armor, fear of responsibility, incapacity for freedom, and, last but not least, as an endemic crippling of biologic functioning. These are grave facts. The fate of future centuries depends upon our ability or inability to cope with them in a natural scientific way. All leading circles have an enormous responsibility. Not a single one of these decisive tasks can be solved with political chatter and formalities. Our basic slogan, "Enough! No more politics! Let's get down to the vital social issues!" is not a play on words. Nothing is more staggering than the fact that a world population of two billion people does not muster the energy to eliminate a handful of suppressors and biopathic warmongers. Man's intense desire for freedom fails to become a reality owing to the many views as to how freedom can be best achieved without also assuming the direct responsibility for the painful readjustment of the human structure and its social institutions.

The *anarchists* (i.e., the syndicalists) strove to achieve social self-government, but they refused to take cognizance of the profound problem of the human incapacity for freedom, and they rejected all guidance of social development. They were utopians and they went down in Spain. They saw only the intense desire for freedom, but they confounded this intense desire with the actual capacity *to be* free and the ability to work and live without authoritarian leadership. They rejected the party system, but they were at a loss to say how the enslaved masses of people were to learn to govern their lives by themselves. Not much is accomplished by solely hating the state. Nor with nudist colonies. The problem is deeper and more serious.

The *international Christians* preached peace, brotherhood, compassion, mutual help. Ideologically, they were anti-capitalist, and they conceived of human existence in international terms. Basically, their ideas were in accord with international socialism, and they called themselves, e.g., in Austria, *Christian Socialists*. Yet, concretely speaking, they rejected and continue to reject every step of social development that moves precisely toward that goal that they have proclaimed to be their ideal. Catholic Christianity in particular has long since divested itself of the revolutionary, i.e., *rebellious*, character of the primitive Christian movement. It seduces its millions of devotees into accepting war as an act of fate, as a "punishment of sin." Wars are indeed the consequences of sins, but entirely different sins from those conceived of by Catholicism. For the Catholics, peaceful existence is possible only in heaven. The Catholic Church preaches the acceptance of distress in this world and thereby systematically ruins man's ability to achieve the goal of freedom, to fight for it in an honest way. It does not protest when its rival churches, the Greek Orthodox churches, are bombed; but it importunes God and culture when bombs fall on Rome. Catholicism produces structural helplessness in masses of people with the result that, instead of relying upon their own strength and self-confidence when they are in distress, they call upon God for help. Catholicism makes the human structure both incapable and afraid of pleasure. A good portion of human sadism derives from this. German Catholics give their blessings to German weapons and American Catholics give their blessings to American weapons. One and the same God is supposed to lead two arch enemies to victory in war. The irrational absurdity of this is conspicuous.

Social Democracy, which followed the Bernsteinian adaptation of Marxian sociology, also failed on the question of mass structure. It lived, as did Christianity and anarchy, on the compromise of the masses between strivings after happiness and irresponsibility. Thus it offered the masses a hazy ideology, an "education in socialism," which was not backed up by a strong and genuine tackling of concrete life-tasks. They *dreamed* of social democracy, but they refused to understand that the structure of masses of people would have to undergo basic changes to become capable of being social democratic and of living in a "social democratic" way. In actual practice it had no inkling of the idea that the public schools, trade schools, kindergartens, etc., had to operate on a self-regulatory basis. Moreover, it failed to realize that every reactionary tendency—including *those in one's own camp*—had to be countered sharply and objectively, that, finally, the term "freedom" had to be imbued with a concrete content to bring about social democracy. It would be far more sensible to use all one's forces against fascist reaction while one is in power than to develop the courage to do so only after one has relinquished it. In many European countries Social Democracy had all the necessary power at its disposal to dethrone the patriarchal power in and outside of man, a power that had been accumulating over thousands of years and finally celebrated its most bloody triumph in the fascist ideology.

Social Democracy made the fatal mistake of assuming that those who had been crippled by thousands of years of patriarchal power were capable of democracy without any further preliminaries and were capable of governing themselves. Officially, it rejected the rigorous scientific efforts—those of Freud, for instance—to comprehend man's complicated structure. Hence, it was forced to assume dictatorial forms within its own ranks and to make compromises outside of them. We can understand a compromise in the good sense of the word, i.e., the awareness that the viewpoint of the other person, the opponent, has to be *understood* and agreed with where it is superior to one's own viewpoint; but there is no justification for a compromise in which principles are sacrificed for fear of precipitating a confrontation. In the latter, rash efforts are often made "to get along" with an arch enemy bent on murder. Unadulterated Chamberlainism existed in the camp of socialism.

In ideology, Social Democracy was radical; in actual practice, it was conservative. A phrase such as "His Royal Highness and Majesty's socialist opposition" shows how ludicrous its position often was. Without intending to, it helped fascism, for the fascism of the masses is nothing other than disappointed radicalism plus nationalistic "petty bourgeoisism." Social Democracy foundered on the contradictory structure of the masses, a structure that it did not understand.

It cannot be denied that the *bourgeois governments* of Europe had a democratic orientation, but in practice they were conservative administrative bodies, which were averse to freedom efforts based on fundamental scientific knowledge. The enormous influence of the capitalist market economy and of profit interests far exceeded all other interests. The bourgeois democracies of Europe separated themselves from their original revolutionary character of the 1848 years much more quickly and thoroughly than Christianity separated itself from its revolutionary character. Liberal measures were a kind of decorum, a voucher that one was after all "democratic." None of these governments would have been able to state how the enslaved masses of people were to be extricated from their condition of blind acceptance and craving for authority. They had all the power in their hands, but social self-government and self-regulation was a book with seven seals to it. In such government circles it was impossible even to hint at the basic problem, i.e., the sexual question of the masses. The extolling of the Austrian Dollfuss government as a model of democratic administration bears witness to a complete lack of social awareness.

The powerful capitalists who emerged from the bourgeois revolution in Europe had a great deal of social power in their hands. They had the influence to determine *who* should govern. Basically, they acted in a short-sighted and self-damaging way. With the help of their power and their means, they could have spurred human society to unprecedented social achievements. I am not referring to the building of palaces, churches, museums, and theaters. I mean the *practical realization of their concept of culture.* Instead, they completely alienated themselves from those who had but one commodity to sell, their working power. In their hearts they held "the people" in contempt. They were petty, limited, cynical, contemptuous, avaricious, and very often unscrupulous. In Germany they helped Hitler to obtain power. They proved themselves to be completely unworthy of the role society had relegated to them. They abused their role, instead of using it to guide and educate the masses of people. They were not even capable of checking the dangers that threatened their own cultural system. As a social class they deteriorated more and more. Insofar as they themselves were familiar with the processes of work and achievement, they understood the democratic freedom movements. But they did nothing to help them. It was ostentation and not knowledge that they encouraged. The encouragement of the arts and sciences was once in the hands of the feudal lords, whom the bourgeoisie later dethroned. But the bourgeois capitalists had far less of an objective interest in art and science than the leading aristocracy had had. While in 1848 the sons of the bourgeois capitalists bled to death at the barricades, fighting for democratic ideals, the sons of the bourgeois capitalists between 1920 and 1930 used the university platforms to deride democratic demonstrations. Later, they were the elite troops of fascist chauvinism. To be sure, they had fulfilled their function of opening up the world economically, but they stifled their own accomplishment with the institution of tariffs and they had not the least notion of what to do with the internationalism that originated from their economic accomplishment. They aged rapidly, and as a social class they became senile.

This assessment of the so-called economic magnates does not derive from an ideology. I come from these circles and know them well. I am happy to have rid myself of their influence.

Fascism grew out of the conservatism of the Social Democrats on the one hand and the narrow-mindedness and senility of the capitalists on the other hand. It did not embody those ideals that had been advocated by its predecessors in a practical way, but solely in an *ideological way* (and this was the only thing that mattered to

233

the masses of people whose psychic structures were ridden with illusions). It included the most brutal political reaction, the same political reaction that had devastated human life and property in the Middle Ages. It paid tribute to so-called native tradition in a mystical and brutal way, which had nothing to do with a genuine feeling for one's native country and attachment to the soil. By calling itself "socialist" and "revolutionary," it took over the unfulfilled functions of the socialists. By dominating industrial magnates, it took over capitalism. From now on, the achievement of "socialism" was entrusted to an all-powerful führer who had been sent by God. The powerlessness and helplessness of the masses of people gave impetus to this führer ideology, which had been implanted in man's structure by the authoritarian school and nourished by the church and compulsive family. The "salvation of the nation" by an all-powerful führer who had been sent by God was in complete accord with the intense desire of the masses for salvation. Incapable of conceiving of themselves as having a different nature, their subservient structure eagerly imbibed the idea of man's immutability and of the "natural division of humanity into the few who lead and the many who are led." Now the responsibility rested in the hands of a strong man. In fascism or wherever else it is encountered, this fascist führer ideology rests upon the mystical hereditary idea of man's immutable nature, upon the helplessness, craving for authority, and incapacity for freedom of the masses of people. Admitted that the formula, "Man requires leadership and discipline," "authority and order," can be justified in terms of man's present antisocial structure, the attempt to eternalize this structure and to hold it to be immutable is reactionary. The fascist ideology had the best of intentions. Those who did not recognize this subjective honesty failed altogether to comprehend fascism and its attraction for the masses. Since the problem of the human structure was never brought up or discussed, let alone mastered, the idea of a nonauthoritarian, self-regulatory society was looked upon as chimerical and utopian.

234

It was precisely at this point, in the period between 1850 and 1917, that the critique and constructive policies of the founders of the Russian revolution made a start. Lenin's standpoint was this: Social Democracy had failed; the masses cannot achieve freedom spontaneously on their own volition. They need a leadership that is constructed along hierarchical lines and acts authoritatively on the surface, but at the same time has a strict democratic structure internally. Lenin's communism is always conscious of its task: The "dictatorship of the proletariat" is that social form that leads from an authoritarian society to a nonauthoritarian, self-regulatory social order requiring neither police force nor compulsive morality.

Basically, the Russian Revolution of 1917 was a politico-ideological revolution and not a purely social revolution. It was based on political ideas which derived from politics and economics and not from the science of man. We have to have a thorough comprehension of Lenin's sociological theory and his accomplishment to understand the weak spots that later made possible the authoritarian totalitarian technique of the Russian mass leadership. It is necessary to stress that the founders of the Russian Revolution had no inkling of the biopathic nature of the masses of people. But then no reasonable person expects that social and individual freedom lie ready-made in the desk drawer of the revolutionary thinker and politician. Every new social effort is based on the errors and omissions of earlier sociologists and revolutionary leaders. Lenin's theory of the "dictatorship of the proletariat" embodied a number of preconditions for the establishment of a genuine social democracy—but by no means all of them. It pursued the goal of a self-governing human society. It held the view that present-day man is not capable of achieving social revolution without an organization constructed along hierarchical lines and that the enormous social tasks cannot be accomplished without authoritarian discipline and loyalty. As Lenin conceived it, the dictatorship of the proletariat was to become the authority that had to be created to *abolish every kind of authority*. In the beginning it was fundamentally different from the fascist ideology of dictatorship in that *it set itself the task of undermining itself,* that is to say, *of replacing the authoritarian government of society by social self-regulation.*

In addition to establishing the economic preconditions for social democracy, the dictatorship of the proletariat had the task of effecting a basic change in man's structure by means of a complete industrialization and technicalization of production and commerce. Granted that Lenin himself did not speak of it in these terms, the effecting of basic change in man's structure was an essential and integral part of his sociological theory. According to Lenin's conception the social revolution had the task not only of eliminating surface formality and actual conditions of servitude, but also, and essentially, *of making men and women incapable of being exploited.*

The creation of the economic preconditions of social democracy, i.e., socialist-planned economy, proved in the course of time to be a trifle compared with the task of effecting a basic change in the character structure of the masses. To understand the victory of fascism and the nationalistic development of the Soviet Union, one must first comprehend the full magnitude of this problem.

The *first* act of Lenin's program, the establishment of the "dictatorship of the proletariat," was a success. The state apparatus that developed consisted entirely of the sons of workers and peasants. Descendents of the former feudal and upper classes were excluded.

The *second and most important act, the replacement of the proletarian state apparatus by social self-administration failed to materialize.* In 1944, twenty-seven years after the victory of the Russian Revolution, there is still no sign that points to the implementation of the second, genuinely democratic act of the Revolution. The Russian people are ruled by a dictatorial one-party system with an authoritarian führer at the top.

How was this possible? Had Stalin "defrauded," "betrayed," the Leninian revolution—had he "usurped power"?

Let us see what happened.

THE "WITHERING AWAY OF THE STATE"

The pursuance of a socially and historically impossible goal is at variance with the scientific view of the world. It is not the task of science to concoct systems and to chase after fantastic dreams of a "better future," but solely to comprehend development *as it really takes place*, to recognize its contradictions, and to help those forces that are progressive and revolutionary to achieve victory, to solve difficulties, and to make it possible for human society to become master of the conditions of its existence. The "better future" can become a reality only when its social preconditions are present and the structure of the masses of people is capable of utilizing these conditions to its own best advantage, i.e., is capable of assuming social responsibility.

Let us begin by summarizing Marx's and Engels' views on the development of a "communist society." In this we will follow the basic writings and expositions on Marxism that Lenin published in the period between March of 1917 and the October Revolution in *State and Revolution*.

ENGELS AND LENIN ON SELF-GOVERNMENT

In his most popular work, *The Origin of the Family, Private Property, and the State*, Engels destroyed the belief in the "absolute and eternal state"—in our context, the belief in the indispensability of the authoritarian leadership of society. On the basis of investigations made by Lewis Morgan on the organization of the pagan society, Engels came to the conclusion: *The state was not here from all eternity. There have been societies that functioned without it, that had no trace of state and state power.* When society began to split up into classes, when the opposition between the emerging classes threatened to undermine the existence of the society as a whole, a state power developed *of necessity*. Society rapidly approached a stage of development in production at which the existence of classes not only ceased to be a necessity but, over and above this, became a direct hindrance to the development of production. "They (the classes) will disappear just as inevitably as they once appeared. With them, the state will also disappear inevitably. That society that reorganizes *production on the basis of free and equal association of those who produce* will relegate the entire machinery of the state to where it belongs: the museum of antiquity, beside the spinning wheel and the bronze axe [my italics, WR]."

Voluntary association and self-government of social life prevail in pagan society.[5] The state came into being with the emergence of classes "to keep the opposition between classes in check" and *to safeguard the continuation of society.* Soon and "as a rule" the state entered the service of the "most powerful, economically superior class, which, owing to this, also became the ruling class politically," and thereby acquired new means of dominating and exploiting the suppressed classes. *What will take the place of state, authoritarian leadership from above and obedience from below, if the social revolution is victorious?*

Engels gives us a picture of the transition to a new social order. *To begin with* "the proletariat seizes state power" and transforms the means of production into state property. In so doing, it annuls itself as a proletariat, annuls the opposition between classes and "*also the state as a state.*" Until then the state was the official representative of the society as a whole, its condensation in a visible body; but it was this only insofar as it was the state of that class that acted as the representative of society as a whole *for its time.* In antiquity it was the state of slave-owning citizens; in the Middle Ages, the state of the feudalists, and later that of the bourgeoisie. *If the state should one day really become the representative of society as a whole, then it makes itself superfluous.* Engels' formulation is easily understood if the state is regarded as that which it *had become.* It was no longer *a bond that held together the class society,*

---

[5] See Malinowski's report on the work-discipline in the matriarchal Trobrianders; elucidated in *Der Einbruch der Sexualmoral,* 2nd edition, 1934.

but an instrument used by the economically superior class to dominate the economically weaker class. As soon as there is no longer any social class to be held in suppression and as soon as class rule and the struggle for individual existence—a struggle that originates in the anarchy of production—are eliminated along with the resulting excesses and clashes, there is no longer anything to be suppressed that would necessitate a special suppressive power such as the state. The first act in which the state appears as the representative of the society as a whole, namely the take-over of the means of production in the name of the *society*, is also its last independent act as a "state." From now on, "the intervention of a state power in social relations . . . *will become superfluous in one sphere after the other until it dies out by itself." The government over people is replaced by the administration of things and the management of production processes. The state is not "abolished"; it "withers away."*

Lenin elucidated this idea in *State and Revolution* and stressed it again and again: In the beginning the capitalist state (state *apparatus*) will not merely be taken over or only changed. It will be *"annihilated,"* and the capitalist state apparatus, the capitalist police, capitalist officialdom and bureaucracy, will be replaced by the "power apparatus of the proletariat" and the peasants and workers allied with it. This apparatus is *still* a *suppressive* apparatus, but now a majority of producers will no longer be suppressed by a minority of those in possession of capital. Instead, the minority, those who had formerly wielded power, will be held in check by the majority, the working people. This is what is known as: *"dictatorship of the proletariat."*

Thus, the withering away of the state described by Engels is preceded by the abolition of the capitalist state apparatus and the establishment of the "revolutionary-proletarian state apparatus." Lenin also went into great detail to point out why this transition in the form of the dictatorship of the proletariat is "necessary" and "indispensable," and why a *direct* realization of a *nonauthoritarian, free* society and "true social democracy" is *not possible*. The social democratic slogan "free republic" was criticized as claptrap by both Engels and Lenin. The proletarian dictatorship serves as a *transition* from the previous social form to the desired "communist" form. The character of the transitional phase can be comprehended only in terms of the final goals toward which the society aspires. These final goals are capable of being compassed only insofar as they have already become visibly developed in the womb of the old society. Examples of such final goals in the organization of a communist society are *"voluntary respect"* for the rules of social cohabitation, the establishment of a *free* "community" in place of the state (of the proletarian state also) as soon as the function of the latter has been fulfilled; in addition, efforts are made to achieve *"self-administration"* in industries, schools, factories, transportation organizations, etc. In short, what is aimed at is the organization of a "new generation" which, reared under new, free social conditions, will be capable of jettisoning the entire trumpery of the state . . . "the democratic-republican included [Engels]." To the extent to which the state "withers away," a "free organization" derives from it in which, as Marx postulated, "the free development of each individual" becomes the basic condition of the "free development of everyone."

In this connection two very important questions arose for the Soviet Union:

1. The "organization of a free generation in a free self-administrative community," cannot be "created." It has to "grow out" of the "dictatorship of the proletariat" (in the form of the "gradual withering away of the state"), must reach a state of development and ripeness in this transitional phase, in the same way that the "dictatorship of the proletariat" developed out of the dictatorship of the bourgeoisie—the "democratic" bourgeoisie included—as a *temporary* form of state. *Was there a "withering away of the state" and a gradual realization of a free, self-administrative community in the Soviet Union between 1930 and 1944—and how was this evident?*

240

2. If so, what was the nature of this "withering away of the state," and what were the *concrete, tangible,* and *guidable* indications of the "development of the new generation"? If this was not the case: *Why didn't* the state wither away? How were the forces that sustained the "proletarian state" related to the other forces that represented the withering away of the state? *What kept the state from withering away?*

Neither in Marx's nor in Engels' and Lenin's writings are these possible outcomes dealt with. In 1935 they were urgent questions. They demanded an immediate answer. *Is the state in the Soviet Union in the process of withering away? If not, why not?*

In contrast to the authoritarian order of the state, the essence of work-democracy can be described as *social self-government.* Quite obviously, a society that is to consist of "free individuals," to constitute a "free community" and to administrate itself, i.e., "govern itself," cannot be suddenly created by decrees. It has to *evolve* organically. And it can create all the preconditions for the desired condition in an *organic* way only when it has succeeded in creating a *freedom of movement,* that is to say, when it has freed itself of those influences that are in opposition to such a condition. The first precondition toward this end is a knowledge of the *natural organization of work,* the *biologic* and *sociologic* preconditions of *work-democracy.* The founders of socialism were *not aware* of the *biologic* preconditions. The *social* preconditions were related to a period (1840 to around 1920) in which there was only capitalistic private enterprise on the one hand and masses of wage earners on the other hand. There was still no politically oriented middle class to speak of, no development toward *state*-capitalism, and there were no masses to be joined together in a reactionary way to carry *National Socialism* to victory. Hence, the picture that emerged was related more to 1850 than it was to 1940.

In Engels' writing, the difference between the "seizure of power by the proletariat," i.e., the establishment of the "proletarian *state,*" and the "cessation of the state altogether," is not clearly worked out as it is in Lenin's writings. This is understandable, for Engels, unlike Lenin, was not faced with the immediate task of making a sharp distinction between the two stages. In 1917, on the threshold of the seizure of power, Lenin had to attach a greater importance to the "period of transition" than Engels had. Lenin determined the tasks of the period of transition more definitively.

To begin with, he demanded that the institution of the "bourgeois" state be replaced by the *proletarian* state, i.e., a *"fundamentally different kind"* of state leadership. What was *fundamentally* "different" about the proletarian state? With the abolition of the bourgeois state, Lenin said, it will be necessary to convert the bourgeois form of democracy into a proletarian democracy with the *"greatest conceivable completeness and consistency,"* to convert the state as a special power for the purpose of suppressing a certain class into an institution "which is no longer a real state." When the majority of the population suppresses its own suppressors, then a special repressive power is no longer necessary. In short, Lenin was not content with a sham, purely formal democracy. He wanted *the people* to determine production, distribution of products, social regulations, increase of population, education, sex, international relations, etc., in a *living* and *concrete* way. And this was the essence of that which Lenin, in accordance with Marx and Engels, so forcefully and repeatedly stressed as the *"withering away of the state."* "In place of special institutions," Lenin wrote, "in place of a minority having special privileges (officials, staff of command of the standing army), the majority itself will take care of these things, and *the greater the entire people's share in the carrying out of the functions of the state power, the less it has need of this power."*

Lenin did not equate "state" and "bourgeoisie rule" in any way, otherwise he would not have been able to speak of a "state" *after* the "defeat of the bourgeoisie." Lenin conceived of the state as the sum of "institutions," which had been in the service of the ruling class, the monied bourgeoisie, but now disappeared from their position *"above* the society" to that extent to which the majority of the *people themselves* took care of the business of social administration ("self-administration"). Thus, the withering away of the state, the evolution toward social self-government, is to be measured by the extent to which those organizations that have become autonomous and stand *above* the society are gradually *abolished*, and the extent to which the masses, the *majority* of the population, are included in the administration, i.e., *"self-government of the society."*

> The Communes will replace the corrupt and rotten parlia-mentarianism of the bourgeois society by public bodies in which *freedom of opinion and discussion* do not degenerate into decep-tion, for the members of parliament have to do their own work, implement their own laws, and check the results themselves. Repre-sentative bodies continue to exist, but parliamentarianism as a special system, as a division between legislative and executive activity, as a privileged position for members of parliament, *does not* exist here. Without representative bodies, we cannot conceive of a democracy [i.e., the phase preceding communism], not even proletarian democracy. *We can and must conceive of it without parliamentarianism.* If our criticism of bourgeois society is not to be a hollow phrase; if our efforts to overthrow the bourgeoisie rulership is to be honest and serious—and not just an "election" slogan to catch the workers' votes. . . .
>
> —*State and Revolution*

Hence, we see that a sharp distinction is drawn between "repre-sentative bodies" and "parliaments." The former are affirmed and the latter are rejected. *Nothing is said about what these bodies represent and how they represent.* We will see that it was this crucial lacuna in Lenin's theory of the state that enabled latter-day "Stalinism" to establish its state power.

The representative bodies, called "Soviets" in the Soviet Union, which had evolved from the workers', peasants', and soldiers' councils, were supposed, on the one hand, to take over the function of the bourgeois parliament by transforming it from a "chatter hovel" (Marx's term) into a *working* body. It is evident from Lenin's train of thought that this very transformation of the *charac-ter* of the representative bodies implies a change in the representative himself. He ceases to be a "chatterbox" and becomes a functionary who *works out* and *carries out* plans and is responsible *to the people*. On the other hand, they are *not stagnant* institutions. They *are constantly growing*. More and more members of the population are included in the functions of social administration. And this self-administration of the society, i.e., the performing of the social functions by the people themselves, will be that much more complete, the greater the number of people who participate in it. At the same time this means that the less the Soviets are elected "representatives," the more the total population takes over those functions that *determine* and *carry out* social planning. For until then the Soviets themselves are *still* more or less isolated from the society as a whole, notwithstanding the fact that they are organs and bodies that evolved from the society itself. It is also clear from Lenin's conception that the proletarian representative bodies serve *transitional functions*. They are conceived of as mediators between the "proletarian state power," which is *still* necessary, *still* in operation, but *already withering*, and the *self-government of society*, which is not yet an accomplished fact, not yet fully capable of functioning by itself. It is a self-government which *still has to be fully developed*. The Soviets can either coincide more and more with the society as a whole, which is developing toward self-government, *or* they can become mere appendages and executive organs of the proletarian state power. They operate between two forces: *one power that is still a state power* and a *new social system of self-government*. What is it that determines whether the Soviets fulfill their progressive revolutionary function, or whether they deteriorate into hollow, purely formalistic fabrics of a state administrative body? Apparently, it is determined by the following:

1. Whether the proletarian state power remains true to its function *of gradually eliminating itself*;

2. Whether the Soviets regard themselves not only as the helpmates and executive organs of the proletarian state power, but also as its surveillant and as that institution, so heavily saddled with

responsibility, that *transfers the function of social leadership more and more from the proletarian state power to the society as a whole;*

3. *Whether the individual members of the masses increasingly measure up to their tasks of gradually and continually taking over the functions of the still operative state apparatus as well as those of the Soviets, insofar as the latter are only "representatives" of the masses.*

This third point is the decisive one, for upon its fulfillment depends the "withering away of the state" in the Soviet Union, as well as the take-over of the functions of the Soviets by the working masses of people.

Hence, the dictatorship of the proletariat is not intended as a permanent condition but as a process, which is *to begin* with the destruction of the authoritarian state apparatus and the establishment of the proletarian state and *to end* with *total self-administration, the self-government of the society.*

To arrive at an accurate appraisal of the course of the social process, one has to study the function and development of the Soviets. The course of this process cannot be concealed by any illusions if one considers the following: It is not a question whether 90 percent of the population participates in the elections of the Soviet bodies, as compared with 60 percent formerly, but whether the Soviet voters (not the Soviet representatives) also *assume more and more of an actual part in social leadership.* A "90 percent election turnout" is not proof of a progressive development toward social self-government, if only because it tells us nothing about the *substance* of the activity of the masses, and, moreover, is not solely characteristic of the Soviet system. The bourgeois democracies, indeed even the fascist "plebiscites" showed "election turnouts of 90 percent and more." It is an essential part of work-democracy to assess the social maturity of a community, not in terms of quantity of votes but in terms of the *actual, tangible substance of its social activity.*

Thus, we always come back to the cardinal question of *every* social order: *What is taking place in the masses of the population? How do they experience the social process to which they are subject?*

Will the working population become capable, and how will it become capable of causing the withering away of the authoritarian state, which rises above and against the society, and taking over its functions, i.e., developing social self-government organically?

Apparently, this is the question Lenin had in mind when he made it clear that a complete elimination of bureaucracy in all spheres all at once was impossible, but that the old, bureaucratic apparatus would certainly have to be replaced by a new one, *"which gradually makes every bureaucracy superfluous and abolishes it."* "This is *not* a utopia," Lenin wrote, "this is borne out by the experience of the commune. It is the immediate task of the revolutionary proletariat." Lenin did not discuss why the "abolition of bureaucracy" was not a utopian aspiration, nor how life *without* bureaucracy, *without* leadership "from above," was not only by all means possible and necessary but, what was more, was the *"immediate task of the revolutionary proletariat."*

Lenin's emphasis can be understood only if one bears in mind man's (and most of his leaders') deeply ingrained, seemingly ineradicable belief in the infantilism of the masses, above all, the belief in the impossibility of getting along without authoritarian leadership. "Self-administration," "self-government," "nonauthoritarian discipline,"—such new concepts, in view of fascism, only evoked an indulgent smile of contempt! The dreams of anarchists! Utopian! Chimerical! Indeed, these shouters and sneerers could even point to the Soviet Union, to Stalin's statement that *the abolition of the state was out of the question,* that, on the contrary, *the power of the proletarian state had to be strengthened and extended.* Lenin had been wrong after all, then! Man is and remains a subservient being. Without authority and coercion he will not work, but merely "indulge his pleasures and be lazy." Don't waste your time and energy with empty chimera! But if this was so, then an official correction of Lenin's ideas was to be demanded from the state leadership of the Soviet Union. It would have to show that Lenin had erred when he wrote the following:

> We are not utopians. We do not "dream" about how we can get along without any administration, without any subordination *all at once*. These anarchistic dreams, which are based on a misunderstanding of the tasks of the dictatorship of the proletariat, are foreign to the nature of Marxism. In reality, they merely serve to put off the socialist revolution to a time when men will have become different. No, we have to carry out the socialist revolution with people as they are now, that is to say, with people who will not be able to get along without subordination, control, "managers and bookkeepers". . . . But one has to subordinate oneself to the armed avant-garde of all those who have been exploited, to the workers, the proletariat. What is specifically "bureaucratic" in government offices can and must be replaced by the simple functions of "managers and bookkeepers." Work on this must begin immediately, from one day to the next. . . . Workers, we *ourselves* shall organize the large industries; we shall organize them on the basis of our own experience; we shall take over where capitalism left off; we shall create a strict, iron discipline, which will be maintained by the state power of the armed workers; we shall convert the state officials into simple executors of our instructions; we shall convert them into responsible, replaceable, modestly paid "managers and bookkeepers" . . . that is our proletarian task. With this we can and must *begin* the implementation of the proletarian revolution. Such a beginning on the basis of large industries will automatically lead to a gradual withering away of every form of bureaucracy, to the gradual creation of a new order without quotation marks, an *order which will have nothing to do with wage-slavery* [my italics, WR]. We will create an order in which the functions of management and rendering of accounts will become more and more simplified and will be performed by the people themselves on a rotation basis. As time goes on, these functions will become a habit and finally disappear altogether as *special* functions of a special class of people.
>
> —*State and Revolution*

Lenin failed to see the dangers of the new state bureaucracy. Apparently, he believed that the proletarian bureaucrats would not abuse their power, would stick to the truth, would teach the working people to be independent. He failed to take into account the abysmal biopathy of the human structure. Indeed, he had no notion of it.

Sociologic literature has paid far too little regard to the fact that in his main work on the revolution, Lenin did not devote most of his attention to the "overthrow of the bourgeoisie" but to the *subsequent* tasks: the replacement of the capitalistic state apparatus by a proletarian apparatus *and* the replacement of the proletarian dictatorship (social democracy = proletarian democracy) by the self-government of the society, which was supposed to be the outstanding characteristic of communism. If one paid special heed to Soviet literature from 1937 on, one saw that it was the *strengthening* (not the loosening) of the power of the *proletarian state appartus* that took priority over all other efforts. *There was no longer any talk of the necessity of its eventual replacement by self-administration.* To understand the Soviet Union, however, it is precisely this point that is of decisive importance. Obviously, Lenin had good reason for discussing it in detail in his main work on the Revolution. It was, is, and will continue to be the living nerve system of every genuine social democracy. It was not and is not mentioned by any politician.

THE PROGRAM OF THE COMMUNIST PARTY OF THE SOVIET UNION (EIGHTH PARTY CONGRESS, 1919)

Under Lenin, Russian despotism was transformed into Russian "social democracy." The program of the Communist party of the Soviet Union of 1919, two years after the Revolution, is proof of the *genuine democratic* character of its efforts. It demands a state power, which is to ward off a return of despotism and is to guarantee the establishment of the *free, self-administration* of the masses of people. But it contains *no hint of the nature of the incapacity for freedom of the masses of people.* It has no knowledge of the biopathic degeneration of man's sexual structure. The revolutionary sexual laws that were enacted between 1917 and 1920 were in the right direction, i.e., they were a *recognition* of man's biologic functions. But they got stuck in legal formalism. I made an effort to demonstrate this in Part II of my book *Die Sexualität im Kulturkampf* (1936). It was on this issue that the reconstruction of the human structure foundered, and with it the fulfillment of the democratic program. This catastrophe of an enormous social effort should be a lesson to every new democratic revolutionary effort: *No program advocating freedom has any chance of success unless a basic change is also effected in man's present biopathic sexual structure.*

The following is an excerpt from the program of the 8th Party Congress of the Communist party of the Soviet Union.*

1. A bourgeois republic, even the most democratic, sanctified by such watchwords as "will of the people," "will of the nation," "no class privilege," remains in fact, owing to the existence of private property in land and other means of production, the dictatorship of the bourgeoisie, an instrument for exploitation and oppression of the broad masses of workers by a small group of capitalists. In opposition to this, proletarian or Soviet democracy transformed mass organizations precisely of the classes oppressed by capitalism, of proletarian and poorest peasantry or semi-proletarian, i.e., the vast majority of the population, into a single and permanent basis of the state apparatus, local and central. *By this act, the Soviet State realized among other things local and regional autonomy without the appointment of authorities from above, on a much wider scale than is practised anywhere.*[6] The aim of the Party is to exert the greatest efforts in order to realize fully this highest type of

---

* The English translation of the program of the 8th Party Congress of the Soviet Union is quoted from *Soviet Communism: Programs and Rules*, edited by Jan. F. Triska (Chandler Publishing Co., San Francisco, 1962). All italics are by Wilhelm Reich.

[6] In this connection: cf. the principle of local self-government in the United States after the emancipation of 1776.

democracy, which to function accurately requires a continually rising *standard of culture, organization and activity on the part of the masses.*

2. In contrast to bourgeois democracy, which concealed the class character of the state, the Soviet authority openly acknowledges that *every state must inevitably bear a class character*[7] until the division of society into classes has been abolished and *all government authority disappears.* By its very nature, the Soviet state directs itself to the suppression of the resistance of the exploiters, and the Soviet constitution does not stop short of depriving the exploiters of their political rights, bearing in mind that any kind of freedom is a deception if it is opposed to the emancipation of labor from the yoke of capital. The aim of the Party of the proletariat consists in carrying on a determined suppression of the resistance of the exploiters, in struggling against the deeply rooted prejudices concerning the absolute character of bourgeois rights and freedom, and at the same time explaining that deprivation of political rights and any kind of limitation of freedom are necessary as *temporary measures* in order to defeat the attempts of the exploiters to retain or to reestablish their privileges. With the disappearance of the possibility of the exploitation of one human being by another, the necessity for these measures will also gradually disappear and the Party will aim to reduce and completely abolish them.

3. Bourgeois democracy has limited itself to formally extending political rights and freedom, such as the right of combination, freedom of speech, freedom of press, equality of citizenship. In practice, however, particularly in view of the economic slavery of the working masses, it was impossible for the workers to enjoy these rights and privileges to any great extent under bourgeois democracy. *Proletarian democracy on the contrary, instead of formally proclaiming those rights and freedoms, actually grants them first of all to those classes which have been oppressed by capitalism, i.e., to*

---

[7] This important democratic point of view was later lost. One stressed the "state," but failed to add that "class rule" was an essential character of every state apparatus. For if there were no classes, ruling and suppressed, there would be no state apparatus, but merely a simple apparatus of social administration [WR].

the proletariat and to the peasantry. For that purpose the Soviet state expropriates premises, printing offices, supplies of paper, etc., from the bourgeoisie, placing these at the disposal of the working masses and their organizations. The aim of the All-Russian Communist Party is to encourage the working masses *to enjoy democratic rights and liberties, and to offer them every opportunity for doing so.*

4. Bourgeois democracy through the ages proclaimed equality of persons, irrespective of religion, race or nationality and the equality of the sexes, but capitalism prevented the realization of this equality and in its imperialist stage developed race and national suppression. The Soviet Government, by being the authority of the toilers, for the first time in history could in all spheres of life realize this equality, destroying the last traces of woman's inequality in the sphere of marriage and the family. At the present moment the work of the Party is principally intellectual and educational with the aim of abolishing the last traces of former inequality and prejudices, especially among the backward sections of the proletariat and peasantry.

The Party's aim is not to limit itself to the formal proclamation of woman's equality, but to liberate woman from all the burdens of antiquated methods of housekeeping, by replacing them by house-communes, public kitchens, central laundries, nurseries, etc.

5. The Soviet Government, guaranteeing to the working masses incomparably more opportunities *to vote and to recall their delegates, in the most easy and accessible manner, than they possessed under bourgeois democracy and parliamentarianism, at the same time abolishes all the negative features of parliamentarianism,* especially the separation of legislative and executive powers, *the isolation of the representative institutions from the masses, etc.*

In the Soviet state *not a territorial district, but a productive unit (factory, mill) forms the electoral unit and the unit of the state.* The state apparatus is thus brought near to the masses.

The aim of the Party consists in endeavoring to bring the Government apparatus into still closer contact with the masses, for the purpose of realizing democracy *more fully and strictly in practice, by making Government officials responsible to, and placing them under the control of the masses.*

6. The Soviet state includes in its organs—the Soviets—workmen and soldiers on a basis of complete equality and unity of interests, whereas bourgeois democracy, in spite of all its declarations, transformed the army into an instrument of the wealthy classes, separated it from the masses, and set it against them, depriving the soldiers of any opportunity of exercising their political rights. The aim of the Party is to defend and develop this unity of the workmen and soldiers in the Soviets and to strengthen the indissoluble ties between the armed forces and the organizations of the proletariat and semi-proletariat.

7. The urban industrial proletariat, being the more concentrated, united and educated section of the toiling masses, hardened in battle, played the part of leader in the whole Revolution. This was evidenced while the Soviets were being created, as well as in the course of development of the Soviets into organs of authority. Our Soviet Constitution reflects this in certain privileges it confers upon the industrial proletariat, in comparison with the more scattered petty-bourgeois masses in the village.

The All-Russian Communist Party, explaining the temporary character of these privileges, which are historically connected with difficulties of socialist organization of the village, must try undeviatingly and systematically to use this position of the industrial proletariat in order closer to unite the backward and the scattered masses of the village proletarians and semi-proletarians, as well as the middle-class peasantry, as a counter-balance to narrow craft professional interests, which were fostered by capitalism among the workmen.

8. The proletarian revolution, owing to the Soviet organization of the state, was able at one stroke to destroy the old bourgeois, official and judicial state apparatus. *The comparatively low standard of culture of the masses,*[8] the absence of necessary experience in

---

[8] "The comparatively low standard of culture of the masses" is a rationalistic conception of the biopathic structure. It shows not the least comprehension of the fact that slave mentality is deeply rooted in the body itself, has become a second nature, as it were, so that *the masses of people pass on their suppression from generation to generation* [WR].

state administration on the part of responsible workers who are elected by the masses, *the pressing necessity, owing to the critical situation of engaging specialists of the old school, and the calling up to military service of the more advanced section of city workmen, all this led to the partial revival of bureaucratic practices within the Soviet system.*[9]

The All-Russian Communist Party, carrying on a *resolute struggle with bureaucratism, suggests the following measures for overcoming the evil:*

(1) Every member of the Soviet is obliged to perform a certain duty in state administration.

(2) *These duties must change in rotation, so as gradually to embrace all the branches of administrative work.*

(3) *All the working masses without exception must be gradually induced to take part in the work of state administration.*

The complete realization of these measures will carry us in advance of the Paris Commune, and the simplification of the work of administration, together with the raising of the level of culture of the masses, will eventually lead to the abolition of state authority.

The following points of the program are singled out as being characteristic of Soviet democracy:

1. Local and regional self-administration without the appointment of authorities from above.

2. Activity on the part of the masses.

3. Deprivation of political rights and limitation of freedom as a *temporary* measure to defeat the exploiters.

4. Not a formal, but an *actual* granting of all rights and freedom to all noncapitalistic classes of the population.

5. Immediate, simple, and direct franchise.

6. The right to elect and recall delegates.

7. Elections not according to districts but according to productive units.

---

[9] The intimate connection between bureaucracy and the human incapacity for freedom is clearly seen here [WR].

8. The responsibility and obligation of those in office to render an account of their activities to the workers' and peasants' councils.

9. Rotation of members of the Soviet in the administrative branches.

10. Gradual inclusion of the entire working population in the work of the administration of the state.

11. Simplification of the administrative functions.

12. Abolition of the state power.

There is *one* thought that struggles to gain clarity among these historically decisive principles, namely: *How can social life be simplified in actual practice?* Struggle as it may, however, it remains stuck in formal political thinking. The *nature* of the politics of state is not described. Admitted that the masses themselves are given the scope of freedom, yet they are still not set any *practical social tasks.* It is not stated that *the masses of the people, as they are today, cannot take over state and (later) social functions.* The present political thinking related to the state was derived from the first hierarchical representatives of the state and was always directed *against* the masses. Politically, we are still stuck in the systems of thought of the Greek and Roman slave states, no matter how much we rant about "democracy." If social self-administration is to become a reality, it is not only the form of the state that has to be changed. *Social existence and its management must be changed in accordance with the tasks and needs of the masses of people.* Social self-administration must gradually replace the state apparatus or take over its rational function.

THE "INTRODUCTION OF SOVIET DEMOCRACY"

The Eighth Party Congress of the Communist party of the Soviet Union founded Soviet democracy in 1919. In January of 1935, the Seventh Soviet Congress announces the "introduction of Soviet Democracy." What is the meaning of this nonsense?

We want to tell a little story to illustrate the process that led to the "introduction of Soviet democracy" in 1935, sixteen years after the introduction of Soviet democracy.

In the course of his studies, a student of criminal jurisprudence realizes that man's antisocial acts are not to be looked upon as crimes, but as sicknesses; therefore, they should not be punished. They should be healed, and efforts should be made to prevent their recurrence. He gives up his study of law and turns to the study of medicine. He replaces formal ethical activities with practical and pertinent activities. After awhile, he further realizes that his medical work will require the use of some nonmedical methods. For example, he would like to dispense with the use of straitjackets as a method of treatment for mental patients and replace their use by preventive educational measures. Despite his better judgment, however, he is forced to make use of the straitjacket—there are just too many mental patients. He cannot cope with all of them, so he has to continue to use antiquated and poor methods, but always bearing in mind that they *must be replaced someday by better methods.*

As time goes by the task becomes more than he can handle. He is not equal to it. Too little is known about mental sicknesses. There are too many of them; education produces them by the thousands every day. As a physician he has to protect society from mental illnesses.

He cannot carry out his good intentions. On the contrary, he has to revert to the old methods, the very methods he had formerly condemned so severely and had wanted to replace with better ones. He makes use of straitjackets more and more. His educational plans come to naught. His efforts to become a physician who prevents sicknesses, instead of one who has to cure them, also fail. He has no choice but to revert to the old laws. His effort to treat criminals as patients does not bear fruit. He is forced to have them *locked up* again.

But he doesn't admit his fiasco, neither to himself nor to others. He doesn't have the courage. Perhaps he isn't even aware of it. Now he asserts the following nonsense: *"The introduction of straitjackets and prisons for criminals and people who are mentally ill represents an enormous step forward in the application of my medical art.* It is the *true* medical art; it constitutes the attainment of *my original goal!"*

This story applies in the minutest detail to the "introduction of Soviet democracy," sixteen years after the "introduction of Soviet democracy." It becomes comprehensible only when it is assessed against the basic conception of *"social democracy"* and the "abolition of the state" as set forth by Lenin in *State and Revolution.* The explanation for this measure given by the Soviet government is not so important here. Only one sentence from the explanation, printed in the *Rundschau,* 1935, no. 7, p. 331, shows that with this act, whether justified or not, Lenin's conception of social democracy was *annulled.* It is stated:

> The proletarian dictatorship has always been the only true power of the people. It has successfully fulfilled both of its main tasks: the destruction of the exploiters as a class, their expropriation and suppression, and the socialist education of the masses. *The proletarian dictatorship continues to exist undeterred. . . .*

If the exploiters have been destroyed as a class and the socialist education of the masses has been a success, and yet the dictatorship continues to exist "undeterred," we see just how nonsensical the whole idea is. If the preconditions have been fulfilled, then why does the dictatorship continue to exist undeterred? Against whom or what is it directed if the exploiters have been crushed and the masses have already been educated to assume responsibility for social functions? Such a ridiculous formulation always conceals an all-too-true meaning: The dictatorship continues, but now it is no longer directed against the exploiters of the old school, but against the masses themselves.

The *Rundschau* continues: "This higher socialist phase, the alliance between workers and peasants, gives the proletarian dictatorship, as *the* democracy of the workers, a new and higher

256

content. This new content also requires new forms, i.e., . . . the transition to equal, direct, and secret ballots for the workers."

We don't want to engage in any hairsplitting: *The proletarian dictatorship* (which in time was supposed to give way to the self-administration of masses of people) *exists simultaneously with the "most democratic" democracy.* This is sociologic nonsense, a confusion of all sociologic concepts. We are concerned here with one central question: Was the main goal of the social revolutionary movement of 1917, the *abolition of the state* and the *introduction of social self-administration, actually achieved?* If so, then an essential difference must exist between the "Soviet democracy" of 1935 and the "proletarian dictatorship" of 1919 on the one hand, and the bourgeois parliamentary democracies of England and America on the other hand.

Mention is made of the "further democratization" of the Soviet system. How is this possible? We were under the impression that, in terms of its nature, the conception of its founders, and also as it *actually* was in the beginning, the "proletarian dictatorship" is completely identical with *social democracy* (= proletarian democracy). If, however, the dictatorship of the proletariat is the same as social democracy, then a Soviet democracy cannot be introduced sixteen years after the establishment of social democracy, nor can there be a "further democratization." The "introduction of democracy" certainly implies—and there can be no doubt about this—that social democracy had not existed previously and that the dictatorship of the proletariat was *not* identical with social democracy. Quite apart from this, it is absurd to say that social democracy is the "most democratic" system. Is *bourgeois* democracy only "a little" democratic, while social democracy is "more" democratic? What does "a little" and what does "more" mean? In reality, bourgeois parliamentary democracy is a formal democracy; masses of people elect their representatives, but they do not govern themselves through their own workers' organizations. And Lenin's *social democracy* was supposed to be a *qualitatively* completely different

257

form of social regulation and not merely a kind of *quantitative* improvement of formal parliamentarianism. It was supposed to replace the proletarian dictatorship of the state by the actual and practical self-administration of the workers. The parallel existence of the "dictatorship of the proletariat" and the self-administration of the working masses, is an impossibility. As a political demand it is confusing and nonsensical. In actual fact it is a dictatorship of party bureaucracy that rules over the masses under the guise of a formal democratic parliamentarianism.

We must never lose sight of the fact that Hitler always built upon the justified hate of masses of people against sham democracy and the parliamentary system—and with great success! In view of such political maneuvers on the part of Russian Communists, fascism's potent slogan, "unity of Marxism and parliamentary bourgeois liberalism," must have been very impressive! Around 1935 the hope that broad masses of people throughout the world had placed on the Soviet Union began to dwindle more and more. Actual problems cannot be solved with political illusions. One has to have the guts to face difficulties squarely. Clearly established social concepts cannot be confused with impunity.

In the establishment of "Soviet democracy," the participation of the masses in the administration of the state was stressed, the protectorate of the industries over the respective branches of the government was made explicit and the fact that workers' and peasants' councils have a voice "in" the people's commissariats was extolled. However, this is not the issue. It is the following that is important:

1. How do the masses *actually* participate in the administration of the state? Is this participation an *increasing take-over of administrative functions,* as is called for by social democracy? What is the form of this "participation"?

2. *A formal protectorate of an industry over a branch of the government is not self-administration. Does the government branch control the industry or vice versa?*

3. Councils having a voice "in" the people's commissariat

means that they are appendages or, at best, executive organs of the commissariat, whereas Lenin's demand reads: *Replacement of all official bureaucratic functions by Soviets, which spread more and more among the masses.*

4. If Soviet democracy is "introduced" *at the same time* that the dictatorship of the proletariat continues to be "consolidated," this can only mean that the goal, *the continuous withering away of the proletarian state and the proletarian dictatorship, has been given up.*

On the basis of the available facts and the assessment of these facts, the introduction of "Soviet democracy" sixteen years after the introduction of Soviet democracy means that: *The transition from authoritarian state government to self-administration of society was not possible.* This transition failed to materialize because the biopathic *structure of the masses* and the *means of effecting a basic change in this structure were not recognized.* There can be no question that the disappropriation and curbing of individual capitalists was a complete success; but *the education of the masses, the attempt to make them capable of abolishing the state, which was only an oppressor to them, to effect its "withering away" and to take over its functions, was not a success.* It was for this reason that the social democracy that had begun to develop during the first years of the Revolution had to die out little by little. It was also for this reason that the state apparatus, which had not been replaced by anything, had to be *consolidated* to secure the existence of society. Besides a shifting of the political emphasis to the masses of the kolkhoz peasants, the "introduction of universal suffrage" in 1935 meant the reintroduction of *formal* democracy. In essence, it meant that the bureaucratic state apparatus, which was becoming more and more powerful, granted a meaningless parliamentary right to a mass of people who had not been able to destroy this apparatus and had not learned to administrate its own affairs. There is no indication whatever in the Soviet Union that the slightest effort is being made to prepare the working masses to take over the administration of society. It is certainly necessary to teach people to read and write, to be sanitary, and to understand the technique of motors, but this has nothing to do with social self-administration. Hitler does as much.

The development of Soviet society was characterized by the formation of a new autonomous state apparatus, which had become strong enough to give the mass of the population the *illusion* of freedom without endangering its own position in any way, in precisely the same way as Hitler's National Socialism had done. The introduction of Soviet democracy was not a step forward, but a step backward, one of many regressions to old forms of social life. *What guarantees are there that the state apparatus of the Soviet Union will abolish itself by educating the masses to administrate their own affairs?* Sentimentality serves no purpose here: The Russian Revolution encountered an obstacle, of which it had no knowledge and which was therefore shrouded in illusions. *The obstacle was man's human structure, a structure that had become biopathic in the course of thousands of years.* It would be absurd to set the "blame" down to Stalin or anyone else. Stalin was only an instrument of circumstances. Only on paper does the process of social development appear as easy and as pleasant as taking a stroll through the woods. In hard reality it encounters new and unrecognized difficulties one after the other. Regressions and catastrophes result. One has to learn to recognize, investigate, and master them. However, *one* reproach remains: The veracity of a promising social plan has to be examined again and again. It must be honestly decided whether the plan is true or false, and whether anything has been overlooked in its development. Only in such a way can the plan be *consciously* changed and improved, and its development more effectively mastered. It may often be necessary to mobilize the thinking of many people to overcome those forces that obstruct the development toward freedom. But to befog the masses with illusions is a social crime. When an honest leader of the masses reaches an impasse and knows that he cannot make any headway, he *resigns* and makes room for others. If a better leader does not appear, the present leader honestly tells the community exactly where it stands, and he waits with them to see whether a solution cannot be found after all, either from the course of events themselves or from an individual insight. But the politician is afraid of such honesty.

In defense of the international workers' movement, it must be pointed out that its fight for a real and genuine democracy—not a mere rhetorical one—was made incredibly difficult. One always sided with those who declared: "The dictatorship of the proletariat is a dictatorship like any other dictatorship. This has become clear, for why is it only now that democracy is 'introduced'?" There was no reason to be happy about the praise given to the Soviet Union ("introspective," "democracy," "finally") by the Social Democrats. It was a bitter pill, a formality. *An objective regression in the course of a development is often necessary and has to be accepted,* but to shroud such a regression in illusions by the fascist method of lying cannot be justified. When Lenin introduced the "New Economic Policy" (NEP) in 1923, he did not say: "We have advanced from a lower phase of proletarian dictatorship to a higher phase. The introduction of the NEP constitutes an enormous step forward toward communism." Such a statement would have immediately undermined confidence in Soviet leadership. When Lenin introduced the NEP, he said:

> It is sad and cruel, but there is no way of getting around it right now. The economy imposed upon communism by the war has confronted us with unforeseen difficulties. We have to go back a step in order to proceed that much more securely. True, we are giving private enterprise a bit of freedom—we have no other choice—but we know exactly what we are doing.

In the case of the "introduction of Soviet democracy," such self-evident perception and frankness were missing. In 1935 they were more necessary than ever before. Such a direct and honest approach would have won millions of friends throughout the world. It would have made people think. It might even have averted the pact with Hitler, the responsibility for which was shoved off on the Trotskians. As it was, however, a new Russian nationalism was super-imposed on Lenin's social democracy.

The *Leningrad Red Times*, the central organ of the Russian Bolsheviks, stated on February 4, 1935:

> All our love, our faithfulness, our strength, our hearts, our heroism, our life—everything for you, take it, O great Stalin, everything is yours, O leader of our great homeland. Command your sons. They can move in the air and under the earth, in water and in the stratosphere.[10] Men and women of all times and all nations will remember your name as the most magnificent, the strongest, the wisest, the most beautiful. Your name is written on every factory, on every machine, in every corner of the world, in every human heart. When my beloved wife bears me a child, the first word I will teach him will be "Stalin."

In *Pravda* of March 19, 1935 (quoted in the *Rundschau*, No. 15, p. 787, 1935), we find an article entitled "Soviet Patriotism," in which "Soviet patriotism" begins to vie with "fascist patriotism":

> Soviet patriotism—that flaming feeling of boundless love, unconditional devotion to one's native country, deepest responsibility for its fate and for its defense—surges forth from the deepest depths of our people. Never before has heroism in the fight for one's own country reached such stupendous heights. The unparalleled and glorious history of the Soviet Union shows what the working people are capable of when it is a question of their homeland. The immortal song of our dear, liberated and new-formed country resounds from the illegal work, the barricades, the storming and sweeping of Budënny's crack mounted army, the grape-shot fire of the imperishable army of the revolution, the harmony of the plants and factories of socialist industries, the rhythm of work between city and town, and the activity of the Communist Party.
>
> Soviet Russia, the country bred and reared by Lenin and Stalin! How it is caressed by the rays of Spring, which began with the

---

[10] As if the sons of the "great German homeland" or of the United States couldn't do the same!

October revolution! Streams swelled up, dammed-up currents broke forth, all the forces of the working people began to move and to pave the way for new historical developments. The grandeur of the Soviet Union, the splendor of its fame and its power shone forth from every corner of the country. The seeds of a rich life and a socialist culture sprang up rapidly. We have raised the Red banner of Communism to new heights and far into blue distant skies.

Soviet patriotism is the love of our people for the land, the land which we have wrung from the capitalists and landowners with blood and sword. It is the attachment to the beautiful life which our great people have created. It is the militant and powerful guard in West and East. It is the dedication to the great cultural heritage of human genius which has blossomed so perfectly in our country and *in our country only* [my italics, WR]. Is it surprising, then, that foreigners come to the borders of the Soviet Union, people with different educational backgrounds, to bow reverently to the haven of culture, to the state of the Red flag?

Soviet Union—the fountainhead of mankind! The name of Moscow rings forth to the workers, peasants, to all honest and cultured people the world over, rings forth like a bell in the fog at sea, a hope for a brighter future and for the victory over fascist barbarism.

. . . In our socialist country, the interests of the people cannot be separated from the interests of the country and its government. Soviet patriotism derives its inspiration from the fact that the people themselves, under the leadership of the Soviet Party, have shaped their own life. It derives its inspiration from the fact that only now, under Soviet power, has our beautiful and rich country been opened to the working people. And the natural attachment to one's native country, one's native soil, to the skies under which one first saw the light of this world, grows and becomes a powerful pride in one's socialist country, in one's great Communist Party, in one's Stalin. The ideas of Soviet patriotism breed and rear heroes, knights and millions of brave soldiers who, like an all-engulfing avalanche, are ready to hurl themselves upon the enemies of the country and obliterate them from the face of the earth. With the milk from their mothers, our youth are imbued with love for their country. It is our obligation to educate new generations of Soviet patriots, for whom the interests of their country will mean more than anything else, even more than life itself. . . .

. . . The great invincible spirit of Soviet patriotism is nurtured with the greatest care, skill and creativity. Soviet patriotism is one of the outstanding manifestations of the October revolution. How much strength, boldness, youthful vigor, heroism, pathos, beauty and movement it contains!

In our country, Soviet patriotism glows like a powerful flame. It drives life forward. It heats the motors of our storm tanks, our heavy bombers, our destroyers, and loads our cannons. Soviet patriotism guards our borders, where vile enemies, doomed to perish, threaten our peaceful life, our power and our glory. . . .

This is the emotional plague of politics. It has nothing to do with the natural love of one's native country. It is the maudlin raving of a writer who knows of no objective means of stirring people's enthusiasm. It is comparable to the erection of an impotent man, forcefully brought about by the use of yohimbine. And the social effects of such patriotism are comparable to the reaction of a healthy woman to a sexual embrace made possible by yohimbine.

Perhaps this "Soviet patriotism," in view of the extinction of revolutionary enthusiasm, was a necessary preparation for the later fight against the "Wotan patriotism." Work-democracy has nothing to do with such "patriotism." Indeed, one can safely infer that rational social leadership has failed when such yohimbine patriotism begins to crop up. The love of a people for its country, attachment to the earth and devotion to the community speaking the same language, are human experiences, which are too deep and too serious to be made the objects of political irrationalism. Such yohimbine forms of patriotism do not solve a single objective problem of the human society of the working man; they have nothing to do with democracy. Outbreaks of sentimental pathos always point to fear on the part of those who are responsible. We want to have nothing to do with it.

When a genuine democratic, i.e., work-democratic effort is made to effect a basic change in the structure of masses of people, it is easy to appraise the progress or lack of progress that is being made. For instance, when masses of people begin to clamor for super-dimensional pictures of their "führer," then they are on their way to becoming irresponsible. In Lenin's time, a spoonfed führer-cult did not exist, and there were no sky-high pictures of the führer of the proletariat. It is known that Lenin wanted no part of such things.

The attitude taken toward technical achievements is also indicative of a peoples' progress or lack of progress toward genuine freedom. In the Soviet Union the construction of the airliner "Gorki" was extolled as a "revolutionary achievement." But wherein lies the essential difference between the construction of this airliner and those of Germany or America? The construction of airplanes is indispensable in order to provide the broad industrial basis necessary for modern work-democracy. This much is clear, and there should be no arguing about it. What is important is whether the broad masses of workers identify with the construction of airplanes in an illusionary nationalistic-chauvinistic way, i.e., derive a feeling of superiority toward other nations on the basis of the construction of these airplanes, or whether the construction of airplanes serves to bring about a closer human relationship among the various nations and nationalities, i.e., serves to promote internationalism. In other words, as far as man's character structure is concerned, the construction of airplanes can serve a reactionary or work-democratic purpose. Under the management of power-thirsty politicians, the construction of airplanes can easily be exploited to create nationalistic chauvinism. But airliners can also be used to transport Germans to Russia, Russians to China and Germany, Americans to Germany and Italy, and Chinese to America and Germany. In this way the German worker would have a chance to see for himself that he is not essentially different from the Russian worker, and the English worker would be able to learn that the Indian worker is not to be looked upon as a born object of exploitation.

Here again we see clearly that the technical development of a society is not identical with its cultural development. The structure of the human character represents a social power in itself, a power that can be directed toward reactionary or international goals, even when the technical basis is one and the same. The tendency to see everything in terms of economy is catastrophic. Every effort must be made to correct this tendency.

It boils down to this: The working masses of people must refuse to be content with illusionary gratifications, which always end in a kind of fascism, and to insist upon the *real* gratification of the necessities of life and *to bear the responsibility for it*.

The Social Democratic organization of Viennese workers regarded the introduction of the trolley system by the Social Democratic community of Vienna as a *specifically social democratic achievement*. The communist workers of Moscow, that is to say, workers who were fundamentally hostile toward the Social Democratic party, regarded the subway constructed by the communist city administration of Moscow as a *specifically communist achievement*. And the German workers regarded the planned Baghdad railroad as a *specifically German* achievement. These examples are evidence of the plaguelike nature of the illusionary gratification fostered by political irrationalism. Such irrationalism conceals the simple fact that a German railroad and a Viennese railroad and a Moscow railroad are based on precisely the same internationally valid principles of *work*, which the Viennese, Berlin, and Moscow workers follow in precisely the same way. These workers of various nationalities don't say to themselves: "We are all related to one another by the principle of our work and accomplishment. Let us get to know one another and also consider how we can teach the Chinese worker to make use of our principles." No! The German worker is firmly convinced that his railroad is different and better, let us say more Wotanistic, than the Russian railroad. Thus, it never enters his mind to help the Chinaman to build a railroad. On the contrary, hypnotized by his illusionary nationalistic gratification, he follows some plague-ridden general or another, who wants *to deprive* the Chinese of whatever railroad they have. In this way the emotional plague of politics engenders division and deadly hostility within the same class; in this way it engenders envy, boastfulness, unprincipled conduct, and irresponsibility. The elimination of illusionary gratification and its replacement by the genuine gratification derived from a genuine interest in and relationship to work and the establishment of international cooperation among workers are indispensable preconditions for the uprooting of the craving for authority in the character structure of the workers. Only then will the working masses of people be able to develop the forces necessary to adapt technology to the needs of the masses.

In an essay printed in the *Europäische Heften* of November 22, 1934, Hinoy reached the conclusion: ". . . The workers [in the Soviet Union] do not feel themselves to be the direct rulers of their country, nor do the youth. The state is the ruler, but the youth look upon this state as their own creation, and it is from this conception that it derives its patriotism."

Such statements were common at that time, and they left no room for doubt that, no matter how one appraised it, the society of the Soviet Union of the 1930s had nothing whatever to do with the original program of the Communist party, a program that called for the gradual abolition of the state. *This is an objective and factual statement and not a political program against the Soviet Union.* I call upon the KGB* agents in Europe and America to take cognizance of this. The murdering of those who make such statements will not change the facts of the case in the least.

THE DEVELOPMENT OF THE APPARATUS OF THE AUTHORITARIAN STATE FROM RATIONAL SOCIAL RELATIONSHIPS

World War II has reconfirmed what has been general knowledge from time immemorial: The *fundamental* difference between the reactionary politician and the genuine democrat is revealed in their attitude toward state power. A man's social character can be *objectively* appraised on the basis of this attitude, regardless of his

---

* The Soviet secret service.

political party. It follows from this that there are genuine democrats among the fascists and pure fascists among the party democrats. Just as the character structure, this attitude toward state power is not confined to any one class or political group. Here, too, to paint everything in black and white colors is wrong and inadmissible from a sociological point of view. Mental attitudes and political parties cannot be mechanically equated.

It is typical of the reactionary to advocate the supremacy of the state over society; he advocates the *"idea* of the state," which leads in a straight line to dictatorial absolutism, whether it is embodied in a royal, ministerial, or open fascist form of state. The genuine democrat, who acknowledges and advocates natural work-democracy as the natural basis of international and national cooperation, always aims at overcoming the difficulties of social cooperation by eliminating the social causes of these difficulties. It is this aim that characterizes him as a genuine democrat! This requires a thorough discussion of the development and the rational function inherent in the authoritarian state. It is fruitless and senseless to fight an irrational social institution, without first asking oneself how it is possible that, despite its irrationality, this institution is capable of surviving and even appearing necessary. From our study of the Russian state apparatus we learned that this state apparatus became necessary in the course of time. And it was not difficult to see that, notwithstanding all its irrationality, it very definitely had the rational function of holding together and leading the Russian people, after the masses had failed to achieve social self-government.

We would not hesitate to call a mother's behavior irrational if she were to treat her neurotic child in a strict and authoritarian manner. We will readily understand that it is this strictness that makes the child sick, but we must not overlook the fact—and this is the cardinal point in the fighting of authoritarian education—that a child who has become a neurotic, and is living in a neurotic family situation, cannot be held in check in any other way than with authoritarian means. In other words, although it is not fundamentally rational, the mother's strictness has a rational side, however conditional and circumscribed it may be. We will have to concede this *conditional* rational function if we ever hope to convince the educator, who adheres to the authoritarian principle from sheer necessity, that it *can* be eliminated by preventing the child from becoming neurotic.

This *conditional* and *circumscribed* rational character also applies to the authoritarian state, as reluctant as we are to admit it, knowing how dangerous such a statement could become in the hands of a mystical dictator. He would be capable of saying: "Do you hear! Even the liberal work-democrats admit the necessity and rationality of an authoritarian leadership." We know now that *it is the irrational character structure of masses of people that offers a "justification" for authoritarian leadership*. Only in this way can a dictatorship be comprehended, and this comprehension is the only hope of eliminating it from man's life. The recognition of the irrationality in the structure of the masses gives us a social basis from which to overcome this irrationality and, with it, dictatorship itself—to overcome it, not with illusions, but objectively and scientifically. When social cooperation is disrupted, state power is always strengthened. This is in keeping with the moralistic-authoritarian method of dealing with the difficulties *superficially*. This approach does not of course really remove the social evil, but merely pushes it into the background, from which it later breaks forth much more violently and extensively. If there are no other means of dealing with rape murders than the execution of the murderer, then one uses this method. This is the approach followed by the authoritarian state. Work-democracy, however, goes to the core of the matter and asks: How can we eliminate the phenomena of rape and murder altogether? Only when we comprehend the compulsion of execution and simultaneously condemn it is the problem of elimination brought into sharp focus. Undoubtedly, the elimination of social evils is one of the chief means of causing the authoritarian state to wither away. In all probability moralistic-authoritarian social leadership will continue to function only so long as and insofar as it cannot be superseded by the methods of self-government. This applies to the state in general, as well as to all other areas of social life.

True enough, the authoritarian state is essentially a suppressive apparatus, but it is not exclusively so. At the same time, and indeed originally, before it became a suppressive apparatus of the society, it was an aggregate of autonomous social relations. Originally, the state was identical with society. In the course of time it detached itself from the society and became more and more alien to it, eventually assuming the form of a raging force above and against it.

As long as there was a social organization (such as in the clan society) that was not driven by serious inner contradictions, there was no need for a special power having the task of holding the social organisms together. The nature of society is such that it requires a power to prevent its disintegration, its decline, and its dissolution when it is riven by powerful opposing interests and difficulties of life. Among other things it was the schism of German society caused by the many different and hostile political parties that enabled German fascism to achieve power. Fascism's rapid and powerful rise to power clearly shows that, for masses of German people, the promise that the society would be held together by means of the state was more essential than the individual party programs. But this does not change the fact that ideas and political ideologies cannot eliminate the inner schisms of society, and it makes no difference whether this political idea is totalitarian or nontotalitarian. The fascists were not the only ones who played up the idea of the state. They merely did so more urgently and more effectively than the social democratic government, the Communists, and the liberals. And it was precisely for this reason that they were victorious. Thus, it is the political schism of a society that gives birth to the idea of the state, and vice versa, the idea of the state that creates social schism. It is a vicious cycle from which one can extricate oneself only if both the schism and the idea of the state are traced to their source and given a common denominator. As we already know, this common denominator is the irrational character structure of masses of people. Neither those who advocated the idea of the state nor those having other political programs had any inkling of this common denominator. The assertion that this or that dictator imposed himself upon a society against its will and from the outside was one of the gravest errors made in the assessment of dictatorships. In reality, every dictator in history did nothing more than bring already existing ideas of the state to a head. He had merely to seize upon this idea and to exclude all nonrelated ideas to achieve power.

The rational and irrational dual function of the state and of the idea of the state was clearly assessed by Friedrich Engels in the last century:

> Hence, the state is definitely not a power imposed upon society from the outside. Nor, for that matter, is it "the reality of the moral idea," "the image and reality of reason," as Hegel claimed. It is the product of society at a certain stage of its development. It is the admission that a society has become entangled in an insoluble contradiction with itself, has split up into irreconcilable opposing interests, which it is powerless to cope with. To prevent these oppositions, these classes with conflicting economic interests, from consuming themselves and society in a fruitless fight, a power which apparently stands above society becomes necessary, a power which is supposed to have the function of checking the conflict and keeping it within the limits of "order." This power which originates from society but, placing itself above it, becomes more and more alien to it, is the state.

This sociological elucidation of the concept of the state by the industrialist and German sociologist Friedrich Engels completely undermined all philosophies of the state, which in one way or another were derived from Plato's abstract and metaphysical idea. Friedrich Engels' theory does not trace the apparatus of the state from higher values and nationalistic mysticism; in a very simple way it gives a picture of the state's dual nature. Inasmuch as it clarifies the social basis of the state apparatus and at the same time points out the contradiction between state and society, it offers the shrewd statesman—one, for instance, having the stature of Masaryk or

271

Roosevelt—as well as each individual working man of the world, a powerful means with which to comprehend the schism of society and the consequent necessity of a state apparatus . . . and the means *to eliminate* it.

Let us try to elucidate the genesis of the dual nature of the state with a simple example:

In the initial stages of human civilization the social tasks of living and working together presented no problem. Hence, the relationship between man and man was also simple. We can study this factor in the remnants of the old and simple civilizations which have continued intact into our own times. Once again let us illustrate our point with the well-known organization of the Trobrianders. They have a natural economy, i.e., a use economy. Whatever market economy they practice is of no account. One clan catches fish, another grows fruit. The one clan has too many fish and the other has too much fruit. Hence, they exchange fish for fruit and vice versa. Their economic relationships are very simple.

Besides the economic relationships there is a definite familial relationship among the members of the clan. Since marriage is exogamous, the Trobriander adolescents of one clan form sexual relations with adolescents of another clan. If by a social interpersonal relationship we understand every relationship that serves to gratify a basic biologic need, then the sexual relationship coexists on an equal par with the economic relationship. The more work itself becomes separated from the gratification of a need, whereby the needs themselves become more complicated, the less is the individual member of the society capable of fulfilling the manifold functions that fall to his share. For example:

Let us transplant the Trobriander society and its natural economy to any place in Europe or Asia. This is an admissible supposition, for all nations of the earth were formed from tribes, and the tribes were originally formed from groups of clans. In the same way, market economy and exchange economy were developed from natural economy. Let us now assume that in one of these small communities, consisting of two to three hundred people, the need arises to establish contact with other small communities. This need is very small. Only one of the two hundred members of the community has something to tell a member of another community. He gets on his horse and rides to the other community and delivers his message. The art of writing has made a beginning and the need for social contact with other communities grows little by little. Until this time everyone delivered his own mail, but now the rider is requested to deliver several letters. In the meantime the communities have grown and now comprise as many as two to five thousand members. The need to enter into a correspondence with members of other communities also grows. Already hundreds of people are exchanging letters. With the development of commerce, the writing of letters ceases to be a rare curiosity. The delivery of letters becomes a daily, vitally necessary task, which is more and more difficult to solve in the old way. One community discusses the matter and decides to employ a *"letter carrier."* It relieves one of its, still nondescript, members from all other duties, guarantees him a definite income and charges him to take care of the community's mail. *This first letter carrier is the human embodiment of the interpersonal relationship between letter writing and letter delivery.* In this way a *social organ* comes into being, the sole function of which is to deliver letters. Our letter carrier is a primitive type of social administrator, whose vitally necessary work is still very definitely and solely in the service of the social community.

Let us further assume that in the course of many years the primitive communities have grown into small towns of, let us say, fifty thousand inhabitants each. Among other things the growth of these communities is to be ascribed to the new function of letter writing and the social intercourse related to it. One letter carrier is no longer enough; one hundred letter carriers are needed now. They require their own administration; therefore, one of them is given the job of *chief letter carrier.* He is a letter carrier who has been relieved of his former duties. In place of these he has assumed the more extensive duty of organizing the work of the one hundred letter carriers in the most practical way possible. As yet, he does not "supervise," and he does not give orders. He does not stand above the community of letter carriers. He merely facilitates their work; he decides when the letters will be picked up and when they will be delivered. He now gets the idea of producing postage stamps, which simplify the entire function.

In this way a very simple and vitally necessary function has become autonomous. "The postal system" has become an "apparatus" of the society; it has grown out of the society for the purpose of improving its coordination. It still does not set itself up against this society as a *superior power*.

How is it possible for such an administrative apparatus of society to become a suppressive apparatus? It does not become a suppressive power on the basis of its original function. The administrative apparatus retains these social functions, but it gradually develops characteristics other than those related to its vitally necessary activity. Let us now assume that in our large community, conditions of authoritarian patriarchy have begun to develop, wholly independent of the postal system. For example, there are already "aristocratic" families, which have developed from the original tribal chiefs. By accumulating dowries, they have developed a twofold power: first of all the power that is inherent in property, and second of all the power to forbid their own children to have sexual intercourse with the less well-to-do strata of the community. In the development of economic and sexual slavery these two power functions always go hand in hand. The authoritarian patriarch who becomes more and more powerful wants to prevent other, weaker members of the community from maintaining contact with other communities. He also wants to make it impossible for his daughters to exchange love letters with whomever they please. It is of interest to him that his daughters form relations only with certain well-to-do men. His interests in sexual and economic suppression cause him to seize upon those autonomous social functions that were originally managed by the society as a whole. On the basis of his growing influence, our patriarch will introduce a new regulation forbidding the post office to deliver all letters without distinction. Under the new regulation, for example, love letters in general and certain business letters will not be delivered. To fulfill this novel function, the post office charges one of its letter carriers with the task of "*censoring the mail.*" In this way the social administration of mail service takes on a second function, one which makes it an *authoritarian power* separated from and above society. This constitutes the first step toward the development of an authoritarian state apparatus from a social administrative apparatus. Letter carriers still continue to deliver letters, but already they have begun to poke their noses into the contents of the letters and to determine who is allowed and who is not allowed to write letters and what one can write about and what one cannot write about. To this the social community reacts in one of two ways: toleration or protest. The first gap in the social community has been created, whether it is called "class conflict" or something else. It is not a question of words, but of the differentiation between a social function which is vital and one which curtails freedom. From now on, arbitrary practices have a free hand. For instance, Jesuits can exploit the postal censorship for their own purposes. The security police might make use of the existing postal censorship to increase their own power.

Without distorting things, this simplified example can be easily applied to the complicated machinery of present-day society. It applies to our banking system, our police, and our school system, the administration of food distribution, and certainly to the bearing of society toward other nations. We begin to make order of chaos if, in the evaluation of any state function, we consistently ask ourselves what part of it relates to its original function of executing social tasks, and what part of it relates to the later-acquired function of suppressing the freedom of the members of the society. Originally, the police of New York, Berlin, or any other city had the task of protecting the community from murder and theft. Insofar as they still perform this task, they are a useful and autonomous function of society. But when the police take it upon themselves to prohibit harmless games in private homes, to prescribe whether a man or woman can receive a member of the opposite sex in his or her apartment alone, to determine when they have to get up and when they have to go to bed, then we have a picture of a tyrannical and authoritarian state power, a state power *above* and *against* society.

It is one of work-democracy's inherent tendencies to eliminate those functions of social administration that operate above and/or against society. The natural work-democratic process tolerates *only* those administrative functions that serve to promote the unity of society and to facilitate its vital operations. It clearly follows from this that one cannot be "against" or "for" the "state" in a mechanical and rigid way. One has to distinguish between its original social functions and its suppressive functions. It is also clear that the state apparatus will become and will have to become the executive organ of society when, in fulfilling its natural work functions, it operates in the interest of society as a whole. When this happens, however, it ceases to be a "state apparatus." It divests itself of those very characteristics that alienate it from society, place it above and against society, and thus implant in it the seed of authoritarian dictatorships. This constitutes the genuine withering away of the state, i.e., a withering away of its irrational functions. The rational functions are vitally necessary and they continue.

This distinction makes it possible to examine every vitally necessary administrative function to see whether it is attempting to place itself above and against society, to see whether it is beginning to become a new authoritarian instrument of the state. As long as it is in the service of society, it is also a part of society. It is desirable, necessary, and it belongs in the sphere of vitally necessary work. If, however, the state apparatus sets itself up to be the master and tyrant of society, if it claims autonomous power for itself, then it becomes the arch enemy of society and must be dealt with accordingly.

It is clear that a modern and complicated social organism could not exist without an administrative apparatus. It is equally clear that it is no easy task to eliminate the tendency of the administrative apparatus to deteriorate into a "state apparatus." Here is a vast field of research for sociologists and social psychologists. After the authoritarian state has been overthrown, the task still remains of preventing administrative functions from becoming autonomous powers again. However, in view of the fact that authoritarian autonomy is the direct result of the inability of working masses of people to regulate, administrate, and control their own affairs, the problem of the authoritarian state can no longer be dealt with and mastered independently of the problem of man's structure, and vice versa.

This leads directly to the question of so-called "*state capitalism,*" which was still unknown in the nineteenth century and did not begin to develop until World War I, 1914–18.

THE SOCIAL FUNCTION OF STATE CAPITALISM

Until around the end of World War I in Russia and until the worldwide economic crisis around 1930 in the United States, the relationship between the system of private capitalism and the system of the state was a simple one. For Lenin and his contemporaries the "capitalist state" was simply the power instrument of the "class of private capitalists." The simplicity of this relationship was depicted somewhat as follows in Russian revolutionary films:

The private owner of a factory attempts to depress wages; the workers demand higher wages. The capitalist refuses to comply with this demand, whereupon the workers go on strike to push through their demand. The capitalist telephones the police commissioner and charges him "to reestablish order." In this case, the police commissioner figures as a public tool of the capitalist, and as such merely attests to the fact that the state is a "*capitalist state.*" The police commissioner orders his force to the factory and has the "ringleaders" arrested; the workers are without leadership. After awhile they begin to feel the pangs of hunger and willingly or unwillingly return to their jobs. The capitalist has won. This demands better and stricter organization of the workers. In the opinion of the sociologists who took the part of the workers, this film reflected the relationship between state and capitalism in America. But the enormous social readjustments of the past twenty years have effected changes which no longer coincide with this simple conception. More and more corporations, which were generally described as "state-capitalistic," grew out of the private capitalist system. The Russian society replaced private capitalism with the unlimited power of the state. It makes no difference what it is called, but in the strict Marxist sense *state capitalism has taken the place of private capitalism*. As we already pointed out, the concept of capitalism is not determined by the existence of individual capitalists, but by the existence of market economy and wage labor.

As a result of the worldwide economic crisis 1929–33, social processes that tended toward state capitalism also set in in Germany and America. The state as an organization above society also began to assume an autonomous position toward the system of private capitalism. In part, it took over functions that had formerly been left to private capitalists: for instance, the replacement of philanthropy by social security. The state also imposed wage controls on private capitalism, in some areas more and in others less. All of this was brought about by the pressure exerted by masses of wage laborers and employees. It was in this way that they exercised their social influence: not by a direct take-over of administrative social functions by *their* organizations, but in a fundamentally different way, namely by exerting the necessary pressure upon the state apparatus to force it to restrict the interests of private capitalism and to safeguard the rights of the laborers and the employees.

In other words: As a result of the revolutionary events in the Soviet Union and the economic slumps in other large societies, which had a more gradual effect, severe crises had been created and with them also the need to mobilize the existing state apparatus to prevent disintegration. "The state" as an autonomous social power again stressed its original function of holding society together at all costs.

This process was very evident in Germany. The need for cohesion in the acute crisis years 1929–39 was so great that the totalitarian and authoritarian idea of the state had hardly any difficulty in gaining wide acceptance. Admitted that the society was held together, the fact remains that the problems that had precipitated the social crisis were not solved. This is easily understood, for the ideology of the state is incapable of dealing with opposing interests in a *factual* and *practical* way. Many of the anti-capitalistic measures adopted by fascism are to be explained on the basis of this process, measures that seduced some sociologists into looking upon fascism as a revolutionary social movement. But fascism was anything but a revolutionary movement. It was merely a precipitant change from the autocracy of private capitalism to state capitalism. In the Göring industries, state capitalism and private capitalism merged into one. Since anti-capitalistic tendencies had always been strong among German workers and employees, this change could be effected only by the use of anti-capitalistic propaganda. It was precisely this contradiction that made the victorious campaign of fascism the prototype of social irrationalism and, consequently, so difficult to grasp. Since fascism promised the masses of people a revolution against private capitalism and at the same time promised private capitalism salvation from the revolution, its moves could be nothing but contradictory, incomprehensible, and sterile. This also accounts to a large extent for the compulsion that drove the German state apparatus into an imperialistic war. There was no possibility of regulating the conditions within the German society in an objective way. The use of police clubs and pistols to create the semblance of peace can hardly be called a "solution of social problems." The "unification of the nation" had been brought about in an *illusionary* way. We have learned to ascribe just as great, if not a greater, effectiveness to processes that are based on illusions as to processes that are based on hard reality. The effect of the church hierarchy has been an incontestable proof of this for thousands of years. Even though not a single factual problem of social life had been actually solved, the illusionary unification of the state created the impression that it was a fascist achievement. The untenability of such a solution was clearly brought out in the course of time. Social discord was greater than it had ever been, yet the illusionary cohesion of the state was sufficient to keep the German society from formal collapse for ten years. The *factual* solution of the existing discord was reserved for different and more fundamental processes.

Whether we are concerned with a capitalist state or a proletarian state, the function of effecting a unity of social discords is the same. Still we must bear in mind the difference in the original intention: In fascism the authoritarian state becomes the fixed prototype of the idea of the state, which means that masses of people are relegated to the status of permanent subjects. Lenin's proletarian state had the intention of undermining itself continuously and of establishing self-administration. In both cases, however, the core is given by the "state control of consumption and production."

Let us return to our common denominator, the inability on the part of working masses of people to administrate society themselves. We will then have a better understanding of the logicality of the development of private capitalism to state capitalism which has taken place during the past twenty-five years. In Russia the working masses of people were capable of overthrowing the old czarist state apparatus and replacing it by a state apparatus whose leaders stemmed from their own ranks. But they were not capable of going on to self-administration and of assuming the responsibility themselves.

In other countries the working masses of people who were highly organized formally were not capable of advancing and putting into practice the self-administration that was a part of the ideology of their own organizations. Hence, the state apparatus was forced to take over more and more functions that actually devolved upon the masses. It took them over in their stead, as it were, for instance, in Scandinavia and in the United States.

As basically different as the state control of social production and consumption was in Russia, Germany, Scandinavia, and the United States on the basis of their historical development, there was still a common denominator, the incapacity on the part of masses of people to administrate society themselves. And the danger of authoritarian dictatorships follows logically and simply from this common basis of a development toward state capitalism. Whether a state functionary has democratic orientation or whether he is an authoritarian representative of the state is purely accidental. Viewed from the perspective of the structure and ideology of the working masses of people, there is in reality not a single concrete guarantee that a dictatorship will not develop from state capitalism. It is precisely for this reason that, in the fight for genuine democracy and social self-administration, it is of decisive importance to single out and stress the role of man's character structure and the shifting of man's responsibility to the processes of love, work, and knowledge.

As painful and embarrassing as it may be, the fact remains that we are confronted with a human structure that has been shaped by thousands of years of mechanistic civilization and is expressed in social helplessness and an intense desire for a führer.

The German and Russian state apparatuses grew out of despotism. For this reason the subservient nature of the human character of masses of people in Germany and in Russia was exceptionally pronounced. Thus, in both cases, the revolution led to a new despotism with the certainty of irrational logic. In contrast to the German and Russian state apparatuses, the American state apparatus was formed by groups of people who had evaded European and Asian despotism by fleeing to a virgin territory free of immediate and effective traditions. Only in this way can it be understood that, until the time of this writing, a totalitarian state apparatus was not able to develop in America, whereas in Europe every overthrow of the government carried out under the slogan of freedom inevitably led to despotism. This holds true for Robespierre, as well as for Hitler, Mussolini, and Stalin. If we want to appraise the facts impartially, then we have to point out, whether we want to or not, and whether we like it or not, that Europe's dictators, who based their power on vast millions of people, always stemmed from the suppressed classes. I do not hesitate to assert that this fact, as tragic as it is, harbors more material for social research than the facts related to the despotism of a czar or of a Kaiser Wilhelm. By comparison, the latter facts are easily understood. The founders of the American Revolution had to build their democracy from scratch on *foreign* soil. The men who accomplished this task had all been rebels against English despotism. The Russian Revolutionaries, on the other hand, were forced to take over an already existing and very rigid government apparatus. Whereas the Americans were able to start from scratch, the Russians, as much as they fought against it, had to drag along the old. This may also account for the fact that the Americans, the memory of their own flight from despotism still fresh in their minds, assumed an entirely different—more open and more accessible—attitude toward the new refugees of 1940, than Soviet Russia, which closed its doors to them. This may also explain why the attempt to preserve the old democratic ideal and the effort to develop genuine self-administration was much more forceful in the United States than anywhere else. We do not overlook the many failures and retardations caused by tradition, but in any event a revival of genuine democratic efforts took place in America and not in Russia. It can only be hoped that American democracy will thoroughly realize, and this before it is too late, that fascism is not confined to any one nation or any one party; and it is to be hoped that it will succeed in overcoming the tendency toward dictatorial forms in the people themselves. Only time will tell whether the Americans will be able to resist the compulsion of irrationality or whether they will succumb to it.

I want to stress that we are not concerned with the question of guilt or evil will, but solely with the elucidation of developments on the basis of definite, already existing conditions.

Let us briefly summarize the connections between the structure of the masses and the form of the state.

The influence of the character structure of masses of people is decisive in determining the form that the state assumes, whether this structure is expressed passively or actively. It is the structure of the masses that tolerates imperialism. It is this structure that actively supports it. By the same token it is the structure of masses of people that is capable of overthrowing despotism, even though it does not have the ability to prevent the emergence of new despotism. It is this structure that promotes and supports genuine democratic efforts when the state operates in this direction. It is this structure that gives rise to national revolutionary movements when the genuine democratic *international* freedom movement fails. It is this structure that takes refuge in the illusionary unity of family, people, nation, and state when democracy fails; but it is also this structure that passes on and develops the process of love, work, and knowledge. Hence, *only* this structure is capable of *imbibing the genuinely democratic tendencies of a state administration* by taking over the administrative functions "above it" piecemeal and learning to execute them through its *own work organizations*. It is beside the point, i.e., it is not of crucial importance, whether the change from state administration to self-administration takes place quickly or slowly. It is better for everyone if it takes place organically and without bloodshed. But this is possible only if the representatives of the state above society are fully conscious of the fact that they are nothing but the delegated executive organs of the working human community; that, in the strictest sense of the word, they are executive organs from necessity, i.e., they are executive organs made necessary by the ignorance and wretchedness in which millions of people live. Strictly speaking, they have the tasks of good educators, namely the task of making self-reliant adults of the children entrusted to their care. A society that is striving to achieve genuine democracy must never lose sight of the principle that it is the task of the state to make itself more and more superfluous, just as an educator becomes superfluous when he has done his duty toward the child. If this principle is not forgotten, bloodshed can be and will be avoided. Only to the extent to which the state clearly and unequivocally abolishes itself is it possible for work-democracy to develop *organically*; conversely, to the same extent to which the state tries to eternalize itself and to forget its educational task, it provokes human society to remind it that it came into being from necessity and must also disappear from necessity. Thus, the responsibility rests upon the state as well as upon masses of people, a responsibility in the good and not the bad sense of the word. It is the state's duty not only to encourage the passionate yearning for freedom in working masses of people; *it must also make every effort to make them capable of freedom.* If it fails to do this, if it suppresses the intense longing for freedom or even misuses it and puts itself in the way of the tendency toward self-administration, then it shows clearly that it is a fascist state. Then it is to be called to account for the damages and dangers that it caused by its dereliction.

X

Biosocial Function of Work

Work is the basis of man's social existence. This is stressed by every social theory. In this respect, however, the problem is not *that* work is the basis of human existence. The problem relates to the nature of work: Is it in *opposition* to or in *harmony* with the biologic needs of masses of people? Marx's economic theory proved that everything that is produced in the way of economic values comes about through the expenditure of man's *living* working power, and *not* through the expenditure of *dead* material.

Hence, as the sole force that produces values, human working power deserves the greatest interest and care. In a society under the compulsion of market economy and not use economy, it is out of the question to speak of the care and careful treatment of human working power. Just as any other commodity, this working power is bought and used by the owners of the means of production (the state or individual capitalists). The "wage" received by the working man corresponds approximately to the minimum of what he needs to reproduce his working power. Profit economy has no interest in sparing labor power. As a result of the progressive mechanization and economization of work, so much labor power is made superfluous that there is always a ready replacement for expended labor power.

The Soviet Union abolished *private* but not *state* profit economy. Its original intent was to transform the *capitalist* "economization" of work into a socialist "economization" of work. It liberated the productive forces of the country and shortened working hours in general; in this way it succeeded in getting through the acute economic crisis of 1929–32 without unemployment. There can be no doubt that the Soviet Union's economizing measures, which were partially socialistic in the beginning, enabled it to satisfy the needs of society as a whole. However, the basic problem of a genuine democracy, a *work*-democracy, is more than just a problem of economy of labor. *More than anything else it is a matter of changing the nature of work so that it ceases to be an onerous duty and becomes a gratifying fulfillment of a need.*

The character-analytic investigation of the human function of work (an investigation that is by no means finished) offers us a number of clues which make it possible to solve the problem of alienated work in a practical way. Two basic types of human work can be differentiated with satisfying exactness: work that is *compulsive* and *does not give any pleasure* and work that is *natural* and *pleasurable*.[1]

To comprehend this differentiation, we must first of all free ourselves of several mechanistic "scientific" views of human work. Experimental psychology considers only the question of which methods lend themselves to the greatest possible utilization of the human labor power. When it speaks of the *joy* of work, it means the joy an independent scientist or artist derives from his accomplishments. Even the psychoanalytic theory of work makes the mistake of solely and always orienting itself on the model of *intellectual* accomplishments. *The examination of work from the point of view of mass psychology correctly proceeds from the relationship of the worker to the product of his work.* This relationship has a socio-economic background and relates to the *pleasure* the worker derives from his work. Work is a basic biologic activity, which, as life in general, rests on pleasurable pulsation.

---

[1] Cf. Reich, *Character-Analysis*.

The pleasure an "independent" researcher derives fom his work cannot be set up as the yardstick of work in general. From a social point of view (any other view would have nothing to do with sociology) the work of the twentieth century is altogether ruled by the *law of duty* and the *necessity of subsistence*. The work of hundreds of millions of wage earners throughout the world does not afford them the least bit of pleasure or biologic gratification. Essentially it is based on the pattern of *compulsory work*. It is characterized by the fact that *it is opposed to the worker's biologic need of pleasure*. It ensues from duty and conscience, in order not to go to pieces, and is usually done for others. The worker has no interest in the product of his work; hence, work is onerous and devoid of pleasure. Work that is based on compulsion, regardless of what kind of compulsion, and not on pleasure, is not only nonfulfilling biologically, but not very productive in terms of economy.

The problem is momentous and not very much is known about it. To begin with, let us try to get a general picture. It is clear that mechanistic, biologically unsatisfying work is a product of the widespread mechanistic view of life and the machine civilization. Can the biologic function of work be reconciled with the social function of work? This is possible, but firmly entrenched ideas and institutions must be radically corrected first.

The craftsman of the nineteenth century still had a full relationship to the product of his work. But when, as in a Ford factory, a worker has to perform one and the same manipulation year in and year out, always working on one detail and never the product as a whole, it is out of the question to speak of *satisfying* work. The specialized and mechanized division of labor, together with the system of paid labor in general, produce the effect that the working man has no relationship to the machine.

At this point one will demur that there is indeed a *need* to work, a "natural" gratification in work, which is inherent in the *act* of work itself. True, there is a biologic gratification in activity, but the forms into which this activity is pressed in the market economy kill the pleasure of work and the urge to work, and prevent them from manifesting themselves. Doubtless, it is one of work-democracy's most urgent tasks *to harmonize the conditions and forms of work with the need to work and the pleasure of work,* in short, *to eliminate the antithesis* between pleasure and work. Here a vast new field is opened for human thought: Would it be possible and how would it be possible to retain the economization and mechanization of work and still not kill the pleasure of work? It is definitely conceivable that the worker can have a relationship to the finished product of work of which he performs only a part, without eliminating the division of labor. The joy of life received from working is an essential, indispensable element of man's restructuralization from the slave of work to the master of production. If man could again have a direct relationship to the product of his work, he would also be happy to bear the responsibility for his work, a responsibility that today he does not have or refuses to have.

One could cite the Soviet Union and say: "You work-democrats are utopians and visionaries, though you pride yourselves on viewing reality unsentimentally. In the workers' paradise of the Soviet Union, where is the abolition of the division of labor? Where is the pleasure of work? Where is the abolition of the wage system and market economy? Can't you see from the results of the workers' revolution itself just how impossible and illusionary your epicurean views of work are?"

The answer to this argument is: In 1944 the mysticism of the masses is stronger than ever before, notwithstanding the progress of natural science. This is indisputable; but when one fails to achieve a goal toward which one strives—in this case, the rationality of masses of people—this in itself does not mean that it *cannot* be achieved. The fundamental question remains: Is the goal of pleasurable work a realistic goal or is it a utopian goal? If it is a realistic goal, if it is intensely desired by everyone, then we must ask what is obstructing its realization. This question applies to the field of technology as well as it applies to the field of science. If it has not yet been possible to climb to the peak of Mount Everest, that does not mean that it is an impossible feat. It is a question of the last eight hundred meters!

It is precisely on this point that the antithesis between work-democracy and politics is clearly and simply disclosed: Our newspapers are full of political discussions which fail to take into consideration a single difficulty of the work process of masses of people. This is understandable, for the politician knows nothing whatever about work. Now let us imagine that a work-democratic community would exclude all irrationalism from its newspapers and would dedicate itself to the discussion of the conditions of pleasurable work. Working masses of people would immediately come forth with a flood of suggestions and proposals which would preclude any kind of politicizing once and for all. Just imagine how pleased a boss, an engineer, a specialist, would be to describe every aspect and step of the work process and to offer suggestions and advice for improvement. They would argue and compete with one another. There would be hot debates. How wonderful this would be. It took centuries before one hit upon the idea of building factories like recuperation homes and not like prisons, to build them with lots of light, good ventilation, and washrooms and kitchens, etc. The pressure of the war economy caused radio music to be introduced into factories. It is incalculable how far this process would continue if the working people and not the politicians were in control of the press.

In the first five years of the Soviet economy there were signs of work-democracy. For example, *one-sided* specialized training of the emerging generation was avoided and every effort was made to give young men and women an *all-round* preparation for professional life. In this way an attempt was made to offset the damages of the division of labor. The gap between "mental" and "physical" work was narrowed. The youth received such an all-round mental and physical preparation for their later professional life that any member of society could be employed in any other place of the work process. For example, employees in large firms were periodically changed from one job to another. Employees of different firms were exchanged. When well-trained specialists became part of the management of the firm, they were sent back to the machines after awhile to prevent them from losing contact with their work and becoming administrative bureaucrats.

The *self-administration of firms* was expressed in the establishment of the so-called "triumviral directorship." Every firm was managed by employees who were elected for this purpose by the firm as a whole. In this way the entire body of employees participated directly in the management. Special "production conferences" were held. These and many other facts showed that an effort was made to reestablish the unity of pleasure and work. At this point the opponents of work-democracy will take pleasure in pointing out that most of these improvements could not be maintained, that, for example, the production conferences of the firm's body of employees degenerated into mere formalities in the course of time or were completely eliminated. To this we answer: Didn't the Wright brothers make flying possible, though Daedalus and Icarus in antiquity and Leonardo da Vinci in the Middle Ages failed in their efforts to fly? *The first attempts at a work-democratic management of the firms in the Soviet Union failed because the reorganization of the firm's management did not go hand in hand with the restructuralization of the human structure.* This was a lesson and the next time it can be done better.

The *triumviral directorship* and the *self-administration of firms* were abolished when a *single* manager became the *director* of a firm, assumed individual responsibility, and advanced to an independent position of leadership. True enough, this "director" still stemmed from the workers, i.e., from the body of workers of the individual firm, but this *autonomous* manager of the firm was soon forced to develop all the characteristics of an overseer, bureaucrat, or ruler who was no longer a part of the mass of working people. Indeed, it is here that we find the roots of the Soviet Union's "ruling class." But this does not refute the fact that every work process is by nature and of necessity a *work-democratic process.* The self-regulation of work is spontaneously present. It is a matter of changing the structure of the working man in such a way as to liberate this natural work-democracy from the encumbrances of bureaucracy and to help it to develop *its own forms and organizations*. The work-democrat who is familiar with work processes does not deny the difficulties; on the contrary, he focuses all his energies on them because it is important for him to comprehend and overcome all difficulties. He does not derive any pleasure from the fact that there are difficulties, setbacks, and failures. Only the politician, who builds his power over masses of people upon these difficulties, etc., sees reason to triumph here. The work-democrat does not use these failures to try to show that use economy is impossible and that man is immutable; it is precisely from his failures that he learns to do it better. One who is lame can easily laugh when a runner misses a hurdle.

One of the major difficulties the Soviet government encountered very early was the fact that precisely the skilled and interested workers showed little enthusiasm for politics. Let it suffice to quote the statement of one functionary in support of this: "The love of one's occupation," he said,

> is what is most important. Qualified workers are the Party's best reserve. They are always gratified by their occupation and are always looking for new ways of improving their work. They are very conscious. When one converses with them and asks why they do not join the Party, the answer is that they don't have the time. "I am interested," they say, "in finding ways to improve steel and mixing concrete." Then they invent something of their own, a tool, etc. *It is precisely in such workers that we are interested, but we have still not found a way of engaging their political interests*; nevertheless, they are the best and the most developed workers. They are always busy and are always looking for ways of improving their production [italics are mine, WR].

This functionary touched upon one of the basic questions of the relationship between politics and work. In Germany, too, one often heard it said: "Those of us who strive for freedom are surely on the right track and the workers understand us, but they want

291

nothing to do with politics; we have the same difficulty with the industrial workers." Apart from the political disappointments that alienated the German industrial workers from the Communist party in the years after 1923, there was a very important circumstance which one repeatedly overlooked or could not comprehend. *As a group, politicians understood nothing whatever about technical problems, and they were completely isolated from the domain of concrete work.* The worker who had a keen interest in the technical problems of his work had "to attune himself to politics" if he listened to a party politician in the evening. The politicians were not capable of developing social revolutionary attitudes and ideas from the work process itself; they simply knew nothing at all about work. And yet they tried to get around the workers with abstract ideas about high politics, which was of no interest to the workers. However, every detail of work-democracy can be organically developed from the *technical aspects of work. How are we going to set up our firm when we have to administrate it? What difficulties will we have to overcome? What measures are we going to adopt to make our work easier? What do we still have to learn to run our firm in a better way? What arrangements are we going to make about living quarters, meals, child care, etc.?"* Such questions will imbue all those who perform responsible work with the feeling: *This firm is our problem child.* The alienation of the worker from his work can be overcome only if the workers themselves learn to master the technical aspects of their firm, which, after all, they keep going to all intents and purposes. In this way the gap between skilled work and social responsibility, which is the ruination of society, is closed. Skilled work and social responsibility must go hand in hand, then the antithesis between *work that gives pleasure and the mechanical conditions of work* will be eliminated. Under fascism in Germany, the worker was not the least bit interested in the work process. He was a "guided," irresponsible subject who had to obey the orders of the firm manager who bore all the responsibility. Or he had the nationalistic illusion that he represented the firm as a "German," not as a socially responsible producer of use values, but as a "German." This illusionary, nationalistic attitude was characteristic of the entire NSBO* work in Germany, which made every effort to conceal the worker's very evident lack of interest in his work by the illusionary identification with the "state." Well now, society is society and machine is machine, whether in Germany, America, or Honolulu. As work itself, society and machine are *international* facts. *"German work" is nonsense!* Natural work-democracy eliminates lack of interest. It does not conceal it by an illusionary identification with the "state," hair color, or nose shape; it eliminates lack of interest by making it possible for the workers to feel a real responsibility for their product and have the feeling: "This firm is ours." It is not a matter of having a *formal* "class consciousness" or of belonging to a specific class, but of having a technical interest in one's occupation, of having an objective relationship to one's work, a relationship that replaces nationalism and class consciousness by a *consciousness of one's skills.* Only when one is objectively and intimately related to one's work is one capable of comprehending just how destructive the dictatorial and formal democratic forms of work are, not only for work itself but also for the pleasure of work.

When a man takes pleasure in his work, we call his relationship to it "libidinous." Since *work* and *sexuality* (in both the strict and broad senses of the word) are intimately interwoven, man's relationship to work is also a question of the sex-economy of masses of people. The hygiene of the work process is dependent upon the way masses of people use and gratify their biologic energy. *Work and sexuality derive from the same biologic energy.*

The political revolution that was borne by the workers failed to inculcate the feeling that the workers themselves are responsible for everything. This failure resulted in a regression to authoritarian measures. Almost from the very beginning, the government of the Soviet Union had to cope with the difficulty that the workers had

---

* Nationalsozialistische Betriebszellen-Organization (a Betriebszelle is an administrative subdivision of the German Labor Service).

no respect for their tools. There was no end to the complaints about desertions from places of work and enormous turnover of workers in the various firms, etc. *Börsen* of May 22, 1934, carried a thorough report on the "unsatisfactory" conditions existing in the coal districts, especially in the very important "Donbas" district. The report stated that it was only by adopting extraordinary measures, namely by taking supernumerary engineers and technicians from their offices and sending them into the mines that they succeeded in raising the daily production from 120 to 148 thousand tons in January of that year; but even then not all of the machines were in operation, and in March of 1934 the daily output again fell to 140 thousand tons. One of the chief causes of this production slump was the "negligence" shown in the treatment of the machinery. Another cause was that, *"with the approach of Spring," many workers sought to get away from the mines.* According to the press, this was due to "lack of interest." In the months of January and February, 33,000 (!) workers left the mines and 28,000 new workers were employed. One is inclined to believe that this large migration could have been averted if the management had provided *better living conditions for the workers and recreational possibilities for their leisure hours.*

To the asceticism and human alienation of the pure economist, this was like a bee in his bonnet. Certainly "leisure time" is intended for amusement and *the partaking of the joy of life.* To be sure, clubs, theaters, and other recreational facilities were set up in the firms. Thus, one sensed the importance of enjoyment for the hygiene of the work process. But officially, and especially in social ideology, "work" was defined as *"the substance* of life" and declared to be the *antithesis* of sexuality.

In the film *The Way to Life,* a revolt breaks out in *spring* in a factory operated and administered by juvenile delinquents. They smash the machines and refuse to work. In the film this outbreak was ascribed to the fact that a rail line had been flooded, thus preventing the delivery of work material. That is to say, the "explosion" was attributed to the "absence of work material." It was clear, however, that the young men, who lived on their collectives without girls, had spring fever, which was merely released but not caused by the absence of work. *Ungratified sexuality is readily transformed into rage.* "Prison explosions" are outbreaks of sadism resulting from the absence of sexual gratification. Hence, when 33,000 workers leave their employment site all at once *precisely in spring*, there can be no doubt that the unsatisfying sex-economic conditions in the Soviet Union are the cause. By "sex-economic conditions" we mean more than just the possibility of a regulated and satisfying love life; over and above this we mean everything that is related to pleasure and the joy of life in one's work. However, Soviet politicians practiced a kind of work therapy against sexual needs. Such practices are sure to backfire. In the course of more than a decade, during which I have been reading official Soviet literature, I have not encountered a single hint of such decisive biologic relations.

The relationship between the worker's sexual life and the performance of his work is of decisive importance. It is not as if work diverted sexual energy from gratification, so that the more one worked the less need one would have for sexual gratification. The opposite of this is the case: *The more gratifying one's sexual life is, the more fulfilling and pleasurable is one's work,* if all external conditions are fulfilled. *Gratified* sexual energy is spontaneously converted into an interest in work and an urge for activity. In contrast to this, one's work is *disturbed* in various ways if one's sexual need is not gratified and is suppressed. Hence, a basic principle of the work hygiene of a work-democratic society is: *It is necessary to establish not only the best external conditions of work, but also to create the inner biologic preconditions to allow the fullest unfolding of the biologic urge for activity. Hence, the safeguarding of a completely satisfying sexual life for the working masses is the most important precondition of pleasurable work.* In any society the degree to which work kills the joy of life, the degree to which it is represented as a duty (whether to a "fatherland," the "proletariat," the "nation," or whatever other names these illusions may have), is a sure yardstick on which to measure the anti-democratic character of the ruling class of this society. Just as "duty," "state," "discipline and order," "sacrifice," etc., are intimately related to one another, so too "joy of life," "work-democracy," "self-regulation," "pleasurable work," "natural sexuality," belong together inseparably.

In academic philosophy there is a lot of barren hair-splitting over whether or not there is a biologic need to work. Here, as in many other areas, the lack of vital experience precludes the solution of the problem. The urge for activity originates in the organism's biologic sources of excitation; therefore, it is a natural urge. But the forms of work are not biologically but socially determined. Man's urge for activity, which is both natural and effortless, fulfills itself spontaneously with objective tasks and aims and enters the service of the gratification of social and individual needs. *Applied to work hygiene: Work must be arranged in such a way that the biologic urge for activity is developed and gratified.* This function excludes every form of moralistic-authoritarian work performed under the compulsion of duty, for it brooks no bossiness. It requires:

1. *The establishment of the best external conditions of work (protection of labor, reduction of working hours, variety in the work function, establishment of a direct relationship of the worker to his product).*

2. *The liberation of the natural urge for activity* (the prevention of the formation of rigid character armoring).

3. The creation of the preconditions that will enable sexual energy to be converted into an interest in work. To this end, sexual energy *must*

4. be *capable of being gratified* and *actually gratified.* This requires the safeguarding of all the preconditions that are necessary for a completely *satisfying, sex-economic, socially affirmed sexual life* of all working men and women (decent living quarters, contraception, affirmative sex-economy in the governing of childhood and adolescent sexuality).

The regressions in the Soviet Union must be comprehended objectively, then we shall see that: The difficulties involved in changing the structure of the masses were incorrectly assessed. It

was believed that one was dealing with a secondary, merely "ideologic" factor. That which was more or less *moralistically* condemned
as "old traditions," "indolence," "proclivity for lower middle-class
habits," etc., was, as it turned out, a problem that was far more
complex and difficult to solve than the mechanization of industry.
Threatened by belligerent imperialistic powers, the Soviet government was forced to implement industrialization with all possible
haste. To do this, it reverted to authoritarian methods. The initial
efforts toward social self-administration were neglected and even
dropped.

Above all, the effort to convert compulsive, authoritarian work
into voluntary, biologically pleasurable work, failed. Work was still
performed under the pressure of rigid competition or under the
illusionary identification with the state. As Stalin noted at the
Seventeenth Congress of the Communist Party of the Soviet Union,
a "depersonalization of work" set in, an "indifference toward the
material" with which one worked and the products intended for
consumers. The workers' and peasants' inspectorate, which was set
up in the Central Committee in 1917 to act as a control on the
Central Committee, proved to be inadequate, despite the fact that
it was a fully democratic organization. Stalin stated:

> According to its organization, the workers' and peasants' in-
> spectorate cannot adequately *control* the execution of the work. A
> few years ago, when our work in the economic sphere was simpler
> and less satisfactory and one was able to reckon with the possibility
> of an inspection of the work of all commissars and all industrial
> organizations, the workers' and peasants' inspectorate was in order.
> But now that our work in the economic sphere has grown and
> become more complex and there is no longer any necessity or possi-
> bility of supervising it from a central position, the workers' and
> peasants' inspectorate has to be changed. Now we have no need of
> supervision, but a *surveillance of the implementation of the deci-*
> *sions of the Central Committee.* Now we need a control over the
> implementation of the decisions of the central courts. Now we have
> need of an organization which, without setting itself the unpleasant

goal of supervising everything, is capable of concentrating its entire attention on the task of controlling and checking the implementation of the decisions of the central institutions. Such an organization can only be the Soviet Control Commission of the Council of the Commissariat of the Soviet Union. This Commissariat shall be responsible to the Council of Commissars and shall have local representatives *who are independent of the local organizations.* However, to insure that it shall have sufficient authority and shall be in the position, if the need arises, to call any responsible functionary to account, it is necessary that the candidates for the members of the Soviet Control Commission *be appointed* by the Party Congress and ratified by the Council of the Commissars and the Central Committee of the USSR. It is my belief that only such an organization will be capable of strengthening Soviet control and *Soviet discipline. . . .*

It is necessary *that the members of this organization shall be appointed and dismissed only by the highest organ, the Party Congress.* There can be no doubt that such an organization will really be capable of *safeguarding the control over the execution of the decision of the central Party organs and of strengthening Party discipline* [all italics are mine, WR].

Here we have a clear articulation of the shifting of the self-administration of firms in the direction of authoritarian control. The workers' and peasants' inspectorate, which originally had the function of controlling the state leadership, disappeared completely and was replaced by organs appointed by the state having the function of controlling the work assigned to the workers and peasants. The workers and peasants said nothing; the fiasco of social democracy was *complete.* The incapacity for freedom on the part of masses of people was neither named nor perceived.

This shift had become necessary in the interest of holding the Russian society together. *The self-administration that had been aimed at had not developed* or had not developed enough. It could not develop because the Communist party, though proclaiming the principle of self-administration, did not recognize the means of allowing this self-administration to unfold itself. Whereas, in the beginning the workers' and peasants' inspectorate had the task of controlling and supervising all the Soviet commissariats and economic organizations as the elected representatives of the Soviet Congress; whereas, in other words, masses of working people, who of course elected the Soviet, once had *control of the party and the economy,* this function was now transferred to the party and its *organs, which were independent of the local Soviet organizations.* If the workers' and peasants' inspectorate was an expression of the social tendency toward the *self-regulation* and *self-administration of the masses,* the new "*Control Commission*" was the *expression of the authoritarian implementation of party decisions.* In short, it was only one of the many regressions from the intention of self-government to authoritarian control of society and its economy.

Could this step be regarded as a consequence of the questionable nature of the Soviets? The answer is: It was not the Soviets, as the representatives of working men and women, that were a fiasco, but the manipulation of these Soviets by politicians. At all events, the Soviet government *had* to cope with the problems of economy and those of work discipline. In view of the failure of the principle of self-government, the reemergence of the authoritarian principle was inevitable. This does not mean that we condone the authoritarian principle. On the contrary, if we stress this catastrophic regression, we do so because we want to know the *reasons* for this setback in order, then, to *eliminate* the difficulties and help self-government to achieve victory after all. *The responsibility for this failure falls heavily upon the working masses of people themselves.* Unless they learn to eliminate their own weaknesses with their own ingenuity, they cannot hope to rid themselves of authoritarian forms of government. No one can help them; they and they alone are responsible. This and this alone is true and affords hope. The Soviet government cannot be reproached for reverting to authoritarian and moralistic methods of control; it *had* no other choice if it did not want to endanger everything. It is to be reproached for neglecting self-government, for blocking its future development, and for not creating its preconditions. The Soviet government is to be reproached *for forgetting that the state has to wither away.* It is to be reproached for neglecting to make the failure of the self-government and self-regulation of the masses the point of departure for new and greater efforts; for trying to make the world believe that, despite everything, this self-regulation was developing and that "complete socialism" and genuine democracy prevailed. Illusions always prevent that which they pretend to be from *really* materializing. Hence, it is clear that the first duty of every genuine democrat is to recognize such difficulties of development, to expose them, and to help to overcome them. Open confession of dictatorship is far less dangerous than sham democracy. One can defend oneself against the former; the latter is like a creeper attached to the body of a drowning man. The Soviet politicians cannot escape the reproach of dishonesty. They did more harm to the development of genuine democracy than Hitler did. This is a heavy reproach, but it is unavoidable. It is useless merely to talk about self-criticism. As painful as it may be, one must also *exercise it.*

The failure of self-administration and self-government in the Soviet Union led to an organization of work discipline, which was clearly manifested in the militaristic display of the first five-year plan. The science of economics was a "fortress," and it was youth's objective to "capture" it. The press carried reports on the "campaign" and "fronts" as at a time of war; armies of workers "fought battles"; brigades stormed "narrow passes." "Iron battalions" took "combat sectors under heavy fire." "Cadre" was appointed. "Deserters" were exposed to public ridicule; "maneuvers" were held; people were "alarmed" and "mobilized." The "light cavalry" took possession of "commando outposts" in dangerous "attacks."

These examples from Soviet literature suffice to show that the implementation of the gigantic five-year plan was possible only with the help of an ideology borrowed from a climate of war and creating a *climate of war.* The concrete fact of the masses' incapacity for freedom was at the basis of all this. The acceleration of industrialization served to build up the military power of the country. Since the social revolution in the West failed to materialize, and since, above all, the self-administration of the Soviet society had not developed, the situation in Soviet Russia was indeed comparable to a state of war. The Soviet diplomacy of that time had the difficult task of delaying every military confrontation, especially the confrontation with Japan over the East Chinese railroad and Manchuria. And yet, owing to the objective developmental circumstances of that time, that which was unavoidable and also immediately useful—insofar as it did actually enable the Soviet Union to arm itself against imperialistic attacks—had two devastating aftereffects:

1. If a country having a population of 160 million is held in a climate of war for years on end and is imbued with a militaristic ideology, this inevitably has an influence on the formation of the human structure, even if the purpose of this war ideology is attained. The militaristic structure of the mass leadership received autonomous powers. "Selfless devotion," held up as the *ideal* of life in the education of the masses, gradually shaped the mass psychology that made it possible to carry out the dictatorial processes of purges, executions, and coercive measures of all kinds. In view of all this, it is clear that the role of biopsychology in the development toward a free society should not be underestimated.

2. If a government that feels itself to be surrounded by belligerent powers exercises a definite kind of militaristic-ideologic influence on the masses for years on end and forgets its own task in the turmoil of solving the most difficult immediate tasks, then it can easily come about that it will maintain this atmosphere and continue to intensify it, even *after*, its purpose fulfilled, it has become superfluous. The masses of people are and remain alien, stand apart, vegetate, or go beyond their needs into irrational chauvinism.

The authoritarian regulation of the work process fits in perfectly with the militaristic atmosphere in which the Soviet man lived. There was and could be no thought of converting the methods of work into self-administration. As far as that goes, the heroism, especially the heroism displayed by the Comsomol in the struggle to build up industry, was worthy of admiration. And yet, how is the nature of the Comsomol's heroism to be differentiated from that of the Hitler youth or an imperialistic warrior? What about the fight for *human* (not national) freedom? It is deceptive to think that the heroism of an English or German soldier in the world wars was inferior to the heroism of a Comsomol youth in the building up of Soviet industry. If we fail to make a sharp and clear distinction between the emotion of heroism and the goal of freedom, we easily fall into a rut which no longer has anything to do with the pursuit of the goal (*self-administration!*). Okay, the heroism was "necessary," but the effort to effect a basic change in the structure of masses of people failed to bear fruit and, as a consequence thereof, the establishment of that social state, for which generations of freedom-fighters had given the best of their minds and their lives, also failed to materialize. Since the worker no longer had a "personal" interest in his work, it was necessary to revert to his "drive for acquisition." The bonus system was reintroduced. Workers were assessed according to the value of their working power; those who did more were given better nourishment and living quarters. But this was not the worst of it: The most rigid form of the competitive wage system was reintroduced. All of this was "necessary," but it should have been clear that it was diametrically opposed to the original goal.

The fact that "locks" were made use of to keep the workers from leaving their work sites was also a clear indication of the moralistic, authoritarian regulation of work. For instance, the workers had to commit themselves to remain until the end of the five-year plan. At that time about 40 percent of the industry of the Soviet Union was producing war materials. This meant that the work in industries producing consumer goods had to be considerably stepped up to keep it at the same level. "Work evenings" were introduced for the purpose of spurring ambition. On such "evenings" competitions were held to see who could set type the fastest, who could wrap confetti the fastest, etc. *Black* and *red* bulletin boards were introduced in various factories. The names of the "lazy" workers were put on the black bulletin boards and the names of the "good and diligent" workers were put on the red bulletin boards. Nothing was learned about the effect the moral elevation of some and the moral degradation of others had on character formation. But from all that we know about the use of such measures, it can be safely concluded that the effect on the formation of the human structure was disastrous. Those whose names appeared on the black bulletin boards could not help but have a feeling of shame, envy, inferiority, indeed, bitter hatred; whereas those whose names appeared on the red bulletin board could triumph over their competitors, could feel themselves to be winners, could give vent to their brutality and allow their ambition to overstep all natural bounds. For all that, those who lost out in such a competition were not necessarily the "inferior" ones. On the contrary, we can assume that, with respect to their structures, some of the "blacks" were freer human beings, even if more neurotic. And those who came out on top did not necessarily have to be free human beings, for we know that the traits that were spurred in them are precisely those traits we find in the overambitious man, the go-getter, the show-off, in short, the plague-ridden man.

Just how little one still thought about the withering away of the state and the transferring of its functions to man is shown by a poem that was used as a means of spurring work discipline.

Es braucht der Staat für die Kolchose
zahllose stählerne Agitatoren.
Vom Pazifik bis Minsk, von Wjatka bis Krim
harrt fetter Ackerboden der Traktoren.

Es ruft der Staat!
Voran, voran! Mann für Mann!
Tretet an!

Den Hammer Nacht und Tag
schwingen wir Schlag auf Schlag,
bauen täglich hundertmal
dem Land ein neues Ross aus Stahl.

[The state needs for the kolkhozes
A host of agitators made of steel.
From the Pacific to Minsk, from Vyatka to the Crimea
Rich soil awaits the tractors.

The state calls you!
Forward! Forward! One and all!
Form ranks!

Day and night the hammer
We swing, blow by blow,
And a hundred times each day we build
A steed of steel for our land.]

"The state needs"—instead of *"We* need." Such distinctions may mean nothing to the politician who sees everything in terms of economy, but they are of decisive importance for the restructuralization of man's character.

The so-called Stakhanov movement was a glaring indication of the misery of the work function. Those workers whose productivity was far above average were called Stakhanovists. Stakhanov was the first industrial worker to set a record in the performance of his work. It is clear that the lack of interest of masses of workers in their work lay at the basis of Stakhanovism. Pretense to superiority has little meaning here. The Soviet Union was forced to step up its production. Since the workers as a whole failed to meet production quotas voluntarily, the Soviet government was forced to adopt measures intended to exploit the workers' ambition to excel. It was also forced to introduce rigid pay scales. But we must not allow the necessity of this process to divert us from the main problem: A *minimal* increase in the individual worker's interest and ability in his work would have made the Stakhanov movement superfluous. In turn, this would have required a complete reversal in the sexual policies and sexual education of the Russian society. The knowledge and the will needed to accomplish this was lacking.

The relapse into Stakhanovism had disastrous effects on the formation of man's character structure. Only those who are inordinately ambitious and brutal are capable of excelling at competitive piecework. The great majority of the workers either fall far behind or leave off altogether. A gap arises between the majority of average workers and a small minority of work-athletes, who readily develop into a new ruling class. As long as the *vast majority* of workers have no enthusiasm for their work and no consciousness of *personal responsibility* about it, it is out of the question to speak of a change from coercive discipline to pleasurable work. Complaints will continue about the workers, poor production, absenteeism, and negligent handling of machinery. This new gap produces envy and ambition among the weaker workers and presumption and racial arrogance among the stronger workers. A collective feeling of belonging and working together cannot emerge. Denunciations and reactions characteristic of the emotional plague will prevail.

The way in which National Socialism or fascist ideologists appraise the democratic or nondemocratic character of a process is a good standard. When nationalistic, chauvinistic, militaristic, imperialistic disciplinary politicians lavish praise on something, one has to be on the alert. For example, this is what Mehnert has to say:

> It very often happens that the Comsomols who come to a factory to help boost production are not received very cordially, for the methods which they use to incite the workers to achieve greater production are not, as a rule, very considerate. Especially hated are the workers' correspondents who drag everything into the open and print it in their newspapers. The lack of tools and raw materials, the living conditions, which are usually bleak, the passive resistance of many workers, are often too much for the Comsomols. There have been times when they have come singing victorious songs and have had to depart with tears of desperation.

So much for the factual report. And now follows fascist praise of the Soviet spirit:

This myth is simple and clear. In our time, which is so devoid of and hungry for myths, it has a fascinating effect. And as every myth, it has created an ethos, an ethos which millions of people today bear in themselves and which seizes others every year. To the Russians, this ethos means: "Our need is great and the goals we have set ourselves are far off. We can achieve them only by struggling against the whole world, which fears and hates us, against enemies around us and in our own ranks. To the degree that we approach socialism, our distress will be lessened. But we can be victorious only if we all stand up for one and one stands up for all. We are all responsible to one another. When a plant produces poor weapons in a time of war, it commits a crime against the nation as a whole, not only against the soldiers who lose their lives because of them. When a plant produces poor machinery today, it commits a crime against socialism, against all of us who are fighting to build it. Desertion from the front at a time of war is not an offense against an officer, but a betrayal of one's comrades. Desertion from the front of the five-year plan and from socialism is not a strike against an employer, but a crime against each and every one of us. For this is our country, our factories and our future!

The human structure that is formed from such a "disciplination" of work is also infused with religious fanaticism and dull passive resistance. It has always been the case that the "ethos" of the few, with their discipline, leads to the incompetence of the large majority of people. Myth and ethos may be heroic, but they are always dangerous, undemocratic, and reactionary measures. *It is a question of the character, the will, the conviction, joy of assuming responsibility, and enthusiasm of the broad masses of working men and women.* They themselves must be willing and capable of sticking up for their own lives and insisting on the wealth of their own experience. An ethos based on the misery of masses and demanding such great sacrifices and discipline that only a few are capable of measuring up to it, an ethos that is so severe and continues to be so severe that even those who support it cannot keep the pace, may have an elevating effect; but it will never solve a single objective problem of the social community. A genuine democrat, a work-democrat, who cannot get to the masses owing to such an ethos, will simply exclaim: *To hell with this ethos!*

Was the authoritarian, nationalistic regulation of work in the Soviet Union necessary?

Yes!

Was it capable of arming the country?

Yes!

Was this regulation a progressive measure intended to establish the self-administration of the Russian society?

No!

Did it solve any of the mounting social problems, or pave the way to their solution? Did it, and what did it, contribute to the satisfaction of society?

Nothing!

On the contrary, it produced a human nature imbued with and confined in nationalism, thus laying the foundation for the Red one-man dictatorship.

The military power of a society plays no role whatever in assessing the structure and tendencies of that society with respect to its freedom. The conducting of war, the building of industry, the waving of banners, the holding of parades, are child's play compared with the task of creating a human species that is free. Friend and foe readily come to terms where militarism and chauvinistic patriotism prevail. But the babble of Babylon was nothing compared with the confusion surrounding the concept "freedom." We want to find our bearings again on a statement made by a military disciplinarian, a man who would fight with the same subjective honesty and conviction for an America striving for democracy as he would fight for an America regressing toward fascism.

In 1943 Captain Rickenbacker paid an official visit to the Soviet Union. Following his return, a detailed article on his impressions appeared in the August 18 issue of *The New York Times*. I quote:

> . . . Captain Rickenbacker remarked that whereas for the last several years Russia has been moving to the right, the United States, at the same time, has been "tending to the left."

"If they keep going on as they are you'll find Russia coming out of this war the greatest democracy in the world, while if we keep going on the way we are we'll be where they were twenty-five years ago," he declared.

"Do you mean to suggest that Russia is moving toward capitalism while we are moving toward bolshevism?" Captain Rickenbacker was asked.

"Yes, in a sense," he replied.

. . . Among the things he was particularly impressed with in Russia was the iron discipline in industrial plants, severe punishment for chronic absenteeism, to the extent of removal from the job to the bread line, incentive pay, compulsory overtime work and "no labor difficulties." The Russians, Captain Rickenbacker said, work eight hours a day, six days a week, with an additional three hours a day overtime at time and one-half. . . .

". . . Bolshevism in Russia is not what we have been led to believe by communistic enthusiasts in this country. They have been constantly turning to the right, as evidenced in many ways, during the last twelve months. Nowhere in the world have I seen so much respect for progressive rank in the Army as I witnessed in Russia from the bottom to the top, which is in the direction of capitalism and democracy. Officers' uniforms have in great measure been copied from the old Czaristic design, and the press is selling prerevolutionary heroes to the people."

We have learned to listen to conservative voices, to comprehend them and to admit the validity of their factual statements when they coincide with the truth. We have also learned to understand that conservative facts and reactionary developments issue from the biopathy of masses of people. We differ from an authoritarian such as Rickenbacker in that we do not feel any sense of triumph over the discovery of unpleasant facts. We simply ferret out the natural processes, for it is when these processes are blocked that the disciplinarian's views are correct. If that which Rickenbacker understands by democracy prevails in the Soviet Union, then we want nothing to do with it. "Capitalism" and "democracy" cannot be equated. Freedom cannot be inferred from military fitness. To praise the Soviet Union of today and to reject the development of social democracy in Russia during Lenin's time is to eliminate every possibility of establishing clarity. Statements as ridiculous as the one quoted above are possible only if the history of a country and its bitter fight for liberation from slavery are not known. Rickenbacker recommended the Soviet Union of 1943 as a model for America. He recommended it because he was annoyed by the absenteeism in American factories. He was impressed by the facility with which the dictatorship appears to be capable of coping with social difficulties. But if that is the case, what is all the fuss about freedom, liberation war, the new world? This Babylonian babble is a consequence of "politicalism." In conclusion, I should like to add this word of warning while there is still time: If things continue as they have, there is a very real possibility that America will soon be at war with Russia. The Soviet Union will tolerate neither a genuinely democratic America nor a genuinely democratic Germany. One of the many reasons for this will be the bad conscience that weighs heavily upon the leadership of a state that started out to conquer freedom for the world and ended in an antiquated chauvinism, so bitterly fought against by its founders.

XI

Give Responsibility to Vitally
Necessary Work!

Social conditions throughout the world have recently fallen into a state of flux. The capitulation of the führer of Italian political irrationalism set this process in motion. Sooner or later it will be followed by the capitulation of German political irrationalism. The process of social reconstruction in Europe will begin with a vacuum in social life, which will be chiefly characterized by political chaos. To cope with this social chaos, the working men and women of all vitally necessary occupations and organizations must be made conscious of the importance of fulfilling their social obligation of work. It cannot be assumed that anyone of the old or any newly founded political party will be capable of engineering a *factual* and rational reorganization of social conditions. Hence, as soon as circumstances permit, it is necessary that the most outstanding, most perceptive and politically unattached representatives of all vitally necessary spheres of work get together at national and international conferences to discuss and solve in work-democratic cooperation the practical tasks of individual and social life for which they are responsible. Once such nonpolitical and strictly practical work conferences have begun to function, their activity will develop with the logic and consistency that are characteristic of objective and rational work. It has been clear for some time that the responsibility for all future developments rests upon the vitally necessary work of all occupations. In short, it rests upon the shoulders of the representatives of these occupations, and not upon any one body having a purely ideologic orientation. This is a conclusion that has been arrived at independently in various countries of Europe and in America.

WHAT IS "WORK-DEMOCRACY"?

Work-democracy is the natural process of love, work, and knowledge that governed, governs, and will continue to govern economy and man's social and cultural life as long as there has been, is, and will be a society. Work-democracy is the sum total of all functions of life governed by the rational interpersonal relations that have come into being, grown, and developed in a natural and organic way.

Work-democracy is not an ideological system. Nor is it a "political" system which could be imposed upon human society by the propaganda of a party, individual politicians, or any group sharing a common ideology. There is no single, formal political measure by means of which work-democracy could be "introduced." Work-democracy cannot be introduced in the same way as a republic or a totalitarian dictator is introduced. There is a very simple reason for this: *Natural work-democracy is always present and is always functioning, whether this or that political party or ideological group know of its existence or not.* The process of natural work-democracy can be in diametrical opposition to social institutions or it can be more or less in accord with them. Wherever it functions, however, this work-democratic process demands that the social ideologies and institutions be brought into line with natural needs and interpersonal relations, in the same way as it is clearly expressed in natural love, vitally necessary work, and natural science. These vital social functions can be thwarted or they can be encouraged; working men and women can be conscious or unconscious of them. But *they can never be destroyed.* Hence, they form the solid basis of every rational social process.

Ideological political systems are based on views of the natural process of life. They can further or thwart the natural process of life. However, these systems are not part of the *foundation* of human society. They can be democratic, in which case they advance the natural process of life; or they can be authoritarian and dictatorial, in which case they become involved in a deadly conflict with this process.

Work-democracy cannot be imposed upon people as a political system. Those who perform vitally necessary work either are conscious of their responsibility for social processes or this consciousness evolves organically, as a tree or the body of an animal. This growth of the consciousness of social responsibility is the most important precondition to prevent political systems from proliferating like tumors on the social organism, political systems that sooner or later *have* to lead to social chaos. Moreover, the consciousness of social responsibility on the part of the working men and women of all occupations is the most important precondition for the gradual harmonizing of the institutions of human society with the natural functions of work-democracy. Political systems come and go, without any essential change taking place in the foundation of social life. Nor does social life cease to function. But the pulse of human society would stop once and for all if the natural functions of love, work, and knowledge would cease even for just a day.

Natural love, vitally necessary work, and natural science are *rational* functions of life. By their very nature, they cannot be anything but rational. Hence, they are arch enemies of any form of irrationalism. Political irrationalism, which plagues, disfigures, and destroys our life, is, in the true psychiatric sense of the word, a perversion of social life, a perversion brought about by the failure to recognize the natural functions of life and by the exclusion of these functions from the regulation and determination of social life.

Every form of totalitarian-authoritarian rulership is based on the irrationalism inculcated in masses of people. Every dictatorial political view, regardless who is its exponent, hates and fears its arch enemy, the functions of love, work, and knowledge. They cannot coexist. Dictatorship is capable only of suppressing the natural functions of life or of exploiting them for its narrow purposes; it can never promote and protect these functions or perform them itself. In doing so, it would destroy itself.

From this it follows that:

1. It is not necessary and would only be catastrophic to introduce newly conceived political systems. What is needed is the coordination of the natural functions of life with the regulation of future social processes. It is not necessary to create anything new; we must merely remove the obstacles that thwart the natural social functions, no matter in what form these obstacles turn up.

2. The representatives of these natural functions of life are those who perform the best work in all vitally necessary occupations. It is not their political inclinations that enable them to function in a work-democratic way, but solely their activity as industrial workers, farmers, teachers, physicians, child educators, writers, administrators, technicians, scientists, researchers, etc. If the representatives of vitally necessary work would form an international organization having concrete social and legal authority, such an organization would be invincible. It would foredoom international political irrationalism.

3. Social production and consumption are naturally and organically interlaced with one another. The establishment of organizations giving practical and formal expression to this natural nexus would be a strong social guarantee against further catastrophes brought about by irrationalism. The responsibility for the course of the gratification of human needs would rest exclusively on the producers and consumers; it would not have to be imposed upon them, against their will and protest, by an authoritarian state administration. This assuming of responsibility for one's own fate, represented in the already existing (i.e., not to be newly created) organizations of producers and consumers in all fields, would be a decisive step toward the establishment of the work-democratic self-administration of society. Since all work processes are dependent upon one another; since, moreover, consumption determines production, a naturally evolved and organically functioning organization is given in the social

basis, which is alone in a position to assume the responsibility for Europe's further social development.

4. Politically, work-democracy is oriented neither toward the "Left" nor toward the "Right." It includes everyone who performs vitally necessary work; hence, it is oriented solely toward the *future*. It is not part of its inherent intention to be against ideologies, nor against political ideologies. But, if it is to function at all, it must of necessity and in terms of its nature be sharply opposed to every ideological orientation and certainly to every political party that obstructs it in an irrational way. At bottom, however, work-democracy is not "against," as is usually the case in politics. It is *for* the concrete formulation and solution of problems.

WHAT IS NEW IN WORK-DEMOCRACY?

Neither the idea that democracy is the best possible form of social cohabitation nor the idea that work and consumption are the natural foundation of social existence is new; neither its anti-dictatorial attitude nor its determination to fight for the natural rights of all working men and women of all the nations of this planet is new. All of these demands, ideals, programs, etc., have been advocated in the liberal, socialist, early communist, Christian Socialist, and other political organizations for centuries.

But this much *is* new: The representatives of work-democracy neither established political parties as a means of pushing through a work-democratic organization nor did they merely reiterate the old demands, ideals, and programs and let it go at that. In a genuinely *scientific* way, work-democrats asked themselves why it has been that until now all democratic demands, programs, and ideals have met with so many failures and, in Europe and in Asia, have had to give way to reactionary dictators.

For the first time in the history of sociology, a *possible* future regulation of human society is derived not from ideologies or conditions that must be created, but from natural processes that have been present and have been developing from the very beginning.

314

Work-democratic "politics" is distinguished by the fact that *it rejects all politics and demagogism*. Masses of working men and women will not be relieved of their social responsibility. They will be *burdened* with it. Work-democrats have no ambition to be political führers, nor will they ever be permitted to develop such an ambition. Work-democracy consciously develops formal democracy, which is expressed in the mere election of political representatives and does not entail any further responsibility on the part of the electorate, into a genuine, factual, and practical democracy on an international scale. This democracy is borne by the functions of love, work, and knowledge and is developed organically. It fights mysticism and the idea of the totalitarian state, not through political attitudes, but through practical functions of life, which obey their own laws. All this is new in work-democracy.

Work-democracy adds a decisive piece of knowledge to the scope of ideas related to freedom. The masses of people who work and bear the burden of social existence on their shoulders neither are conscious of their social responsibility nor are they capable of assuming the responsibility for their own freedom. This is the result of the century-long suppression of rational thinking, the natural functions of love, and the scientific comprehension of the living. Everything related to the emotional plague in social life can be traced back to this incapacity and lack of consciousness. It is work-democracy's contention that, by its very nature, politics is and has to be unscientific, i.e., that it is an expression of human helplessness, poverty, and suppression.

In short, work-democracy is a newly discovered bio-sociologic, natural, and basic function of society. It is not a political program.

I alone bear the responsibility for this brief summary and statement.

XII

The Biologic Miscalculation in the
Human Struggle for Freedom

OUR INTEREST IN THE DEVELOPMENT OF FREEDOM

This chapter will deal with the biologic miscalculation that, as
history proves, all freedom movements have made. It is a miscalculation that nipped freedom efforts in the bud or frustrated
satisfactory regulations of social life, which had already been attained. This endeavor is prompted by the conviction that only *work-
democracy* can create the basis of *genuine* freedom. My experiences
in social discussions lead me to believe that the exposure of this
miscalculation will very likely be taken amiss. It imposes the highest
demands upon the will to truth of each and every one of us. In
actual practice it implies a great burden in the daily struggle for
existence, for *it transfers all social responsibility to the working men
and women in factories, on farms, in clinics, offices, laboratories,
etc.*

We have found that facts of a *fundamental* nature, i.e., facts
that, over and above the political hubbub of everyday life, relate to
the ancient history of the human species, relate, indeed, to man's
biologic constitution, are rejected with various arguments. At bottom, however, the motive is always irrational. When peace reigns,
when everything is proceeding at a leisurely pace, then it is said:
"Everything is quite all right as it is; the League of Nations is a
guarantee of peace; our diplomats settle conflicts in a peaceful way;
the generals are only decorations. So why pose questions that would

be relevant only in the event of a war? We have just ended a war to end all wars—there is no need to get excited." Then, when it is shown that such arguments were based on illusions, when the League of Nations and the diplomats have given ample testimony of their inability to cope with pressing problems, when a new war rages—this time one that is worldwide and more brutal than anything known in history, then all attention is concentrated on "winning the war." Then it is said: "We have to win the war first. This is no time for profound truths. We will need those when the war has been won, for then we will also have to secure peace." Thus, a clear-cut distinction is made between the conduct of war and the winning of the war, between the termination of hostilities and the conclusion of peace. Only after the war has been won and the peace concluded, does one want to proceed to secure peace. One fails to see that it is precisely in *the heat of the war that those deep social convulsions take place that destroy old institutions and remold man*, that, in other words, *the seeds of peace germinate in the devastations of war*. Man's intense longing for peace is never so strong as it is at a time of war. Hence, in no other social circumstance are there so many strong impulses intent on changing the conditions that produce war. Man learned to construct dams when he suffered from floods. *Peace can be hammered out only at a time of war, then and only then.*

Instead of learning the lessons of war on the spot, so that a new world can be built immediately, important decisions are put off until diplomats and statesmen are so involved in peace treaties and reparations that again there is no time for "basic facts." In the transition period from the cessation of hostilities to the conclusion of a sham peace, we hear statements like this: "First the damages of war must be repaired; the war production has to be converted to peace production; our hands are full. Before dealing with these basic facts, let us arrange everything peacefully." In the meantime the lessons of war have been forgotten; once again everything has been arranged in such a way that in the course of *one* generation a new, even more horrible war has broken out. Once again there is "no

time" and one is "too busy" to concern oneself with "basic truths."
The emotions of wartime rapidly give way to the old rigidity and
emotional apathy.

If someone, as I myself, has gone through this procrastination
of essential questions and heard these same arguments for the
second time in forty-five years of life; if he recognizes in the new
catastrophe all the characteristics of the old catastrophe; he has to
admit, however reluctantly, that no essential change has taken place
since the first catastrophe (unless one considers the improvement of
the means of destruction and a more widespread development of
human sadism as essential changes). Slowly and surely the conviction takes shape in such a man that: *For some curious reason or
another, masses of people do not want to get to the root of the
secret of war. They fear the truths* that could bring them a painful
cure.

People like to think of war as a "social thunderstorm." It is said
that it "purifies" the atmosphere; it has its great benefits—it
"hardens the youth" and makes them courageous. As far as that
goes, people say, we have always had and will always have wars.
They are biologically motivated. According to Darwin, the "struggle
for existence" is the law of life. Why, then, were peace conferences
organized? Nor have I ever heard that bears or elephants split up
into two camps and annihilate one another. *In the animal kingdom
there are no wars within the same species. Like sadism, war among
one's own kind is an acquisition of "civilized man."* No, for some
reason or another, man shies away from putting his finger on the
causes of war. And there can be no doubt that better ways than war
exist of making youth fit and healthy, namely, a satisfying love life,
pleasurable and steady work, general sports, and freedom from the
malicious gossip of old maids. In short, such arguments are hollow
chatter.

What is this fact anyhow?

Why do people fear it?

Is it possible that in his inmost self every man knows this fact,
but is afraid to admit it to himself and to his neighbor?

318

It boils down to this: *As a result of thousands of years of social and educational distortion, masses of people have become biologically rigid and incapable of freedom. They are not capable of establishing peaceful coexistence.*

As cynical and hopeless as these two succinct sentences may sound, they contain the answer to the three above questions. No one wants to acknowledge the truth they contain, or even listen to them. No democratic statesman would know what to make of it. Every honest man knows it. *All dictators have built their power on the social irresponsibleness of masses of people.* They have made no bones about consciously exploiting this fact. For years on end, far more than half the civilized German people heard the assertion that the masses merely regurgitate what has been funneled into them. They reacted to this with slavish loyalty. They themselves brought about this ignominious situation. It is ridiculous to contend that the psychopathic general was capable of oppressing seventy million people all *by himself.*

"How's that?" the suave politician and philanthropist will ask. "You say that the Americans are incapable of freedom? And what of the heroic rebels of Czechoslovakia, Yugoslavia, the British Commandos, the martyrs in Norway, the armies in Soviet Russia? How can you dare to cast a slur upon democracies!"

We do not mean military groups, governments, minorities, individual scientists or thinkers! But genuine social freedom is more than a question of groups. *The trend of society is determined solely by the overwhelming majority of working men and women,* whether they passively tolerate or actively support tyranny. Are the *masses themselves* capable of administering society without their statesmen or parties telling them what to do and how to do it? They are, to be sure, capable of enjoying *given* freedoms, of performing *assigned* work, of being against war and for peace. Thus far, however, they have not been capable of safeguarding work against abuse, regulating it through their own organizations, promoting rapid development, preventing wars, mastering their own irrationalism, etc.

319

The masses cannot do these things because until now they have never been in the position to acquire and practice this ability. The self-administration of society by the masses, their administration of the organizations in charge of production and consumption, can be the only possible answer to this war. *One who takes the masses seriously demands their full responsibility, for they alone are peacefully disposed.* The responsibility and the capacity to be free must now be added to the love of peace.

As bitter as it may be, the fact remains: It is the irresponsibleness of masses of people that lies at the basis of fascism of all countries, nations, and races, etc. Fascism is the result of man's distortion over thousands of years. It could have developed in any country or nation. It is not a character trait that is confined specifically to the Germans or Italians. It is manifest in every single individual of the world. The Austrian saying *"Da kann man halt nix machen"* expresses this fact just as the American saying "Let George do it." That this situation was brought about by a social development which goes back thousands of years does not alter the fact itself. It is man himself who is responsible and not "historical developments." It was this shifting of the responsibility from living man to "historical developments" that caused the downfall of the socialist freedom movements. *However, the events of the past twenty years demand the responsibility of the working masses of people.*

If we take *"freedom"* to mean first and foremost the *responsibility of each individual to shape personal, occupational, and social existence in a rational way,* then it can be said that *there is no greater fear than the fear of the creation of general freedom.* Unless this basic problem is given complete priority and solved, there will never be a freedom capable of lasting more than one or two generations. The solution to this problem will require more thought, more decency, more conscientiousness, more of an economic, educational, and social readjustment in the social life of masses of people than all the efforts which were made in former wars (and will have to be made in wars still to come) and postwar reconstruction programs taken together. This one problem and its solution contain everything that the most audacious and most agonized thinkers of history have tried to grasp by the idea of international social revolution. We are the protagonists and bearers of a stupendous revolutionary upheaval. If one must indeed suffer, then "blood, sweat, and tears" should at least have a rational goal, namely: *the responsibility of the working masses of people for social life!* This conclusion follows with hard logic from the following statements:

1. Every social process is determined by the attitude of the masses.

2. *The masses are incapable of freedom.*

3. *When the masses achieve the capacity to be free through their own efforts, this will be genuine social freedom.*

What prompts me to depart from the usual policy of veiling such generally known facts, especially as I make no claim to political leadership?

There are several motives. For years I demurred from pursuing them, simply because I feared the consequences. Again and again I hesitated to put my ideas down on paper. I tried to extricate myself from this perplexity by telling myself that I of course was not a politician and that political events were no concern of mine. Or I evaded the issue by persuading myself that I had more than enough to keep me busy with my orgone biophysics and saw no reason why I should burden myself with an embarrassing, thankless basic social question, which seemed hopeless for the time being anyhow. I tried to make myself believe that it was my secret political ambition that was prompting me to get involved in the turmoil of irrational political ideologies. I demurred to give in to such an ambition. The responsible politicians and statesmen were bound to come out with these facts sooner or later!

After years of painful and harassing oscillations and attempts to fight shy of these facts, I had finally to yield to the pressure exerted on me as well as on all of my coworkers by our investigation of the phenomena of life. A researcher has an *allegiance to truth,* over which no other allegiance, however highly esteemed, can take precedence. What makes it particularly difficult to fulfill this allegiance is the fact that communications of truth, instead of being looked upon as natural, have a highly dangerous potential as things now stand.

Basically speaking, this is merely a summary of facts, which, in an isolated way, have been well known to us for a long time:

1. Mankind is biologically sick.

2. Politics is the irrational social expression of this sickness.

3. Whatever takes place in social life is actively or passively, voluntarily or involuntarily, determined by the structure of masses of people.

4. This character structure is formed by socio-economic processes and it anchors and perpetuates these processes. Man's biopathic character structure is, as it were, the fossilization of the authoritarian process of history. It is the biophysical reproduction of mass suppression.

5. The human structure is animated by the contradiction between an intense longing for and fear of freedom.

6. The fear of freedom of masses of people is expressed in the biophysical rigidity of the organism and the inflexibility of the character.

7. Every form of social leadership is merely the social expression of the one or the other side of this structure of masses of people.

8. It is not a question of the Versailles Peace Treaty, the oil wells of Baku or two to three hundred years of capitalism, but a question of four to six thousand years of authoritarian mechanistic civilization, which has ruined man's biologic functioning.

9. Interest in money and power is a substitute for unfulfilled happiness in love, supported by the biologic rigidity of masses of people.

10. The suppression of the natural sexuality of children and adolescents serves to mold the human structure in such a way that masses of people become willing upholders and reproducers of mechanistic authoritarian civilization.

11. Thousands of years of human suppression are in the process of being eliminated.

These are more or less the results of our research on the character and its relationship to social processes.

We have a threefold interest in the development of a free world: personal, objective, and social.

1. The *personal* interest is determined by the threat to our existence as members of this mortally sick society. Those, like myself, who lost their home, family, and possessions, who experienced three and a half years of murder in war at first hand, who saw many friends die and go to pieces, who witnessed mass migrations and destruction of property, etc., in World War I, understand what millions upon millions of men and women are going through on this planet today. We want an end to this ignominy! It is ignominious that a handful of Prussian crooks and perverse neurotics, functioning as the "führer" of one thing or another, are able to exploit the social helplessness of hundreds of millions of industrious and decent men and women. The ignominy is all the more poignant in view of the fact that these same millions of men and women unwittingly and naively allowed themselves to be taken in by these political swindlers (and this was the case not only in Germany, but elsewhere also). All we want is to be able to perform our work in peace, to love our wives or husbands without danger, to raise our children free of the miasma of the plague. In short, we do not want to be bothered, deceived, and led around by the nose by a handful of political swindlers in this short life of ours. Our lives have been crushed by politics long enough! We want an end of it! Once and for all!!

2. The protagonists of the fascist plague have looked through the incapacity for freedom of masses of people and have declared that it is *an absolute biologic fact*. They have put alluring irrational race theories into the world, have divided mankind into biologically immutable superior and inferior races, and have conferred upon themselves, who are the most sick and most vicious, the biologic title of "superman." We have the answer to this fraud: *The race theory is a mystical view of life. Man's natural happiness in love and security in life will be the doom of this view.*

3. Our institute is faced with a momentous task. We have to prepare ourselves for two basically different possibilities:

a. In the event that this Second World War will force the answer to social chaos to the surface and into social consciousness, we will be called upon to deal with great tasks. We will have to assume an enormous responsibility. We *have to prepare* ourselves for this possibility in advance. We must have a clear conception of our tasks. Our knowledge of human reactions and the effects of the fascist pestilence will have to be clearly organized if we do not want to fail. Our tasks can be fulfilled only within the framework of the general struggle for the establishment of *genuine* freedom. If we cherish the illusion that man's structure is immediately capable of freedom and self-administration, that, in other words, we need merely eliminate the plague of party fascism to make it possible for social freedom to function, to put justice before injustice, truth before falsehood, decency before meanness, then we too will be doomed together with everything else that is based on such illusions. This much is clear. *The development of freedom requires that one be ruthlessly free of illusions, for only then will one succeed in rooting out irrationalism from masses of people* to open the way to *responsibility* and *freedom.* To idealize masses of people and to commiserate with them will only produce fresh misfortunes.

The various freedom organizations in Europe treated this sickness on the part of masses of people as a quack might treat a paralyzed patient, namely by persuading him that he was *not* really paralyzed and would surely be able to dance a polka if it were not for the bad wolf (in 1914, the war industrialists; in 1942, the psychopathic generals). A paralyzed patient may like to hear such a consolation and rejoice in it, but he still won't be able to walk. The *decent* physician would proceed "ruthlessly"; he would be very careful not to arouse any false hopes in the patient. He would use every means at his disposal to determine the nature of the paralysis and to decide whether it is curable or not. If, fundamentally, it is curable, then he will find the means of curing it.

The fascist dictator declares that the masses of people are

324

biologically inferior and crave authority, that, basically, they are slaves *by nature*. Hence, a totalitarian authoritarian regime is the only possible form of government for such people. It is significant that all dictators who today plunge the world into misery stem from the suppressed masses of people. They are intimately familiar with this sickness on the part of masses of people. What they lack is an insight into natural processes and development, the will to truth and research, so that they are never moved by a desire to want to *change* these facts.

On the other hand, the formal democratic leaders made the mistake of assuming that the masses of people were automatically capable of freedom and thereby precluded every possibility of *establishing* freedom and self-responsibility in masses of people as long as they were in power. They were engulfed in the catastrophe and will never reappear.

Our answer is *scientific and rational*. It is based on the fact that masses of people are indeed incapable of freedom, but it does not—as racial mysticism does—look upon this incapacity as absolute, innate, and eternal. It regards this incapacity as the result of former social conditions of life and, therefore, as *changeable*.

Two important tasks follow from this:

i. The investigation and elucidation of the forms in which man's incapacity for freedom expresses itself;

ii. The investigation of the medical, pedagogic, and social tools necessary to establish the *capacity* for freedom in a more and more thorough and more and more extensive way.

At this point the "mistakes" made by democratic governments will be recalled: pacts with plague-ridden dictators, the many acts of treachery committed against democratic allies (England-Spain; Russia-Czechoslovakia, etc.), the priority given to business interests over principles (Russian oil for Italy during the Ethiopian war; Mexican oil for Germany during the Spanish anti-fascist fight; Swedish steel for Nazi Germany; American steel, American coal, etc., for Japan; English behavior in Burma and India; the religious-mystical faith of the socialists and Communists, etc.). But the gravity of these "mistakes" diminishes when compared with the mistakes of masses of people, their social apathy, passivity, craving for authority, etc. The ineluctable fact remains: *The working masses of men and women, they and they alone, are responsible for everything that takes place, the good things and the bad things.* True enough, they suffer most from a war, but it is their apathy, craving for authority, etc., that is most responsible for making wars possible. It follows of necessity from this responsibility that *the working masses of men and women, they and they alone, are capable of establishing lasting peace.* The quintessence of this accomplishment can be nothing but the elimination of the incapacity for freedom. Only the masses of people themselves can accomplish this. *To become capable of freedom and of securing peace, masses of people who are incapable of freedom will have to have social power.* This is the contradiction and its solution.

b. In the event that the outcome of this war will *not* bring the basic facts to the surface of social consciousness and that the old illusions continue to exist, it is to be assumed that our present position will not change much. If such is the case, we will not be able to escape the conclusion that the illusionary "pills," the *formal* freedoms, the *formal* joys and *formal* democracies, will soon give birth to new dictators and a new war. In such a case we will continue to be "isolated" and in opposition to this social misery; our task will be no less difficult. Within this general framework of illusions we will have to maintain a subjective and objective honesty. We will have to make every effort to keep our insights into the nature of man *unadulterated,* and at the same time to deepen them. It will not be easy for the workers in the field of orgone biophysics, structure psychology, and sex-economy to elude the influences of illusions and to preserve their knowledge in a *pure* and *crystal clear* form for future generations. Their knowledge must be practically applicable if the insight into the psychic mass plague should still have to be asserted after the sixth, twelfth, or twentieth world war. In this case we will not pass on to our descendants deeds of heroism, war decorations, "heroic remembrances," and front-line experiences, but a modest, unobtrusive, unostentatious knowledge, *pregnant with the seed of the future.* This task can be accomplished even under the worst social conditions. *When the time is ripe to overcome the emotional plague, we do not want that generation to make any unnecessary mistakes, and we do not want it to have to cast about for answers to the arguments of the plague. We want it to be able to fall back on old, though neglected, truths and to be able to shape its life more honestly and more decently than the generation of 1940.*

At this point, some friend or other may well feel prompted to ask: "For Christ's sake, why don't you fight for social power to push through the important truths you have perceived? Isn't it cowardly of you to sit there, politically passive, though you claim to be in possession of vital facts. Damn it, fight for positions as ministers of health, ministers of education, statesmen, etc.!"

We understand this argument. Many of us have set it forth again and again. There were many sleepless nights because of it. The dilemma is this:

Without the power to put them into practice, truths are of no use. They remain academic.

Power, no matter what kind of power it is, without a foundation in truth, is a dictatorship, more or less and in one way or another, for it is always based on man's fear of the social responsibility and personal burden that "freedom" entails.

Dictatorial power and truth do not go together. They are mutually exclusive.

It is a historical fact that truth has always died when its protagonists have gained social power. *"Power" always means the subjugation of others.* However, truthful facts can never be put into practice by subjugation, but only by persuasion. We learned this from the French and Russian revolutions. Not a single one of their truths survived more than a few decades at the most. Jesus proclaimed a truth which was stupendous at his time. It died in the Christian world when he was replaced by the popes. Deep insights into human misery of two thousand years ago gave way to formulas;

327

the simple cowl gave way to the gold-draped ornament; the rebellion against suppression of the poor gave way to consolations of happiness beyond the grave. The truths of the great French Revolution died in the French Republic and ended in political power-mongering, in the ignorance of a Pétain and the business dealings of a Laval. The truths of Marxian economy died in the Russian Revolution when the word "society" was replaced by the word "state" and the idea of an "international mankind" was replaced by nationalistic patriotism and the pact with Hitler. They died in Germany, Austria, and Scandinavia, notwithstanding the fact that the heirs of the great European freedom-fighters had all the social power in their hands. Almost one hundred years after the birth of the truths of 1848, the muck, which goes back thousands of years, still prevails. *Power and truth do not go together. This too is a bitter, unfortunate truth.*

It is true that those of us who have political experience could wrestle for power just as any other politician. *But we have no time; we have more important things to do.* And there is no doubt that the knowledge we hold to be sacred would be lost in the process. To acquire power, millions of people have to be fed illusions. This too is true: Lenin won over millions of Russian peasants, without whom the Russian Revolution would have been impossible, with a slogan which was at variance with the basic collective tendencies of the Russian party. The slogan was: "Take the land of the large landowners. It is to be your *individual* property." And the peasants followed. They would not have offered their allegiance if they had been told in 1917 that this land would one day be collectivized. The truth of this is attested to by the bitter fight for the collectivization of Russian agriculture around 1930. In social life there are *degrees* of power and degrees of falsity. *The more the masses of people adhere to truth, the less power-mongering there will be;* the more imbued with irrational illusions the masses of people are, the more widespread and brutal individual power-mongering will be.

It would be stupid to try to win over masses of people with the assertion that *they themselves* and not individual psychopaths are responsible for social misery, that *they themselves* and not one of their elected or acclaimed leaders bear the responsibility for their fate, that *they alone* are responsible *for everything* that happens in the world. This is completely at variance with what they have always been told and what they have imbibed. It would be stupid to try to acquire power with such truths.

On the other hand, it is *definitely* conceivable that the world catastrophe will reach a stage at which the masses of people will be *forced to get an insight into their social attitudes, be forced to change themselves and to assume the heavy burden of social responsibility.* But in such a case, *they themselves* will acquire power and will rightfully reject groups who "conquer" power "in the interest of the people." Hence, there is no reason for us to fight for power.

We can be assured that the masses of people will need us, will call upon us and will entrust us with important functions, if they should ever get in a position to transform themselves in a rational direction. We will be a part of these masses, not their leaders, not their elected representatives, not their "custodians." Then, as was the case in Austria and Germany many years ago, masses of people will throng to our clinics, schools, lectures, and demonstrations of scientific facts to get answers to basic questions of life. (They will not demand or expect us to tell them how to solve their life tasks.) But they will throng to us *only if we shall have remained honest.* Then, when masses of people *will have to bear* the responsibility for social existence themselves, they will inevitably run against their own weaknesses, against the heritage of a vicious past. In short, they will run against those facts in their structures, thoughts, and feelings that we include under the term "incapacity for freedom." And as a social institution, together with thousands of friends, we will expose the mechanism of the incapacity for freedom and all the obstructions to the development of freedom to help masses of people to achieve genuine freedom.

For this we need no power. The *confidence* of men and women—of all ages, all occupations, every color of skin and every view of life—in our absolute integrity as physicians, researchers, teachers, social workers, biologists, physicists, writers, technicians, etc., will be far more enduring than any power ever acquired by a politician. This confidence will be that much greater, the more our scientific and practical activity reflects reality. This confidence cannot be conquered; it comes about of itself when one adheres to one's work honestly. In no case should we want to adapt our insights to the masses' present way of thinking for the purpose "of winning influence." Widespread confidence in our activities can proceed only from the deepening of our general knowledge about the nature of the plague.

When we are called upon, it will be a sign that self-administration in social life is indeed taking hold, that the will to "profound truth," to fruitful self-criticism, is awakening in the working masses of men and women. Since our organization is the only organization that sees through the irrationality of politics and the old ideologies, it cannot be any other way. Conversely, if we continue to remain in the "opposition," it will be a sure sign that society is not ready to see through and eliminate the irrationality in its mechanism. In such a case, however, no power would be of any help to us, and we ourselves would only degenerate into irrationality.

Don't let this conscious renunciation of power cause anyone to underestimate our work. We do not play the role of "humble," "unassuming" scientists. Our work is accomplished at the source of life, in line with fundamental natural science. False modesty here would be tantamount to self-destruction. It is true that, beside "Dneprostroi Dam," "orgastic potency" sounds small; "character armoring," insignificant, compared with "blackout"; "orgone," academic beside "Bataan and Tobruk." It seems this way from a *contemporary* point of view. But compared with Kepler's laws, what remains of Alexander the Great? What remains of Caesar compared with the laws of mechanics? What of Napoleon's campaigns compared with the discovery of micro-organisms or unconscious psychic life? And what will remain of the psychopathic generals compared with cosmic orgone? Renunciation of power does not mean renunciation of rational regulation of human existence. It is the effect that is different: long-sighted, deep, and revolutionary, true and life-securing. It does not matter whether we feel the effects tomorrow or the day after tomorrow. It will be up to working masses of men and women to pick the fruits of new knowledge today and not the day after tomorrow. The responsibility they bear for their life and activity is no less than the responsibility the individual shoemaker bears for the shoe, the physician for the patient, the researcher for his statements, the architect for his constructions. We do not strive to be people's benefactors or commiseraters. *We take people seriously!* When they need us, they will call us. Then we shall be there. For my part, I reject the struggle for power with the intent of obtruding my knowledge.

BIOLOGIC RIGIDITY, INCAPACITY FOR FREEDOM, AND MECHANICAL AUTHORITARIAN VIEW OF LIFE

We are confronted with the incontrovertible fact: *At no time in the history of human society did masses of people succeed in preserving, organizing, and developing the freedom and peace that they had achieved in bloody battles.* We mean the *genuine* freedom of personal and social development, the freedom to face life without fear, freedom from all forms of economic suppression, freedom from reactionary inhibitions of development; in short, the *free self-administration of life.* We have to rid ourselves of all illusions. In the masses of people themselves there is a retarding power which is both reactionary and murderous and which thwarts the efforts of the freedom-fighters again and again.

This reactionary power in masses of people appears as a general *fear of responsibility* and *fear of freedom.* These are not moralistic evaluations. This fear is deeply rooted in the biologic constitution of present-day man. However, this constitution is not, as the typical fascist believes, native to man; it has become that way in the course of history and is therefore changeable, fundamentally speaking. It is not easy to give a brief and lucid exposition of the social role of the fear of freedom. Perhaps it would be best to begin with a report by

331

James Aldridge, which appeared in *The New York Times* of June 24, 1942, under the title, "British in Africa Lack Killer Urge." I quote:

> The German Afrika Corps defeated the Eighth Army because it had speed, anger, virility and toughness. As soldiers in the traditional sense, the Germans are punk, absolutely punk. But Marshal Erwin Rommel and his gang are angry men, they are tough to the point of stupidity. They are virile and fast, they are thugs with little or no imagination. They are practical men, taken from a most practical and hard life to fight practically: Nazis trained to kill. The German commanders are scientists, who are continually experimenting with and improving the hard, mathematical formula of killing. They are trained as mathematicians, engineers and chemists facing complicated problems. There is no art in it, there is no imagination. War is pure physics to them. The German soldier is trained with a psychology of the daredevil track rider. He is a professional killer, with no distractions. He believes he is the toughest man on earth. Actually, he cracks very easily and is not so tough, and can be beaten soundly and quickly by a foe using the same ruthless speedy methods he uses. . . . The British soldier is the most heroic on earth, but do not confuse that with military toughness. He has the toughness of determination but he has not the toughness which makes him scientifically kill his enemy.

This is the best description of mechanical militarism that I have ever read. It discloses at one blow the complete *identity of mechanistic natural science, mechanical human structure, and sadistic murder*. This identity found its highest and most consummate expression in the totalitarian dictatorship-ideology of German imperialism. This mechanical trinity is set in relief against that view of life that regards man not as a machine, the machine not as the master of man, and militarism not as his greatest asset. This living functional view has found its last refuge in the Western democracies. It remains to be seen whether it will survive the chaos.

As strange as it may sound to the ears of a general, I maintain that the defeats of the democracies, as tragic and dangerous as they were, were imbued with a deep humanity, which is diametrically opposed to mechanical automatism: *the appreciation of human life.* Aldridge is wrong in reproaching the democratic commanders-in-chief for attempting to spare human life, instead of imitating the human robots. He is wrong in demanding that the anti-fascist fighters learn to kill even more mechanically, more automatically, more scientifically, than the Prussian automatons. Those who attempt to beat the mechanical automatons with their own methods will only jump out of the frying pan and into the fire, i.e., in their efforts to become more efficient scientific killers, they will transform *themselves* into mechanical automatons and perpetuate the process their opponents have set in motion. In such a case the last vestiges of all living hope for a different kind of human society, a permanently peaceful one, will vanish altogether.

Our conception of the anti-fascist fight is different. It is a clear, relentless recognition of the historical and biological causes that lead to such murders. The deracination of the fascist plague will come about solely from such a recognition, and not by imitating it. One cannot vanquish fascism by imitating and subduing it with its own methods, without becoming a fascist oneself. The way of fascism is the way of the automaton, death, rigidity, hopelessness. The way of the living is fundamentally different; it is more difficult, more dangerous, more honest, more hopeful.

Let us strip the matter of all current political interests and concentrate on the *one* question: *How does such a complete functional identity of machine, man, and scientific murder come about?* This question may not bear any relevance to such questions as whether ship-building is keeping pace with ship-sinking or whether the mechanical monstrosity will reach the oil wells of Baku or not. We do not fail to appreciate the importance of these current questions. If my house should suddenly catch fire, naturally I would first try to extinguish the fire and to save what could still be saved of important manuscripts, books, and apparatus. But sooner or later I shall have to build a new house, and I shall give considerable thought to what it was that caused the fire in the old house, so that I can prevent a repetition of the misfortune.

MAN IS FUNDAMENTALLY AN ANIMAL. In contrast to man, animals are not mechanical or sadistic, and their societies (within the same species) are incomparably more peaceful than man's societies. The basic question runs: *What caused the human animal to deteriorate and become robotlike?*

When I use the word "animal," I do not mean something vicious, terrible, or "inferior," but a biologic fact. However, man developed the peculiar idea that he was not an animal; *he* was a "man," and he had long since divested himself of the "vicious" and the "brutal." Man takes great pains to disassociate himself from the vicious animal and to prove that he "is better" by pointing to his culture and his civilization, which distinguish him from the animal. His entire attitude, his "theories of value," moral philosophies, his "monkey trials," all bear witness to the fact that he does not want to be reminded that he is fundamentally an animal, that he has incomparably more in common with "the animal" than he has with that which he thinks and dreams himself to be. The theory of the German superman has its origin in man's effort to disassociate himself from the animal. His viciousness, his inability to live peacefully with his own kind, his wars, bear witness to the fact that man is distinguished from the other animals only by a boundless sadism and the mechanical trinity of an authoritarian view of life, mechanistic science, and the machine. If one looks back over long stretches of the results of human civilization, one finds that man's claims are not only false, but are peculiarly contrived to make him forget that he is an animal. *Where and how did man get these illusions about himself?*

Man's life is dichotomized: One part of his life is determined by *biologic* laws (sexual gratification, consumption of food, relatedness to nature); the other part of his life is determined by the machine civilization (mechanical ideas about his own organization, his superior position in the animal kingdom, his racial or class attitude toward other human groups, valuations about ownership and

334

nonownership, science, religion, etc.). *His being an animal and his not being an animal, biologic* roots on the one hand and *technical* development on the other hand, cleave man's life and thought. All the notions man has developed about himself are consistently derived from the machine that he has created. The construction of machines and the use of machines have imbued man with the belief that he is progressing and developing himself to something "higher," in and through the machine. But he also invested the machine with an animal-like appearance and mechanics. The train engine has eyes to see with and legs to run with, a mouth to consume coal with and discharge openings for slag, levers, and other devices for making sounds. In this way the product of mechanistic technology became the extension of man himself. In fact, machines do constitute a tremendous extension of man's biologic organization. They make him capable of mastering nature to a far greater degree than his hands alone had enabled him. They give him mastery over time and space. Thus, the machine became a part of man himself, a loved and highly esteemed part. He dreams about how these machines make his life easier and will give him a great capacity for enjoyment. The enjoyment of life with the help of the machine has always been his dream. And in *reality? The machine became, is, and will continue to be his most dangerous destroyer, if he does not differentiate himself from it.*

The advance of civilization which was determined by the development of the machine went hand in hand with a *catastrophic misinterpretation of the human biologic organization.* In the construction of the machine, man followed the laws of mechanics and lifeless energy. This technology was already highly developed long before man began to ask how *he himself* was constructed and organized. When, finally, he dared very gradually, cautiously and very often under the mortal threat of his fellow man to discover his own organs, he interpreted their functions in the way he had learned to construct machines many centuries before. He interpreted them in a mechanistic, lifeless, and rigid way. *The mechanistic view of life is a copy of mechanistic civilization.* But living functioning is fundamentally different; it is not mechanistic. The specific biologic energy, orgone, obeys laws which are neither mechanical nor electrical. Trapped in a mechanistic picture of the world, man was incapable of grasping the specifically living, non-mechanistic functioning. Man dreams about one day producing a homunculus à la Frankenstein or at least an artificial heart or artificial protein. The notions of homunculus, which man has developed in his fantasy, project a picture of a brutal monster, manlike, but mechanically stupid, angular, and possessing powerful forces, which, if they are set loose, will be beyond control and will automatically cause havoc. In his film *Fantasia* Walt Disney brilliantly captured this fact. In such fantasies of himself and his organization, we miss every expression of that which is vitally alive, kind, social, and related to nature. On the other hand, it is striking that man invests the animals he portrays precisely with those traits he misses in himself and does not give to his homunculus figures. This, too, is excellently brought out in Disney's animal films.

In his fantasies, man appears as a mechanical, vicious, overbearing, heartless, inanimate monster, while the animal appears as a social, kind, and fully alive creature, invested with all the human strengths and weaknesses. We have to ask: Does man reflect a reality in these fantasies? The answer is: *Yes.* He very vividly portrays his inner biologic contradiction:

1. In ideology: vicious animal—majestic man;
2. In reality: kind, free animal—brutal robot.

Thus, the machine has had a mechanical, mechanistic, "dulling," and "rigidifying" effect on man's conception of his own organization. This is how man conceives of himself: The brain is the "most consummate product of development." His brain is a "control center," which gives the individual organs commands and impulses just as the "ruler" of a state orders his "subjects" about. The organs of the body are connected with the master, the "brain," by telegraph wires, the nerves. (A complete misconception naturally, for the organs of the organism had an expedient biologic function long before there was a brain in billions of organisms. And as physiology has experimentally proven, the essential functions of life continue for some time in a dog or chicken from which the brain has been removed.) Infants have to drink a precise quantity of milk at fixed intervals and have to sleep a precise number of hours. Their diet has to have exactly x ounces of fat, y ounces of protein and z ounces of carbohydrates. Until the day of marriage, a man does not have a sex drive; it begins to operate precisely on this day. God created the world in exactly six days and rested on the seventh, as man rests from his machines. Children have to study x hours of mathematics, y hours of chemistry, z hours of zoology, all exactly the same, and all of them have to acquire the same amount of wisdom. Superior intelligence is equal to one hundred points, average intelligence to eighty points, stupidity to forty points. With ninety points one gets a Ph.D., with eighty-nine, one does not.

Even in our own time, psychic life itself is only something nebulous and mysterious to man, or at best a secretion of the brain, which, as it were, is neatly stored away in individual compartments. It has no greater significance than the excreta that are discharged from the bowels. For centuries man has not only denied the existence of a soul; what is worse is that he repudiated every attempt to comprehend sensations and psychic experiences. At the same time, however, he devised mystical conceptions which embodied his emotional life. Those who questioned his mystical conceptions of life were persecuted and punished with death, whether it was the "saints," "racial purity," or the "state" that was questioned. In this way man developed mechanistic, mechanical, and mystical conceptions of his organization at one and the same time. Thus, his understanding of biology remained far behind his dexterity in constructing machines, and he abandoned the possibility of comprehending himself. The machine he had created sufficed to explain the performances of his organism.[1]

---

[1] The tragic duality between biologic and technical organization, between what is vitally alive and what is automatic and mechanical in man, is clearly expressed in the following fact. Not a single one of the individuals who make up the masses of this world wanted the war. All of them, without exception, have fallen prey to it, hopelessly, as to a monstrous automaton. *But it is rigid man himself who is this monstrosity.*

Is this gap between outstanding industrial dexterity and biologic understanding only the result of a lack of knowledge? Or can we assume that there is an unconscious intention, an, as it were, unconscious arbitrary banishment of the insight into one's own organization? (In the experimental studies of the orgone, I never cease to marvel that atmospheric orgone was so completely overlooked by tens of thousands of outstanding researchers.)

The irrefutable answer is: The lagging behind of our understanding of the living, its mechanistic misinterpretation, and the overestimation of the machine were and are unconscious intentions. There is no reason whatever why man could not have constructed machines mechanistically and at the same time comprehended the living, nonmechanical in a *living* way. A thorough consideration of human behavior in important life situations betrays the nature of this intention.

For man the machine civilization constituted not only an improvement of his animal existence; over and above this it had the subjectively far more important, but *irrational,* function of constantly stressing that he was *not an animal,* that he was fundamentally *different from the animal.* The next question is this: What interest does man have in constantly crying out, whether in his science, his religion, his art or his other expressions of life, that he is indeed a *man* and *not* an animal; that the highest task of human existence is the "slaying of his animal side" and the cultivation of "values"; that the child has to be transformed from a "little wild animal" into a "higher man"? How is it possible, we have to ask, that man should want to cut himself off from the biologic branch on which he grew and of which he is inveterately a part? How is it possible, we must ask further, that he does not see the damages (psychic illnesses, biopathies, sadism, and wars) to his health, culture, and mind that are caused by this biologic renunciation? Is it possible for human intelligence to admit that human misery can be done away with only if man fully acknowledges his animal nature? Doesn't man have to learn that that which distinguishes him from the other animals is merely an improvement of the security factor of life, and that he has to give up the irrational renunciation of his true nature?

"Away from the animal; away from sexuality!" are the guiding principles of the formation of all human ideology. This is the case whether it is disguised in the fascist form of racially pure "supermen," the communist form of proletarian class honor, the Christian form of man's "spiritual and ethical nature," or the liberal form of "higher human values." All these ideas harp on the same monotonous tune: "We are not animals; it was we who discovered the machine—not the animal! *And we don't have genitals like the animals!*" All of this adds up to an overemphasis of the intellect, of the "purely" mechanistic; logic and reason as opposed to instinct; culture as opposed to nature; the mind as opposed to the body; work as opposed to sexuality; the state as opposed to the individual; the superior man as opposed to the inferior man.

How is it to be explained that of the millions of car drivers, radio listeners, etc., only very few know the name of the inventor of the car and the radio, whereas every child knows the name of the generals of the political plague?

Natural science is constantly drilling into man's consciousness that fundamentally he is a worm in the universe. The political plague-monger is constantly harping upon the fact that man is not an animal, but a "zoon politikon," i.e., a non-animal, an upholder of values, a "moral being." How much mischief has been perpetuated by the Platonic philosophy of the state! It is quite clear why man knows the politicos better than the natural scientists: He does not want to be reminded of the fact that he is fundamentally a sexual animal. *He does not want to be an animal.*

Viewed in this way, the animal has no intelligence, but only "wicked instincts"; no culture, but only "base drives"; no sense of values, but only "material needs." It is precisely the human type who sees the whole of life in the making of money who likes to stress these "differences." If a war as murderous as the present one has any trace of a rational function, then it is the function of exposing the abysmal irrationality and mendacity of such ideas.

Man would have good reason to be happy if he were as free from sadism, perversions, and meanness, and as filled with a natural spontaneity, as any one of the animals, whether an ant or an elephant. As vain as man's assumption was that the earth is the center of the universe or the sole inhabited planet, even so unreal and pernicious was his philosophy that represented the animal as a "soulless" creature devoid of any morals, indeed, as morally repulsive. If, while professing myself to be a benevolent saint, I should take an ax and crack my neighbor's skull, there would be good reason for putting me in a mental institution or in the electric chair. But this juxtaposition exactly reflects the contradiction in man between his ideal "values" on the one hand and his actual behavior on the other hand. His expressing of this contradiction in high-sounding sociological formulas such as "the century of wars and revolutions," or "elevating experiences at the front," or "the highest development of military strategy and political tactics," does not in the least alter the fact that it is precisely with respect to his biological and social organization that man gropes in the dark and is so hopelessly confused.

It is clear that this frame of mind did not evolve naturally; it is the result of the development of the machine civilization. It is easy to prove that, when the patriarchal organization of society began to replace the matriarchal organization, suppression and repression of genital sexuality in children and adolescents were the principal mechanisms used to adapt the human structure of the authoritarian order. The suppression of nature, of "the animal" in the child, was and has remained the principal tool in the production of mechanical subjects.[2] Society's socio-economic development has continued its mechanical course until today in an independent way. The basis of all ideologic and cultural formations developed and branched out hand in hand with the socio-economic development: "Away from genitality" and "away from the animal." Man's effort to disassociate

---

[2] This socio-economic process and its effects on the formation of human ideology and human structure are described in *Der Einbruch der Sexualmoral.*

himself from his biological origin became more and more pronounced and comprehensive in the course of these two processes, the social and the psychological. Sadistic brutality in business and war, mechanicalness in his nature, ambiguity in his facial expression, armoring against feelings, perverse and criminal tendencies, all of these became more and more pronounced and comprehensive.

It hasn't been too long since we began to take cognizance of the devastating effects of this devious biological development. One is easily tempted to look upon the state of affairs too optimistically. One could argue as follows: There can be no doubt that man went astray when he interpreted his own nature in terms of the machine civilization. Now that we recognize this error, it will be easy to correct it. Civilization has to be mechanical, but man's mechanistic attitude toward life can easily be converted into an attitude based on functional living processes. An astute minister of education could issue appropriate edicts for the purpose of reshaping education. The error would be corrected in one or two generations. That's the way some clever men spoke at the time of the Russian Revolution, 1917–23.

This argument would indeed be correct if the mechanical view of life were merely an "idea" or "attitude." However, the character analysis of the average man in all social situations brought a fact to light which we cannot afford to underestimate. It turned out that the mechanical view of life was not merely a "reflection" of the social processes in man's psychic life, as Marx had assumed, but much more than that:

Over the course of thousands of years of mechanical development, the mechanistic view of life has become more and more ingrained in man's biological system, continuously from generation to generation. In the process of this development, man's functioning was actually changed in a mechanical way. Man became plasmatically rigid in the process of killing his genital function. He armored himself against the natural and spontaneous in himself and lost contact with the function of biological self-regulation. Now he is filled with mortal fear of the living and the free.

341

This *biologic rigidity* is essentially manifested in a general stiffening of the organism and in a demonstrable reduction of plasmatic mobility: Intelligence is impaired; the natural social sense is blocked; psychosis is rampant. I gave a thorough exposition of the facts that support this assertion in *The Function of the Orgasm*. So-called civilized man actually did become angular and mechanical, and he lost his spontaneity, i.e., he developed into an automaton and "brain machine." Thus, he not only believes that he functions as a machine, but *he actually does function automatically, mechanistically, and mechanically*. He lives, loves, hates, and thinks more and more mechanically. With his biological stiffening and the loss of his native function of self-regulation, he acquired all the characterological attitudes, which culminated in the outbreak of the dictatorship plague: a hierarchical view of the state, a mechanical administration of society, fear of responsibility, an intense longing for a führer and craving for authority, insistence upon commands, mechanistic thinking in natural science, mechanical killing in war. It is no coincidence that the Platonic idea of the state was born in the Greek slave society. Nor is it a coincidence that it has continued to exist into the present day: serfdom was replaced by inner slavery.

The question of the fascist plague has led us deeply into man's biologic organization. It relates to a development that goes back thousands of years, and not, as those who view society in purely economic terms believed, to the imperialistic interests of the past two hundred years or even past twenty years. On no account, therefore, can the present war be confined to the imperialistic interests in the oil wells of Baku or the rubber plantations in the Pacific. The Treaty of Versailles plays the same role in World War II as the wheel of a machine in the transmission of the energy of coal to the steam piston. The purely economic view of life, as much as it may have been of service, is totally unsuited to cope with the convulsive processes of our life.

The biblical legend of the creation of man as an image of God, of his dominion over the animals, clearly reflects the repressive action man carried out against his animal nature. But he is reminded of his true nature every day by his body functions, procreation, birth and death, sexual urge, and dependency upon nature. His efforts to fulfill his "divine" or "national" "calling" become more and more strenuous; the deeply rooted hatred of all genuine natural sciences, i.e., sciences that are not concerned with the construction of machines, stems from this source. It took several thousand years before a Darwin succeeded in unmistakably proving man's animal descendancy. It took just as long until a Freud discovered the fact, banal as it is, that the child is altogether, and *above all*, sexual. And what a fuss the animal, man, made when he heard such things!

There is a direct connection between the "dominion" over animals and racial "dominion" over the "black man, the Jew, the Frenchman, etc." It is clear that one prefers to be a gentleman than an animal.

To disassociate himself from the animal kingdom, the human animal denied and finally ceased to perceive the sensations of his organs; in the process he became biologically rigid. It is still a dogma of mechanistic natural science that the autonomous functions are not experienced and that the autonomous nerves of life are rigid. This is the case, notwithstanding the fact that every three-year-old child knows very well that pleasure, fear, anger, yearning, etc., take place in the belly. This is the case, notwithstanding the fact that the experience of oneself is nothing but the total experience of one's organs. By losing the sensation of his organs, man lost not only the intelligence of the animal and the ability to react naturally, but he ruined his own chances of overcoming his life problems. He replaced the natural self-regulatory intelligence of the body plasma by a goblin in the brain, which he invested with both metaphysical and mechanical characteristics in a way that was metaphysical in every respect. Man's body sensations did *indeed* become rigid and mechanical.

In his education, science, and philosophy of life, man is constantly reproducing the mechanical organism. Under the slogan "Away from the animal" this biologic deformity celebrates the most amazing triumphs in the fight of the "superman against the lower-man" (is equal to abdominal man) and in scientific, mathematical, and mechanical killing. But more than mechanistic philosophies and machines are needed to kill. This is where sadism comes in, this secondary drive which is the offspring of suppressed nature and is the only important trait differentiating man's structure from that of the animal.

However, this tragic mechanical-mechanistic development, distorted as it is, did not eradicate its opposite. At the bottom of his nature, man still remains an animal creature. No matter how immobile his pelvis and back may be; no matter how rigid his neck and shoulders may be; or how tense his abdominal muscles may be; or how high he may hold his chest in pride and fear—at the innermost core of his sensations he feels that he is only a piece of living organized nature. But as he denies and suppresses every aspect of this nature, he cannot embrace it in a rational and living way. *Hence, he has to experience it in a mystical, other-worldly, and supernatural way,* whether in the form of religious ecstasy, cosmic unification with the world soul, sadistic thirst for blood, or "cosmic seething of the blood." It is known that such an impotent monster senses his strongest urges to kill in the spring. The Prussian military parades betray all the characteristics of a mystical and mechanical man.

Human mysticism, which thus represents the last traces of vitality, also became the fountainhead of mechanical sadism in Hitlerism. From the deepest sources of biologic functioning still remaining, the cry for "freedom" wins through again and again, notwithstanding all the rigidity and enslavement. There is not a single social movement that could advocate the "suppression of life" as part of its program and hope to win over masses of people. Every single one of the many different social movements that suppress the self-regulation of life energy, advocates "freedom" in one form or another: freedom from sin; redemption from the "earthly"; the freedom of lebensraum; the freedom of the nation; the freedom of the proletariat; the freedom of culture; etc., etc. The various cries for freedom are as old as the ossification of the human plasma.

The cry for freedom is a sign of suppression. It will never cease as long as man feels himself to be trapped. No matter how different the cries for freedom may be, at bottom they always express one and the same thing: *the intolerableness of the organism's rigidity and the mechanical institutions of life, which are sharply at variance with the natural sensations of life.* If there should ever be a society in which all the cries for freedom fade away, then man will have finally overcome his biological and social deformity and have achieved genuine freedom. Not until man acknowledges that he is fundamentally an animal, will he be able to create a genuine culture.

Man's "upward strivings" are nothing but the biologic development of vital powers. Such strivings are conceivable only within the framework of the laws of biologic development and *not in opposition to* them. The *will* to freedom and the *capacity* for freedom are nothing but the will and the capacity to recognize and promote the unfolding of man's biologic energy (with the aid of the machine). It is out of the question to talk about freedom if man's biologic development is choked and feared.

Under the influence of politicians, masses of people tend to ascribe the responsibility for wars to those who wield power at any given time. In World War I it was the munitions industrialists; in World War II it was the psychopathic generals who were said to be guilty. *This is passing the buck. The responsibility for wars falls solely upon the shoulders of these same masses of people, for they have all the necessary means to avert war in their own hands.* In part by their apathy, in part by their passivity, and in part actively, these same masses of people make possible the catastrophes under which they themselves suffer more than anyone else. *To stress this guilt on the part of masses of people, to hold them solely responsible, means to take them seriously.* On the other hand, to commiserate masses of people as victims, means to treat them as small, helpless children. The former is the attitude held by the genuine freedom-fighters; the latter the attitude held by the power-thirsty politicians.

THE ARSENAL OF HUMAN FREEDOM

Kings and emperors always inspect their troops. Money magnates keep a sharp eye on the sums of money that give them power. All fascist dictators measure the degree of irrationality in human reactions, for it is this irrationality that makes it possible for them to win and maintain their power over masses of people. The natural scientist measures the degree of knowledge and the methods of research. But thus far no freedom organization has taken stock of the *biologic arsenal* in which the weapons necessary to establish and maintain human freedom are to be found. Despite the exactness of our social machinery, there is still no natural scientific definition of the word *freedom*. No other word is so abused and so misunderstood as this one is. To define freedom is to define sexual health. *But no one wants to state it openly.* One often has the impression that the advocacy of personal and social freedom is associated with fear and guilt feelings. As if to be free were a forbidden sin, or at least not quite decent. Sex-economy comprehends this guilt feeling: Freedom without sexual self-regulation is a contradiction in itself. According to the prevailing human structure, however, to be sexual means to be "sinful" or guilty. There are only a few people who experience love without feelings of guilt. "Free love" became a defamatory word and lost the meaning given to it by the old freedom-fighters. In films, to be a criminal and to have a strong sexuality are represented as *the same thing*. It is not surprising, therefore, that the ascetic and the reactionary man are more highly esteemed than the amorous peoples of the South Seas; that a high social position is incompatible with natural behavior in sex; that, officially, "authority" is not supposed to have a "private life"; that a great researcher such as De La Mettrie could be defiled and persecuted; that any perverse moralist can insult a happy couple with impunity; that adolescents can be imprisoned for having sexual intercourse, etc.

In this chapter we set out to show the miscalculation that all freedom-fighters until now have made: *The social incapacity for freedom is sexual-physiologically anchored in the human organism.* It follows from this that the overcoming of the physiologic incapacity for freedom is one of the most important basic preconditions of every genuine fight for freedom. It cannot be the aim of this chapter to give an exposition of those elements of freedom that are generally known and advocated, i.e., freedom of expression, freedom from economic suppression and exploitation, freedom of assembly and coalition, freedom of scientific research, etc. For us it is essential to focus upon and elucidate the *most powerful obstacles* to all these efforts.

We understand why the general characterological incapacity for freedom on the part of masses of people has never been a subject of public debate. This fact is too dark, too depressing, and too unpopular to be discussed openly. It demands that the overwhelming majority subject themselves to a self-criticism, which is sure to prove embarrassing, and to undertake an enormous reorientation in their total approach to life. It demands that the responsibility for all social events be shifted from minorities and islands of society to the overwhelming majority, on whose work society is dependent. This working majority has never managed the affairs of society. The best that they were able to attain so far was the entrusting of the leadership of their lives to decent and not mean individuals. The "parliamentary" form of "government" could not stand up to the pressure of facts, for *other* social groups and majorities invested brutal sadists and imperialists with power over their fates. The danger is too great that a formal democratic social organization will deteriorate into a dictatorial organization when it is forced to defend itself against the authoritarian dictator of its life. Since the working masses of people themselves do not determine their life in a *factual* and *practical* way, the germ of oppression is already present in the course of the chance makeup of the government. This seems to be a generally known fact. It is heard more and more clearly from all sides that one can no longer count on a return of the old and that a fundamentally new world order has to be put together. This is absolutely correct, but concrete words are missing. *What is missing is the burdening of the working majority of the population, which until now has assumed only a passive social role, with the full responsibility for their future fate.* It is as if there were a widespread secret fear of shifting the responsibility from the shoulders of a democratic and well-meaning government to the shoulders of those who had until now been only electors, but not *responsible supporters* of society. This fear does not relate to evil-mindedness or a wicked orientation, but to the knowledge of the given biopsychic structure of masses of people. The Russian Revolution, which began in the direction of mass responsibility, fell to pieces and ended in a dictatorship precisely for this reason. Nonetheless, social revolution by means of transforming formal democracy to a complete, factual democracy is the most essential conclusion to be drawn from this war and everything that led to it. I want to repeat the inevitable conclusion to be drawn from the above facts:

1. Masses of people are incapable of freedom.

2. A general capacity for freedom can be acquired only in the daily struggle for the free formation of life.

3. Hence: *Masses of people who are incapable of freedom at present have to have the social power to become capable of being free and of establishing freedom.*

I should like to illustrate the present practical task with an example from plant life. For some time I have been observing the effect of weeds on the growth of fir seedlings. Those seedlings that are not surrounded by many weeds grow fully on all sides; hardly above the ground, the stem shoots forth far-reaching branches. The needles are full and sappy. The plant strives upward toward the sun free of any hindrances; it is "healthy"; its development is "free." But if the fir seed has chanced to fall on a spot where there are a lot of weeds, then it develops, hemmed in by weeds, a needleless, crooked stem. It does not develop full branches; the needles are shriveled, others don't develop at all. Many such seedlings are not capable of pushing their way up through the weeds. The influence of the weeds is directly manifested in the deformity of the plant. It has to fight a hard battle to get to the sun, and it is distorted in the process. If such a seedling is freed of its weeds, it grows better, develops more fully; but the early influence of the weeds cannot be eradicated. The growth of the fir is stunted, its stem will be crooked and its needles will not be full and sappy. Yet every *new* seed that falls on a patch of earth free of weeds develops freely and fully from the start.

I think that we can definitely compare the free development of a society to the fir seedling that is free of weeds; the dictatorship society to the stem hedged in by weeds; and that formal democracy which is at the mercy of pressure groups can be compared to the stem that, though it fights its way through, is biologically distorted in the process of its growth. At the present time there is no democratic society that can develop according to natural, free, self-regulatory laws, i.e., free of the deforming influence of dictatorial-authoritarian conditions within or outside of the society. The experience of fascism has put at our disposal numerous means of recognizing inchoative Hitlerism within or outside of its own borders. *Biopsychically viewed, Hitlerism is nothing other than the consummate form of mechanical mechanism plus mystical irrationalism in masses of people.* The crippling of individual and social life is nothing other than the accumulated secular influence of all authoritarian and irrational institutions on present-day man. Fascism did not create these conditions anew; it merely exploited and perfected the old conditions which were used to suppress freedom. The generation that bears the remnants of an age-old authoritarian order in its nature can only hope to be able to breathe more freely. Even after the weeds have been uprooted, i.e., after the fascist machine has been smashed, it will not be able to live and grow according to the natural laws of a fir tree.

In other words: *The biologic rigidity of the present generation can no longer be eliminated, but the living forces that are still operative in it can attain space to develop in a better way. However, new human beings are born every day, and in the course of thirty years the human race will have been biologically renewed; it will come into the world without any trace of fascist distortion.* It is a question of the conditions under which and in which this new generation will be born; will they be conditions safeguarding freedom or will they be authoritarian? From this, the task of social hygiene and social legislation is clear and emphatic:

Every effort must be made and all means employed to guard future generations against the influence of the biologic rigidity of the old generation.

German fascism was born of the biologic rigidity and deformity of the preceding German generation. With its mechanical discipline, its goose-stepping, and its "stomach in, chest out," Prussian militarism was an extreme expression of this rigidity. German fascism was able to rely on the biologic rigidity and deformity of masses of people in other countries. This accounts for its international success. In the course of a single generation it succeeded in uprooting the last vestiges of the biologic will to freedom in the German society and in remolding the new generation into rigid, robotlike, war-machine automatons in a little more than a decade. Hence, this much is clear: Social freedom and self-regulation are inconceivable with biologically rigid, mechanized human beings. *The principal weapon in the arsenal of freedom is each new generation's tremendous urge to be free. The possibility of social freedom rests essentially upon this weapon and not upon anything else.*

Let us assume that the formal democracies will be victorious in this war. Let us further assume that in the struggle for freedom they will overlook or refuse to admit the social importance of the biologic miscalculation, i.e., the general biologic rigidity of masses of people. In such a case, each new generation will reproduce this rigidity of necessity. They will produce new life-fearing, authoritarian views of life in this or that form. Though bitterly fought for, the freedoms achieved under such conditions will be full of loopholes and gaps and their functioning will be biologically hampered. Masses of people will never be capable of developing full responsibility for social existence. Thus, those who have *no* interest in the self-regulation of society, need only *prevent* each new generation from liberating itself from the pressure of the old generation's rigidity, using any one of the power means of money, position, or force.

The task consists of social, medical, and educational acts:

Socially, it is a matter of seeking out all the sources of man's biologic desolation and of enacting appropriate laws to safeguard free development. General formulations such as "freedom of the press, assembly, and expression," etc., are obvious, but they are not enough by a long shot. Under these laws the irrational man has the same rights as the free man. Since weeds always proliferate and grow more rapidly than a sturdy tree, the Hitlerite would have to win out in the long run. It will be a question of realizing that "Hitlerism" is not confined to those who bear the overt insignia of fascism, a question of seeking it out and fighting it in everyday life in a scientific and human way. Only in this process of weeding out fascism in everyday life will the appropriate laws against it be formulated as a matter of course.

Let one example suffice: A person who wants to drive a car has to pass a driver's test; this is a necessary requirement to guarantee the safety of others. A person who owns a bigger house than he can afford is forced to rent or buy a smaller house. A person who wants to open a shoe store must show proof of his ability to do so. But in this twentieth century of ours, there is no law to protect the newly born against the parents' inability to bring them up and the parents' neurotic influence. Scores of children can, indeed *should*, according to the fascist ideology, be put into the world; but no one asks whether they can be nourished properly and whether they can be educated in keeping with the highly extolled ideals. The sentimental slogan about the large family is typical of fascism, no matter who propagates it.[3]

With respect to medicine and education, the deplorable fact will have to be corrected that hundreds of thousands of physicians and teachers hold the weal and ill of every new generation in their

---

[3] Unfortunately, it appeared in the progressive Beveridge Plan in England, 1942.

hands, though they know nothing about the laws pertaining to the biosexual development of the small child. And this is still the case forty years after the discovery of childhood sexuality. Fascist mentality is hourly and daily inculcated in millions upon millions of children and adolescents owing to the ignorance of educators and physicians. Two demands shoot into the foreground at this point. First: Every physician, educator, and social worker etc., who is to deal with children and adolescents will have to prove that he himself or she herself is healthy from a sex-economic point of view and that he or she has acquired exact knowledge on human sexuality between the ages of one and about eighteen. In other words, *the education of the educators in sex-economy must be made mandatory*. The formation of sexual views must not be subject to the hazard, arbitrariness, and influence of neurotic compulsive morality. Second: *The child's and adolescent's natural love of life must be protected by clearly defined laws*. These demands may sound radical and revolutionary. But every one will admit that the fascism that grew out of the frustration of childhood and adolescent sexuality has had a far more radical and revolutionary effect, in the *negative* sense of the words, than the social protection of nature ever could have in a positive respect. Every modern democratic society is full of individual attempts to effect a change in this area. But these islands of understanding perish in the swath of the plague spread by the biologically rigid, moralistic educators and physicians who stand above the society as a whole.

There is not much sense in going into detail here. Each individual measure will result spontaneously, if only the *basic principle of sexual affirmation* and *the social protection of childhood and adolescent sexuality is adhered to*.

With respect to economy, only natural relationships of work, i.e., men's natural economic dependencies upon one another, are capable of creating the framework and basis for the biologic restructuralization of masses of people.

We call the sum total of all natural work relationships, work-democracy; it is the form of the natural organization of work. In terms of their nature, these work relationships are *functional* and not mechanical. They cannot be arbitrarily organized; they ensue spontaneously from the work process itself. The reciprocal dependency between a carpenter and a blacksmith, a natural scientist and a glass grinder, a painter and a paint manufacturer, an electrician and a metal worker, is determined by the interrelationships of the work *functions*. One cannot conceive of an arbitrary law that could change these natural work relationships. The man who works with a microscope cannot be made independent of the glass grinder. The nature of lenses is solely dictated by the laws of light and technology, just as the form of induction spools is dictated by the laws of electricity and the activities of man are dictated by the nature of his needs. The natural functions of the work process are divorced from every kind of human-mechanistic and authoritarian arbitrariness. They function *freely* and are *free* in the strict sense of the word. They alone are rational; hence they alone can determine social existence. Even the psychopathic generals are dependent upon them. Love, work, and knowledge embrace everything that is implied in the concept work-democracy.

Though it is true that the natural functions of work, love, and knowledge can be abused and stifled, they regulate themselves by virtue of their nature. This has always been the case from the very beginning of human work, and they will continue to regulate themselves as long as there is a social process. They constitute the *factual* basis (not the "demand") of work-democracy. The concept work-democracy is not a political program; it is not an intellectual anticipation of an "economic plan," nor is it a "New Order." Work-democracy is a *fact* that has eluded human perception until now. Work-democracy cannot be organized any more than freedom can be organized. The growth of a tree, an animal, or a man cannot be organized. *By virtue of its biologic function, the growth of an organism is free in the strictest sense of the word.* The same applies to the natural growth of a society. It is self-regulating and requires no legislation. To repeat, it can only be hindered or abused.

The problem lies in the fact that it is the function of all forms of authoritarian rulership to *hinder* the natural self-regulatory functions. Hence, the task of a *genuinely* free order must be to *eliminate* all hindrances to natural functions. Strict laws are needed to accomplish this. In this way, a democracy that has a serious and genuine intent is a direct manifestation of the natural self-regulation of love, work, and knowledge. And dictatorship, in other words man's irrationality, is a direct manifestation of the obstruction of this natural self-regulation.

It clearly follows from this that the fight against dictatorship and the irrational craving for authority on the part of masses of people can consist only in one fundamental deed:

Those forces in the individual and in the society that are natural and vital must be clearly separated from all the obstacles that operate against the spontaneous functioning of this natural vitality.

The former have to be promoted, the latter have to be eliminated.

The human regulation of social existence can never relate to the natural functions of work. Civilization in the positive sense of the word can have no other meaning than to create the best conditions for the *unfolding* of the natural functions of love, work, and knowledge. Though freedom is not capable of being organized, since any organization is contrary to freedom, the *conditions* that are to clear the way to the free unfolding of the life forces can, indeed must, be organized.

We do not tell those who work with us how or what they should think. We do not "organize" their thinking. But we demand that every worker in our field free himself or herself from the false ways of thinking and acting that he or she acquired through his or her upbringing. In this way, his or her ability to react spontaneously and in a rational way is set free.

It is ridiculous to conceive of freedom to mean that a lie has the same right as a truth before a court of law. A genuine work-democracy will not accord mystical irrationality the same right as truth; nor will it allow the suppression of children the same scope as it allows their freedom. It is ridiculous to argue with a murderer about his right to murder. But this ridiculous mistake is made again and again in dealing with fascists. Fascism is not comprehended as state-organized irrationality and meanness; it is regarded as a "state form" having equal rights. The reason for this is that everyone bears fascism *in himself*. Naturally, even fascism is right "sometimes." The same is true of the mental patient. The trouble is that he doesn't know when he is right.

Viewed in this way, freedom becomes a simple, easily comprehensible and easily manageable fact. Freedom does not have to be achieved—it is spontaneously present in every life function. *It is the elimination of all obstacles to freedom that has to be achieved.*

Viewed in this way, the arsenal of human freedom is enormous and has an abundance of means at its disposal, both biological and mechanical. Nothing extraordinary has to be fought for. The living must merely be set free. When reality is comprehended, the age-old dream can become reality. In this arsenal of freedom, we find:

A *living, spontaneous knowledge* of the natural laws of life, a knowledge that men and women of all ages, every social situation, and every color of skin have. What has to be eliminated is the thwarting and distortion of this knowledge by hard, rigid mechanical-mystical views and institutions, which are hostile to life.

The natural work relationships of men and women and their natural pleasure in work are full of energy and promise. What has to be eliminated is the thwarting of natural work-democracy by arbitrary, authoritarian restrictions and regulations, which are hostile to life.

Natural sociability and morality are present in men and women. What has to be eliminated is the disgusting moralization which thwarts natural morality and then points to the criminal impulses, which it itself has brought into being.

As no other war, the present war is eliminating many obstacles to natural self-regulation, the elimination of which appeared inconceivable in times of peace, e.g., the authoritarian relegation of the woman to the kitchen, wild business dealings, rank exploitation, artificial national boundaries, etc. We do not belong to those who contend that wars are necessary for the development of human culture. It is like this: The mechanical, mystical, and authoritarian organization of human society and of the human structure constantly precipitates the mechanical destruction of human lives in war. That which is living and free in man and in society rebels against this. Since the biological crippling of man and society surpasses all bounds in war, that which is truly alive is *forced* to make efforts it would not have been capable of making under less vicious circumstances, for it had not previously comprehended itself.

At this point a justified objection will be raised, namely:

We admit that for the past thousands of years man has allowed his body to become more and more like a machine and his thinking to become more and more irrational, especially since he fell under the influence of machine production. But we fail to see how it is possible to undo the mechanical degeneration of the organism and to liberate man's self-regulatory forces, if masses of people continue to live under the pressure and influence of the machine. No reasonable person will demand or expect us to abolish the machine civilization. The biologically destructive influences of machine technology are not offset by any significant counterbalance. Facts more tangible than scientific expositions are needed to rid man of his biologic rigidity. It is more likely that this war, by making human activity more rigid and more thoughtless, will increase, not eliminate, biologic rigidity.

This objection is entirely correct. With man's present technical means, there is indeed no prospect of undoing the devious biologic development of the race of animals called man. In fact it took me a long time to decide to publish the insight I had obtained into the biologic reproduction of the machine civilization. I told myself that it could serve no purpose to proclaim truths that could have no practical effect.

The way out of this painful dilemma offered itself spontaneously when I asked myself how I had arrived at the functional formulations in psychiatry, sociology, and biology, formulations that so successfully succeeded in clarifying the mechanization and the mysticism in these three fields and were capable of replacing this mechanization and mysticism. I do not regard myself as some sort of exceptional superman. I am not much different from the average man. How, then, did I manage to hit upon the solution that had eluded others. Gradually it became clear that my professional involvement with the problem of biologic energy over several decades had forced me to free myself from mechanistic and mystical views and methods. If I had not freed myself from these views and methods, I would not have been able to perform my work on the living organism. In short, *my work forced me to learn to think functionally*. If I had cultivated solely the mechanical-mystical structure that my education had inculcated in me, I would not have discovered a single fact of orgone biophysics. However, the hidden path to the discovery of the orgone was discerned the moment I set foot in the prohibited domain of orgastic plasma contraction. In retrospect, I saw that I had got past any number of critical points in this development which could have diverted me from the living, functional way of looking at things to the mechanical-mystical view of the world. I have no idea how I managed to escape the pitfalls. It is certain that the functional view of life, which contains so many essential answers to the present chaos, was nourished by my work with biologic energy, i.e., orgone energy.

The *ignorance* of the laws of biological functioning was responsible for mechanization and the substitution of mysticism for living reality. However, cosmic orgone, i.e., the specific biologic energy in the universe, does not function mechanistically, and it is not mystical. This orgone energy follows its own *specific functional* laws, which cannot be comprehended materially, mechanistically, or rigidly, nor in concepts of positive and negative electric fluids. It obeys *functional* laws, such as attraction, disassociation, expansion, contraction, radiation, pulsation, etc. I doubt that orgone energy is suited for any kind of killing, and hence of any use to the mechanistic technique of murder. This war or the next war will enormously increase the need of life-securing functions. The orgonotic radiation is no mean contribution on the part of sex-economy to the further development of the human race. Sooner or later, larger and larger groups and circles will familiarize themselves with the functions of orgone. In the process of working with the cosmic life energy, men and women will be *forced* to learn to think in functional, living terms in order to be able to master cosmic orgone. In the same way, they learned to think in psychological terms when the doors to the knowledge of childhood sexuality were opened and to think in economic terms when the economic laws were discovered. In the process of comprehending and mastering the mechanistic laws of inanimate nature, man himself was forced to become mechanically rigid. In the same way, as each new generation masters the orgonotic functions of life to an ever-increasing degree, it will comprehend *the living* and learn to love, protect, and develop it. This analogous conclusion is definitely justified.

Therefore, I ask you not to confuse this line of reasoning with the proclamation of messianism. As I have stressed again and again in many of my writings, I regard myself as a "worm in the universe" and as the mere tool of a certain scientific logic. That great delusive characteristic that helps the plague-ridden general to accomplish his criminal deeds is definitely missing in my case. I lack the conviction of being a superman, and it follows from this that I also lack the conviction that the masses are racially inferior. The far-reaching conclusion I drew from the discovery of orgone for the social problem of man's biological desolation is a modest but *true* conclusion, comparable perhaps to the conclusion that the earth's force of gravity can be overcome by filling a balloon with a gas specifically lighter than air. I do not, as many of my friends expect, have a remedy which would enable us to effect immediate political changes. Facts such as "biologic and natural self-regulation," "natural work-democracy," "cosmic orgone," "genital character," etc., are weapons that sex-economy has put at the disposal of the human race for the purpose of eradicating enslaving conditions, such as "biologic rigidity," "character and muscular armoring," "pleasure anxiety," "orgastic impotence," "formal authority," "enslavement to authority," "social irresponsibility," "incapacity for freedom," etc. It is of the very nature of this work that it was done with pleasure, pleasure in research and discovery, pleasure in the perception of nature's spontaneous decency and wisdom. It was not done in the expectation of medals, riches, academic recognition, and popularity, and certainly not from any sadistic pleasure in torture, suppression, the procreation of lies and deception, the conduct of war, and the killing of life. That's all!

XIII

On Natural Work-Democracy

INVESTIGATION OF THE NATURAL SOCIAL FORCES FOR THE
PURPOSE OF OVERCOMING THE EMOTIONAL PLAGUE

The material I want to present in this chapter is general and
spontaneous human knowledge, a knowledge that is not socially
organized and, therefore, has not yet been able to evolve and have a
practical effect on the general public.

Social events have once again been caught up in the flux of
enormous convulsions. The world over, people are asking: Where
do we go from here? What's to be done now? Which party, which
cabinet, what kind of political group, will assume the responsibility
for the future fate of European society? I have no answer to these
questions, which are on everyone's lips. Nor is it the intent of this
chapter to offer political suggestions. Its sole intent is to draw attention to a concrete, practical, and rational fact, which will not be
referred to in the many political debates on how the world is to be
organized after the war. It is the fact that has been designated as
natural work-democracy. Now I want to describe what natural work-
democracy is; please note, what it *is* and *not* what it should be.

In 1937, i.e., two years before the outbreak of World War II, as
the storm clouds were gathering over Europe, a pamphlet entitled
"The natural organization of work in work-democracy," appeared in
Scandinavia. It did not bear the name of its author. It was merely
stated that it had been written by a laboratory worker with the

consent of other men and women engaged in practical work in this field. It appeared in German, not in a printed form, but merely mimeographed. Later it was translated into English. It was not widely circulated, for it was not backed up by any political propaganda apparatus and had no political pretensions. But it was acclaimed wherever it was read. It was circulated in small circles in Paris, Holland, Scandinavia, Switzerland, and Palestine. Several dozen copies were also smuggled across the German border. It was reviewed only once, in a German Socialist weekly in Paris; otherwise, it did not cause the slightest stir. Far from playing a revolutionary role in the political events of that time, it was soon lost in the turmoil. Nor, for that matter, was it a political pamphlet; quite the contrary, it was a pamphlet *against* politics, written by a working man. Yet, somehow two things stuck in one's mind, and they were brought up again and again—*en passant*, one might almost say—in discussions among men and women of various political orientations and occupations. One thing was the word "work-democracy." The other was two sentences. They sounded unworldly, alienated from politics, utopian, and, at bottom, hopeless: *"Enough, let's have done with politics once and for all! Let's get down to the practical tasks of real life!"*

Strangely enough, the political newspaper, which accorded the pamphlet a long article, also centered its critique around the word "work-democracy" and around those sentences that read like a slogan. The article took a sympathetic attitude toward work-democracy, but flatly rejected the slogan. This contradiction showed those who were familiar with the pamphlet that it had not been really understood. Apparently, the pamphlet had been written by a former socialist. It clearly detached itself from all Socialist party methods and concerns. In contradiction to its basic slogan, however, it was full of political formulations and political discussions.

In spite of its deficiencies and its lack of clarity, it was enthusiastically read by a German socialist and smuggled into Germany. In the ensuing six years of war, nothing more was to be heard about it. In 1941, however, a continuation of this first pamphlet appeared under the title, "Additional problems of work-democracy." Like its predecessor, it too was smuggled into several European countries, and was even "intercepted" by the American secret police, the FBI.

The word *work-democracy* gained a permanent footing in the circles of the entirely informal sex-economists and vegetotherapists. The word began a life of its own. It was used more and more frequently; one spoke of work-democratic institutions, "work-family," etc., and one began to think about these things in a serious way. In the middle of the chaos of war, a letter arrived from an occupied European country; in this letter, a sex-economist wrote that the pamphlet had been translated and was ready for immediate circulation as soon as circumstances allowed.

In the course of the last four years of the war, I delved into the conceptual content of *work-democracy*. I made an effort to comprehend and elaborate on the content of the word. In this effort I relied upon discussions which I had had in Norway with friends of various occupations. The more I immersed myself in this concept, the more clearly I saw its outlines, the more completely and forcefully I perceived its substance, and finally I had a picture that coincided perfectly with a large number of neglected but decisive sociological facts.

As well as I can, I want to describe what this picture purports. I have no intention of engaging in any kind of propaganda for it. Nor do I have the intention of engaging in time-consuming debates about it.

What follows is what I have come to understand by natural work-democracy.

WORK IN CONTRAST TO POLITICS

A medical student who wants to be admitted to the medical profession must offer satisfactory proof of his practical and theoretical knowledge of medicine. On the other hand, a politician who takes it upon himself to determine the fate, not of hundreds, as the medical student, but of millions of working men and women, is not required in our society to prove his qualifications and knowledge.

It is this circumstance that seems to be one of the essential causes of the social tragedy that has pockmarked the society of human animals for thousands of years with individual acute outbreaks. Let us pursue this briefly described contradiction as well and as far as we can.

The man who performs practical work in any field whatever, whether he comes from a rich or poor family, has to go through a definite schooling. He is not elected by "the people." Experienced workers whose skills have been tested over a long period must determine in a more or less thorough way whether the apprentice in their field is qualified to perform his or her job professionally. This is the demand, even if it often runs ahead of the facts. It gives the direction in any event. In America, this demand has been carried to such an extreme that a salesgirl in a department store has to have a university education. As exaggerated and as socially unjust as this demand may be, it shows clearly just how much social pressure is exerted on the simplest work. Every shoemaker, cabinet-maker, turner, mechanic, electrician, stone mason, construction worker, etc., has to fulfill strict requirements.

A politician, on the other hand, is free of any such demands. One need merely possess a good dose of cunning, neurotic ambition and will to power, coupled with brutality, in order to take over the highest positions of human society when suitable chaotic social conditions arise. In the past 25 years we have witnessed how a mediocre journalist was capable of brutalizing the fifty million strong Italian nation and finally reducing it to a state of misery. For twenty-two years there was a great fuss about nothing, coupled with much blood and thunder, until one day the hubbub faded out without a flourish. And one was overcome by the feeling: *And all to no avail!* What remained of this great tumult, which had made the world hold its breath and had torn many nations out of their accustomed life? *Nothing*—not a single, permanent thought; not a single useful institution; not even a fond memory. Facts such as this show more clearly than anything else the social irrationalism that periodically brings our life to the brink of the abyss.

A young house painter who fails miserably in his choice of profession is capable, also for a period of twenty years, of having himself talked about the world over, without having accomplished a single, useful, objective, practical piece of work. In this case, also, it is a tremendous noise that one day quietly fades away into an "all to no avail." The world of work continues on its calm, quiet, vitally necessary course. Of the great tumult, nothing remains but a chapter in falsely oriented history books, which are only a burden to our children.

If one takes the trouble to ferret them out, one will find unprecedented consequences for practical social life in this clear-cut antipathy between work and politics, this antipathy that is intelligible to everyone and that every working man and woman has long since been aware of. First and foremost, these consequences relate to the system of political parties that determines the ideologic and structural formation of the human animal everywhere on this earth. It is not our purpose here to enter into the question of how the present system of political parties developed from the first patriarchal-hierarchal European and Asian systems of government. What is important here is solely the effect of the system of political parties on the development of society. The reader will have already divined that natural work-democracy is a social system that already exists. It does not have to be established, and it bears the same relationship to the system of political parties as water bears to fire.

The contradiction between work and politics leads us on as follows: The elucidation and elimination of chaotic conditions, whether in a social, animal, or dead organism, require lengthy scientific work. Without going into details, let us briefly designate as *scientific* that man who performs some kind of *vitally necessary* work that requires the comprehension of facts. In this sense of the word a lathe operator in a factory is scientific, for his product is based on the fruits of his own work and research as well as the work and research of others. Now let us contrast this scientific man with the mystic, including the political ideologist.

Every scientific person, whether he is an educator, lathe operator, technician, physician, or something else, has to fulfill and safe-guard the social work process. Socially, he has a very responsible position: He has to prove each one of his assertions in a practical way. He has to work industriously, to think, to seek out new ways of improving his work, to recognize errors. As a researcher he has to examine and refute false theories. Whenever he succeeds in accomplishing something fundamentally new, he has to contend with human viciousness and fight his way through. He has no need of power, for no motors can be constructed with political power, no sera can be produced with it, no children can be brought up, etc. The working, scientific man lives and operates without weapons.

Compared with the working man and woman, the mystic and political ideologist have an easy social position. No one demands proof for their assertions. They can promise to bring down God from Heaven, to raise the Devil from Hell, and to establish paradise on earth from their ministerial buildings, and in all this they know very well that they will not be called to account for fraud. Their wild assertions are protected by the inviolable democratic right of free speech. If we think about it very carefully, we find that there must be something wrong with the concept of "free speech," when it is possible for a foiled painter to use this right to conquer in a *completely legal* way and in the course of a few years a position in the world that has never in human history fallen to the share of the great pioneers of science, art, education, and technology. It clearly follows from this that our thinking in social matters is catastrophically wrong in a certain area and requires radical correction. On the basis of careful sex-economic clinical investigations, we know that it is the authoritarian upbringing of little children, the teaching them to be fearful and submissive, that secures for the political power monger the slavery and the gullibility of millions of adult industrious men and women.

Let us pursue the contradiction between work and politics in another direction.

The following motto always appears on the title page of the Orgone Institute's official publication: *"Love, work and knowledge are the source of human existence. They should also govern it!"* Without the function of natural *love* between husband and wife, mother and child, coworkers, etc., without *work* and without *knowledge*, human society would fall to pieces overnight. It is not incumbent upon me as a physician to make allowances for some political ideology or another or for some current diplomatic necessity, no matter how important it may appear. It is my task solely to elucidate important but unknown facts. And it is a fact, however embarrassing it may be, that none of the three basic functions of social life is affected by universal suffrage and the secret ballot, or ever had an effect in the history of parliamentary democracy. On the other hand, political ideologies, which have nothing to do with the functions of natural love, work, or knowledge, enjoy unhampered and unlimited access to every kind of social power on the basis of universal suffrage and the party system. Let me hasten to make it clear that I am and have always been *for* universal suffrage. This does not alter the firmly established fact that the social institution of universal suffrage of parliamentary democracy in no way coincides with the three basic functions of social existence. It is left to chance whether the basic social functions are safeguarded or damaged by parliamentary vote. There is no stipulation in the legislation of parliamentary democracy that accords love, work, and knowledge any kind of prerogative in the regulation of the fate of society. This dichotomy between democratic suffrage and basic social functions has catastrophic repercussions on the basis of social processes.

I want only to mention the many institutions and laws that explicitly hamper these functions. I don't think that any scientific or political group has ever clearly and sharply pointed out this basic contradiction in a way that would be intelligible to everyone. And yet, it constitutes the core of the bio-social tragedy of the human animal. The system of political parties does not at all fulfill the

---

* This motto has appeared in the various publications in the following translation: "Love, work and knowledge are the well-springs of our life. They should also govern it."

conditions, tasks, and aims of human society. This is clearly and plainly shown by the fact, one of many, that a shoemaker cannot simply decide to be a tailor, a physician to be a mining engineer, and a teacher to be a cabinet-maker. On the other hand, a Republican in America can become a Democrat from one day to the next without undergoing any objective change in his thinking; and in Germany before Hitler, a Communist could simply become a Fascist, a Fascist a Communist, a Liberal a Communist or Social Democrat, and a Social Democrat a German National or Christian Socialist. Such changes were capable of strengthening or weakening the ideology of the party program of any of the respective parties; in short, they were capable of deciding the fate of a whole nation in the most unconscionable way.

This clearly shows politics' irrational nature and its antithesis to work. I do not want to go into the question whether the political parties ever had an objective and rational basis in the social body. It has no relevance here. The political parties of *today* have nothing concrete to say. The practical and positive events of a society have nothing to do with party boundaries or party ideologies. Something like Roosevelt's New Deal is a proof of this. So-called party coalitions are makeshifts in default of an objective orientation, a bridging of difficulties without really solving anything. Firmly established realities cannot be mastered with opinions, which are changed as one changes one's shirt.

These initial steps in the clarification of the concept of work-democracy have already yielded a number of important insights into the social chaos. This obligates us to follow up our train of thought on natural work-democracy. It would be an inexcusable omission not to do so. For no one can foresee where and when human thinking will disclose the answer to the chaos produced by politics. Thus, we shall follow the path we have taken, as one might look for a suitable settlement site in a primeval forest.

Even this attempt to orient oneself in social chaos must be regarded as a piece of practical and rational work. Since natural work-democracy is based on work and not on politics, it is possible that this "work on the social organism" might lead to a practical and applicable result. It would be the first time that *work* got control of social problems. And this work would be work-*democratic*, insofar as it might induce other sociologists, economists, psychologists, to work on the social organism. Since this work attacks politics as a principle and as a system, there can be no doubt that it will be countered with political ideologies. It will be interesting and important to see how work-democratic sociology will stand up in practice. Work-democracy, as far as I understand it, counters political ideologies with the point of view of *social function* and *social development*, in short, with facts and possibilities. It does not counter them with another political view. It follows an approach similar to the one followed in the field of morality: Sex-economy deals with the damages caused by compulsive morality, not, as is politically customary, with another kind of morality, but with concrete knowledge and practical data on the natural function of sexuality. In other words, work-democratic socio-economy will have to prove itself in practical life, just as the assertion that steam contains energy is proven by the locomotion of engines. Thus, we have no reason whatever to engage in ideological or political arguments concerning the existence or nonexistence of work-democracy, its practical applicability or nonapplicability, etc.

The working men and women who think and act in a work-democratic way do not come out *against* the politician. It is not his fault or his intention that the practical result of his work exposes the illusionary and irrational character of politics. Those who are engaged in practical work, regardless what field they are in, are intensely concerned with practical tasks in the improvement of life. Those who are engaged in practical work are not *against* one thing or another. It is only the politician who, having no practical tasks, is always *against* and never *for* something. Politics in general is characterized by this "being against" one thing or another. That which is productive in a practical way is not accomplished by politicians, but by working men and women, whether it is in accord with the politicians' ideologies or not. Years of experience have clearly demonstrated that the men and women who perform practical work always come into conflict with the politician. Thus, those who work *for* living functioning are and operate against politics, whether they want to or not. The educator is *for* the objective upbringing of small children; the farmer is *for* the machines necessary in agriculture; the researcher is *for* proofs for scientific findings. One can easily satisfy oneself that wherever a working man or woman is *against* this or that achievement, he or she is not speaking up as a worker, but under the pressure of political or other irrational influences.

It sounds improbable and exaggerated to say that a positive accomplishment of work is never against, but always for something. The reason for this is that our work life is interfused with irrationally motivated expressions of opinion, which are not differentiated from objective evaluations. For instance, the farmer is against the worker and the worker is against the engineer. This or that physician is against this or that drug. It will be said that democratic free speech means that one is "for" *and* "against." It is my contention, on the other hand, that it was precisely this formalistic and nonobjective comprehension of the concept of free speech that was chiefly responsible for the failure of the European democracies. Let us take an example: A physician is *against* the use of a certain drug. There can be one of two reasons for this:

Either the drug is really harmful and the physician is conscientious. In this case, the manufacturer of the drug did *poor* work. His work was not crowned with success and, evidently, he was not motivated by strong objective interests to produce an effective and harmless drug. The manufacturer did not have the function of the drug in mind, but was motivated, let us say, by pecuniary interests, i.e., was irrationally motivated. The motive did not suit the purpose. In this case the physician acted in a *rational* way. He spoke up in the interest of human health, that is to say, he was automatically against a bad drug because he is *for* health. He acted rationally, for the goal of work and the motive of the expression of opinion are in accord with one another.

369

Or the drug is a good one and the physician is unscrupulous. If this physician is *against* a good drug, his action is not motivated by an interest in human health. Perhaps he has been paid by a rival firm to advertise a different drug. He does not fulfill his work function as a physician; the motive for the expression of his opinion has no more to do with its content than it has to do with any work function. The physician speaks out against the drug because secretly he is for *profit* and not for health. But profiteering is not the purpose of a physician's work. Hence, he speaks out strongly *"against"* something and not "for" it.

We can apply this example to any other field of work and any kind of expression of opinion. We can easily satisfy ourselves that it is an inherent part of the rational work process always to be *for* something. The "being against" something ensues not from the work process itself, but from the fact that there are irrational functions of life. It follows from this that: *In terms of its nature, every rational work process is spontaneously against irrational functions of life.*

The attentive reader who is not unfamiliar with the ways of the world will readily agree that this clarification of the concept of free speech invests the democratic movement with a new and better point of view. The principle: *What is harmful to the interests of life is poor work, hence not work at all* imbues the concept of work-democracy with a rational meaning, a meaning that is lacking in the concept of formal or parliamentary democracy. In formal democracy the farmer is against the worker and the worker is against the engineer because political and not objective interests predominate in the social organization. If responsibility is shifted from the politician, not to the working men and women, but to *work*, then cooperation between farmer and worker automatically takes the place of political opposition.

We shall have to pursue this idea further, for it is of decisive importance. To begin with, we want to dwell upon the question of so-called democratic criticism, which also rests upon the democratic right of free speech.

NOTES ON OBJECTIVE CRITICISM AND IRRATIONAL CAVILING

The work-democratic way of life insists upon the right of every working man and woman to free discussion and criticism. This demand is justified, indispensable, and should be inviolable. If it is not fulfilled, the source of human productivity is easily dried up. Owing to the effects of the general emotional plague, however, "discussion" and "criticism" become more or less grave jeopardies to serious work. We want to illustrate this with an example:

Let us imagine an engineer who is having a difficult time repairing a defective motor. It is a complicated piece of work; the engineer must exercise every bit of his intelligence and energy to master the difficulty. He sacrifices his leisure hours of pleasure and works until late in the night. He grants himself no rest until he has finished his job. After awhile an unconcerned man comes along, looks on for a bit, then picks up a stone and smashes the conducting wires. That morning his wife had nagged him at the breakfast table.

Another completely unconcerned man comes along; he derides the engineer. He tells him that he, the engineer, knows nothing about motors, otherwise he would have had it repaired long ago. And just look at how filthy he is—his body is literally covered with sweat and grease. And that isn't all. He is an immoral man also, for otherwise he would not leave his family at home alone. Having insulted the engineer to his heart's content, he moves on. That morning he had received a letter from his firm informing him that he is being dismissed from his job as an electrical engineer. He is not a very good worker in his field.

A third totally unconcerned man comes along, spits in the engineer's face and moves on. His mother-in-law, who has a special talent for torturing people, had just given him a hard time.

The intent of these examples is to illustrate the "criticism" of unconcerned passers-by, who, like highwaymen, wantonly disturb honest work, a piece of work about which they know nothing, which they do not understand and which does not concern them.

These examples are typical of a good portion of what is known as "free discussion" and the "right of criticism" in wide sectors of society. The attacks of the hereditary school of psychiatrists and cancer theoreticians on the, at that time, still-embryonic bion research was of this nature. They were not interested in helping and improving, but merely in wantonly disrupting a difficult job. They of course did not betray their motives. Such "criticism" is harmful and socially dangerous. It is prompted by motives that have nothing to do with the matter being criticized, and it has nothing to do with objective interests.

Genuine discussion and *genuine* criticism are different. Again we want to illustrate this with an example:

Another engineer passes by the garage where the first engineer is working on the motor. With his wealth of experience in this field, he immediately sees that the first engineer has his hands full. He takes off his jacket, rolls up his sleeves, and attempts, first of all, to comprehend any mistakes in his approach. He points out an important place the first engineer had overlooked; they both consider the error that may have been made in the work. He gives the first engineer a hand, discusses and criticizes the work, and helps *to do it better*. He is not motivated by the nagging of his mother-in-law or his failure in his own profession, but by an objective interest in the success of the work.

The two kinds of criticism described above are often difficult to distinguish from one another. Irrational caviling is often very cunningly disguised behind a sham objectiveness. These two kinds of criticism, which are so different from one another, are usually included under the *one* concept "scientific criticism."

In the strict objective and scientific sense of the word, only so-called immanent criticism is admissible, that is to say, the person exercising criticism must first fulfill a number of demands before assuming the right to criticize:

1. He himself must have a complete grasp of the field of work that he criticizes.

2. He must know this field at least as well as, if not better than, the one whom he criticizes.

3. He must have an interest in seeing the work succeed—not in seeing it fail. If he is merely intent upon disrupting the work, if he is not motivated by objective interests, then he is a neurotic grumbler, but not a critic.

4. He has to exercise his criticism *from the point of view of the field of work under criticism.* He cannot criticize from an alien point of view, i.e., from a point of view that has nothing to do with the field of work. Depth psychology cannot be criticized from the point of view of surface psychology, but surface psychology can be criticized from the point of view of depth psychology. The reason for this is simple. Depth psychology is forced to include surface psychology in its investigations. Hence, it is conversant with it. Surface psychology, on the other hand, is precisely that, *surface* psychology; it does not look for biologic motives behind psychic phenomena.

We cannot criticize an electric machine from the point of view of a machine that has the function of heating a room. The thermal theory plays a part in the electric machine only insofar as it enables the electrical engineer to prevent the overheating of the electric motor. And in this respect, the helpful suggestions of a thermal theorist are definitely welcomed by the electrical engineer. But it would be ridiculous to blame the electromachine for not being able to heat a room.

It follows from this that sex-economy, which wants to liberate the *natural* sexuality of children, adolescents, and adults from neuroses, perversions and criminality, cannot be criticized from the point of view of anti-sexual moralism, for the moralist wants to suppress and not to liberate the natural sexuality of children and adolescents. A musician cannot criticize a miner, and a physician cannot criticize a geologist. Our feelings about a particular kind of work may be pleasant or unpleasant, but that does not affect the nature or usefulness of that work.

The sole purpose of these observations on criticism and caviling has been to alleviate the position of young sex-economists and orgone biophysicists toward critics.

WORK IS INHERENTLY RATIONAL

The analysis of the concept of work-democracy has, as we see, led us into a sphere of human life that, though it has been ascribed enormous importance for thousands of years, has been looked upon as overwhelming and beyond mastery. It is the complicated and vast sphere of so-called "human nature." That which philosophers, poets, superficial politicians, but also great psychologists, designate and bemoan with the sentence "That's the way human nature is" completely coincides with sex-economy's clinical concept, *"emotional plague."* We can define it as the *sum total of all irrational functions of life in the human animal.* If "human nature," which is conceived of as immutable, is identical with the emotional plague, and if, in turn, the emotional plague is identical with the sum total of all irrational functions of life in the human animal; if, moreover, the functions of work, in themselves and independent of man, are rational, then we are confronted with two enormous fields of human activity, which are mortally opposed to one another: vitally necessary work as the rational function of life on the one hand and the emotional plague as the irrational function of life on the other hand. It is not difficult to divine that work-democracy views as being a part of the emotional plague all politics that is not based upon knowledge, work, and love and that, therefore, is irrational. This is work-democracy's answer to the timeless and age-old question of how we could finally come to grips with our "notorious" human nature in a simple way: Education, hygiene, and medicine, which have been grappling with the problem of human nature since time began without achieving satisfactory results, find in the rational function of vitally necessary work a powerful ally in the fight against the emotional plague.

To follow work-democracy's train of thought to the end, we

must first of all wholly free ourselves from conventional political and ideological thinking. Only in this way is it possible to compare the fundamentally different train of thought that springs from the world of love, work, and knowledge to the train of thought that springs from the world of pomp and circumstance, of diplomatic and political conferences.

The politician thinks in terms of "state" and "nation"; the working man *lives* "sociably" and "socially." The politician thinks in terms of "discipline" and "law and order"; the average working man experiences "pleasure of work" and "order of work," "regulation" and "cooperation of work." The politician thinks in terms of "morals" and "duty"; the working man experiences or would like to experience "spontaneous decency" and a "natural feeling for life." The politician speaks of the "ideal of the family"; the working man enjoys or would like to enjoy the "love of husband, wife, and children." The politician speaks of the "interests of the economy and the state"; the simple working man wants "gratification of needs and an untrammeled food supply." The politician speaks of the "free initiative of the individual" and thinks of "profit"; the simple working man wants the freedom to try things on his own, the freedom to become what he is or could be.

In an irrational way, the politician holds sway over precisely those spheres of life that the working man copes or could cope with in a rational way, if he were not severely hampered by political irrationalism. Though the irrational and rational labels relate to the same spheres of life, they are diametrically opposed to one another; they are not words that could be substituted for one another. In actual practice they are mutually exclusive. This is borne out by the fact that, throughout the history of human society, the authoritarian discipline of the state has always thwarted natural sociability and the pleasure of work; the state has thwarted society; the compulsive sacredness of the family has thwarted the love of husband, wife, and children; compulsive morality has thwarted the natural decency that springs from the joy of life; and the politician has continually thwarted working men and women.

Fundamentally, our society is ruled by concepts—by political-irrational concepts, let it be noted—that exploit human labor to compass irrational goals by force. Effective institutions are needed to secure freedom of action and development for the life activity of masses of people. The social basis for these institutions cannot be any old arbitrary, interchangeable political orientation or ideology; it can be only the social function of vitally necessary work as it results naturally from the interlacing of the various vitally necessary fields of work in the sphere of work as a whole.

Let us pursue work-democracy's train of thought a step further into the thicket of entangled rational and irrational functions of life. In this pursuit we want to stick strictly to the logical sequence of thoughts and to exclude our personal interests as much as possible. To reach an applicable conclusion, we have to put ourselves, even in these considerations of the concept of work-democracy, in its position, i.e., we have to act as if we *wanted to burden natural work-democracy with the responsibility for social existence*. In short, we have to test its tenability from all angles in a strictly *objective* way. If we should allow our personal interests in some unnecessary activity or another to influence us, we would automatically exclude ourselves from the framework of this discussion.

If there were nothing but the emotional plague in its various forms, the human species would have met its doom long ago. Neither political ideology nor mystical ritual, the military power apparatus nor diplomatic discussions, would be able, by themselves, to provide the population of any country with food, even for just an hour, to keep the traffic system running smoothly, provide living quarters, cure diseases, safeguard the rearing of children, ferret out nature's secrets, etc. According to the work-democratic concept, political ideologies, mystic rituals, and diplomatic maneuvers are necessary only within the framework of social irrationalism. They are not necessary in the factual sphere of life, which is ruled by love, work, and knowledge. These vitally necessary functions obey their own self-generated laws; they are not accessible to any irrational ideology. Love, work, and knowledge are not "ideas," "cultural values," "political programs," "mental attitudes," or "confessions of creed." They are *concrete realities*, without which human society could not exist for a day.

If human society were rationally organized, the priority of love, work, and knowledge would be unquestioned; they, and not unnecessary institutions, would have the right to determine social existence. In accordance with the work-democratic conception, individual groups could arm themselves and kill one another; other groups could glory in mystical rituals, and still other groups could take delight in the discussion of ideologies. *But they would not be able to dominate, exploit, and lay claim to the basic biologic functions of society for their own selfish purposes. Moreover, they would not be able to deprive them of every right to exercise a determining influence.*

The social irrationalism in the attitude toward these two spheres of human activity is enormous:

A politician is in a position to deceive millions of people, e.g., he can promise to establish freedom without actually having to do so. No one demands proof of his competence or of the feasibility of his promises. He can promise one thing today and the exact opposite tomorrow. Without let or hindrance, a mystic can imbue masses of people with the belief that there is a life after death—and he need not offer the least trace of proof. Let us now compare the rights of a politician or a mystic to the rights of a railroad engineer. The latter would be immediately put in jail or a mental institution if he would try to persuade as few as two dozen people who wanted to travel from one town to another that he could fly to the moon. Let us further imagine that this same railroad engineer, armed with a gun now, *insisted* that his assertions were true and that he would have the waiting passengers locked up if they refused to believe him. The railroad engineer *has to* transport people from one place to another; he has to do so as practically and as safely as possible if he wants to hold his job.

It is wholly immaterial whether an architect, physician, teacher, lathe operator, educator, etc., is a Fascist, Communist, liberal, or

Christian when it comes to building a school, curing the sick, making a piece of furniture, or taking care of children. No one of these workers can hold long speeches or make fantastic promises; he has to perform concrete, practical work. He has to place one brick upon another and, before he begins, he must give careful thought to and draw blueprints of the number of rooms a school is to have, where the ventilation and exits are to be placed, where the windows are to be, and where the administration office and kitchen are to be placed. Liberal, social democratic, religious, fascist, or communist ideologies are of no use whatever when it comes to performing practical work. No worker can afford to fritter away his time in idle chatter. Each worker must know what he has to do, and he must do it. But an ideologist can go on giving free rein to his fantasy, without ever performing one piece of solid work. Long after a group of politicians has completely bankrupted some country or another, it continues its threadbare ideologic debates in some other country. Real processes are totally foreign to the politician. Actually, there would be nothing to object to in this if the politicians would content themselves with debating among themselves and not try to impose their ideology on others, or even to determine the fate of nations.

I once made the attempt of testing the above exemplified system of thought of work-democracy on myself. In 1933, when I began to divine the existence of a universal biologic energy as a hypothesis, if I had openly asserted that such an energy really did exist, that it was capable of destroying cancerous tumors, I would only have confirmed the diagnosis of schizophrenia that overzealous psychoanalysts had passed around and would have been confined to a mental institution. On the basis of my research in the field of biology, I could have promulgated any number of ideologies and could have founded a political party, let us say, a work-democratic freedom party. There is no doubt that I could have done this as well as others who had less practical experience. By virtue of my influence on people, it would have been an easy matter to surround myself with my own SS and to have thousands of people provided with work-democratic insignia. All of this would not have brought me one step closer to the problem of cancer or to a comprehension of the cosmic or oceanic feeling of the human animal. I would have firmly established a work-democratic ideology, but the naturally present, but as yet unperceived, process of work-democracy would have remained undiscovered. For years on end, I had to work very hard, to make observations, to correct mistakes, to overcome my own irrationalism as well as I could, to comprehend why biology is both mechanistic and mystical at the same time. I did not complain. I had to read books, to dissect mice, to deal with various materials in a hundred different ways, until I actually discovered orgone, until I was able to concentrate it in accumulators and make it visible. Only after this had been accomplished was I able to pose the practical aspect of the question, namely whether orgone contained curative effects. In this I was guided by the organic development of the work process. This means that every vitally necessary and practical work is a rational, organic development in itself, and it cannot be surmounted or circumvented in any way whatever. This formulation contains an essential biologic principle, which we call "organic development." A tree must first have reached the height of one yard before it can reach the height of two yards. A child must first learn to read before he can find out what other people are saying in their writings. A physician must first study anatomy before he can understand pathology. In all these cases the *development ensues from the organic progress of a work process. Working men and women are the functional organs of this work.* He or she can be a good or poor functioning organ, but the work process itself does not undergo any fundamental change. Whether a man or woman is a good or poor functioning organ depends essentially upon the degree of irrationalism in his or her structure.

As might be expected, this "law of organic development" is absent in irrational functions. In such functions the goal is there as an idea from the very beginning, long before any practical work is begun. The activity follows a fixed, preconceived plan; by its very nature, therefore, it has to be irrational. This is clearly and plainly shown by the fact that, of the world-famous irrationalists, literally nothing remains behind that could be put to use by posterity.

Over thousands of years the law of organic development has been clearly manifested in all technical and scientific arts. Galileo's achievements originated in the criticism of the Ptolemaic system and extended the work of Copernicus. Kepler took up the work of Galileo, and Newton took up the work of Kepler. Many generations of working and searching men and women were developed from each of these functional organs of objective natural processes. Of Alexander, the so-called Great, Caesar, Nero, Napoleon, on the other hand, nothing whatever remains behind. Nor do we find any trace of a continuity among the irrationalists, unless the dream of a Napoleon to become a second Alexander or Caesar is regarded as a continuity.

In these men, irrationalism is completely exposed as a nonbiologic and nonsocial, indeed anti-biologic and anti-social, function of life. It lacks the essential characteristics of the rational functions of life, such as germination, development, continuity, nondeviation of process, interlacing with other functions, fragmentation, and productivity.

Now let us apply these insights to the question whether the emotional plague can be fundamentally overcome. The answer is in the affirmative. No matter how sadistic, mystical, gossipy, unscrupulous, fickle, armored, superficial, and given to idle chatter human animals may be, they are *naturally predisposed to be rational in their work functions.* Just as irrationalism vents and propagates itself in ideological processes and mysticism, man's rationality is confirmed and propagated in the work process. It is an inherent part of the work process and, therefore, an inherent part of man that he *cannot be irrational* in his work function. By his very nature and by the nature of work itself, he is *forced* to be rational. Irrationalism automatically excludes itself by virtue of the fact that it *disrupts* the work process and makes the goal of work unattainable. The sharp and irreconcilable opposition between the emotional plague and the work process is clearly expressed in the following: As a working man or woman, one can always come to an understanding with any technician, industrial worker, physician, etc., in a discussion on work functions. As soon as the conversation shifts to ideology, however, the understanding falls to pieces. It is indicative of so many dictators and politicians that they regularly give up their work when they enter the province of politics. A shoemaker who loses himself in mystical ecstasy and begins to think of himself as a savior of the people, sent by God, will inevitably cut the soles the wrong way and mess up his stitches. As time goes on, he will be faced with starvation. It is precisely by this process, on the other hand, that the politician becomes strong and rich.

Emotional irrationalism is capable only of disrupting work; it is never capable of accomplishing work.

Let us examine this work-democratic train of thought *from its own point of view*. Are we dealing here with an ideology, a glorification or idealization "of work"? I asked myself this question in view of my task to teach physicians and educators. It is incumbent upon me as a physician, researcher, and teacher to differentiate between vitally necessary, rational work and unnecessary, irrational ideology, i.e., to ascertain the rational and rationally effective character of work. I cannot help one of my students of vegetotherapy to overcome a practical difficulty in his own structure or in his work with patients by feeding him hopes of a better Beyond or by appointing him "Marshal of Vegetotherapy." The title of Marshal of Vegetotherapy would not make him the least bit more capable of dealing with difficulties. By appointing him Marshal of Vegetotherapy, I would only endanger him and possibly even precipitate a disaster. I must tell him the whole truth about his weaknesses and shortcomings. I have to teach him to recognize them by himself. In this I am guided by the course of my own development and my practical experience. I do not have an ideology that compels me to be rational for ethical or other reasons. Rational behavior is imposed upon me by my work in an objective way. I would starve if I did not strive to act rationally. I am immediately corrected by my work if I try to cover up difficulties with illusions, for I cannot eliminate a biopathic paralysis with illusions any more than a machinist, an architect, a farmer or teacher, can perform his work with illusions. Nor do I demand rationality. It is objectively present in me, independent of what I am and independent of the emotional plague. I do not order my students to be rational, for that would serve no purpose. I teach them and advise them, in their own interest and in the light of practical work processes, to distinguish the rational from the irrational in themselves and in the world. I teach them to promote the former and to check the latter. It is a basic feature of the emotional plague in social life to escape the difficulties of responsibility and the actualities of everyday life and work by seeking refuge in ideology, illusion, mysticism, brutality, or a political party.

This is a fundamentally new position. It is not the rationality of work that is new, nor its rational effect on working men and women, but the fact that work is rational and has a rational effect *in itself* and of itself, whether I know it or not. It is better if I know it. Then I can be in harmony with the rational organic development. This is also a new position for psychology and sociology. It is new for sociology because, until now, sociology has looked upon society's irrational activities as rational; and it is new for psychology because psychology did not doubt society's rationality.

VITALLY NECESSARY AND OTHER WORK

The deeper one delves into the nature of natural work-democracy, the more villainy one discovers in human thinking, villainy caused by political ideologies. Let us try to elucidate this statement by examining the content of the concept of *work*.

Thus far we have contrasted work and political ideology, equating work with "rationality" and political ideology with "irrationality." But vital life is never mechanical. Thus, we catch ourselves setting up a new irrational black-white dichotomy. But this blunt dichotomization is justified insofar as politics is indeed essentially irrational and, compared with it, work is essentially rational. For instance, is the construction of a casino work? This example forces us to differentiate *vitally necessary* work from work that is not vitally necessary. Under the heading of "vitally necessary work," we have to list every kind of work that is *indispensable* to the maintenance of human life and the social machinery. Hence, that work is vitally necessary the absence of which would be harmful to or would inhibit the living process. That work, on the other hand, the absence of which would not change the course of society and human life is not vitally necessary. We have to designate as *nonwork* that activity that is detrimental to the life process.

For centuries on end it has been precisely vitally necessary work that the political ideology of the ruling but nonworking classes has depreciated. On the other hand, it has represented nonwork as a sign of noble blood. All socialist ideologies reacted to this appraisal with a mechanistic and rigid reversal of valuations. The socialists conceived of "work" as relating solely to those activities that had been looked down upon in feudalism, i.e., essentially to manual labor; whereas the activity of the ruling classes was represented as nonwork. To be sure, this mechanical reversal of ideologic valuations was wholly in keeping with the political concept of the two economically and personally sharply demarcated social classes, the ruling and the ruled. From a purely economic point of view, society could indeed be divided into "those who possessed capital" and "those who possessed the commodity, working power." From the point of view of bio-sociology, however, there could be no clear-cut division between one class and another, neither ideologically nor psychologically, and certainly not on the basis of work. The discovery of the fact that the ideology of a group of people does not necessarily have to coincide with its economic situation, indeed, that economic and ideologic situation are often sharply opposed to one another, enabled us to understand the fascist movement, which had remained uncomprehended until then. In 1930 it became clear that there is a "cleavage" between ideology and economy, and that the ideology of a certain class can develop into a social force, a social force that is not confined to that one class.

It was first shown in connection with the suppression of the natural sexuality of children and adolescents that there are fundamental biologic functions of the human animal that have nothing to do with the economic distribution of the classes and that class boundaries overlap and cut across one another. The suppression of sexuality relates not only to all strata and classes of every patriarchal society; it is precisely in the ruling classes that this suppression is often most pronounced. Indeed, sex-economy was able to show that a large part of the sadism made use of by the ruling class to suppress and exploit other classes is to be ascribed chiefly to the sadism that stems from suppressed sexuality. The connection between sadism, sexual suppression, and class suppression is excellently expressed in De Coster's famous *Till Eulenspiegel*.

The real social functions of work also overlap and cut across the politico-ideological class boundaries. In the socialist parties there were many leading politicians who had never performed vitally necessary work and who knew nothing about the work process. A worker usually gave up his job when he became a political functionary. On the other hand, the classes that political socialism designated as the "ruling nonworking" classes, as opposed to the workers, comprised essential bodies of workers. There is probably nothing more suited to demonstrate the blindness to reality of the typical political ideologies than the fact that the leading members of the political reaction, in Austria for example, were recruited from the circles of the University of Technology. These technicians were engineers in the coal mines, constructors of locomotives, airplanes, bridges, public buildings, etc.

Now let us apply work-democracy's criticism to the concept of the capitalist. In political ideology, the capitalist was either the "leader of economy" or the "nonworking parasite." Both conceptions were mechanical, ideological, politically unrealistic, and unscientific. There are *capitalists who work*, and there are *capitalists who do not work*. There are capitalists whose work is vitally necessary and others whose work is unnecessary. A capitalist's political orientation or ideology is wholly immaterial in this respect. The contradiction between work and politics relates to the capitalist as well as the wage earner, in one and the same person. Just as a stonemason can be a fascist, a capitalist can be a socialist. In short, we have come to realize that it is not possible to orient oneself in the social chaos on the basis of political ideologies. The possibility of a concrete reorientation is offered by work-democracy's scope of ideas, which is based on a realistic appraisal of the concept of work. Accordingly, with respect to vitally necessary work, the political class of capitalists is divided into two groups, which are not only opposed but often antagonistic to one another: One group comprises those who possess capital and who neither work nor plan but make others work for their profit. A Henry Ford may hold this or that political view; ideologically, he may be an angel or a noxious person; but this does not alter the fact that he was the first American to construct an automobile and totally change the technical face of America. Politically and ideologically, Edison was undoubtedly a capitalist; but one would like to meet the political functionary of a workers' movement who would not use the incandescent lamp, which Thomas Edison took great pains to invent, or who would dare to state publicly that Edison was a nonworking parasite of society. From the point of view of work-democracy, the same applies to the Wright Brothers, Junkers, Reichert, Zeiss. There are any number of names that could be added to this list. There is a clear distinction between these capitalists, who perform objective work, and the *non*working capitalists, who *merely exploit* the fact that they possess capital. With respect to work, the latter do not constitute a special class type, for they are fundamentally identical to any socialist party bureaucrat who sits in this or that office, from which he determines "the policies of the working class." We have had our fill of the catastrophic effects of the nonworking possessors of capital and the nonworking political functionaries. We know better than to orient ourselves on ideologic concepts; we have to orient ourselves on practical activities.

From the point of view of vitally necessary work, many deeply ingrained political concepts, and the "political sciences" dependent upon them, are supplemented and changed. The concept of "the worker" has to be extended. The concept of economic classes is supplemented by the fact of the human structure, whereby the social importance of the economic classes is extremely reduced.

In what follows, the essential changes are to be brought forward that have obtruded themselves upon concepts as a result of the fundamentally new social events and the discovery of the fact of natural work-democracy. I have no illusions about how these changes will be received: This and that political ideology will raise a loud, very dignified, and high-sounding cry. But this will not have any effect upon the reality of the facts and processes, whether force is applied or not. No matter how far-reaching a political process is, no matter how many hundreds of "ists" are executed, the fact remains that a physician or a technician, educator or farmer, in America, India, Germany, or elsewhere, performs vitally necessary work. In practical everyday life, moreover, they accomplish far more, for better or for worse, for the course of life processes than the Comintern as a whole even remotely accomplished since 1923. There was no change in the life of man when the Comintern was dissolved in 1943. But let us imagine that China or America would exclude all teachers or all physicians from the social process on a certain day!

The history of the past twenty years leaves no doubt that the party ideologies advocating the "elimination of class differences," "the establishment of national unity," etc., not only did not effect any change in the existence of class differences, in the fragmentation of the human community, and in the suppression of freedom and decency; they merely brought matters to a head, indeed to a catastrophic degree. Hence, the natural scientific solution of the social tragedy of the human animal must begin with the clarification and correction of those ideologic party concepts that perpetuate the fragmentation of human society.

Work-democracy does not limit the concept of "the worker" to the industrial worker. To avoid any misunderstanding, work-democracy calls everyone who performs vitally necessary social work a *worker*. The concept of the "working class," a concept that was politically and ideologically limited to the body of industrial workers, estranged the industrial worker from the technician and educator, and it created a hostility among the representatives of the various vitally necessary work processes. Indeed, this ideology caused the medical and teaching professions to be subordinated to the "revolutionary proletariat"; they were designated as the "servants of the bourgeoisie." Not only the medical and teaching professions, but also the industrial proletariat, objected to such a relegation. This is understandable, for the objective and factual relationship and cooperation between the physician and the workers in an industrial center are much deeper and more serious than the relationship between the industrial workers and those who wield political power. Since the working community and the interlacing of the various branches of vitally necessary work derive from the natural processes and are nourished by natural interests, they alone are in a position to counter political fragmentation. It is clear that when a vitally necessary group of industrial workers degrades an equally vital group of physicians, technicians, or teachers to the status of "servants" and elevates itself to the status of "masters," then the teachers, physicians, and technicians fly into the arms of those who preach racial superiority because they do not want to be servants, not even "servants of the revolutionary proletariat." And the "revolutionary proletariat" flies into the arms of a political party or trade union, which does not burden them with any responsibility and imbues them with the illusion that they are the "leading class." This does not alter the fact that this "leading class," as has been clearly shown, is not in a position to assume social responsibility and that it even goes so far as to practice racial hatred, as in America, where unions of *white* workers deny membership to *black* workers.

All of this is the result of deeply ingrained ideological party concepts, under whose sway the community, which is produced by work, is suffocated. Hence, it is only the new concept of the *worker*, i.e., as a person who *performs vitally necessary work*, which is in a position to bridge the gap and to bring the social bodies into line with the organizations of vitally necessary work.

There can be no doubt that this clarification of concepts will not be welcomed by the party ideologists. We can be just as certain that in the attitude toward this clarification of concepts, the ideologic chaff will be clearly and spontaneously separated from the practical wheat, this or that power apparatus notwithstanding. Those who affirm and advocate the natural work community, the basis for which is given by the interlacing of all vitally necessary work, will be practical wheat. On the other hand, those to whom party ideologies and concepts, i.e., ideologies and concepts that obstruct and hamper our society on all sides, are more important than the community of all working men and women, will make a big fuss under one pretext or another, and thus prove themselves to be chaff. But the clarification of these concepts will fall in with the naturally present knowledge surrounding these relationships and, therefore, with the need to arrange social life in accordance with the interrelation of all branches of work.

In this discussion of the concept of the worker, I have merely followed the logic imposed on me by work-democratic thinking. I *had* to arrive at the above results, whether I wanted to or not. There is a very simple reason for this. Just at the time I was writing these pages, I had to have some signs and placards made up for Orgonon.* I am not a carpenter, and therefore I am not able to make the placards myself. Nor am I a painter, so I cannot produce neat lettering. But we needed placards for our laboratory. Hence, I was forced to put myself in contact with a carpenter and a painter and, on terms of equality, discuss the best way of making and lettering the placards. I would not have been able to deal with this need without their experience and practical counsel. It was wholly immaterial whether or not I regarded myself as a very erudite academi-

---

* Reich's home and research laboratory in Rangeley, Maine.

cian and natural scientist; and it was just as immaterial whether the painter or carpenter held this or that "view" on fascism or the New Deal. The carpenter could not regard me as the "servant of the revolutionary proletariat," nor could the painter regard me as a highly superfluous "intellectual." The work process made it necessary for us to exchange knowledge and experience with one another. For instance, if the painter wanted to do a good job, he had to understand our symbol of the functional method of research. As it turned out, he glowed with enthusiasm for his work when he learned its meaning. From the painter and the carpenter, on the other hand, I learned a great deal about the arrangement of letters and the placards themselves, which had the purpose of correctly expressing the function of the Institute to the outside world.

This example of the objective and rational interlacing of branches of work is clear enough to make more comprehensible the abysmal irrationalism that governs the formation of public opinion and thus burkes the natural process of work. The more concretely I sought to visualize the course of my work in relationship to other branches of work, the better I was able to comprehend work-democracy's scope of thought. There was no doubt about it: The work process went well when I allowed myself to be instructed by microscope manufacturers and electrical engineers, and when they, in turn, allowed me to instruct them on the function of a lens or an electrical apparatus in their special orgone-physical use. I would not have been able to proceed a single step in orgone research without the lens grinder and the electrical engineer. In turn, the electrical engineer and the lens grinder struggle hard with the unsolved problems of the theory of light and electricity, some aspects of which can hope for clarification by the discovery of orgone.

I have described this obvious fact of the interrelation of the various branches of work at some length and in an intentionally primitive way because I had good reason to know that, as simple as all this is, it nonetheless appears to be strange and new to working men and women. To be sure, this sounds hard to believe, but it is true and it is understandable: The fact of the natural interrelationship and indissoluble interdependence of all work processes is not clearly and plainly represented in the thinking and feeling of working men and women. True enough, every working man and woman is automatically familiar with this interrelationship on the basis of his or her practical work, but it sounds strange when they are told that society could not exist without their work or that they are responsible for the social organization of their work. This gap between vitally necessary activity and the consciousness of one's responsibility for this activity was created and perpetuated by the political system of ideologies. These ideologies are responsible for the hiatus between practical activity and irrational orientation in working men and women. This assertion also sounds peculiar and strange. But one can easily convince oneself of its veracity by picking up and studying very carefully any newspaper in Europe, Asia, or anywhere else, regardless of date. It is only seldom and as if by chance that one finds anything about the basic principles and nature of the processes of love, work, and knowledge, their vital necessity, their interrelationship, their rationality, their seriousness, etc. On the other hand, the newspapers are full of high politics, diplomacy, military and formal events, which have no bearing upon the real process of everyday life. In this way the average working man and woman are imbued with the feeling that actually they are of little significance, compared with the elevated, complicated, and "clever" debates on "strategy and tactics." The average working man and woman get the feeling that they are small, inadequate, superfluous, oppressed, and not much more than an *accident in life*. The veracity of this assertion with respect to mass psychology can easily be tested. I have often carried out such tests and have always attained the same result:

1. Some worker comes up with a good idea, which enables him to effect a considerable improvement in his work. We ask him to put his small or big discovery down in writing and to publish it. When we do so, we meet with a peculiar reaction. It is as if the worker, whose work is important and indispensable, wanted to creep into a shell. It is as if he wanted to say—and often he puts it into

precisely these words—"Who am I to write an article? My work doesn't count." This attitude on the part of the worker toward his work is a typical phenomenon of mass psychology. I described it very simply here, but this is its essence, and anyone can easily persuade himself that it is so.

2. Now let us approach the editor of any newspaper. We'll suggest that he reduce the formal, strictly political "questions of strategy and tactics" to two pages of the newspaper and that he reserve the *first* and *second* pages of the newspaper for extensive articles on practical everyday questions of technology, medicine, education, mining, agriculture, factory work, etc. He will gaze at us devoid of all understanding and in complete perplexity, and he will have doubts about our state of mind.

These two basic attitudes, i.e., that of masses of people and that of the molders of public opinion, supplement and determine one another. The nature of public opinion is essentially *political,* and it has a low estimation of the everyday life of love, work, and knowledge. And this is in keeping with the feeling of social insignificance experienced by those who love, work, and have knowledge.

However, a rational reassessment of the social conditions is out of the question as long as political irrationalism contributes 99 percent, and the basic functions of social life contribute only 1 percent, toward the formation of public opinion and, therefore, toward the formation of the human structure. A complete reversal of the relationship would be the minimal requirement if one wants to deprive political irrationalism of its power and to achieve the self-regulation of society. In other words: *The factual process of life must also have an emphatic voice in the press and in the forms of social life, and it must coincide with them.*

In this extension and correction of political concepts, we encounter an argument that is difficult to counter. It runs as follows: Political ideologies cannot be simply eliminated, for workers, farmers, technicians, etc., determine the trend of society not only through their vitally necessary work, but also through their political ideologies! The Peasants' War of the Middle Ages was a political revolt that had a revolutionizing social effect. The Communist party in Russia changed the face of Russia. One cannot, it is stated, prohibit or prevent "politicizing" and the formation of political ideologies. They too are human needs and have social effects, just as love, knowledge, and work. These arguments are to be countered as follows:

1. Work-democracy's scope of thought does not want to prohibit or prevent anything. It is directed exclusively to the fulfillment of the biologic life functions of love, work, and knowledge. When it is backed by some political ideology, then natural work-democracy is only promoted. But if a political ideology with irrational claims and assertions gets in the way, then work-democracy will act just as a lumberman would act who, in the process of felling a tree, is attacked by a poisonous snake. He will kill the snake to be able to continue his work unobstructed. He will not give up his lumberman's job because there are poisonous snakes in the woods.

2. It is true that political ideologies are facts that also have actual social effects and that they cannot be simply dismissed or talked away. However, it is work-democracy's point of view that it is precisely these facts that constitute a terrible portion of the tragedy of the human animal. The fact that political ideologies are tangible realities is not a proof of their vitally necessary character. The bubonic plague was an extraordinarily powerful social reality, but no one would have regarded it as vitally necessary. A settlement of human beings in a primeval forest is a vitally important matter and a real and tangible social fact. But a flood is also such a fact. Who would equate the destructive force of a flood to the activities of the human settlement only because both of them have social effects? Yet, it was precisely our failure to differentiate between work and politics, between reality and illusion; it was precisely our mistake of conceiving of politics as a rational human activity comparable to the sowing of seeds or the construction of buildings that was responsible for the fact that a painter who failed to make the grade was able to plunge the whole world into misery. And I have stressed again and

again that the main purpose of this book—which, after all, was not written merely for the fun of it—was to demonstrate these catastrophic errors in human thinking and to eliminate irrationalism from politics. It is an essential part of our social tragedy that the farmer, the industrial worker, the physician, etc., do not influence social existence solely through their social activities, but also and even predominantly through their political ideologies. For political activity hinders objective and professional activity; it splits every profession into inimical ideologic groups; creates a dichotomy in the body of industrial workers; limits the activity of the medical profession and harms the patients. In short, it is precisely political activity that prevents the realization of that which it pretends to fight for: peace, work, security, international cooperation, free objective speech, freedom of religion, etc.

3. It is true that political parties sometimes change the face of a society. However, from the point of view of work-democracy we maintain that these are *compulsive achievements*. Originally, when Karl Marx began his critique of political economy, he was not a politician, nor was he a member of a party. He was a scientific economist and sociologist. It was the emotional plague in masses of people that prevented him from being heard; it was the emotional plague that caused him to fall into poverty and wretchedness; it was the emotional plague that forced him to found a political organization, the notorious "Communist Alliance," which he himself dissolved after a short time. It was the emotional plague that turned scientific Marxism into a Marxism of political parties, which no longer had anything to do with scientific Marxism and even bears a large share of the responsibility for the emergence of fascism. Marx's exclamation that he was "not a Marxist" is a precise confirmation of this fact. He would never have resorted to the founding of a political organization if rational, and not irrational, thinking were the rule in masses of people. True, political machinery was often a necessity, but it was a compulsive measure made necessary by human irrationalism. If work and social ideology were

in accord with one another, if needs, the gratification of needs, and the means of gratifying needs were identical with the human structure, there would be no politics, for then politics would be superfluous. When one does not have a house, one might be forced to live in a hollow tree trunk. A tree trunk may be better or worse than a house, but it is not a house. A decent home remains the goal, even if one is forced for a time to live in a tree. The elimination of politics and of the state from which it springs was precisely the goal that was forgotten by the founders of socialism. I know that it is embarrassing to be reminded of such things. It requires too much thought, honesty, knowledge, self-criticism, for a physician to regard the main goal of his activity as the prevention of those diseases from the cure of which he makes a living. We shall have to regard as objective and rational sociologists those politicians who help human society to expose the irrational motivations of the existence of politics and its "necessity" so completely that every form of politics becomes superfluous.

This work-democratic critique of politics does not stand alone. In America the hatred of political power mongering and the insights into its social harmfulness is widespread. From the Soviet Union we hear that there too the technocrats are prevailing more and more against the politicians. Perhaps, even the execution of leading Russian politicians by politicians has a social meaning that is concealed from all of us, despite the fact that we have learned to look upon these executions as the manifestation of political irrationalism and sadism. The politics of the European dictators was unrivaled for a whole decade. If one wants to recognize effortlessly the essence of politics, let one reflect upon the fact that it was a Hitler who was able to make a whole world hold its breath for many years. The fact that Hitler was a political genius unmasks the nature of politics in general as no other fact can. With Hitler, politics reached its highest stage of development. We know what its fruits were, and we know how the whole world reacted to them. In short, it is my belief that, with its unparalleled catastrophes, the twentieth century marks

394

the beginning of a new social era, free of politics. Of course, it is impossible to foresee how much of a role politics itself will still play in the uprooting of the political emotional plague, and how much of the role will be played by the consciously organized functions of love, work, and knowledge.

INDEX